REMAKING WOMEN

EDITORS

Sherry B. Ortner, Nicholas B. Dirks, Geoff Eley

A LIST OF TITLES

IN THIS SERIES APPEARS

AT THE BACK OF

THE BOOK

PRINCETON STUDIES IN

CULTURE / POWER / HISTORY

REMAKING WOMEN

FEMINISM AND MODERNITY

IN THE MIDDLE EAST

Edited by Lila Abu-Lughod

PRINCETON UNIVERSITY PRESS

PRINCETON, NEW JERSEY

Library of Congress Cataloging-in-Publication Data

Remaking women : feminism and modernity in the
Middle East / edited by Lila Abu-Lughod.
p.   cm. — (Princeton studies in culture/power/history)
Includes bibliographical references and index.
ISBN 0-691-05791-5 (cl : alk. paper).
ISBN 0-691-05792-3 (pb : alk. paper)
1. Women—Middle East—Social conditions. 2. Women in Islam—
Middle East. 3. Feminism—Middle East.
I. Abu-Lughod, Lila, 1952– II. Series.
HQ1726.5.R45 1998   305.42'0956—dc21
97-46125   CIP

Contents

Preface

THIS BOOK grew out of my strong sense that emerging in Middle East studies was a fundamentally new way of thinking about the implications for women of the projects of modernity. This new thinking was enabled by the mature scholarship on "the woman question" that had been developing over the last two decades, scholarship characterized by fine historical research, critical social analysis of the contemporary scene, and intense intellectual debate. It was also enabled by the wider reading by feminist scholars of the Middle East of contemporary theory and historical work about and from other regions, whether Europe or South Asia.

Although there are some differences in theoretical approach and interpretation among the contributors to this volume, four features distinguish our collective effort. First, we question the familiar dichotomy that has opposed tradition to modernity, relegating women's domesticity to the realm of conservatism and tradition and labeling women's emergence into the public sphere, whether in politics, employment, or education, as radical and new. Several of the chapters examine the modernity of early-twentieth-century domesticity itself and the discourses about nationalism that supported it. Others consider the modernity of the gender politics of contemporary Islamism.

Second, we are suspicious about the way modernity is so easily equated with the progress, emancipation, and empowerment of women. Some chapters reexamine iconic figures and institutions in the narrative of modern Middle Eastern women's progress. Others explore the ambiguities and contradictions of the programs intended to make women modern, programs related in particular to education, marriage, and rational, scientific forms of conduct, including child rearing. We ask not just what new possibilities but what hidden costs, unanticipated constraints, novel forms of discipline and regulation, and unintended consequences accompanied such programs.

Third, we take seriously the vexed question of the relationship of Europe to Middle Eastern projects of remaking women. We try to steer a measured course between glossing over and overemphasizing the role of the West (in its variety and its local appropriations), looking for ways to acknowledge the specificities of local feminisms while interrogating the complex ways in which European colonial power was fundamental to the historical development of the Middle East. This inescapable history and its postcolonial legacy, as the chapters on the late twentieth century show, have profoundly affected, in sometimes counterintuitive ways, its gender politics.

Finally, we use a broad definition of feminism in this volume, not confining ourselves to women's movements per se (ably studied by others before us) but including the wide range of projects having women as their object. We try to set such projects, whether initiated and promoted by men or by women, within their historical, political, and social contexts. This has meant placing such projects not along a trajectory of liberation from patriarchy but squarely within the messy situations of state building, anticolonial nationalism, changing social orders, and the emergence of new classes. At the same time, although we have not focused specifically on women's activism, we have tried to remain attuned to the ways in which women shaped and reshaped the projects that affected them; in the case of feminism, this has usually meant middle-class and elite women.

The volume does not claim to be comprehensive, either in its coverage of the Middle East or its inclusion of all those working on the issues we consider. The Middle East is too broad a region and the field of Middle East gender studies too rich for a single book to dream of being comprehensive. The fact that we discuss only three countries, Egypt, Iran, and Turkey, with a decided weight on Egypt, can be justified in intellectual terms but is also to be explained by the accidents of personal history. On the one hand, these are the three major countries with long histories of modernizing reform in the Middle East. More pertinent, I think, is that these are three countries for which there are, as the bibliographic references in all our chapters indicate, both untapped original sources and impressive bodies of research and analysis on which feminist scholars can draw—and build. This critical mass enabled the inchoate emergence I noted above of a shift in ways of thinking about feminism and the politics of modernity.

I have tried to give form to this shift by bringing together those scholars I knew had work in progress that was relevant to the questions about women and the politics of modernity outlined above. And this is where accidents of personal history enter in. By no means have I included all those working along these lines; and surely the book would have been even better could others have been included or could we have had studies of other Middle Eastern nations. What I hope is that these essays by a group of scholars whose material and ideas speak so directly to each other will be suggestive, sparking further conversation and research on the story of gender and feminism in the Middle East. I also trust that our thinking about Middle Eastern history and contemporary society, though by necessity specific, will be useful for students of other postcolonial societies and their histories. Their work has certainly been instructive for us.

This book has been a truly collective endeavor. I have learned an enormous amount from all the contributors and am grateful to them for their brilliant scholarship and their spirit of cooperation. Others have contributed to this book in various ways and I want to thank them all. Abouali Farmanfarmaian first urged me to bring together what I considered exciting new work in Middle East gender studies; I did not dream then how much I would learn in the process. Annette Weiner, then Dean of the Graduate School at New York University, offered valuable support for a symposium called "Women, Culture, Nation: Egyptian Moments" that enabled many of us to exchange ideas, even though none of the papers presented there appear in this volume. Two conferences on "Questions of Modernity" that brought together Middle East and South Asia scholars have been critical to shaping my ideas. I am grateful to the Social Science Research Council (grants program for Transnational and Comparative Studies and the Committee on the Near and Middle East) and to New York University's Dean of the Humanities, Thomas Bender, for funding those meetings. Mary Murrell and Lauren Lepow were exemplary editors, the anonymous readers for Princeton University Press provided very thoughtful suggestions for improving the volume, and Omnia Shakry and Jessica Winegar gave invaluable help in the final stages. Finally, I am deeply grateful to the National Endowment for the Humanities and the John Simon Guggenheim Memorial Foundation for fellowships in 1996 and 1997 that opened up the unexpected possibility of bringing this book into being.

Rough Park, Cornwall, England
June 30, 1997

Note on Transliterations

THE CHALLENGES of devising a system for transliterating three languages, Arabic, Persian, and Turkish, in a book meant for both regional specialists and a more general readership in gender studies and colonial and postcolonial studies are not insignificant. For the most part, we have adopted a simplified version of the system recommended by the *International Journal of Middle East Studies*. We have avoided diacriticals in our Arabic and Persian transliterations, assuming that specialists who know the languages will be able to recognize the words while nonspecialists would only find the diacriticals confusing. The exceptions are the ʿayn (ʿ) and the hamza ('). For Turkish, however, diacriticals have been indicated. We use common English spellings for proper names of well-known figures and places. We also use the preferred spellings of names of those who write in English. Otherwise, we transliterate.

REMAKING WOMEN

Feminist Longings and Postcolonial Conditions

LILA ABU-LUGHOD

IN TURKEY, the fabulously popular transsexual singer Bülent Ersoy, known for her seductive poses and low-cut dresses, is now voicing her desire to become a good Muslim woman.[1] In Iran, the Islamic Republic turned the *chador*, worn by some feminists in antishah demonstrations, into a mandatory form of dress. In Egypt, progressive intellectuals feel threatened by the public repentance of born-again movie stars who have taken on the veil and by certain guests on a television talk show hosted by a woman whose autobiography is titled *My Journey from Unveiling to Veiling*.[2] Meanwhile, in Iran magazines edited by women sometimes calling themselves "Islamic feminists" carry stories critical of the representation of women in textbooks and of the glass ceiling in occupations, support women's education, and even, in one case, cite the work of Simone de Beauvoir and Susan Faludi.[3] Other young women who are politically active in state-sponsored religious organizations can actually gain enough independence from recalcitrant fathers and brothers to seriously undermine the usual dynamics of the patriarchal family, if in the name of more powerful authoritarianism.[4] Veiled feminists in Egypt, like their counterparts in other countries, are busy reinterpreting Islamic law and the Qur'an; some find fault with what they consider the Western division between public and private spheres, arguing that the same democratic principles that should guide leadership in the political sphere should apply within the family.[5]

These phenomena point to three issues this book addresses. First is the way that in the postcolonial world women have become potent symbols of identity and visions of society and the nation. Issues of women's rights, as Deniz Kandiyoti has put it so well for the Muslim world, are invariably "part of an ideological terrain where broader notions of cultural authenticity and integrity are debated and where women's appropriate place and conduct may be made to serve as boundary markers."[6] Second is the way that women themselves actively participate in these debates and social struggles, with feminism, defined in sometimes quite different ways, having become by now an inescapable term of reference. Third are the complex ways that the West and things associated with the West, embraced, repudiated, and translated, are implicated in contemporary gender politics.

In the Middle East, the stage for this state of affairs was set over a century
ago. In Turkey, Iran, Egypt, and elsewhere, the turn of the century was a
moment of intense preoccupation with women and family—not to mention
nation and society—in part because of the encounter with Europe, whether
desired (as by reformers of the Ottoman Empire), ambivalent (for the Persian-
speaking areas), or imposed through colonial occupation (for many in the
Arab world). The arguments that would later be called arguments about
"feminism," about redefining women's rights, clothing, and roles in and
beyond the family, were lively topics for men and women interested in social
reform.

What went on? How have the earlier debates and the social transformations
that went hand in hand with them shaped the present? The Islamists of today
are often branded "medieval" by their opponents. They themselves invoke the
past and self-righteously denounce certain versions of modernity. And yet they
are very much part of and a product of modernity and best seen as striving—
like all contemporaneous social movements—for an alternative modernity.[7]
The essays in this book may help us understand how and why.

The book consists of detailed explorations of that earlier historical moment
when "new" women and men were talking about remaking women. It also
contains critical analyses of how that moment figures in contemporary political argument and social life. Needless to say, the discourses we analyze are
related in complex ways to local and global economic and political forces, and
their impact has been uneven across the social spectrum. But we have chosen
to foreground the terms of the debates themselves because they are part of that
broader history and reveal much that feminists, historians, and other analysts
of the Middle East can now begin to appreciate.

Although all the chapters deal with the Middle East, and most in fact with
Egypt, the concerns and the insights are of wide relevance. In India, not just
Muslim but Hindu communities have made women symbols of identity and
debated their proper roles in light of specific visions of the nation and society.[8]
And feminism there has a complex history, beginning with nationalism,
moving into postindependence concerns about the impoverished, and now, as
Mary John suggests, turning its critical lens onto its own middle-class Hindu
location.[9] In Malaysia, women are charged symbols in contests over ethnicity,
markers of class politics, and magnets of the ambivalence felt about the effects
of multinational capitalism.[10] There, as in Egypt, young women are voluntarily
taking on the veil. In fact, wherever Christian missionaries and European
colonists set down, and wherever nationalist movements sought to shape new
nations, marks were left on gender ideals and possibilities. Yet we can theorize
only through carefully researched analyses of historically and regionally specific situations, something we have done in this book for three major countries
of the Middle East.

In this introduction, which relates the issues to two critical terms, modernity and postcoloniality, I want to try to trace the inspirations for the individual studies and to draw out their theoretical implications. The inspirations include previous studies of women and feminism in the Middle East, a critical post-structuralist literature on modernity (and the feminist critiques of modern Western gender relations it has enabled), and a body of writing on postcolonial theory that is developing subtle ways of thinking about the cultural dimensions of the colonial encounter and, more broadly, the relationship between the constructs of "East" and "West" as they have shaped anticolonial nationalist projects.

THE HISTORY OF "FEMINISM" IN
THE MIDDLE EAST

A formative context for our work has been the extraordinary energy and richness the last two decades have witnessed in the field of Middle East women's studies. In particular there has been some crucial new work on the history of what might be called "the woman question" at the end of the nineteenth and beginning of the twentieth century, a topic that until the 1980s had attracted only modest interest.[11]

The way was paved for this book by collections, like Kandiyoti's *Women, Islam and the State*, which insisted that women in the Middle East must be studied not in terms of an undifferentiated "Islam" or Islamic culture but rather through the differing political projects of nation-states, with their distinct histories, relationships to colonialism and the West, class politics, ideological uses of an Islamic idiom, and struggles over the role of Islamic law in state legal apparatuses. Linking attempts at family reform and women's rights to the efforts of modern states to break up the autonomy of local kin groups and thus enhance their own power, to mobilize labor forces or political constituencies to meet national needs, or most recently to meet the requirements of international development agencies, Kandiyoti and her coauthors voiced a certain cynicism about Muslim regimes' calls for women's emancipation.[12]

Yet this groundbreaking work was not able to cover everything. Its emphasis on state policies and nationalist projects tended to make women appear primarily as objects of reform and manipulation, although some essays focused specifically on women's political efforts. Second, with the historical sweep of many of the essays, not enough attention could be paid to the fascinating subtleties of the debates about women at particular historical moments. Third, although the authors recognized that women were caught in polemics about cultural authenticity, they did not investigate in any detail the dynamics by which local and Western discourses and actors played off each other. Fi-

nally, because the relationship of women and nationalism was the central concern, the significance of the links between reforms for women and a politics of
modernity went unexplored.

Some of what Kandiyoti's volume could not do was accomplished by
several books published in the past few years. These paid special attention
to the crucial moment of the late nineteenth and early twentieth centuries
when the terms of the debates about "women's emancipation" were set and
when, it might be said, "the history of the present" regarding feminism and
its possibilities in the Middle East was made. Leila Ahmed's *Women and
Gender in Islam*, Margot Badran's *Feminists, Islam, and Nation*, and Beth
Baron's *The Women's Awakening in Egypt*, all focusing on Egypt, and Parvin
Paidar's *Women and the Political Process in Twentieth-Century Iran* make
extensive use of the writings of Middle Eastern women themselves to analyze the period in question and examine specifically the history of feminist
political movements, and they are the work of feminist scholars whose own
commitment to and faith in some sort of feminist transformation of women's
lives are patent.[13]

The rediscovery of women's writings and the analysis of the active
women's press, especially in turn-of-the-century Egypt but also in Iran and
Ottoman Turkey, have enabled feminist scholars to shift their attention from
the prominent male reformers to the many women who were active participants in the shaping of the new discourses on women.[14] These studies allow us
to see women more clearly as a diverse group of individuals who thought
about, argued for, and managed to transform women's lives in colonial, quasi-
colonial, and nationalist contexts. Moreover, these writings revealed ambiguities and contradictions that rendered any simple story impossible. The outlines
of the projects pursued by such women who can, at least from the 1920s, be
called feminists, are impeccably chronicled, opening up for reflection and
further analysis rich new domains.

In their comprehensiveness and intelligence, however, these books crystallized certain questions that the authors of the essays in *Remaking Women* could
now pursue in detail. First and foremost are questions about the politics of
modernity. In particular, the question arose as to how new ideas and practices
considered "modern" and progressive implanted in Europe's colonies or simply taken up by emerging local elites might usher in not only forms of emancipation but new forms of social control. Second are questions about the politics
of East/West relations. How are we to think about those discourses that borrowed from Europe, were supported by Europeans, or were shaped in response
to colonial definitions of the "backwardness" of the East? Third are questions
about class that enter into both of these, such as who becomes involved in
debates about "the woman question" and what relationship does their involvement have to consolidating class projects and identities?

POSTSTRUCTURALIST CRITIQUES OF MODERNITY

Paul Rabinow has noted that it is impossible to define modernity; rather, what one must do is to track the diverse ways the insistent claims to being modern are made.[15] Certainly "being modern" has been the dominant self-image of Europeans for almost two centuries.[16] Modernity has also been the abiding concern of social theorists, from the great nineteenth- and early-twentieth-century figures of Karl Marx, Max Weber, and Emile Durkheim to the present, if the number of books with "modernity" and now "postmodernity" in their titles is any indication. The preoccupation with modernity lives on in the discourse of developmentalism that marks all national rhetorics in the Third World, just as it characterized until recently the dominant Western understandings of those regions in terms of "modernization theory."

What is important for the study of "the woman question," in the Middle East and elsewhere, is to explore how notions of modernity have been produced and reproduced through being opposed to the nonmodern in dichotomies ranging from the modern/primitive of philosophy and anthropology to the modern/traditional of Western social theory and modernization theory, not to mention the West/non-West that is implied in most of these dichotomies.

Even more crucial for understanding the projects of remaking women over the last century is to ask how modernity—as a condition—might not be what it purports to be or tells itself, in the language of enlightenment and progress, it is. Sociological and cultural studies of science have been chipping away at that cherished sign of modernity, undermining its claims to be a rational enterprise, built on objectivity, devoted to the value-free accumulation and improvement of knowledge.[17] Those thinking seriously about race and modernity have argued for a genealogy of modernity that takes slavery or colonialism as foundational.[18] But for purposes of gender analysis, it is Foucault's provocative exploration of the dark underside of the modern state and its institutions like schools, hospitals, and prisons where the everyday practices of normalization and disciplining that now have spread throughout society were developed, that is most suggestive. The way in which the family, and women and children as part of that, became a site for the intervention and production of discourses about the self and its sexuality was developed in his later work, particularly the first volume of *The History of Sexuality*.[19]

Although feminist scholars have responded ambivalently to Foucault, some finding him inspirational, others reactionary and little concerned with women, there is little doubt that the specific ways that he found power to be at work in the most personal realms of family and sexuality have extended the kinds of critiques of the effects of capitalist modernity on gender that could be made. From a Marxian questioning of how positive capitalism had been for most women, tracing in its separation of the private and public spheres the naturalization of women's exclusion from productive work and political rights and their denigration (and exploitation) as invisible reproducers, scholars could then go on to question even the "emancipations" of the sexual revolution and women's entry into the public sphere and citizenship.[20] The language of rights that promised equality to women could be seen as problematic not only because it was actually unavailable to women but because of the assumptions about personhood and subjection to the state it carried.

How can this kind of critical rethinking of modernity and of gender help us reassess the projects of modernizing Middle Eastern women that have characterized this century? Modernity is certainly the correct frame. The rhetoric of reformers and literate women themselves was full of references to "the new"—with calls for "women's awakening" and "the new woman" reverberating through the magazines, books, and speeches of the era. As Zohreh T. Sullivan in this volume says of the Iranian émigrés and exiles she interviewed, "[M]odernity was a currency that circulated through all their transactions." How best to become modern and what role should be given to Islam and how much of the West to emulate were certainly contentious issues. But that something new was to happen was not doubted.

With regard to remaking women, discussion revolved around their roles as mothers, as managers of the domestic realm, as wives of men, and as citizens of the nation. The proper place of women in public and the merits of educating them were debated within these contexts. Rather than worrying about which aspects of these modernizing projects should be called radical and which conservative, the chapters in this book explore how these projects were conceived and promoted, in all their complexity, contradictions, and, as Sullivan stresses, unintended consequences, but with a critical eye for the ways in which they might not have been purely liberatory.

What seems so confusing about the calls for remaking women at the turn of the century and into the first half of the twentieth century is that they included advocacy of both women's greater participation in the public world—through education, unveiling, and political participation—and women's enormous responsibility for the domestic sphere. As the essays in this book show, nationalism and visions of national development were central to both arguments. The redefinition of women's domesticity is examined by Afsaneh Najmabadi and Omnia Shakry, for Iran and Egypt, respectively. While some might dismiss the cult of domesticity promoted by writers in women's journals as conservative, and others are tempted to see it as a deplorable extension of women's traditional roles, Najmabadi argues instead that it depended on a radical refiguring of gender roles. In other words, as I also argue in my chapter, to be a wife and mother as these modernizers conceived of it was to be a very different kind of subject from the wife and mother of before. It was not insignificant, as both Najmabadi and Shakry show, that the "new" wife and mother was now to be in charge of the scientific management of the orderly household of the modern nation, as well as the rearing and training of the children who now were seen as the future citizens of the modern nation.

Najmabadi is particularly interested in the way that this new vision of wifehood and motherhood underwrote developments in the education of women and intersected with nationalist aspirations. Shakry concentrates on the ways such novel visions of child rearing and household management—and the prescriptive literature through which they were reiterated—not only intersected with nationalist projects but articulated the national struggle in terms of a politics of modernity. Moreover, she shows how this new domesticity worked to enforce a single bourgeois norm, devaluing other forms of marriage and family. Both, as I will discuss in the next section, trace the sources of these new visions of women's roles to Europe, whose prescriptive literatures were being translated and whose definitions of the modern deeply affected the Middle Easterners' images of themselves and their society.

A sharply critical perspective on the implications for women of the projects of modernity has not been completely absent in the Middle East literature. Mervat Hatem, for one, has questioned the implicit endorsement of the projects of "modernization" that runs through even the best feminist scholarship on the Middle East, asking whether one should not be more suspicious of the ways such projects exacerbated class inequalities among women and seriously disadvantaged rural and working-class women.[21] Along these lines, Sullivan's interview with an Iranian woman who directed a project for modernizing rural women gives us the haunting image of village girls in government-sponsored development centers having to be tied to their bunk beds with their *chadors* "for their own good."

But the questioning can go much further to include a critical consideration of the ways that these forms of modernization—the induction of women into new domestic roles as "ministers of the interior" (as Judith Newton has put it for British women of the mid–nineteenth century), the professionalization of housewifery, the 'scientizing' of child rearing, women's drafting into the nationalist project of producing good sons, the organization into nuclear households governed by ideals of bourgeois marriage, and even the involvement in new educational institutions—may have initiated new coercive norms and subjected women to new forms of control and discipline, many self-imposed, even as they undermined other forms of patriarchy.[22]

For example, in an earlier article, titled "Veiled Discourse—Unveiled Bodies," Najmabadi has shown that as Iranian women became educated and gained entrance to a public world that placed them in heterosocial space, their language was stripped of a rich sexual explicitness and they strove to produce their unveiled bodies as disciplined and chaste.[23] Similarly, Kandiyoti argues in this volume that in Turkey, women's entrance into public space might have mandated new forms of puritanism; Badran has similarly noted that the middle-class Egyptian feminist and educator Nabawiyya Musa tried, in the early decades of the twentieth century, to shift the focus of debate from veiling versus unveiling to modesty versus immodesty or seductiveness.[24]

Writing of an institution celebrated in Egyptian nationalist and feminist historiography as the first to give women professional status, Khaled Fahmy in this volume uses archival material including health and police records to analyze the intents and effects of the School of Midwives set up by the modernizer Mohammad Ali in the 1830s. He shows that not only did the low status of the women recruited to the school compromise their social standing even after they were trained, but, more important, that the motives for setting up the school were, on the one hand, to demonstrate to visiting Europeans how progressive and modern Muhammad Ali was, and, on the other hand, to increase the efficiency and reach of the state in enforcing new forms of regulation and surveillance of the population necessary for improving the health of his army. Fahmy sees this School of Midwives, and the new women doctors it produced, as sites where differing ideas over modernization and reform were contested. He is able to trace the tremendous ambivalence toward these women doctors, the ways they were treated as second class vis-à-vis male doctors, and, even more significant, the way that the state usurped the traditional rights of families to control their marriages and movements, sometimes forcing them into domestic partnerships that were unhappy.

Insofar as this remaking of women gathered momentum in relation to the colonial encounter (in ways to be explored in the next section), Timothy Mitchell's interpretation of the turn-of-the-century movement to modernize and uplift women in Egypt is useful to recall. He has linked the British colonial administrators' localization of the backwardness of the Egyptians in the low status of their women and these men's apparent concern to free Egyptian women from the degradations of harem life to the colonial frustration about the inaccessibility of "the harem"—a frustration intimately linked to their efforts to police the population. Moreover, he traced Egyptian nationalist reformers' responsive calls to make women into modern wives and mothers to the general demand to train the population, instituting a new disciplinary regime in everyday life.[25] As he put it, "The family was to be organised as this house of discipline, which would then be able to produce, alongside the schools, the military and the other practices I have mentioned, the proper 'mentality' of the Egyptian."[26]

Shakry's analysis of the similar ways the liberal secular and the Islamist press in Egypt during the early years of the twentieth century dealt with the issues of women and motherhood indicates how, as she puts it, "the sphere of women was localized as a sphere of backwardness to be reformed, regenerated, and uplifted for the benefit of the nation." Her analysis also suggests the ways that children were now to become the objects of training which, as one of the proponents of new forms of scientific child rearing put it, "entails the inculcation of the good virtues in the child and the removal of evil germs." The virtues included thrift and industry, with their unmistakable links to a modern capitalist order.

Even the new visions of companionate marriage can be subjected to scrutiny. It is remarkable, and I think quite revealing, that in a 1958 novel by the Egyptian woman writer Out el Kouloub, the main character, who comes of age and into feminist awakening in the early part of this century, has one cause: love marriage.[27] As a young woman the protagonist Ramza persuaded her father to educate her, listened in while someone sounding much like the reformer Qasim Amin gave speeches on the rights of women in her father's salon, made friends with some French girls who introduced her to romantic novels, and eventually defied her father, family, and society (with tragic consequences) to marry for love.

Someone like Qasim Amin, the turn-of-the-century lawyer whose two controversial books *The Liberation of Women* and *The New Woman* are discussed in three of our chapters (Abu-Lughod, Shakry, and Najmabadi), did not, as the fictional heroine Ramza did, call for marriage based on romantic love. He called for deep friendship between husbands and wives, dedicating *The New Woman* (1900) to his friend and fellow nationalist Saad Zaghloul with the following words:

> I have found in you a loving heart, a thinking mind, and a determined will. You represent for me friendship in its most perfect form. . . . Our friendship has led me to consider the value of such a love when shared between a man and his wife. This is the secret of happiness that I declare to the citizens of my country, men or women.[28]

Who could disagree that calling for marriages based on choice and love—or at least consent, as most interpretations of Islamic law require—would benefit women? From the perspective of women (and men) forced into arranged marriages they do not want, certainly the opposite looks better. However, anyone who has lived in communities where arranged marriages prevail and where "the couple" is not a well-developed ideal or made the quintessential social bond has also found many marriages filled with affection and companionability.

What lay behind this idealization of love and companionate marriage and the condemnation of their opposites? Puzzling over Allen Duben and Cem Behar's finding that there had already been a pronounced shift toward nuclear families well before Turkish reformers boldly denounced the extended patriarchal family as outmoded, Kandiyoti has asked why it was that these reformers staked their claims to modernity and even to political independence on their advocacy of this "new" form of family.[29] Again we see the power of the rhetoric of the new. But she also asks about the larger social context for this promotion of domestic mores and the consequences of reformers' vehement espousal of this new vision. My own argument in this book is that one must be suspicious of Qasim Amin's call for a good wife to be companion to the "new man" because, among other things, it was linked to a denunciation of women's homosocial networks that encouraged certain kinds of subversions of men's authority.[30] Kandiyoti goes further to ask what sorts of male sexualities the privileging of this new heterosexual domesticity rendered perverse, or invisible.

The tricky task in all this is how to be skeptical of modernity's progressive claims of emancipation and critical of its social and cultural operations and yet appreciate the forms of energy, possibility, even power that aspects of it might have enabled, especially for women. How can one question modernity without implying that one longs nostalgically for some premodern formation? Feminist scholars feel this dilemma acutely because they cannot ignore the fact that gendered power has taken and can take many forms. As Hatem's chapter shows, the kinds of constraints within which a late-nineteenth-century woman poet had to work were deeply troubling.

All the chapters in this book offer subtle and compelling ways of assessing the impact for women of the kinds of modernizing projects and discourses that marked the nineteenth and twentieth centuries in the Middle East. As Najmabadi puts it, one needs to become attuned to the ways these projects might have been simultaneously regulatory and emancipatory. Her argument, for example, is that the "discourse of domesticity" provided the very grounds from which the male domain of modern education could be opened up, and with it women's movement into public life and national recognition. Later, women could use notions of serving the state to claim higher education and professions. In her study of the prescriptive biographies of famous women that appeared in the Arab press in the first decades of this century, Marilyn Booth has similarly noted that the ideological work these biographies did was both constrictive and expansive for women's lives.[31]

In sharpening the distinction between the public and private realms, writers of the era could now problematize women's absence from the public (and thus encourage them to enter it) while enforcing new norms of the private, now elaborated as a unique and busy domain in which women should exert themselves. A discourse of scientific domesticity for the middle classes and emergent elite, while appearing to confirm women's place in the home and in fact to tie women more closely to newly redefined households, also gave them a quasi-professional status that may have paved the way for other professions. As Najmabadi argues, if women's education was promoted only in the name of preparing them to become good mothers who could produce the new citizens of the nation (and we should not forget the novelty of each of these roles), girls' experiences in schools gave them valuable practice in "public" life on which they could base later claims to equal citizenship for themselves. This is not dissimilar to Baron's insight that the women's press in Egypt was transformative, not so much through the ideas it promoted, many of which oriented women to domesticity, but through the practices of writing, signing their names, public speaking, publishing, and reading that it encouraged.[32]

Booth's chapter articulates the ambiguity of the historical development of "feminism" in the Middle East most eloquently when it observes that the content of the biographies of famous women published in magazines as models for young women did not always conform to the rhetoric that framed them. In their inconsistency and multiplicity, these biographies may have succeeded in pushing the boundaries of the thinkable. She seeks the key to the popularity of Jeanne d'Arc as a subject of biographies until the 1940s in the way this figure encapsulated struggles over identities and loyalties that young Egyptian women were facing: how to reconcile duties to nation, God, and family. Her value as an exemplar lay not just in her anti-imperialism but in her perseverance and courage.

One can make these arguments about new possibilities without denying the poststructuralist critiques of the liberal discourses and technologies of power of the modern state or forgetting that becoming a citizen or a worker is itself making oneself subject in new ways—not just to family and community but also to the state and economy. One can make them without forgetting that to attend modern educational institutions is to be interpellated into new discourses about the training of minds and characters and new practices of disciplining bodies. Even today, young Bedouin women in Egypt try to resist their elders and the kin-based forms of domination they represent by embracing aspects of a commodified sexuality—buying makeup and negligees—that carry with them both new forms of control and new freedoms.[33] And one can make them without forgetting, as Hatem points out in her biography of ʿAʾisha Taymur, that when women were offered or struggled for more public roles, these made no allowance for their continued—and perhaps enhanced—domestic responsibilities and nurturing roles, placing them under enormous strain. For Taymur, this caused tremendous grief. The chapters in this book show that the forms of feminism in the Middle East tied to modernity ushered in new forms of gendered subjection (in the double sense of subject-positions for women and forms of domination) as well as new experiences and possibilities.

POSTCOLONIAL THEORY AND THE RETHINKING OF EAST/WEST POLITICS

Perhaps the most troubling question, for scholars and Middle East activists alike, concerns the relationship between modernity and the West. In colonial or semicolonial contexts, the distinction between modernity and tradition (with its correlate, backwardness) had a particularly active life because it was

paired with that between the West and the non-West. Europe was modern; the
East was not. How might one become modern when one was not, could not be,
or did not want to be Western? Women have had a prominent place in the
debates and struggles over this question, and many of the images with which
this chapter opened are signs of this continuing centrality.

It is difficult for anyone thinking about "the woman question" today, as
at the turn of the century, to escape the language of accusations and counter-
accusations about cultural authenticity. Are attempts to transform the
condition of women indigenous or foreign? It has become something of a
commonplace in postcolonial studies to talk about the ways that the low status
attributed by missionaries and colonial officials to colonized women—represented as the victims of traditions, whether Hindu, Muslim, or pagan—were
used as a justification for rule. As Gayatri Chakravorty Spivak has asked for
India, to put it bluntly, what are we to think of white men saving brown women
from brown men?[34] Or white women saving brown women from brown men,
as would be the case with those dedicated women missionaries who tell their
tales in *Our Moslem Sisters*?[35]

This colonial legacy of feminism in the Middle East, linked in Mitchell's
work to larger projects of power, has been more directly explored by Leila
Ahmed in her analysis of the way that Lord Cromer, the British governor of
Egypt in the early years of the twentieth century, seemed to champion the
emancipation of Egyptian women while condemning women suffragists back
home in England. She argues that the European obsession with unveiling
women, reflected in the efforts of Lord Cromer (and the even more drastic
efforts Marnia Lazreg has documented for the French in Algeria), has produced the contemporary fixation on the veil as the quintessential sign of
Muslim resistance and cultural authenticity.[36] Ahmed frames her critique of
what she calls "colonial feminism" in terms of the concept of culture. She
argues that what the colonists sought was to undermine the local culture. Like
Lazreg, another feminist scholar from the Arab world who has had to confront
academic feminists in the West, she is particularly disturbed by the resemblances she perceives between the colonial discourses and the discourses of
some Western feminists of today. Ahmed worries that some Western feminists
devalue local cultures by presuming that there is only one path for emancipating women—adopting Western models.

This framing in terms of "cultures" has a long history, great contemporary
currency, and, it must be added, an imperial genealogy. It marked the dominant critical discourse in Iran in the decade and a half before the 1979 revolution when, as Sullivan notes, Jalal Al-Ahmad's notion of "westoxication" was
applied by the radical thinker Ali Shariati to a certain class of women who
epitomized the loss of culture and morals the Pahlavi regime encouraged:
the idle, made-up, consumerist Westernized "painted dolls."[37] As many have
argued for the Arab world, the rhetoric of return to authentic culture runs

through the Islamist discourse that attributes political defeats like the 1967 war with Israel as well as contemporary social problems to the straying from the Islamic path. This kind of argumentation, pitting Islamic culture against Western, is crucial to calls for women's veiling.

But even a century ago, most advocates of changes in women's roles felt the need to justify their programs as being in conformity to Islam—interpreting the Qur'an to support their arguments, even while accepting the Western equation of women's status and level of civilization. As a way out of this bind, as Renée Worringer's research on the Arab press reveals, Japan was often invoked as a model to emulate.[38] Japan was pictured as an "Eastern" country that had successfully borrowed technology and science from the West while preserving its own traditions. Women figured in this discourse in complex ways, as proof that a civilization, to advance, must educate its women, but also that one could modernize women without undermining social hierarchies and morality. Japan was particularly useful, in other words, because it allowed modernizers to argue for and imagine an alternative modernity, a modernity that was not Western. Even today, *Oshin*, a soap opera imported from Japan, generates arguments by secular progressives in Egypt in favor of a moral modernity, distinct from the West (and its soap operas) with its sexual immorality and individualism.[39]

This trafficking in images of East and West, particularly the anti-Western rhetoric of many oppositional movements in the Middle East, has left its mark on current feminist scholarship. As Kandiyoti notes, Ahmed divides Egyptian feminists into two camps, the indigenous or vernacular, and the Western-oriented, implicitly devaluing the latter.[40] Badran, in her careful charting of the history of the Egyptian feminist movement, rejects formulations like this, arguing that "attempts to discredit or to legitimize feminism on cultural grounds . . . are political projects." She argues instead that the origins of feminism cannot be sought in any culturally pure location. " 'External elements'—external to class, region, country—are appropriated and woven into the fabric of the 'indigenous' or local. Egypt has historically appropriated and absorbed 'alien elements' into a highly vital indigenous culture."[41] She implies that Egyptian feminism is part of such an indigenous (fluid and always in process) culture, and locates feminists like the upper-class Huda Sha'rawi and Saiza Nabarawi (who spent most of her youth in France not even knowing who her real Egyptian mother was) squarely within their local context, in part on the basis of their identification with Egypt and their commitment to it.[42] She shows how such women were more nationalist and uncompromising regarding British colonialism than men of their class. She also shows how despite meeting with European feminists and developing their ideas in relationship to European women and feminist organizations, Egyptian feminists were politically independent. They expressed criticism of European support for Zionism and were most concerned with the lot of Egyptian and Arab women.

In short, her argument, like Nelson's about the controversial later feminist Doria Shafik, is that these women were very much part of and concerned about their own societies and cannot be dismissed as Western (hence somehow inauthentic) agents.[43]

However, this construction as indigenous, or in Amrita Basu's more useful term, "local," of the feminism of such women who had strong ties to Europeans, in not only the languages in which they wrote, but their formative influences, their interlocutors, and their liberal ideas, carries with it a risk different from that embodied by the stark opposition of Western/inauthentic versus Eastern/authentic.[44] The danger is that the conjunctures between the projects of Europeans and Middle Easterners and the actual role of European discourses in Middle Eastern ones, often mediated, as argued earlier, through the projects of modernity, are passed over too quickly. The actual dynamics of the processes of colonial cultural hybridization deserve more careful study.

We all write in contexts, and when we come to write the history of "the woman question" in the Middle East, we find ourselves caught: between the contemporary Egyptian or Iranian or Turkish context where Islamists denounce things Western, a label they, like many nationalist men before them, attach to feminism, and a Euroamerican context where the presumption is that only Western women could really be feminist. How to get beyond this? Showing Euroamerican colleagues that there were real feminists in the Middle East, women who fought for women's social, economic, and political rights, means having to dismiss other aspects of their projects (being uninterested in unveiling, asking for limited reforms in family law, arguing in terms of an Islamic moral framework, accepting female difference, and stressing women's maternal roles for the good of the nation) as strategic or expedient. Demonstrating the nationalist fervor of Middle Eastern feminists may vindicate them in the eyes of their secular progressive compatriots but is less persuasive for Islamists whose loyalties might be the larger Muslim community, not the nation-state. The solution is to refuse, as Badran has attempted, to be dragged into the binary opposition between East and West in which so many such arguments are mired. However, the most powerful way to do this is to fearlessly examine the processes of entanglement.

One can look to new work in anthropology and postcolonial studies for ways to question rigid concepts of culture. In particular, one can ask about the ways such notions of separate cultures have themselves been produced by the colonial encounter. This leads to different possibilities for analyzing the politics of East and West in the debates about women, ones that do not take the form of narratives of cultural domination versus resistance, cultural loyalty versus betrayal, or cultural loss versus preservation. It also opens up the possibility of exploring, in all their specificities, the actual cultural dynamics of the colonial encounter and its aftermath.

One of the most productive lines of thought made possible by Edward Said's *Orientalism* has been the reframing of world history as a global phenomenon, with the recognition that the division between West and East, and the representations of each, were produced in the historical encounter broadly labeled imperialism.[45] One can ask how empire was constitutive both of Europe and of the regions that came under its orbit. A scholar of colonialism like Ann Stoler has, for example, asked how the history of European bourgeois culture could be written without reference to the context of empire with which it was so intertwined.[46] Said's recent book *Culture and Imperialism* has explored how the canonic texts of Western high culture must be read in the imperial contexts in which they were written and read.[47] Several scholars have shown how techniques, practices, and institutions we associate with the West were first developed or tested in the colonies.[48]

On the other hand, the new literature on the colonial encounter has been exploring how colonialism was not only a process of capitalist expansion, political domination, and financial extraction but a process that profoundly transformed the everyday lives and discursive terms of the colonized. This is not to make colonialism monolithic: many of its projects failed or were disrupted and diverted; it differed by historical period and location; there were tensions among colonists; the colonized were affected differently depending on their class, gender, geographic location, and other factors.[49] But it is to recognize that one must tell the story of colonialism in part in cultural terms (in the broadest sense of the meaning of culture) while attending to the ways that notions of "cultures"—distinct and antithetical—themselves became reified.[50]

Some recent thinking in postcolonial studies has the potential to get us beyond the impasse of this ossified notion of culture and the binaries that it underwrites. This is especially important, as Partha Chatterjee has shown, in the analysis of how what he calls "the rule of colonial difference" (the difference and inferiority attributed to the colonized) shaped nationalist responses. He has argued that in Bengal, at least, nationalists seeking to overturn the power of Britain initiated a cultural process before a political movement. They divided the world into an inner and an outer domain, a kind of private and public, in which men could safely emulate the ways of the West and appropriate its technologies in order to gain power as long as the home, with women its clearest representatives, could be preserved as a space of spirituality and cultural authenticity.[51] In studies of nationalism and women in the Middle East, most have treated nationalism as a political movement—and one that failed women—rather than seeing it also as a cultural or discursive project in which ideals of womanhood and notions of the modern were key elements.[52]

So how did the colonized, or semicolonized, or even those who just looked westward and saw great power, explain what they could now see only as their own backwardness? How did they seek to remedy it? How did gender enter into their formulations? Two basic processes resulted. First, rhetorical efforts were made by those one could broadly call nationalists to put distance between their proposals and the West, often by arguing for an Islamic modernism. Second, what actually happened was that there occurred complicated and interesting entanglements. Ideals of womanhood were central to both processes.

The history of the "modernizing" world is often written as one of failed imitation of the West—failures of secular democracy, failures of nationalism, failures of enlightened modernity, failures due to the pull of tradition, travesties of modernity. But in recent years, a number of theorists of the postcolonial have been thinking more creatively about the encounter between West and East. They have pursued the analytical implications of the insight that modernity is a construct and an organizing trope, especially for the national developmentalist successors of colonial regimes. They have also suggested that translation, hybridization, and even dislocation might be more useful metaphors than imitation, assimilation (forced or attempted), or rejection for grasping what happened in the colonial encounter.[53]

Such notions as hybridization and translation seem especially appropriate for the complex mixtures one finds in the Middle East where the term "postcolonial" might seem confusing. By privileging the colonial experience in the (de)formation of those parts of the world that were subjected to European control, notions of the postcolonial might seem more appropriate to places like India, the Caribbean, or Algeria. After all, it can be protested, two major countries, Iran and Turkey, were never formally colonized by European powers. The history of the Middle East is far more messy, complicated by a local empire, Ottoman, overthrown by Europe-crazy republicans who were, nevertheless, very much Turks and a Persian region with an imperial history, struggling with constitutionalists, who all hoped to maintain it as a sovereign area when it was threatened by two encroaching imperialisms, British and Russian. Even Egypt, formally occupied by Britain only in 1882, earlier became the site of extensive "indigenous" attempts at modernizing and industrializing by an ambitious Ottoman provincial governor, considered by some a nationalist, who sent students off to France to study and tried to create a new order, carried out its own colonization of the Sudan, and was ruled until a revolution in the middle of this century by a Turkish-Egyptian aristocracy. And as Kandiyoti points out, the Middle East was a site of incredible ethnic diversity where local differences seemed more vivid than those between East and West.

What makes the term "postcolonial" and the mode of thinking and scholarship that has grown up around it pertinent for the Middle East is the unquestionable way that, as even this potted history makes clear, Europe was a crucial context for its historical development and its political and cultural life. One may argue that there persisted alternative "traditions" (in the sense meant by Alasdair MacIntyre and elaborated for the Muslim world by Talal Asad and

Samira Haj) within which argumentation took place, and thus that intellectual life was not only, as earlier intellectual historians of the Middle East have suggested, reactive to Europe.[54] But one must admit that even these could not, certainly from the nineteenth century, have avoided taking into some account the encounter with Europe.

There is an amazing document from South Asia that illustrates the way Muslim thinkers can both be working within a separate Muslim tradition, using its familiar tools and language, and yet be shaped by the colonial encounter. Called *Bihishti Zewar*, or the *Heavenly Ornaments*, it is a still popular guide for the Muslim woman, written at the turn of the century by Maulana Ashraf ʿAli Thanawi, a Deobandi Muslim reformer.[55] It is as odd a mixture as one could imagine. It begins as a literacy primer that also teaches proper forms of address; then moves on to inform women about religious teachings, and to provide models of the good woman (including the Prophet Muhammad himself), a list of one hundred hadith (sayings of the Prophet) women need to know, and guidelines for proper moral conduct. Although the latter draw on a long tradition of guidelines for moral conduct (in the past written for men), they are eerily Foucauldian-modern in their obsession with self-discipline.

And what emerges in the long sections prescribing good Muslim versus sinful behavior is that besides the purification of the Muslim community's practices (sloughing off Hindu accretions), Thanawi is intent on breaking up the independence of the women's community with its rituals, gossip, and visiting. He wants to place women—now educated, now self-disciplined, now properly Muslim—firmly in their homes and under their husbands' control. Thanawi will empower women with literacy but relegate them to a newly created private sphere where they can even develop some modern forms of housewifery (he includes weights and measures and recipes in the concluding sections). As Barbara Metcalf points out in her commentary on the translation, the backdrop to the document is the promotion in South Asia by the British of women's education and the fear of competition from Hindus, now being educated in mission schools, that left the Muslim community feeling vulnerable and backward. Despite being firmly rooted in a distinct community of Muslims uninterested in "Westernization," in its address to women one can hear echoes of that colonial discourse about the relationship between a civilization and the status of its women.

The studies of the Middle East presented here in *Remaking Women* provide evidence of a far more direct link to European discourses on gender and more explicit debates about the value of emulating the West than the South Asian case of the *Bihishti Zewar* just described. It is well known that reformers like the lawyer Qasim Amin studied in France and that the founder of the Egyptian Feminist Union was in her youth close to a Frenchwoman married to an Egyptian and converted to Islam.[56] Najmabadi provides evidence of widespread translation into Persian of French manuals of domestic instruction, not to mention translations of Qasim Amin's work from the Arabic. The biographies of famous women that appeared in the Egyptian press included not just the kind of biographies of Muslim heroines reproduced in texts like *Bihishti Zewar* but also biographies extolling European women's accomplishments. Shakry gives plenty of evidence of translations from the European press and shows the impact of the German kindergarten movement on Egyptian discussions of proper child rearing. Everywhere one looks, in fact, one sees the grafting of European ideas and practices, diverse as these may be.

But as Shakry argues, despite the borrowings and imitations, one also sees differences—either attempted consciously or introduced unconsciously because of the dissimilarities between foreign and local ideas and practices. She suggests that we examine more closely the ways that being framed within an Islamic discourse and argued with some of its tools (reference to the Qur'an, etc.) subtly transformed the translated discourses on motherhood and housewifery. Both Westernized and Islamist reformers in Egypt situated their projects as a defense of Islam and a critique of custom, thus in a complex dialogue with colonial discourse. Here she has followed a lead from Dipesh Chakrabarty's analysis of the public narratives about domesticity in nineteenth-century Bengal.[57] He has shown that what emerged in Bengal as a result of the encounter with the British was a new hybrid concept of the ideal wife. She was to be modern and scientific yet duty-bound within a Hindu "religious" framework. This new middle-class ideal was incommensurate in culturally specific ways with the British concepts that informed it and at the same time quite different from any previous Bengali understanding of women's roles in the household and family. As Chakrabarty concludes, "There are bits [of Bengali modernity] . . . that don't owe their existence to the bourgeois projects that European imperialism brought to India. Nor are these ideas mere historical residues, remnants of a past, left there only because the colonial-Bengali transition to modernity did not afford us the allegedly leisurely pace of the transformation in Europe."[58]

Najmabadi's evidence that translations always involved rewritings of the original text or framing by commentaries that drew from the texts different meanings signals the workings of this kind of dynamic. Booth's analysis of the complex ways that Jeanne d'Arc could be made into an Egyptian heroine reveals other dynamics: in particular the way that the West could be appropriated neither as "Western" nor "universal" but rather piecemeal. Jeanne d'Arc's life was interpreted strategically in local terms and in terms of local battles: her Frenchness was subordinated to her identity as a fighter against British imperialism, the same imperialism Egyptians had to fight; her pastoral origins provided material for a romantic movement that sought to locate authenticity in the countryside; her chastity was used to support arguments for women's public roles by showing that these did not automatically imply moral depravity.

The irony is that these Egyptian women in a context of anti-British politics turned the image of Jeanne d'Arc "against its Western origins."

If one recalls that in most of these chapters it is didactic material, often on the new domestic sciences, that is being analyzed, then Chatterjee's edited volume on the disciplines, such as medicine, art history, political science, and music, in colonial Bengal becomes relevant. On the basis of a number of individual studies' findings, and writing in response to the notions of hybridization and translation elaborated by Homi Bhabha and Gyan Prakash, he argued, "Following its implantation in a different if not entirely alien field, the new discursive formation will open itself to intrusions by various elements in the preexisting linguistic or intellectual practices of the country. . . . What happens is that the new indigenous practitioners of the disciplines actively seek out the various points of entry—equivalence, similarity, adjacency, substitutability, and so forth—through which, in a ceaseless process of translation, the new knowledges are aligned with prior knowledges."[59]

Shakry demontrates this through her exploration of the ways that Western modern notions of child rearing were aligned with Islamic notions of bodily discipline. In general, we need to pursue further, for the Middle East, the way that "Islam" itself might have been transformed by being made the object of derision by missionaries, the sign of barbarism by the Europeans, and, in response, both the banner of authenticity for those opposing domination and the framework in which debates about society and women have come to take place.[60] Hatem's suggestion, based on conversations with Denise Spellberg, that the teaching of *fiqh* (Islamic law) to girls in the nineteenth century might have been a new phenomenon hints at the kinds of transformations that might have been taking place. Like the oppositional movements, and in the case of Iran, regimes, to which its name is attached, Islam's contemporary forms and meanings are products of history and the dynamics of contemporary global society. It would be worth exploring the ways that this, one of the "cultures of postcolonial *contra-modernity*," as Bhabha would say, forged at the borders between East and West, has been forced to "'translate', and therefore reinscribe, the social imaginary of both metropolis and modernity."[61]

The point is that thinking along the lines just proposed may bring new insights into the relationship between the colonizing or dominant Europe and the colonized or aspiring Middle East, so crucial to gender and the politics of feminism. We could escape the binary thinking that these scholars have begun to dismantle—thinking that posits a rigidly distinct West and East and assumes therefore the crude dynamics that correspond to this division, slavish imitation or cultural loss versus nationalist resistance and cultural preservation. We would be able to analyze dynamics like the one I trace in my chapter on contemporary Islamist rhetoric about feminism, whereby certain aspects of social and cultural life that might be considered Western-derived are repudiated for political purposes while other aspects (especially those with broad support in the middle and lower-middle classes) are barely challenged. Or one could make statements like Sullivan's that in postrevolutionary Iran we are witnessing the development of a women's movement that is "articulated in dialectical conflict" both with past narratives and with Western models.

Perhaps we could also interrogate the genealogy of feminism, in the sense of a movement dedicated to achieving political, social, and economic rights for women, in the way that we have already done for other modern movements and concepts like nationalism and, as Chatterjee now argues we might, secularism. Provocatively, he shows that secularism in India has an indisputable European genealogy, indexed among other ways linguistically (like feminism in the Middle East, for which at least in Arabic there is still no fully acceptable term).[62] Asad has long argued that secularism (and its prerequisite "religion") emerged in the history of Christianity.[63] Rather than being a universal idea, it is therefore a local one, tied to a particular history in Europe that one can examine. Further, one can trace, as Asad is beginning to do, the ways in which when linked to colonial and modernist law in a place like Egypt, it worked to actually construct both "religion," in this case Islam, and the problem of its secularization.[64] The essays in this book suggest that feminist projects are similarly rooted in sets of ideas about politics, law, rights, personhood, and community that are part of a modernity that is both related to Europe and developed in particular ways in the Middle East. To concede that such ideas and projects developed in complex interaction with European notions in societies shaped by the encounter with a more powerful Europe that prided itself on being modern is not to deny their relevance to the communities that made use of them. Nor is it to underestimate the ways that such ideas were selectively appropriated, as Kandiyoti points out in the volume's afterword, according to local needs and in terms of local struggles. It is to begin to ask how these ideas that informed projects of reform and political struggle around women were deployed as part of projects of power—colonial and national—as well as how they were translated and renegotiated.

CONCLUSION: TELLING FEMINIST STORIES

Much of the best recent literature in Middle East women's history and anthropology can be conceived of as working against universalizing discourses about patriarchy, Islam, and oppression. Scholars have been seeking to specify, to particularize, and to ground in practice, place, class, and time the experiences of women and the dynamics of gender.[65] Even when they make comparisons, it is with a deep respect for the historical, regional, and political economic specificities. In a variety of senses, these scholars now working on gender and women can be thought of as telling feminist stories—stories about gender and

power of interest to feminists, and, in the literature with which this book engages most closely, the stories of feminism as a social and political movement
in the Middle East.

We have worked with a broad definition of feminism in this book, including
in our purview not just the organized women's movements so ably analyzed
by other scholars who came before us, but the wide range of projects that
have or had as an explicit goal or necessary foundation the remaking of
women. We consider such projects whether initiated by men or women and
whether expressed in practical projects (like starting schools) or in debates
and calls to action in the press, books, speeches, sermons on cassette, or television soap operas.

Among the advantages of such an inclusive definition is that one is not
forced to apologize when local projects do not appear to conform to a particular definition of feminism.[66] Nor need one try to explain away—with arguments about expediency, safe topics, or marketing—stances that seem to
go against a liberal or socialist feminist thrust. One need not be so eager to
enlist historical individuals as heroines and icons of modernity, making
their complex lives signify the story of progress, as Hatem argues Arab feminists and contemporary scholars have done with the nineteenth-century poet
'A'isha Taymur.

More important, this inclusive or loose definition and the very exploration
of the ways in which women have been targeted for reform in projects of social
transformation as well as themselves seeking to change their status, lives, and
societies, make it impossible for us to forget that feminism always occurs in
particular contexts, historical and social. The essays in this book suggest the
kinds of contexts that were crucial to projects with women at their center: state
building with its requirement of controlling and making productive popula-
tions; nationalism and the forging of modernities that could confront colonialism and respond to the sense of backwardness the encounter with Europe had
engendered; changes in political organization with a move against ancien
régimes that were now felt to be outmoded and oppressive; a concomitant
consolidation of new class identities, with the emergence of more powerful
upper-middle and middle classes; and, most recently, failures of "secular modern" states to deliver on their promises to a wide constituency, their violence
against certain groups and ideals coming back, as Sullivan suggests, like the
return of the repressed, to haunt them.

The risk of such a broad definition is that one might fail to make crucial
distinctions among such projects, regarding either their consequences for
women or the motives of those involved. What I think we have managed,
however, is to avoid the pitfalls that critical historians of nationalism in India
have been accused of (several of whom have been cited in this chapter): of
colluding with the nationalists they study by domesticating and silencing
women in their scholarship.[67] Kamala Visweswaran has, like other feminist

scholars, argued that the subaltern studies school is strangely silent on women's agency, though in its earlier phases it was concerned with the agency of subalterns. The essays in this book, while placing all feminist projects within their local and historical contexts, have not ignored women's particular activism on behalf of women. Booth relies exclusively on women's writings in the press and shows how they used biographies of famous women to stretch the boundaries of acceptable gender roles. Hatem's rereading of the biography of the nineteenth-century woman poet uncovers the ways that modernist historians have ignored the role of other women, who might be regarded as traditional, in enabling her rise to this position. While Shakry and Najmabadi examine the writings of both reformist men and women in the early-twentieth-century press, finding broad overlaps between them, they note the specific voices of women. For instance, Najmabadi shows that in Iran women used calls for education as a platform for more radical demands about citizenship, and that they set up and took charge of all the girls' schools in the first decades of the century. Sullivan describes the programs for women of some key Iranian male intellectuals, but she dwells, through her interviews, on women's conflicting personal experiences of such programs. Although I describe the positions of men and women on women's issues among Egypt's contemporary Islamists and secular progressives, I note the "feminist" difference of women in both cases.

Spivak in a famous essay has questioned the very possibility of recuperating subaltern voices, including those of women. Visweswaran, in response, in a more cautious way has explored the special difficulty of recuperating the voices of any but middle-class and elite women in the study of nationalism.[68] This concern certainly applies to the study of feminism in the Middle East. Basing his insights on the archives, Fahmy can speculate that despite the difficulties they faced, the lives of the new women doctors produced by the School of Midwives may have been better than other fates their origins as slaves and orphans might have dealt them, their positions and economic security even enabling them to challenge their subordinate positions within the modern medical establishment. Similarly, based on archives and court records, Judith Tucker's pioneering study of women in nineteenth-century Egypt amply demonstrated the ways rural and lower-class women resisted new forms of power.[69] But these were not women informed by "feminism" or projects for remaking women.[70]

The rest of what we rely on, in the study of those seeking to remake women, is the written word—the productions of the literate and the educated. Without impugning the courage and vision of the upper- and middle-class women who were literate and educated, including feminists like the Iranian Siddiqeh Dawlatabadi or the Egyptian Saiza Nabarawi, we can still consider the contradictions their class positions put them in vis-à-vis other women. Shakry explains how representations of backward mothers and unhealthy children, part of a eugenic patriotism in Britain, in Egypt "served to prop up a bourgeois ideal of motherhood and rationalize a series of pedagogical and philanthropic interventions." Nabarawi, a critic of modernized housewifery, nevertheless supported the Egyptian Feminist Union's 1932 setting up of a Professional and Domestic School to train poor girls to be "excellent housekeepers" so they might find employment as domestics or workers in clothing workshops; she also described a new focus on rural Egypt as part of a duty "to raise the living standard of the peasant materially and morally."[71] Sullivan describes how Dowlatabadi, who was not intimidated when pomegranates were thrown at her during her speeches or when her life was threatened, imposed on the nine-year-old daughter of her father's secretary a marriage to her seventy-year-old father when he was widowed. She later ignored the girl's cries when she went into labor and thereafter, when Dowlatabadi's father died, married off the girl to someone else, taking her daughters. As Sullivan concludes, bringing us back to the links with the West, "She consolidated her feminism along class lines," finding "more common ground with Margaret Ashby [a New York campaigner for women's suffrage and author of *Taking Care of Home and Children* whose journal influenced the journal Dowlatabadi edited in Iran] than with her father's child bride."

One must also be careful not to accept uncritically the terms of the upper-middle- and middle-class women involved in most feminist projects—the notions of "awakening," "women's rights," and "empowerment" that are part of the narratives of progress and enlightenment that still have currency among secular progressives in the Middle East today. To accept these is to get caught up, as I argue in my chapter on the modernity of Islamism, in nonsensical notions like "retraditionalization." It is also to be led to grasp what is happening now in Iran, Algeria, or Egypt, with the more visible assertion of Islamic countermodernities, as a going backward. What we are seeing in the Middle East today in arguments about "the woman question" could not have occurred earlier. While we need to heed Kandiyoti's warning that we should not jump to celebrate the emergence of different feminisms, particularly because veiled women in places like Iran and Algeria are working within movements whose tolerance of pluralism is undemonstrated—and whose intolerance of opposition is quite evident—we should not therefore fail to interrogate the feminist discourses of modernity to which they are counterposed.[72] All these forms of feminism are products of complex histories and the projects of modernity that have been central to the Middle East. And with feminism's having become an unavoidable term of current debates across the Middle East, its stories, which must include not just education, unveiling, political rights, and domesticity but also reveiling and reinterpreting Islamic law, are worth telling in all their messiness and contradictions.

NOTES

I am grateful to all the contributors to this book for stimulating me to think in such broad terms about the issues discussed here. Special thanks to Margot Badran, Marilyn Booth, Deniz Kandiyoti, Tim Mitchell, Afsaneh Najmabadi, and two anonymous readers, one for Princeton University Press and one for the University of California Press, for their critical readings of the introduction. Over the years, students in my courses at New York University on "Theories of Modernity" and "Gender Politics in the Muslim World" have provided good intellectual company for the formulation of many of the ideas brought together here. Amanda Barnhart provided invaluable last-minute transatlantic research assistance. Finally, I want to acknowledge the National Endowment for the Humanities for a fellowship in 1996 that gave me time to write and think.

1. Personal communication, Deniz Kandiyoti. This follows debates and legal cases about wearing headscarves (illegal in government offices), which have raged since the 1980s, and the most recent elections, memorable for an appealing and slick television ad campaign by the Islamic party. See Ayşe Öncü, "Packaging Islam: Cultural Politics on the Landscape of Turkish Commercial Television," *Public Culture* 8, no. 1 (1995): 51–71.

2. See Lila Abu-Lughod, "Movie Stars and Islamic Moralism in Egypt," *Social Text* 42 (1995): 53–67; Fedwa Malti-Douglas, "A Woman and Her Sûfîs" (Washington D.C.: Center for Contemporary Arab Studies Occasional Papers, Georgetown University, 1995).

3. Akbar Mahdi, "Reconstructing Gender in Post-Revolutionary Iran: Two Perspectives on Women in the Islamic Republic," *Middle East Insight* 11, no. 5 (1995): 68–71. For more scholarly examinations of the women's journals, see Ziba Mir-Hosseini, "Stretching the Limits: A Feminist Reading of the *Sharī'a* in Post-Khomeini Iran," in *Feminism and Islam: Legal and Literary Perspectives*, ed. Mai Yamani (New York: New York University Press, 1996), pp. 285–319; and Afsaneh Najmabadi, "Feminisms in an Islamic Republic: 'Years of Hardship, Years of Growth,'" in *Islam, Gender and Social Change*, ed. Yvonne Haddad and John Esposito (Oxford: Oxford University Press, 1998), pp. 59–84.

4. See Sullivan's description of Mohammad Tavakoli's sister's defiance of paternal power and current intimidation of her brothers.

5. Karim El-Gawhary, "'It Is Time to Launch a New Women's Liberation Movement—an Islamic One': An Interview with Heba Ra'uf Ezzat," *Middle East Report* 24, no. 1, #191 (1994): 26–27.

6. Deniz Kandiyoti, "Women, Islam, and the State: A Comparative Approach," in *Comparing Muslim Societies: Knowledge and the State in a World Civilization*, ed. Juan R. I. Cole (Ann Arbor: University of Michigan Press, 1992), p. 246.

7. For arguments along the same lines as Abu-Lughod's and Sullivan's in this volume, see Mervat Hatem, "Egyptian Discourses on Gender and Political Liberalization: Do Secularist and Islamist Views Really Differ?" *Middle East Journal* 48, no. 4 (1994): 661–76; also her "Secularist and Islamist Discourses on Modernity in Egypt and the Evolution of the Post Colonial Nation-State," in *Islam, Gender, and Social Change*, ed. Yvonne Haddad and John Esposito (New York and Oxford: Oxford University Press, 1998), pp. 85–99.

8. The literature on India is large. For highlights, see Partha Chatterjee, *The Nation and Its Fragments* (Princeton: Princeton University Press, 1993); Amrita Chhaachhi, "Forced Identities: The State, Communalism, Fundamentalism and Women in India," in *Women, Islam and the State*, ed. Deniz Kandiyoti (Philadelphia: Temple University Press, 1991), pp. 144–75; Lata Mani, "Contentious Traditions: The Debate on Sati in Colonial India," in *Recasting Women*, ed. Kumkum Sangari and Sudesh Vaid (New Brunswick, N.J.: Rutgers University Press, 1990), pp. 88–126; Zakia Pathak and Rajeswari Sundur Rajan, "Shahbano," *Signs* 14, no. 31 (1989): 558–82; and Susie Tharu and K. Lalita, eds., *Women Writing in India: 600 B.C. to the Present* (New York: The Feminist Press, 1991).

9. Mary E. John, *Discrepant Dislocations: Feminism, Theory, and Postcolonial Histories* (Berkeley and Los Angeles: University of California Press, 1996), esp. pp. 109–44.

10. Aihwa Ong, "State versus Islam: Malay Families, Women's Bodies and the Body Politic in Malaysia" *American Ethnologist* 17, no. 2 (1990): 258–76.

11. See Margot Badran, "Islam, Patriarchy, and Feminism in the Middle East," *Trends in History* 4, no. 1 (1985): 48–71; Mangol Bayat, "Women and Revolution in Iran, 1905–1911," in *Women in the Muslim World*, ed. Lois Beck and Nikki Keddie (Cambridge: Harvard University Press, 1978), pp. 285–308; Juan Cole, "Feminism, Class, and Islam in Turn-of-the-Century Egypt," *International Journal of Middle East Studies* 13 (1981): 397–407; Thomas Phillip, "Feminism and Nationalism in Egypt," in *Women in the Muslim World*, pp. 285–308.

12. Deniz Kandiyoti, ed., *Women, Islam and the State* (Philadelphia: Temple University Press, 1991).

13. Leila Ahmed, *Women and Gender in Islam* (New Haven: Yale University Press, 1992); Margot Badran, *Feminists, Islam, and Nation: Gender and the Making of Modern Egypt* (Princeton: Princeton University Press, 1995); Beth Baron, *The Women's Awakening in Egypt* (New Haven: Yale University Press, 1994); Parvin Paidar, *Women and the Political Process in Twentieth-Century Iran* (Cambridge: Cambridge University Press, 1995).

14. Marilyn Booth has also been working on women's writing and the women's press in Egypt. See her " 'May Her Likes Be Multiplied': 'Famous Women' Biography and Gendered Prescription in Egypt, 1892–1935," *Signs* 22, no. 4 (1997): 827–90; "Exemplary Lives, Feminist Aspirations: Zaynab Fawwaz and the Arabic Biographical Tradition," *Journal of Arabic Literature* 26 (1995): 120–46; "Biography and Feminist Rhetoric in Early Twentieth-Century Egypt: Mayy Ziyada's Studies of Three Women's Lives," *Journal of Women's History* 3, no. 1 (1991): 38–64.

15. Paul Rabinow, *French Modern* (Cambridge: MIT Press, 1989), p. 9.

16. For a classic treatment of this issue, see Marshall Berman, *All That Is Solid Melts into Air: The Experience of Modernity* (New York: Simon and Schuster, 1982).

17. Haraway goes so far as to see scientific knowledge as a form of storytelling—an equation that she does not mean as an insult. See Donna Haraway, *Primate Visions* (New York and London: Routledge, 1989).

18. See Paul Gilroy, *The Black Atlantic: Modernity and Double-Consciousness* (Cambridge: Harvard University Press, 1993); Anne McClintock, *Imperial Leather: Race, Gender and Sexuality in the Colonial Context* (New York: Routledge, 1995); Ann

Laura Stoler, *Race and the Education of Desire* (Durham, N.C.: Duke University Press, 1995).

19. Michel Foucault, *Discipline and Punish: The Birth of the Prison*, trans. Alan Sheridan (New York: Pantheon, 1977); Michel Foucault, *The History of Sexuality: An Introduction*, trans. Robert Hurley (New York: Random House, 1978).

20. In a biting critique of the implications for women of the capitalist transformation of Europe, Jane Collier has noted the usefulness of discourses on Middle Eastern women: "[I]mages of veiled Islamic women and walled harems must also have played a role in constructing understandings of Western women's liberties. It seems no accident, for example, that consent emerges as a key difference between 'oppressed' Islamic women and 'free' Western ones during the nineteenth century, when industrialization was transforming adult women from productive members of family enterprises into economic dependents of wage-earning husbands. . . . [I]mages of oppressed Islamic women, who could neither marry for love nor develop intimate relations with polygamous husbands, must have played a crucial role in constructing images of Western women as consenting to their disempowerment within increasingly privatized and confining homes. And images of 'enslaved' Islamic women must have helped reconcile Western men to marriages that were difficult to distinguish from prostitution as the devaluation of women's work left women only 'love' to offer in return for the money they and their children needed to survive." Jane Collier, "Intertwined Histories: Islamic Law and Western Imperialism," *Contested Polities: Religious Disciplines and Structures of Modernity*, special issue of *Stanford Humanities Review* 5, no. 1 (1995): 162.

21. Mervat Hatem, "Toward a Critique of Modernization: Narrative in Middle East Women Studies," *Arab Studies Quarterly* 15, no. 2 (1993): 117–22.

22. Judith Newton, "'Ministers of the Interior': The Political Economy of Women's Manuals," in *Starting Over: Feminism and the Politics of Cultural Critique* (Ann Arbor: University of Michigan Press, 1994), pp. 125–47.

23. Afsaneh Najmabadi, "Veiled Discourse—Unveiled Bodies," *Feminist Studies* 19, no. 3 (1993): 487–518.

24. Badran, *Feminists, Islam, and Nation*, p. 68.

25. A similar interpretation is given for India of the debates about women's education by Tharu and Lalita in *Women Writing in India*. They write, "On one level education promised freedom and equality and was projected as a program that would shape the child for responsible citizenship. Yet underlying much of the discussion in the nineteenth century was the need felt as urgently by the missionaries . . . as by the new Indian men to break into the *zenana*, or the private spheres of household and family, and make women more fitting homemakers, mothers, and companions for the emerging urban middle-class men" (1:163–64). Cited in Purnima Mankekar, "Reconstituting 'Indian Womanhood': An Ethnography of Television Viewers in a North Indian City" (Ph.D. diss., University of Washington, 1993), p. 384.

26. Timothy Mitchell, *Colonising Egypt* (Cambridge: Cambridge University Press, 1988), pp. 111–13.

27. Out el Kouloub, *Ramza*, trans. Nayra Atiya (Syracuse, N.Y.: Syracuse University Press, 1994).

28. Qasim Amin, *The New Woman*, trans. Samiha Sidhom Peterson (Cairo: The American University in Cairo Press, 1995), p. xi.

29. Allen Duben and Cem Behar, *Istanbul Households* (Cambridge: Cambridge

University Press, 1991). Deniz Kandiyoti, "Gendering the Modern: On Missing Dimensions in the Study of Turkish Modernity," in *Rethinking Modernity and National Identity in Turkey*, ed. Sibel Bozdoğan and Reşat Kasaba (Seattle, Wash.: University of Washington Press, 1997), pp. 113–32.

30. One could link this, perhaps, to what Foucault has analyzed as a shift from a regime of blood and alliance to one of sexuality and bio-power, thus criticizing the modern form without romanticizing the premodern. See Foucault, *The History of Sexuality*.

31. Booth, "'May Her Likes Be Multiplied.'"

32. Baron, *The Women's Awakening in Egypt*.

33. Lila Abu-Lughod, "The Romance of Resistance: Tracing Transformations of Power through Bedouin Women," *American Ethnologist* 17 (1990): 41–55.

34. Gayatri Chakravorty Spivak, "Can the Subaltern Speak?" in *Marxism and the Interpretation of Culture*, ed. Cary Nelson and Lawrence Grossberg (Urbana: University of Illinois Press, 1988), pp. 271–313.

35. Annie Van Sommer and Samuel Zwemmer, *Our Moslem Sisters: A Cry of Need from Lands of Darkness* (New York: Fleming H. Revell Company, 1907).

36. Ahmed, *Women and Gender in Islam*, p. 163; Marnia Lazreg, *The Eloquence of Silence: Algerian Women in Question* (New York: Routledge, 1994). For an earlier treatment of colonialism and the veil in the Algerian context, see Malek Alloula, *The Colonial Harem* (Minneapolis: University of Minnesota Press, 1986).

37. See Valentine Moghadam, *Modernizing Women* (Boulder, Colo.: Lynne Reiner, 1993), pp. 141–43; Najmabadi, "Veiled Discourse"; and Nayereh Tohidi, "Modernity, Islamization, and Women in Iran," in *Gender and National Identity: Women and Politics in Muslim Societies*, ed. Valentine Moghadam (London: Zed Books, 1994), pp. 110–47.

38. Renée Worringer, "Japan as Archetype: Arab Nationalist Considerations as Reflected in the Press, 1887–1920" (paper presented at the Middle East Studies Association Meetings, 1995).

39. Lila Abu-Lughod, "The Objects of Soap Opera: Egyptian Television and the Cultural Politics of Modernity," in *Worlds Apart: Modernity through the Prism of the Local*, ed. Daniel Miller (London: Routledge, 1995), pp. 190–210.

40. Deniz Kandiyoti, Review of *Women and Gender in Islam*, *Contemporary Sociology* 2, no. 5 (1993): 688–89.

41. Badran, *Feminists, Islam, and Nation*, pp. 31–32.

42. Margot Badran, "Alternative Visions of Gender," *Al-Ahram Weekly*, February 13–19, 1997, p. 11; Badran, *Feminists, Islam, and Nation*, p. 98.

43. In her sensitive study of Doria Shafik, Nelson finds herself forced to defend this feminist in the following terms: "It is true that in her dress and physical appearance Doria Shafik appeared the epitome of the Westernized Egyptian woman, but her objectives and her commitment to free herself and her society from the 'chains of the past' were authentically Egyptian, grounded in the cultural roots of her past as well as in the present realities of her own society." Cynthia Nelson, "Biography and Women's History: On Interpreting Doria Shafik," in *Women in Middle Eastern History*, ed. Nikki Keddie and Beth Baron (New Haven: Yale University Press, 1991), pp. 310–33, quotation p. 329. For elaboration, see Nelson's *Doria Shafik, Egyptian Feminist: A Woman Apart* (Gainesville: University Press of Florida, 1996), esp. p. 283.

44. Amrita Basu, ed., *The Challenge of Local Feminisms: Women's Movements in Global Perspective* (Boulder, Colo.: Westview Press, 1995). Deniz Kandiyoti, in "Contemporary Feminist Scholarship and Middle East Studies," in *Gendering the Middle East*, ed. Deniz Kandiyoti (London: I. B. Tauris, 1996), pp. 1–27, uses another term, "local dialects" to speak of feminisms.

45. Edward Said, *Orientalism* (New York: Random House, 1978).

46. Stoler, *Race and the Education of Desire*.

47. Edward Said, *Culture and Imperialism* (New York: Knopf, 1993).

48. Mitchell, *Colonising Egypt*, p. 35; Gwendolyn Wright, *The Politics of Design in French Colonial Urbanism* (Chicago: University of Chicago Press, 1991).

49. For some of the new ways scholars are thinking about colonialism and culture, see Nicholas Dirks, ed., *Colonialism and Culture* (Ann Arbor: University of Michigan Press, 1992); Frederick Cooper and Ann Laura Stoler, eds., *Tensions of Empire* (Berkeley and Los Angeles: University of California Press, 1997); and, most exciting, the work published in the annual *Subaltern Studies*.

50. As Nicholas Dirks, in "Introduction: Colonialism and Culture," in *Colonialism and Culture*, p. 3, puts it, "If colonialism can be seen as a cultural formation, so also culture is a colonial formation."

51. Chatterjee, *The Nation and Its Fragments*, esp. chaps. 2 and 6.

52. For an example of a fine collection that nevertheless remains within this paradigm, see Valentine Moghadam, ed., *Gender and National Identity* (London: Zed Press, 1994).

53. These ideas about translation and hybridity have been developed by Homi Bhabha, *The Location of Culture* (London and New York: Routledge, 1994), esp. chaps. 6 and 12. Gyan Prakash in "Science between the Lines," in *Subaltern Studies* IX, ed. Shahid Amin and Dipesh Chakrabarty (Delhi: Oxford University Press, 1996), pp. 59–82, and in "Science Gone Native," *Representations* 40 (1992): 153–78 makes these arguments in the historical context of the colonial development of science in India. For further thinking that links such ideas directly to the problems of modernity, see Timothy Mitchell, "Introduction: The Stage of Modernity," in *Questions of Modernity* (Minneapolis: University of Minnesota Press, forthcoming).

54. Alasdair MacIntyre, *After Virtue*, 2d ed. (Notre Dame, Ind.: University of Notre Dame Press, 1984); Talal Asad, *Genealogies of Religion* (Baltimore: Johns Hopkins University Press, 1993) and "The Idea of an Anthropology of Islam" (Washington D.C.: Center for Contemporary Arab Studies Occasional Papers, Georgetown University, 1986); Samira Haj, *Reconfiguring Tradition: Islamic Rationality, Reform, and Modern Power* (forthcoming).

55. Barbara Daly Metcalf, *Perfecting Women: Maulana Ashraf ʿAli Thanawi's Bihishti Zewar* (Berkeley and Los Angeles: University of California Press, 1990).

56. See Badran, *Feminists, Islam, and Nation*, pp. 37–38.

57. Dipesh Chakrabarty, "The Difference-Deferral of a Colonial Modernity: Public Debates on Domesticity in British Bengal," *Subaltern Studies* VIII, ed. David Arnold and David Hardiman (Delhi: Oxford University Press, 1994), pp. 50–88.

58. Chakrabarty, "The Difference-Deferral of Modernity," p. 83.

59. Partha Chatterjee, "The Disciplines in Colonial Bengal," in *Texts of Power*, ed. Partha Chatterjee (Minneapolis: University of Minnesota Press, 1995), p. 23.

60. Peter Gran, *Islamic Roots of Capitalism: Egypt, 1760–1840* (Austin: University

of Texas Press, 1979), has begun this process but does not consider the impact on gender.

61. Bhabha, *The Location of Culture*, p. 6.

62. Partha Chatterjee, "Religious Minorities and the Secular State: Reflections on an Indian Impasse," *Public Culture* 8, no. 1 (1995): 11–39. On "feminism," see Karen Offen, "On the French Origin of the Words Feminism and Feminist," *Feminist Issues* 8, no. 2 (1988): 45–51.

63. Asad, *Genealogies of Religion*.

64. Talal Asad, "Notes on Modernizing Religion and the Law in Egypt" (Paper presented at the conference, "Questions of Modernity," New York University, April 1996).

65. Samples of the fine work being done in history are collected in Nikki Keddie and Beth Baron, eds., *Women in Middle Eastern History* (New Haven: Yale University Press, 1991).

66. Perhaps anticipating the objections of her readers, Baron—who evinces great sympathy for the efforts of the turn-of-the-century Arab women writers whose work she analyzes—nevertheless writes of their efforts to link their cause to nationalism and to emphasize their moral influence as mothers in the following way: "[T]hey set limits, defining themselves in their relationships to men *rather than as autonomous human beings* and appealing to men for reform and change rather than trying to implement more of *their own ideas*. They criticized the foreign occupation and Western ways, claiming that these contributed to the nation's and women's plights; but they *rarely condemned Egyptian men* for their role in subordinating women or explored women's own recreation of the social system" (my emphasis).

67. See Kamala Visweswaran, "Small Speeches, Subaltern Gender: Nationalist Ideology and Its Historiography," *Subaltern Studies* IX, ed. Shahid Amin and Dipesh Chakrabarty (Delhi: Oxford University Press, 1996), pp. 83–125.

68. Spivak, "Can the Subaltern Speak?"; Visweswaran, "Small Speeches, Subaltern Gender," p. 89.

69. Judith Tucker, *Women in Nineteenth Century Egypt* (Cambridge: Cambridge University Press, 1985).

70. I would not want to imply, however, that the writings of the elite and middle-class men and women considered in this book's essays should be seen as irrelevant to other classes. The ideas have been diffused through the educational system, which can now be considered a system of mass education. In Egypt, for example, the legacy of the discourses of modern domesticity can be seen in the compulsory home economics classes for girls, where hygienic methods of cooking are taught. For a vivid description, see Linda Herrera, *Scenes of Schooling: Inside a Girls' School in Cairo, Cairo Papers in Social Science* 1 (1992).

71. Cited in Badran, *Feminists, Islam, and Nation*, pp. 112, 118.

72. Deniz Kandiyoti, "Reflections on the Politics of Gender in Muslim Societies: From Nairobi to Beijing," in *Faith and Freedom: Women's Human Rights in the Muslim World*, ed. Mahnaz Afkhami (London: I. B. Tauris, 1995), pp. 19–32; quotation p. 29.

Part One

REWRITING FEMINIST BEGINNINGS:

THE NINETEENTH CENTURY

CHAPTER 1

Women, Medicine, and Power in Nineteenth-Century Egypt

KHALED FAHMY

In 1825 a certain Dr. Antoine-Barthélemy Clot, a French doctor from Marseilles, arrived in Cairo answering a request from Mehmed Ali Pasha, the governor of Egypt, to organize the country's medical system. Two years later Dr. Clot succeeded in founding a modern medical school attached to an impressive new hospital that he also founded in Abu Zaʿbal at the northern outskirts of Cairo and which by the late 1830s had managed to produce 420 medical doctors for the pasha's large army and navy.[1] The hospital, which was later called Qasr al ʿAini (after its new location southwest of Cairo), was mainly aimed at treating the soldiers of the rapidly expanding army of the pasha; the civilian population, on the other hand, was mostly treated in the Civilian Hospital founded in 1837 and located in the elite quarter of Azbakiyya in northwestern Cairo. In Alexandria the Mahmudiyya Hospital that was founded in 1827 admitted naval soldiers, workers in the Alexandria Arsenal, and their families. In addition to founding hospitals and opening what was by all accounts an impressive medical school, the pasha and his chief medical adviser also instituted a nationwide vaccination program against smallpox, introduced free medical care for the urban population, and, by founding a modern press, undertook an ambitious project of translating more than fifty medical titles from various European languages into Arabic.[2]

One of the most interesting of the numerous medical institutions that Egypt witnessed in the first half of the nineteenth century was a School of Midwives. Established in 1832, it was intended to teach young women some basics of modern medicine. During their six years of study the first two focused on Arabic literacy, followed by four years of special training in the following fields: obstetrics, pre- and postnatal care, dressing wounds, cauterization, vaccination, scarification, cupping, and the application of leeches, in addition to identification and preparation of the most common medicines. Thus these girls were educated not only in midwifery and obstetrics but also in basic knowledge of modern medicine. This was a good enough reason for LaVerne Kuhnke, the leading historian of the subject, to refer to them not as *daya*s, the name reserved for the traditional midwives, but as *hakima*s, that is, female doctors.[3] Kuhnke goes on to argue that the school was remarkable for being "the first government educational institution for women in the Middle East."[4] Moreover, if one looks at the contemporary European scene, the school compares very favorably. At a time when medical men in Europe (especially in England and France) were gradually replacing women in the medical profession on the grounds that the latter were weak, unfit for public service, or, with regard to midwives in particular, forming an inferior class of practitioners,[5] the Egyptian School of Midwives was offering women the opportunity to receive modern education in medical science and to be part of the state-sponsored medical system.

The pioneering aspect of the school was a cause for amazement for all contemporary European travelers who not only did not find Egyptian women locked up in their harems but in fact saw them working in modern health establishments. One such traveler, a certain Dr. Wilde who was a fellow of the Royal College of Surgeons in Ireland, was impressed by how Mehmed Ali, "mindful not only of the lives of his soldiers and subjects, but even of the lowest female in his dominions, . . . has re-introduced the female midwives of Egypt."[6] Another traveler was amazed to be admitted into the school and to find "an ʿalim, a Muslim doctor, teaching women—this is truly a revolution. When one has seen this, it seems insignificant to add that the students . . . were not embarrassed in the least to remain with their faces uncovered, even in the presence of Christians. Their head was simply surrounded by a veil of white gauze covering the chin and falling gracefully on the shoulder."[7] One cannot fail to notice how the European traveler in this case was not appalled by the veil, one of two typical motifs constantly highlighted in the writings of European visitors to the Middle East in the nineteenth century (the other being the harem, of course). The argument implicitly put forward in this brief but telling description of the School of Midwives in the early 1840s runs as follows: As a result of the modern education that these women were receiving, they were being enlightened. The medieval institution of the veil that had secluded them and helped to put them in an inferior place could not stand the pressure of modern times: it was now "falling gracefully" and would soon be all but forgotten. Indeed, the veil appears here not as covering the face, blocking vision and light, but "surrounding" the head and sanctifying those graceful figures like the halo of angels and saints. The message is clear: Islam, superstition, and old customs could not be a match for the power and lure of modern science.

More recent historians, moreover, could not but feel impressed by the school. They hail it as "one of the most remarkable reforms of Muhammad Ali"[8] and perceive it as an example of how enlightened the regime of Mehmed Ali was because of its "openness toward women's studying European subjects."[9] Indeed, it is seen as decisively changing the position of Egyptian women in a way that made them more prepared than other women in the

Middle East to ask for their liberation. "[W]as not this rapid incursion into domains beyond those traditionally closed for her [i.e., the Egyptian woman]," a modern scholar wonders about this particular experience, "a factor curbing her retreat into them? Did not the breaking of this weak link, connecting her briefly to life, leave behind a feeling of nostalgia which would explain why the Egyptian woman was the first in the Arab world to claim her right nearly half a century later to greater independence, to work, and to public and political life?"[10]

This is how this particular institution has been viewed and studied: as an example of an enlightened project offered by a reforming government to its secluded female population. The metaphors of light, vision, and enlightenment associated with the introduction of modern science as contrasted with veiling, religion, and superstition abound in the literature on this school as indeed they do regarding all institutions introduced by the "enlightened" Mehmed Ali. In these pages I challenge this positive, modernist view that contemporary observers and later historians alike have commonly held regarding this school. Relying on the school's documents housed in the Egyptian National Archives in Cairo, I ask a set of questions concerning its daily functioning that, it is hoped, will enable us to come to a closer understanding of its nature and the purpose of its establishment, its impact on the students who attended it, and the effect it had on society at large. Specifically I raise the following questions. What were the conditions under which these girls were recruited to and educated in the school? Upon graduation, what problems did they encounter in assuming their new positions and performing their tasks? What was the reaction of their male colleagues to them? What did they themselves think of this whole "experiment" and their role in it? And, finally, what does this particular institution tell us about the introduction of modern "reforms" in a "traditional" society, reforms that were targeted at women and were aimed at "improving" their lot?

Rather than seeing this school only as an institution used by the state to spread modern education to Egyptian women or to improve their status in society, or, alternatively, arguing that it was yet another institution that the state used to spread its influence and control over the population, this paper demonstrates that the School of Midwives and indeed all health establishments were *sites of contestation* on which various battles about "modernity" and "science" were fought. It is in the context of the School of Midwives and its female students as much as in that of any other of Mehmed Ali's "modern" institutions that different ideas concerning "modernization," "reform," and "enlightenment" were contested and challenged; such issues were raised as the proper role of women, the views of religious scholars regarding changes that Egypt was witnessing, and the relative position of various social and ethnic groups within Egypt. By closely studying an institution that was at the forefront of the exciting process of "modernization" that nineteenth-century

Egypt was witnessing, this paper shows how the people mostly concerned with this institution, the graduates of the School of Midwives, were not only objects of discipline and control by the state but also conscious subjects who benefited considerably from the chance that was offered to them to improve their position in society.

SCIENCE AND THE FOUNDING OF THE EGYPTIAN NATION

Before we look closely at the school and its everyday functioning, however, it might be useful to trace the origins of the conventional view of the School of Midwives. One source is, interestingly, the pronouncements of Mehmed Ali himself to his European visitors. These foreign travelers were often keen on adding more color to their already exotic Oriental tour by visiting "the old spider in his den," as one British traveler described the almost ritualized encounter with the pasha in his citadel in Cairo.[11] On his part the pasha, desperate to influence public opinion in Europe and to improve his chances of forcing the Ottoman sultan to grant him hereditary rule of Egypt, used these travelers in his efforts to portray his regime as an enlightened, egalitarian one attempting to introduce modern ideas in his province at a time when the central lands of the Ottoman Empire were suffering from bigotry and superstition. Aware that he lacked the right to appoint political agents (ambassadors or consuls) in European capitals, since technically and legally he was only a governor of an Ottoman province, Mehmed Ali had few tools available for this project of influencing European public opinion. One strategy was to stage the visits of the European tourists and, in a sense, to condition what they would write about.[12] The record these travelers left does suggest that he often succeeded in using them for that purpose. Consider, for example, the following account of an interview he once gave to Sir John Bowring, a British "adviser" whom Lord Palmerston, the British foreign secretary, had sent to Egypt to report on the pasha's finances and government, but who soon struck up a rather intimate friendship with the old pasha. "Do not judge me by the standard of your knowledge. Compare me with the ignorance that is around me. . . . I can find very few to understand me and do my bidding. . . . I have been almost alone for the greater part of my life."[13] How can one remain unmoved by this canny announcement in which the pasha reveals himself as the great lonely reformer, little understood by his own people but determined, nevertheless, to push his country into "modernity?" Coming to the country when it was teetering on near collapse and misery, he uplifted it from the brink of total chaos and stoically and steadily attempted to modernize it. What is of relevance here is his allusion to modern science to justify his position in Egypt and to answer European criticism of his rule and his controversial rebellion against the Ottoman sultan.

It is also significant that in his attempts to influence (and even condition) the views of these foreign visitors and thus what they ultimately wrote about, Mehmed Ali and his top employees often went out of their way to present in the best possible way the various establishments that these visitors were checking, much as is true of "unexpected" visits by modern-day Egyptian officials. For example, in a letter from the Health Council (termed in Arabic *Shura al-Atibba*; hereafter the Shura for short) to the Department of War (*Diwan al-Jihadiyya*, hereafter the Jihadiyya for short), which technically supervised its activities, the Shura writes, "One-quarter of the Qasr al-ʿAini Hospital is [currently] under construction. This section is reserved for the hospital pharmacy and its lab. What we have now is a temporary building that functions as a lab; it has no ceiling and is so inadequate that we do not dare show it to tourists."[14] In another letter the Cairo Department of Health Inspection (*Diwan Taftish Sihhat al-Mahrusa*, hereafter Taftish) wrote to the Cairo Police Department (*Zabtiyyat Masr*, hereafter Zabtiyya) telling them that on touring the streets of Azbakiyya quarter, they found the streets filthy and the garbage uncollected. "This is unacceptable," they explained, "especially since your headquarters are located there and the quarter is where most of the European [residents] and the [European] consuls live. . . . We request that you be diligent in supervising the health and hygiene of the quarter, especially since all tourists constantly go there, and if they find it in this condition, they might assume that all other quarters in Cairo are equally dirty, which is something you certainly would not be pleased by."[15] In yet another letter the Shura wrote to the Schools Department (*Diwan Madaris*, hereafter Madaris) backing the request of one of the teachers in the School of Midwives for some crucial equipment that had been lacking. In its letter the Shura said that this equipment was necessary "to improve the performance of the school, which besides benefiting the students there, is also important for its image especially since all important tourists go there to inspect it."[16]

These preparations must have been very effective, since the archival record shows that there were constant complaints about the actual performance of the various medical establishments, yet the contemporary European writers described the hospitals as without deficiencies. Consider, for example, the following description of Qasr al-ʿAini Hospital by Dr. Wilde, whom we have already come across being mesmerized by the pasha's efforts to educate "the lowest females in his dominions." His visit to the hospital was made on January 27, 1838. "Having a letter of introduction to the chief medical attendant, Dr. Pruner, I this morning visited the military hospital and medical college in Casr-el-Ein [*sic*]. . . . This splendid establishment, decidedly the best constituted, and the one which reflects most credit on the humanity and liberality of the Basha of many of the recent improvements in Egypt is situated in the midst of the most charming parks,. . . and I am bound to say that a cleaner, better regulated, and better conducted medical establishment I never visited."[17] I

quote Wilde here and juxtapose his version of what he saw with letters by
health officials that hint at the possibility that his visit might have been staged
to caution against the uncritical use of travelers' accounts as we formulate our
views about the School of Midwives. More generally, though, it is to point out
that our view of the great pasha has been considerably shaped by the pasha
himself. It is as if the pasha had succeeded in dictating his own biography from
beyond the grave. Again it was "science" to which he resorted in order to affect
how his European visitors saw and judged his reign. These European interlocutors have left us many "eyewitness" accounts of the pasha and his enlightened
reign, accounts that we should read with care, rather than uncritically accept as
do a number of his biographers.[18]

Another important source for this vision of the pasha's enlightenment can
be traced to the writings of his own Egyptian contemporaries, especially those
students whom he had sent to "see with their own eyes . . . how and why [the
West] is superior to us."[19] Over three hundred students were dispatched during
his reign to study in various countries in Europe, but mostly to France. Around
fifty of them were sent to study medicine, and on returning a number of these
students set about translating books from European languages and spreading
the knowledge they had received in Europe among fellow Egyptians who were
now educated in the enlarged Qasr al-ʿAini Hospital. These young doctors,
who were handpicked by the pasha, had no doubt that it was Mehmed Ali who
was to be thanked for introducing modern medicine to Egypt. If the pasha
wanted to portray himself as an enlightened despot, the students he sent to
Europe preferred to see him more as a prophet who through his vision and
determination eagerly improved the lot of his people. Consider, for example,
the writings of one such student, Ahmad al-Rashidi, who was sent to France in
1832, after having finished his studies in Qasr al-ʿAini, and who on returning
to Egypt wrote: "Medical science had all but disappeared from Egypt . . . and
was practiced by all kinds of quacks who . . . did not understand anything
about medicine, its rules or its foundations. . . . [This continued to be the case]
until God sent us the greatest reformer on earth . . . Mehmed Ali . . . who was
determined to resurrect this science by opening medical schools."[20] Eventually
the same doctor took it upon himself to translate a book on childbearing and
child delivery "to be used by the midwives of the [newly founded] School of
Midwives, in the hope that they find it useful."[21]

This discourse about science, modernity, and enlightenment was not restricted to Mehmed Ali, his foreign interlocutors, or his Egyptian students:
nationalist historians in their never-ceasing effort to find a founding father of
the Egyptian nation depict the great pasha as exactly this kind of leader. The
"Founder of Modern Egypt" was, therefore, not only a familiar figure to British historians, reminding them of their civilizing mission in India,[22] or to
French historians who see in his career a logical continuation of what Napoleon left unfinished;[23] he is also seen by Egyptian historians as a true national

hero who was determined to rid Egypt of its Ottoman yoke and also to deliver the country from European and specifically British control.[24] But it is his measures to design a modern public health program, in particular, that are often seen as his greatest achievement because they "helped get rid of clouds of ignorance that have been hovering over the country for centuries."[25] Similarly, the Qasr al-ʿAini School has lately been judged to be "more than another academic institution; . . . it played a central role in the creation of a medical profession in Egypt, and . . . it thereby came to represent a center of civilization that was to have an enlightening effect on the country as a whole."[26]

ORIGINS OF THE SCHOOL OF MIDWIVES

Rather than viewing the founding of a modern medical school in 1827 or a school for midwives five years later as "determined [attempts] to resurrect [medical] science," we should place these "experiments" of the pasha's within his larger military career. It was the founding in the early 1820s of a huge army and navy (a fighting force that at their peak a decade later reached the impressive figure of 180,000) that prompted Mehmed Ali to undertake a costly and controversial medical reform program. For the pasha was aware that creating a conscription-based army entailed gathering and training tens of thousands of conscripts in tightly guarded camps and educating thousands of young cadets in equally packed military schools, acts that by their nature constituted a considerable health risk, not least because of the repeated plague and cholera visitations to which Egypt was prone.[27]

Equally important was the acute concern about the size of the potential fighting force, a concern that grew as the conscription and corvée orders became more frequent.[28] Specifically at issue here was the high infant mortality rate, the result of smallpox infection and stillbirths. Both, it was believed, could be effectively dealt with if attention were given to the creation of a corps of women health practitioners. Clot Bey shared his male contemporaries' prejudice against the traditional midwife, the *daya*, and believed her alone to be responsible, with her superstitious, irrational practice, for the large number of stillbirths every year. He hoped that the opening of a school for midwives would offer an opportunity to supplant the traditional *daya* with a reliable, properly educated *hakima* as a step toward the complete eradication of what he considered to be "the symbol of the whole complex of 'old-wives medicine' with its magic potions, charms and incantations."[29]

But it was smallpox that was deemed to be more damaging to Mehmed Ali's expansionist dreams, if only because of its higher incidence: by the early 1820s fifty to sixty thousand children were falling prey to it annually. It was thus responsible for increasing the infant mortality rate by forty or fifty per thousand, which in turn increased the overall annual death rate by something between three and four per thousand.[30] In response, and as early as 1819, the pasha ordered his deputy to institute a countrywide vaccination program against smallpox.[31] Five years later, the pasha requested of M. Drovetti, the French consul-general, that he secure a number of doctors from France who could administer a vaccination program in the countryside. Three such doctors arrived in Egypt and started to vaccinate people against smallpox in various provinces in Lower Egypt,[32] then moving to Middle Egypt the following year.[33] After Dr. Clot arrived in 1825 and took over the entire health establishment, he convinced the pasha that effective control of smallpox and other diseases required that the health and hygiene of women and children, who had not hitherto been the target of public policy, be checked.[34] Women, Clot Bey reasoned further, "must be trained to help safeguard the health of Egypt's women and children,"[35] and specifically must be entrusted with vaccinating them against smallpox, something that the male barber-surgeons had difficulty accomplishing.

If control of smallpox was the primary objective prompting the pasha in 1832 to accept the counsel of his chief medical adviser and to approve the establishment of a school for midwives, it was not the only factor. There was another more alarming disease whose control necessitated having access to women and making their bodies available to the piercing medical gaze: syphilis. The connection that syphilis had to Mehmed Ali's army was even more apparent than that of smallpox, for in nineteenth-century Egypt as everywhere else syphilis was thought to spread mainly through prostitution, an undesirable, if often unavoidable, concomitant of nineteenth-century standing armies.

There is some evidence to suggest that prostitution in Egypt was on the rise during the first half of the nineteenth century. This is so not so much because of any sudden collapse in morals or a mysterious rise in vice as represented by someone like al-ʿalmeh Kuchuk Hanim[36] on her divan or the khawals[37] of Cairo dancing in the streets in their female dresses to the amusement of the rich and poor alike. Nor is it, as Clot Bey hints, because of the high rise in the rate of divorce or the "voluptuous temperament of Egyptian women."[38] Rather, it was caused by the unprecedented disruption to family life that resulted directly from Mehmed Ali's ravenous conscription policy, which forced tens of thousands of men to move around from city to city and from region to region, leaving their wives, mothers, and daughters behind. "Numbers of young wives thus abandoned are compelled by starvation, or to prevent their children from perishing to join the almé [i.e., prostitutes], all whose profligate habits they must soon acquire."[39] In March 1833, during a visit to Beni Suwaif in Middle Egypt, the British traveler James A. St. John, described what was most probably a typical scene. "On reaching [the town] unusual bustle and activity were observable in the streets. . . . The cause was soon discovered: Ahmad Pasha, with a division of the Egyptian army, had just arrived from the Hedjaz, and the soldiers . . . were spreading themselves through the city, snatching in haste the coarse pleasures within their reach. All the dancing girls, singers and musicians were consequently employed, and we found the cara-vanserai so entirely occupied by this military rabble, that not a single apart-ment could be obtained."[40]

As evinced by this European visitor's contemporary observation, it is clear that the pasha's army was putting pressure not only on the resources of the country but also on the women of any area it happened to march through. As a result, as in all military mobilizations, Mehmed Ali's army helped spread venereal disease wherever it marched.[41] Just after the outbreak of the Syrian War in 1831, for example, the army faced a serious syphilis epidemic.[42] The field hospitals that were quickly established in Syria could not cope with the rapidly increasing numbers of syphilitic soldiers. Many had to be sent back to Egypt for treatment.[43] One medical examination in the army revealed that the number of soldiers afflicted with syphilis was equal to the number of all other patients put together.[44] Recognizing the seriousness of the situation, Mehmed Ali had to order his nephew, Ahmad Pasha Yeğen, to supervise the process of medical checkup himself.[45] Eventually, and as evidence that syphilis (in addi-tion to scabies) received particular care, the preprinted daily reports of the hospitals in Syria had separate entries in which the director of the hospital had simply to fill in the number of syphilitic soldiers.[46]

Faced with a near-epidemic incidence of syphilis, and supervising doctors unqualified to deal with it, Clot Bey had to write a special treatise on the subject.[47] Translated into Arabic and printed by the army press, the treatise took the form of a personal letter from the chief physician of the army to each regimental doctor. However useful this treatise might have been in helping the young medical officers diagnose and treat the disease, the authorities felt that the main problem lay in the military establishment's having failed to prevent the spread of the disease in the first place. Prevention obviously required a strict system of control of the soldiers' sexual lives and a strong prohibition on women's entering the camps or barracks.[48] The men were not allowed to solicit the services of prostitutes. This rule also applied to European officers "who-ever they might be,"[49] and to Turkish-speaking officers.[50]

Once prostitutes were forbidden to enter the camps and strict regulations were passed against soldiers' and officers' soliciting their services, the main problem was the soldiers' wives. As long as the troops were still in Egypt, their families were allowed to join them and to follow them from camp to camp.[51] Eventually, and for health reasons, this practice had to be stopped. Preventing the soldiers from having access to their wives proved to be difficult to enforce, and some women disguised themselves as soldiers to follow their husbands all the way to Syria.[52] When the authorities insisted on forbidding wives to ac-company their husbands, the men grumbled strongly "and in order to counter-act the feeling of despondency as far as possible, the wives, concubines, and parents of the conscripts have been allowed to accompany them."[53]

By conceding the soldiers' needs on that front, Mehmed Ali proved to be more flexible and pragmatic than the contemporary British naval commanders who through "the whole illogical system of indiscriminate pressing with its corollary of not allowing the men shore-leave when in port" were aiming at a standard of morality "altogether too high for the people with whom it dealt."[54] Allowing women to join their husbands in Syria placated the soldiers and helped to stem possible mutinies, but it created serious hygienic problems that contributed to the spread of syphilis and other venereal diseases among the soldiery, and that the authorities now found difficult to address.

In the second section of his treatise on syphilis Clot Bey set out a method that he hoped would be effective in controlling the spread of syphilis through prevention rather than cure. It had to do primarily with the health condition of the wives' lodgings and their bodies. The wives of the soldiers of each regiment were to be divided into four sections corresponding to the battalion divisions within the regiment. They had to be set aside and examined by the wives of the doctors in charge of the men of the battalion.[55] The doctors had to teach their wives how to diagnose syphilis and how to detect any suspicious signs of it on the bodies of the women they had to examine. The "women doctors" then had to report their findings to their husbands after each weekly examination. More important, the soldiers were ordered not to allow into the camps any women except their wives, "even if these women are their mothers or sisters since this will increase the financial burden of the soldiers, plus being a further cause for the spread of diseases."[56]

What is clear from this short excursion into military affairs is that Clot Bey clearly realized that these women, whether wives, concubines, or prostitutes, were a serious health hazard. His initial suggestion that women be prevented from joining their husbands for health reasons faced so much opposition that the military authorities had to give in and to overturn his recommendations. Allowing women into military camps, however, created obvious problems, especially health ones that, as Clot Bey realized, his impressive medical establishment was ill prepared to resolve because it lacked properly trained medical personnel who had access to women.

As alarmed as Clot Bey was by the health condition of the army, he was even more alarmed when he realized that syphilis had spread epidemically among the student population in the military schools in Cairo. In June 1847, when he was informed that the number of syphilitic students was as high as 305 in one such school alone, he wrote a harsh, reprimanding letter to the Schools Department, the Madaris, telling them that they had to take serious action to bring the situation under control.[57] The Madaris replied that, in effect, he was exaggerating the matter since a number of names on his list were in fact repeated more than once and hence the total number of afflicted students was not as large as he had claimed. Clot Bey countered that even if some names had indeed been repeated, the number was still large enough to warrant concern. He concluded that undoubtedly the disease was so prevalent because of "improper behavior and the abominable acts [that the students commit], and if you conduct a regular checkup, you will find that most of the students are afflicted."[58]

Ultimately he determined that the root of the problem was prostitution:

Unlike [the situation in] Europe, prostitutes [al-nisa' al-fawahish] are not required to present themselves for medical examination. One such woman is enough to infect one hundred men. Since we have established clinics and hospitals in the provinces [I suggest] it will be a great move if we force these women to be treated there. This is how European countries have managed to control syphilis, which is graver and more dangerous than the plague. In my opinion there is nothing [morally wrong] in forcing these women to report to the hospitals, since given the fact that these women have no sense of propriety in shamelessly practicing prostitution and adultery, they certainly will have no shame in allowing themselves to be examined regularly. . . . If they refuse [we can force them] to change their profession. This is one of the most important matters regarding health, and I urge you [i.e., Diwan al-Khidiwi], to pay considerable attention to it since examining these women is far better than banning them [from their trade]. This is so because these women are an essential link in maintaining the health of free women [sic], and not banning them [but at the same time examining them] is far better than [allowing the men] to replace them with a much greater vice that is against human nature, by which we mean those young boys who, with the pretext of [public] dancing, commit what is improper even to be uttered.[59]

The key to controlling the spread of syphilis, then, was being able to check and treat the prostitutes who in Clot Bey's mind were solely responsible for spreading the disease among "free women," as he called upper-class women. In addition, lack of proper medical scrutiny of prostitution forced men, in their fear of contracting venereal disease, to seek pleasure elsewhere and to "commit what is improper even to be uttered." Compulsory weekly medical examinations for prostitutes were not instituted until after the British takeover in 1882.[60] However, as early as the 1830s, as has been shown above, there seems to have been a realization that women health practitioners were needed to check the prostitute population of Cairo and other major cities. Indeed, one effort to control this sprawling prostitute population was the attempt to recruit some of these women into the School of Midwives. In a telling letter from the Shura to Madaris, Clot Bey suggested that since "Cairo is a large city having a large number of girls who are orphans or very poor and who out of need are forced to commit indecent vices, . . . it would then be easy to recruit some of these girls [to the school]. . . . We therefore request [permission] to ask the Zabit Bey [the Cairo police commissioner] to summon the shaykhs of the quarters of Cairo and to ask them to supply three such girls from each quarter."[61]

It is obvious from this brief review of the reasons that might have prompted the authorities to found a medical school for women that the aim was not to start an "enlightenment" project among the female population. Clot Bey might have been interested in public morals and was obviously appalled by the "improper behavior" of students in military schools. He might have also been interested in cleansing Cairo of the prostitutes who were littering its streets, and probably he was also genuine in wishing to give them a better chance. However, the prime reason for establishing the School of Midwives with the full backing of Mehmed Ali was not to emancipate the prostitute population of Cairo, nor was it to give its "free women" a chance to acquire modern education; rather, it was the need to preserve the health of the soldiers in the army, which was believed to be threatened by syphilitic prostitutes and by the *dayas*, whose superstitious practices raised the rate of stillbirths, ultimately reducing the size of the potential fighting force. That it was the general hygienic standards of the population, which in turn affected the size of the army, and the objective of keeping a watchful eye on public morality that constituted the main impetus for founding this daring institution is borne out by a review of the duties and responsibilities of the school's students upon graduation and of the tasks that they were entrusted with. But before we follow the graduates of the School of Midwives to see whether they did in fact meet the authorities' expectations after they had assumed their new positions, a word is in order regarding who these women were in the first place and how they came to join the school.

EARLY PROBLEMS: FINDING STUDENTS AND TEACHERS

The first problem that Clot Bey encountered in founding the new school was that of finding girls who would be capable and willing to undertake what was by all standards a lengthy, rigorous, and unorthodox course of training. People in general, not women alone, resisted Mehmed Ali's "progressive" educational policy, and this resistance was not the result of bigotry or an inherent opposition to the values of modern "science" but was a natural consequence of the manner in which this policy was implemented and the logic that informed it. One has to bear in mind that Mehmed Ali was uncomfortable with the idea of educating the masses, let alone the female population, for he was apprehensive concerning the political and social problems that would ensue if his Arabic-speaking subjects were given the chance to challenge the Turkish-speaking military/bureaucratic oligarchy he had so laboriously put together.[62] As a result, the pasha was opposed to opening primary schools to educate girls (or boys for that matter). Indeed, he opened such schools only after their need became desperately obvious when the secondary and advanced schools could not function owing to a lack of literate students. Consequently, his educational policy made little sense and appeared rather as a series of uncoordinated decisions taken in response to crises. This was particularly noticeable in the case of the School of Midwives, which—unlike the Abu Zaʿbal medical school, which recruited its male students from al-Azhar, the old and prestigious religious seminary—lacked a similar institution for girls that could supply Clot Bey with literate and able-bodied female students.

Moreover, Mehmed Ali and his top officials rarely allowed the population to join the supposedly beneficial educational institutions of their free will. The peasantry seriously opposed the recruitment of students for the pasha's schools, and parents often hid their children to prevent their being taken by the pasha's agents. This opposition was triggered not by any inherent loathing of the values of education but rather by the way the authorities conducted the recruiting process: Turkish-speaking officials would be sent from Cairo to grab as many young children as could be found, and these officials would then drag them to their schools, prompting peasants to draw valid comparisons between the recruiters and conscription gangs, corvée officials, and tax collectors. The opposition sometimes took dramatic form, as in the case of a mother who chopped off her son's finger to prevent him from joining one of the pasha's schools; but he was later asked to join it anyway.[63]

Given these problems in finding girls who would volunteer to join the school, the government resorted to "a measure which appears to us now as very queer."[64] Officials were dispatched to the Cairo slave market to acquire ten Abyssinian and Sudanese girls. These girls constituted the first batch of students to join the school, which was initially attached to the Abu Zaʿbal Hospital. The pasha ordered the appointment of two eunuchs from his palace in the citadel to guard them in their new location. Three years later the government bought ten more students from the Cairo slave market, raising the number to twenty. Then the government took ten young girls from the old Mansuri Maristan, which had functioned as a hospice for the poor since the Middle Ages.[65] These girls had been sent there to be cured by parents who had not claimed them back. It was this "queer" mixture of former slaves and inmates of the old Cairo hospice that formed the nucleus of the student body of the School of Midwives.

In spite of the government's pressing need for these women doctors to undertake numerous medical tasks, as will be elaborated below, the difficulty in finding willing and suitable girls for the school remained a perennial problem throughout the school's history. Initially Clot Bey envisaged recruiting as many as a hundred girls, a number representing the absolute minimum needed for the essential female medical corps.[66] However, the number of students rarely reached even half that figure. Immediately after the school was transferred from Abu Zaʿbal in 1837 to be attached to the Civilian Hospital in

Azbakiyya, it had no more than twenty-two girls; by 1840, there were only eleven.[67] In 1844 and according to the regulations of ʿIssawi al-Nahrawi, supervisor of the school (see below), Clot Bey ordered the appointment of six of these female doctors for Cairo: four for the eight "quarters" and two for Bulaq and Old Cairo. However, they had not finished their full course of training, and it was soon realized that "if we discharge these girls now, Egypt will need one hundred years to be self-sufficient in female doctors." It was therefore decided that these girls should not be discharged completely from school, but that they would divide their daily schedule between studying and performing their duties outside school.[68] The Shura was constantly complaining of the insufficient number of female doctors. They fully realized that each quarter of Cairo needed at least one female doctor who, the Shura added in a letter to *Diwan al-Khidiwi* (the Department of Civil Affairs, a precursor to the Department of Interior), might fall ill and hence would need to be replaced by another doctor.[69] Nevertheless, few girls came of their free will to join the school, and those who did were mostly orphans.[70] By 1859 some general criteria were set down by the Shura regarding potential candidates for the school. In a letter to *Majlis al-Ahkam* (the Supreme Court, which also had some legislative and administrative functions), it said that the school should depend less on slaves as a major source of students and should rely instead on orphans, daughters of the soldiers of the Cairo police force, daughters of the army soldiers, and finally the daughters of public employees, in that order.[71] In spite of these regulations, the number of students in 1863 was only twenty-four, which prompted the Shura to encourage the recruitment of thirty-four more girls to increase the number to the sixty now considered a full complement.[72] Nevertheless, the school had no more than twenty-two students in 1876, and the Shura seems to have resigned itself to increasing the number to only thirty.[73]

Besides the difficulty of encouraging suitable girls to enroll in the school, the other obstacle was finding competent teachers. When the school opened in 1832, the first group of students were taught by a Frenchwoman, a Saint-Simonist by the name of Suzanne Voilquin.[74] She was in charge of the school until 1836 when she was replaced by a Parisian compatriot, Palmyre Gault. It is not known how long Mme Gault stayed in Egypt; by 1844, however, an Egyptian male doctor, ʿIssawi al-Nahrawi, was appointed as supervisor of the school and chief instructor there.[75] Three years later, negotiations were conducted by a certain Estefan Efendi who was working on behalf of Clot Bey to find a new Frenchwoman to assume the position of chief instructor. The archival records do not provide the name of this new doctor; what is known, however, is that her contract stipulated an annual salary of 1,500 piasters (approx. £15).[76] At around the same time, 1847, one of the students of the school, Tamruhan, finished her course of training and was appointed as assistant schoolmistress.[77] Tamruhan proved to be an outstanding *hakima* and was eventually promoted to the position of chief instructor of the school in 1857, a position she held till her death in 1863.[78] After her death the chief doctors of the Qasr al-ʿAini and Alexandria Hospitals recommended replacing her with a European doctor, a recommendation that the Health Council (*Majlis al-Sihha*) backed. However, *al-Majlis al-Khususi* (the Privy Council) turned down this recommendation and suggested the selection of a girl from among the students of the school "so as to offer an enticement for the students and encourage them to excel in their studies."[79] In the end a general exam was conducted among the various *hakima*s, and one Zarifa ʿUmar was appointed as chief instructor.[80]

DUTIES OF THE GRADUATES OF THE SCHOOL

During their stay in the school the students received a monthly stipend from the government in addition to free lodging and food; and on graduation they were given a monthly salary of 250 piasters (approx. £2.5), a military rank like that of their fellow male doctors, a means of transportation (usually a donkey), lodgings, and a position within the government health establishment, generally in the clinics created in Cairo and in the provinces to provide free health consultation for the population. The graduates of the School of Midwives, therefore, appear to have improved their position in society and to have succeeded in crossing race, class, and gender boundaries. By closely following these women to their new posts, however, we find a less rosy picture, and their new position in society appears to be much more problematic than the teleological analysis of the introduction of "modern" science to "traditional" society would like us to believe. This is borne out when we review what these women actually did after graduating from the school, and how they performed the duties entrusted to them.

As the official *al-Waqaʾiʿ al-Misriyya*, Mehmed Ali's gazette, would have it, one of the main tasks to be performed by these women was to serve in the newly founded health offices of Cairo, the *makatib al-sihha*. These were clinics offering medical services to the urban population free of charge, in which 21,468 outpatients were reportedly treated in the period between 1845, when six such clinics were first established, and 1848, when their number was raised to eight, six for Cairo's eight "quarters" (*tumn*s), one for Bulaq, and one for Old Cairo. These clinics were supposed to "treat common ailments like ophthalmia, scabies, syphilis, and dislocated or broken limbs. . . . [In addition, they were to offer] free consultation for all the city's inhabitants; emergency aid to victims of drowning or asphyxiation; dressing injuries; free vaccination; dispatching *hakima*s to confinement cases, [and] verifying and certifying causes of death."[81]

This is what the *Waqaʾiʿ* would like us to believe—that these were problem-free, benevolent institutions. Reading the records of these clinics, however, reveals a different picture. It was not such a large number of patients that sought the medical assistance offered, nor was the care free of charge. Further-more, the picture that emerges is one of conflict and confusion, and this is nowhere more clear than in the cases involving the *hakima*s. There is no doubt that vaccination was one of the important duties performed by these women doctors in the clinics as well as in the Civilian Hospital in Azbakiyya. In addition to these tasks, however, these women were entrusted with other re-sponsibilities seldom mentioned in the literature. These were duties instrumen-tal in enabling the authorities to have a wider and tighter grasp of the popula-tion and were arguably more important for the state than were the benevolent ones usually highlighted in the literature. These were also tasks that brought the *hakima*s face-to-face with groups in society that were adversely affected by the reforms of the state and defenseless against its new power. Except, per-haps, to attack its new, fragile agents.

HAKIMAS AND DAYAS

As mentioned above, the number of *hakima*s graduating from the School of Midwives was far below that required to oversee all childbirth in the country and to supplant the *daya*s altogether. The latter continued to be in charge of the overwhelming majority of childbirths throughout Egypt.[82] It was reported, for example, that in a two-year period there were only three deliveries at the Civil-ian Hospital, which prompted the government to offer financial incentives to pregnant women to encourage them to patronize the maternity care facilities of the hospital.[83] The small number of *hakima*s notwithstanding, they were indi-rectly involved in the process of childbirth in that they oversaw the activities of the traditional midwives. The *daya*s were expected to report all difficult delivery cases and to promptly seek the assistance of the *hakima* of the quarter they were working in; if this *hakima* was not to be found, then the *hakima* of the Cairo Police Headquarters, the Zabtiyya (located in Azbakiyya) was to be immediately informed.[84]

Another duty that connected the new midwives to the old ones was the requirement that if a woman requested certification in midwifery, and if she was found lacking in basic knowledge, she would be entrusted to the chief instructor of the school who would educate her. This, however, was to be done privately and outside the school.[85] But the *hakima*s' most important function vis-à-vis the old *daya*s lay in their forcing the latter to supply vital statistics. For the authorities were constantly suspicious that the *daya*s were evading government regulations about recording names and birth dates of the children they delivered and relaying this information regularly. According to the regu-lations the *daya*s were to supply information about the children they delivered on a daily basis; a large number of them, though, were doing so only at the end of every month.[86] This information was supposed to be handed to the shaykhs of the *hara*s (streets) who, in turn, were supposed to hand it to the clinic of the quarter. However, the authorities constantly complained that the number of reported births was inconceivably low and that births were not reported punctually, either by the shaykhs of the *hara*s or by the *daya*s.[87] Often the number of reported deaths exceeded that of births, which looked very suspicious when there were no major epidemics.[88]

One way to control what appeared to be a serious leakage in the system was to have a tighter control over the *daya*s. This was made possible by a requirement that they obtain a certificate authorizing them to perform their trade, a certificate that was to be renewed annually.[89] Any *daya* suspected of laxity in reporting information on the babies she delivered would be fined the first time and would have her certificate revoked if she were found guilty a second time.[90] Those found performing midwifery without certificates were fined and punished.[91] Now, it was the *hakima*s who managed this task: the certificates to be handed to the *daya*s were to be stamped by the *hakima*s.[92] It appears, therefore, that the *hakima*s were an important tool of the authorities, wielded to force the compliance of a section of the population that had hitherto been outside effective government control, namely, the *daya*s. Controlling the *daya*s was important not only because it forced them to seek assistance from their better-educated female superiors but also because it ensured that the government was kept updated with vital information on which "such matters as inheritance, marriage, pensions, conscription, taxation, and vaccination rest," as a government communiqué explicitly stated in 1879.[93]

*HAKIMA*S AND THE DEAD

Another duty these women had to perform was conducting postmortems to verify cause of death.[94] This was of utmost importance especially in times of epidemics, mainly plague and cholera. It was precisely through identification of causes of death that the plague was effectively controlled and finally eradicated from Egypt.

During plague and cholera epidemics no corpse was to be buried without health certificates' having been issued by a doctor certifying that the death was not caused by one of these two diseases or by any other suspicious cause, such as murder. Since burials within the city had been forbidden, it was at the city gates that these certificates were checked.[95] Technically the guards at the city gates were ordered to take the certificates from the hands of the relatives of the deceased and then deliver them to police headquarters. When it was discovered that some of the guards were handing in a suspiciously small number of certificates, they were punished.[96] The system seemed to work, and the only possible problem was that of examining female corpses. Probably in order to placate those opposed to having women's bodies checked by male doctors, the young graduates of the School of Midwives were ordered to conduct postmortems on female corpses, and gradually this became one of their main duties. The *hakima*s conducted postmortems not only in times of epidemics but also in cases in which a woman was suspected of having been murdered. Regardless of the nature of the "unnatural" cause of death, epidemics or suspected homicide, all problematic cases were to be reported immediately to the Qasr al-ʿAini Hospital.[97]

It was in this particular capacity—that is, as coroners—that the *hakima*s faced the strongest opposition from various quarters of society. Sometimes their male superiors accused them of being incompetent; at other times resistance came from the religious authorities who found the *hakima*s to be undertaking unorthodox, controversial tasks. Their dealing with death triggered this opposition because, as will be shown below, autopsy and postmortems in general offered fertile ground for larger disputes between men and women regarding the proper position of women in society, between the religious and secular authorities, among the Turkish-speaking aristocracy, the European advisers in the Egyptian administration, and the Arabic-speaking young doctors who were elbowing their way up the social ladder, and finally between the Health Council and other branches of the government in charge of health and hygiene. If we are to understand the various obstacles and opposition that the *hakima*s faced, a word is in order regarding the social, administrative, and legal framework that governed the School of Midwives.

The most important factor that affected the functioning of the School of Midwives, and, indeed, the whole medical establishment that Clot Bey founded, was lack of administrative autonomy. For the Health Council that the Frenchman headed, the *Shura al-Atibba*, was not an independent government body: technically the Shura was only a subdivision within the War Department, the *Diwan al-Jihadiyya*. This meant that all its operations, finances, requisitions, and correspondence had to approved by the Jihadiyya; Clot Bey and his subordinates complained bitterly of the inevitable bureaucratic complications that this situation entailed. In one letter to the War Department Clot Bey asserted that the military hospitals were issued insufficient medicine and food. "I do not understand," he said, "why there is always a readiness not only to belittle the [entire] medical service but also to abolish [things] related to it. . . . [This in spite of the fact] that the medical regulations used in the various hospitals in Egypt stipulate the expenditure of only one-twentieth of what hospitals in Europe spend."[98] In another letter he countered the accusation of the Jihadiyya that it was *his* department that was causing delays. He said he would not accept such language: "I have been in service for over twenty-two years, in which time I have never been so harshly rebuked."[99]

The situation was even more complicated because the Shura was also supervised by the Schools Department, the Madaris, in matters pertaining to the Qasr al-ʿAini medical school (while the hospital itself was supervised by the

Jihadiyya) and by the Department of the Interior, the *Diwan al-Khidiwi*, in matters concerning civilian hospitals, like the Azbakiyya Hospital, and the urban and provincial health clinics (the *makatib al-sihha*). This cumbersome administrative structure invited all kinds of disputes and tensions. For example, the Madaris complained to the Shura that the head of the Qasr al-ʿAini medical school was addressing the Shura directly and circumventing the Madaris. Clot Bey countered by saying that this was only to save time, and that he was not intending to imply that the Shura was on the same administrative level as the Madaris.[100] Such apparently simple tasks as appointing doctors, admitting patients to hospitals, submitting requisitions, delivering food, medicine, and supplies to the provincial hospitals, or paying rent for the apartments occupied by the urban health clinics were completed only after numerous, and often acrimonious, letters.[101] The best evidence of the tension that characterized the relationship between Clot Bey's Shura and the other government departments that controlled and often interfered in its work is the following sarcastic letter drafted by Clot Bey to the Madaris about the length and nature of the reeds that were needed to cover the roofs of rural dwellings.

> I have received your letter concerning the reeds needed for the rooftops of newly renovated peasant houses, and although I have not clearly understood the connection between the length of reeds and [important] health matters, I answer Your Excellencies, as far as my incompetent mind allows me, by the following. First, any roof could not be covered without [beams of] wood. Second, as far as health matters are concerned, there is no difference between short and long reeds that would be needed to cover these wooden beams. Third, if the intention of dwelling on the length of reeds is to argue that they could be used instead of wood and could therefore help in cutting cost, then this would mean that these houses would necessarily have to be so small as to render them unhealthy and unfit for human occupation. Since Your Excellencies were kind enough to address us concerning this matter, we are more than delighted to remind Your Excellencies that the intention of His Highness [Mehmed Ali] was to rebuild and renovate the villages in the entire country of Egypt, and he had allocated for that purpose the sum of 50,000 *kise*s [i.e., approx. £500] annually and this is something that had been published in the *Waqaʾiʿ* and was reported by all European newspapers. Ultimately, the aim is to improve the health standards of the population. But now we have spent an entire year with only three villages being rebuilt. Accordingly, and God willing, if we continue at this pace we will need four thousand years to renovate all the villages in Egypt.[102]

Besides illustrating the kind of daily problems that Clot Bey and his medical establishment encountered, this letter is also interesting for its caustic tone. This kind of language was not used because Clot Bey had recently arrived in Egypt and was appalled by the incompetence and inefficiency of the local bureaucracy; rather, this is a letter he wrote after spending more than twenty years in Egypt and after his position had been made secure. What triggered this acrimonious language was the very real opposition that Clot Bey encountered every day in his work—opposition that he attributed to the ignorance, superstition, or bigotry both of his superiors and of the general population.[103]

However, his "scientific" arguments notwithstanding, the opposition to Clot Bey's enterprise was not irrational, accidental, or impulsive; rather, it emanated from various factions that deemed the whole institution of modern medicine detrimental to their positions in society. In spite of his repeated allegation that the "members of *Shura al-Atibba* had no intention but to improve the [health] establishment, and they have no other ulterior motives in performing their duties,"[104] the Turkish-speaking members of the bureaucracy saw the Shura as a new powerful and prestigious government body that had the backing of Mehmed Ali and which they were barred from entering owing to their lack of Arabic or French. In addition, the *ʿulema*, the religious scholars, rightly realized that they had no home territory on Mehmed Ali's new social map: they had previously been hit hard when the pasha put their religious endowments (*awqaf*) under tight government control; the educational reform program that the pasha started had no place for al-Azhar in it; the modern legal structure was gradually replacing Islamic law (the *shariʿa*) with an amalgam of Ottoman and European codes that they could not master; and finally the new medical institution was challenging what remained of their position in society especially as regards the performance of rituals relating to death. As far as the population at large was concerned, the modern medical establishment was seen as authorizing interference in people's daily lives in unprecedented ways. For what rural as well as urban folk saw was a powerful institution that through such practices as registering newborns, vaccination, quarantines, and autopsies controlled and manipulated their bodies in unprecedented ways.

It was these considerations, informed by linguistic, religious, and class tensions, that triggered the opposition to Clot Bey's new medical establishment. With regard to the School of Midwives the opposition was more fierce because tensions related to gender and race were added.[105] It follows, therefore, that although the resistance to the new roles that these women were undertaking was sometimes couched in religious language, as will be seen below, the school and its students were often (and rightly) seen as part of a larger establishment that faced opposition for reasons that had little to do with Islam. Similarly, although their gender might have been the reason for some difficulties that the *hakima*s were encountering in their daily jobs, other considerations also often played a role in making their lives less than pleasant, as the following examples illustrate.

In November 1877, a middle-aged woman, Zahra bint Sayyid Ahmad, died suddenly.[106] Her son-in-law, Muhammad ʿAbd al-Rahman, was initially suspected of having caused her death when it was rumored in the neighborhood that he was seen beating her hard in the stomach when she interfered in a dispute between him and his wife. Muhammad was therefore arrested by the head of the neighborhood, the *shaykh al-hara*, and detained in the prison (*karakol*) of Muski in northern Cairo. The *hakima* of the quarter, Amna by name, was summoned to give her verdict on the case and reported that she found no evidence of homicide, that death had been caused by intestinal problems, and that if the relatives of the deceased were still suspicious, they should send the body to Qasr al-ʿAini Hospital for autopsy by a coroner. When Zahra's son, Muhammad the cobbler, heard this, he was frightened and accepted her verdict; he dropped charges against his brother-in-law (*fa min khawfihi min dhalika iqtanaʿa bi-kashfiha*), and so the main suspect, the son-in-law, was released. However, soon afterward the son became suspicious again, went to the Zabtiyya, and requested an autopsy. This time a male coroner conducted it after the body had been exhumed. His report concluded that the woman had been beaten. The detailed report noted that the woman had been living on one lung, that it was obvious that serious concussions had been caused to the liver, and that the ninth rib was found broken. It ended with conclusive evidence that this was not a case of natural death, giving the cause of death as "external pressure on the healthy right lung, which was the only lung that was suitable for respiration and oxygenating the blood. This pressure caused a temporary halt in breathing, . . . added to the damage caused to the liver [as a result of the concussion], death occurred."

Soon afterward, however, the deceased's son and his sister (the accused man's wife) decided to drop the charges and claimed that their mother had been ill for some time and that her death was ordained by God (*bi'l-qada' wa'l-qadar*). They requested that all charges against Muhammad ʿAbd al-Rahman be dropped. The Zabtiyya would not accept their request. Relying on the neighbors' testimony that they had seen the woman being beaten (although it was never ascertained that she had been), they decided to charge Muhammad ʿAbd al-Rahman with murder. This accusation was also based on the Qasr al-ʿAini autopsy report, which contradicted Amna's written testimony and thus implicitly questioned her competence. Amna's position was not improved by the allegation of the deceased woman's son that he had changed his mind about asking for an autopsy because she had confused him: on the one hand, telling him that there was no reason to be suspicious, and on the other, telling him that to confirm that the death was due to natural causes, he had to send the body to Qasr al-ʿAini.

When the case was forwarded to the Cairo Court of First Instance (*Majlis Ibtida'i Masr*), the *hakima* denied ever having told him this. The trial centered not only on the question of whether or not Muhammad ʿAbd al-Rahman was guilty, but on Amna's performance and her competence. A special committee was formed of two senior male physicians to review the report she had written. Probably realizing that it was their own medical establishment and not only Amna's competence that was being questioned, they backed Amna's report, saying that they found nothing wrong in it. They also backed her in her denial of having given conflicting messages to the deceased's son. Nevertheless, they said that she had deviated from their own regulations, which stipulated that at the slightest suspicion, the opinion of a second *hakima* should be sought. Accordingly, the court found Amna guilty of slight negligence (though not incompetence) and sentenced her to ten days' detention, which, however, was commuted and changed to a deduction in pay.

The case did not stop at that, however. Muhammad 'Abd al-Rahman appealed the verdict (he had been found guilty and sentenced to one year in the Alexandria prison, the infamous Liman). The Court of Appeal (*Majlis Isti'naf Masr*) sentenced Amna to one month in the women's prison in Bulaq. Muhammad, on the other hand, rather than having his sentence commuted, was sentenced to two years in the Liman. This time it was Amna's turn to appeal, saying that she preferred the verdict of the Court of First Instance. The Supreme Court (*Majlis al-Ahkam*) accepted the appeal and on reviewing the whole case rejected the verdict of the Court of Appeal: Muhammad 'Abd al-Rahman was sentenced to one year (which by that time he had already spent in jail and so was released), and Amna was to be investigated by the Health Council.[107]

What is interesting about this case is how the *hakima* and her testimony became the subject of conflicting opinions and positions taken up by different people regarding modern medicine, health officials, and the state at large. Consider, for example, the wavering attitude manifested by Muhammad the cobbler (the deceased woman's son) regarding the order that his mother's body be sent to the hospital for autopsy. Naturally, this was a difficult decision, especially since the body had already been buried and since autopsy in this case meant exhuming it, raising many confusing, stressful, and conflicting opinions and emotions. In addition, the person he was accusing was no stranger to him; he was his brother-in-law. (As detailed as this particular case was, it does not offer many insights into the nature of the relationship between the two men, except to hint that they were not particularly fond of each other.) The familial connection might explain why he dropped the charges in the end. The family, coming together, might have decided that this was, after all, a family matter, and that the government had no business meddling in a private affair. Obviously, the authorities would not accept this decision. Frustrated at his wavering, the Zabtiyya asked Muhammad the cobbler why he had not ordered an autopsy from the beginning. In answering this rather important question, he could find no one more vulnerable to blame than Amna. She was subsequently cleared, but this verdict constituted the weakest link in this complicated case. What was being tried here, as much as Muhammad 'Abd al-Rahman, was the young *hakima*'s competence and her ability to ascertain adequately the causes of death. Equally important was the position taken by the senior doctors summoned to give their opinion on Amna's testimony. While finding her guilty of slight negligence, they were not willing to blame her alone for what had happened, and were satisfied to point out that her mistake was that she had deviated from their *own* regulations mandating a second opinion. The final verdict was therefore much to their liking, for they preferred an internal investigation to one whereby other departments of the government would judge their competence and credibility.

This is not the only case in which the testimony of a *hakima* was challenged. When in 1857, for example, a woman by the name of Fattuma bint ʿAli ʿUbayd died, the *hakima*s of the Zabtiyya declared that she had been murdered. Their verdict had to be seconded by the male physicians in Qasr al-ʿAini Hospital. They refuted the *hakima*s' findings and declared that the women must have been confused by the postmortem petrification of the body. Given the body's condition, they explained, the *hakima*s could not have been able to ascertain the cause of death. The senior doctors had to defend their own position, however, lest someone in the legal establishment reviewing the case level accusations against the whole institution of modern medicine, which through postmortems and autopsies was increasingly interfering in the process of criminal investigations. The male doctors had to add, therefore, that these women doctors had not been trained properly in practical sciences. Obviously, it was the verdict of these higher-ranking male doctors that was to be accepted in cases of conflict.[108] Eventually this inferior position of the women doctors was explicitly pronounced in an order in 1879 stating that postmortems were to be conducted first in the *tumn* (the quarter). If the results were inconclusive, the opinion of the doctors in the Cairo Police Headquarters (the Zabtiyya) was to overrule them; then finally if there was still ambiguity in the medical verdict, the case had to be checked by the all-male staff of Qasr al-ʿAini.[109]

Thus these women doctors found themselves occupying the lowest positions in the newly founded medical establishment. While they had occupied marginal places in society before—in their previous lives, as it were—now this marginality, this tangential position that used to accommodate them, albeit with unease and often with hostility, was replaced by one in which they were rigidly and *institutionally* placed at the bottom of the deck. Above them was a rigid, hierarchical establishment that itself was not homogenous. At the head of that hierarchy was the Frenchman Clot Bey and, after his departure, other European physicians. Below this European tier were the young Arabic-speaking doctors (*hukama' awlad ʿArab*) who had been educated in Qasr al-ʿAini or sent to Europe for their medical education. Below these were the uneducated, often illiterate, Arabic-speaking orderlies who were employed by the government and appointed to man the clinics and other health establishments in the capital. And at the very bottom and below all of these men were the women doctors. In spite of having received modern education and in spite of the importance of the tasks that they performed, they still occupied the lowest rung in this new establishment and in times of dispute were the ones who consistently lost out.

An example might help illustrate this point further. As mentioned above, there were not enough women doctors to keep up with the pressure of the job, especially with regard to the conducting of postmortems. The shortage was exacerbated in times of epidemics or when one of these *hakima*s fell ill and her tasks had to shared by the *hakima*s of the nearest quarter. This was especially problematic in the case of the two farthest quarters, namely, Old Cairo in the south and Bulaq in the north. In this case it usually took much longer for the replacement to arrive, causing delays in burials and inciting the opposition of the religious scholars. These *ʿulema* complained, saying that the *hakima*s' failure to perform their jobs properly was resulting in violations of the Islamic principle of prompt burial.[110] In their opposition to the new health establishment the *ʿulema*, already weakened by the reforms that Mehmed Ali and his successors had been introducing in Egypt, did not dare voice their opposition publicly; they also would not dare attack Clot Bey or any of his assistants openly. They could, however, be safe in accusing the women doctors of being slow and inefficient, and of preventing religious rituals from being properly performed. Again it was the precarious position of the *hakima*s in the newly founded medical establishment that allowed the *ʿulema* to do so.

Faced with opposition from various quarters and at the same time expected to perform an inordinate amount of work, some of these *hakima*s occasionally undertook acts of resistance. While not grand or heroic, often taking the form of complaints about the treatment they were getting and the heavy load they were expected to carry, these resistances nevertheless show that the *hakima*s were not the docile, mute objects the authorities might have taken them to be. In 1859, for example, Zaynab bint Muhammad was appointed as *hakima* of the city of Damanhur in the Delta. Her duties were similar to those of her colleagues in Cairo: vaccination, postmortems, registering the midwives, and the like. One day she was asked to assist in a difficult delivery involving a woman living in a small village two hours away from Damanhur who had been in labor for a week. The *hakima* refused, and eventually the pregnant woman died in labor. Zaynab said that she was not responsible for checking cases all over the province. She added that she had been requested to do so before and had incurred a lot of expenses since the government had repeatedly refused to give her a transportation allowance. She added that in this particular case, she had not refused to go on principle; but she had repeated her earlier requests that she be given a transportation allowance, have two guards appointed to accompany her on her long and hazardous trip, and, given that it was an especially difficult case, have a medical tool kit sent to her. It was only after her requests had been turned down, she argued, that she decided not to go. The Health Council heard her case but did not accept her reasoning and found her guilty of negligence. She was sentenced initially to two months' imprisonment. Soon the council discovered that they could not afford to lose her services, so they

decided to substitute a deduction of half her salary in place of the imprisonment. However, before they did so, they checked her previous records and
discovered that this was not the first time she had refused to go out of the town
for medical calls. Accordingly, it was decided that as punishment she should
be sent back to the School of Midwives as a student for a year. When she
appealed this ruling before the Supreme Court, the *Majlis al-Ahkam*, she not
only failed to overturn the verdict of the Health Council but was expelled from
service altogether.[111]

MAIDENS, *HAKIMAS*, AND THEIR HUSBANDS

The evidence reviewed so far regarding the *hakimas*, their background, their
training, their duties, and their position within the medical establishment is far
from being an unambiguous indication of the larger picture of women in society. If the School of Midwives is to be taken as a typical example of the
"modernization" efforts that Egypt witnessed in the nineteenth century, then
the record certainly looks complicated. On the one hand, we see the government grabbing some African slaves and orphaned girls, offering them an opportunity to receive a free education in medical science, giving them a regular
salary, and even awarding them a military rank within the expanding and prestigious bureaucracy. Yet, at the same time, these women found themselves
enmeshed institutionally in a rigid hierarchical structure in which they were
allocated the lowest positions. They were also soon to realize that they were
often the targets of fierce opposition aimed strategically at the medical establishment that they were part of; they, as the most vulnerable component in this
new controversial structure, were the easiest to attack. They attempted to stave
off opposition from different sectors of society, but often to no avail.

The most obvious example of the ambiguous nature of the School of Midwives and how it was often used to control, rather than emancipate, women
concerns a particular task that its graduates were expected to perform in the
urban health clinics and the police stations as part of their routine work:
namely, checking the virginity of young maidens roaming the streets after
escaping from their homes.

Take the case of a poverty-stricken woman by the name of Sabha who
sought help from a friend of hers, Hasna. The latter promised that she would
introduce Sabha to her daughter, and together they would open a brothel (*ka-
rakhana*), "and you would be great and in perfect shape" (*ʿazima wa fi ghayet
al-sihha*). Sabha agreed to the proposal, and on a certain Friday after her father
had left the house, she escaped and went to see Hasna, as promised. Her father,
however, soon found her unconscious in a tavern (*khammara*) and asked her
if she was still a maiden; she answered yes. He did not believe her, though, and
took her to the police station where she was checked by the female doctor
and was found to have lost her virginity.[112] Another case involved a twenty-

year-old woman called Sayyida who was living with her parents in Gam-maliyya in northern Cairo. Her parents had repeatedly turned away her suitors, always asking for a better dowry. Fed up with them, she finally decided to leave the house and seized the opportunity of a quarrel between her parents to secretly seek refuge at some friends' house. There she had sex with their eighteen-year-old son, Hassanein. A couple of days later, her uncle, who happened to be passing by and who knew that his niece had gone missing from her parents' house, found her. He dragged her to the police station of the Gammaliyya quarter to be checked. The *hakima* of the clinic of Gammaliyya could not establish whether Sayyida was a virgin, and the *hakima* residing in the Zabtiyya, the General Cairo Police Headquarters in Azbakiyya, had to be fetched. She declared that the girl was not a maiden (*sayyib*, i.e., *thayyib* = deflowered). In spite of the fact that both Sayyida and Hassanein later agreed to get married, the Zabtiyya still insisted on forwarding the case to a court for trial.[113]

Another case involved a woman called Hafiza who was employed by a cer-tain Ahmad Mahmud, a stoker by profession, to sift wheat in his house. While she was attending to her business in the courtyard of his house, he attacked and raped her. Terrified, she went to the police station, where the *hakima* there had her examined and found her "hymen removed a long time ago and [the girl previously] used" (*wa ghisha al-bikara minzal min mudda qadima wa mustaʿmala*). When they summoned Ahmad, he first denied the charges com-pletely. Then later he admitted that he had slept with Hafiza, but insisted that she had agreed to go along with what he did and that he had not forced her. When Hafiza was confronted with Ahmad's testimony, she admitted that he had not forced her and that she had agreed to go along with him because she had wanted to marry him. Although the religious personal status court, the *mahkama sharʿiyya*, pardoned the couple since Hafiza was willing to drop the charges, the Zabtiyya decided to move the case to the Supreme Court, the *Majlis al-Ahkam*.[114] In another case a woman by the name of ʿAyda employed as a domestic servant in the house of a leading pasha fled the house without giving notice. When she was found, she was sent to the police station, where she was checked by the *hakima* and found deflowered (*sayyib*). She testified that she had lost her virginity to a certain Muhammad Abu al-ʿIla, who had drugged and then raped her. She said, however, that she had visited him twice since then. The religious court which initially reviewed this case decided that it was a clear case of adultery and sentenced the couple to severe corporal punishment, *taʿzir*. The Supreme Court, to which the case was forwarded, however, decided to sentence ʿAyda to six months in the women's prison, the *iplikhane*, and Abu al-ʿIla to six months' hard labor.[115] A more telling case involved a woman, Gazia, who fell in love with a certain Hassan, but her father refused to allow them to marry. She eloped and went to stay with him at the house of a woman named Um al-Rizq. There they had sex and then attempted to get married without Gazia's father's knowledge. Her father had reported her missing, however, and the government had appointed a detective/spy (*bassas*), who did find her. She was sent to the Zabtiyya where she was first examined by the *hakima* of the Bulaq clinic and then by the *hakima* of the Zabtiyya itself. Both *hakima*s found her "*sayyib*" (deflowered). Both Gazia and Hassan stated their request to get married, though, and the father finally agreed after testifying in a religious court that he would accept the *shariʿa*-stated compensation, a suitable "bride-money" (*mahr al-mithl*). But the secular, civil authorities, in this case the Zabtiyya, said that although the case was concluded as far as the *sharʿ* was concerned, both Gazia and Hassan, as well as Um Al-Rizq who had given them refuge, were still to be charged according to *al-siyasa*, a term that by that time referred to secular laws.[116]

What these cases show is that instead of liberating women, the state was beginning to police female "decency" and sexuality, taking over these functions from fathers, brothers, and families. In addition, the period witnessed a conflation of private morality with public security. Prior to Mehmed Ali's "reforms," a father searching for his missing daughter or a master looking for a domestic servant was responsible for finding the woman himself. Urban security had never been a private matter, it is true, but the various Egyptian governments prior to the nineteenth century had never had a municipal body that could impose security and maintain it so thoroughly as did Mehmed Ali. The creation of these municipal agencies in the second quarter of the nineteenth century in Cairo represents a new conception of the city as a corporate entity whose integrity and security were to be protected. Hence the peace and security that were being defended were not only those of the parties concerned; as we saw, even after parties agreed to drop charges, a case would not necessarily be dismissed. It was the city itself that was being defended, and it was the security of urban life per se that was at stake. A girl's loss of her virginity was no longer a private matter. It also ceased to be looked upon as a solely religious matter. It was an act that undermined the authority of the state and its ability to maintain urban security. The employment of the *hakima*s in the police stations—where they were entrusted, among other things, with checking the virginity of girls who had been found after going missing—was a novel encroachment on people's lives. This kind of control over women's bodies and their sexualities was unprecedented and was made possible through the agency not only of the spies and police officers but also of these *hakima*s, who had acquired their education in the School of Midwives.

The most obvious example of how these women found themselves and their bodies at the very bottom of the medical pecking order was in the matter of their own marriages, which the all-embracing bureaucracy of Mehmed Ali attempted to arrange. The *hakima*s were not permitted to leave the school until they found a suitable husband from among the Egyptian doctors. The aim of this policy was to cut down on expenses, since the couple in this case would live together, saving the government the cost of a lodgings allowance for the married *hakima*.[117] Again we see the contradictions in the authorities' logic: on the one hand, they were recruiting women, educating them, and giving them a regular salary and a respectable rank. At the same time, they assumed a paternalistic attitude toward them: first, in allowing them to leave the school only when they married, and second, in finding husbands for them.[118]

Of course, and in true paternalistic fashion, the girls were supposedly given the right to approve the marriage themselves, and the authorities had to "investigate [the suitor's] situation thoroughly in case he was already married and only proposing [to marry one of these *hakimas*] with an eye on her money."[119] In practice, however, things were different, and the *hakimas* occasionally complained of the husbands that had been chosen for them. There is the case of Amna bint Muhammad, for example, who, after finishing her course of study at the school, was given the rank of second lieutenant, with a monthly salary of 250 piasters. She was soon married off to ʿAli Efendi Gibril, given a dowry of 500 piasters (ostensibly by the Shura itself), and sent off to work in Damietta with him. They lived together for three years, both performing their jobs efficiently and receiving the praise of their superiors. Then one day Amna came to the Shura in Cairo and presented a petition for divorce, saying that she could not get along with her husband, that he was rude and rough with her, and that he took all her money. In addition, he had been sleeping regularly with a black slave whom he did not own and, as if this were not enough, he had remarried a woman to whom he had been married before marrying Amna. The Shura ordered the husband to report to Cairo for investigation.[120]

When ʿAli reported to the Shura in Cairo, he was reunited with his wife in the presence of Clot Bey in the Shura headquarters. After two days of negotiations, the problem was resolved in the following manner. First, ʿAli was to divorce the wife he had remarried and get rid of the black slave "since the whole dispute was caused by their constant chattering." Second, Amna herself was ordered to leave her mother's house in Cairo, where her sister was also living and where she had sought refuge after she could no longer endure living with her husband. The Shura justified asking her to leave her mother's home by saying that both her mother and her sister had helped to turn her against her husband. Third, and for similar reasons, ʿAli was to tell his brother, who had come to live with him in Damietta, to leave for Cairo. Fourth, ʿAli was to desist from taking all his wife's salary and was to be allowed to take only half of it. "The other half she is to do with as she pleases."[121]

As the case of Amna illustrates, the record of the School of Midwives shows the complexities that accompanied the introduction of "modern" institutions in nineteenth-century Egypt and characterized the "project of modernity" at large. On the one hand, one can clearly see how the school helped the girls who joined it by turning them into *hakimas* and thus saved them from a worse fate: they were picked from the streets, educated, cared for, and given a regular salary and lodgings during their stay in the school. On graduation, they were given an even higher salary and assigned to various places not only in Cairo but also in the provinces, where they were entrusted with important and arguably prestigious tasks. They were thus offered free education, economic power, mobility, and an enviable social status—in short, they received all the benefits that scholars of modernity and modernization programs represent as accruing to women under such programs. Yet as we have seen, these women found themselves strongly enmeshed in a hierarchical system in which they occupied the lowest positions. When disputes arose, as they often did, these women wrote petitions, protested against what they considered an unjust system, and often complained of their inferior positions in the new medical structure. Nevertheless, they found themselves and their bodies tightly controlled and had no one to turn to except their families and friends. They soon realized that the school was at once both an agent of discipline and regulation *and* an "enlightening" and even "empowering" institution. In short, while it is clear that the sojourn of the *hakima*s in the school and their subsequent jobs had given them the opportunity to become empowered, emancipated actors, and even in some cases strong-willed subjects capable of undertaking small acts of resistance, they were also clearly aware that they were intentionally used by the state as agents of discipline and regulation. In addition, they realized that their own bodies were rigidly controlled and vigilantly watched. It is this paradoxical nature of the modern School of Midwives, one of the most illustrious institutions of Mehmed Ali and Clot Bey, that makes one wonder, contemplating Amna's case, if she would have agreed to join the school had she known what her life with ʿAli Gibril would be like.

NOTE ON THE SOURCES

All of the primary material referred to is from the Egyptian National Archives in Cairo, the *Dar al-Watha'iq al-Qawmiyya*. Below is a brief description of those that were found to be most useful and the codes used to refer to them.

Registers of the Health Council, the **Shura:** *Referred to by the Code S/3*

They are of two kinds:

Outgoing (Sadir)—code: "S/3/122." These are nine registers of around 800–900 letters each, all covering the period between A.H. 1261 and 1278, i.e., A.D. 1845–1861. The letters were addressed mainly to three departments: the Schools Department (for such matters as medical checkups on students in the government schools, reports on exams taken by various medical students, appointments of doctors and pharmacists to the different schools); the *Diwan Khidiwi*, i.e., Department of Civil Affairs (for matters concerning civilian hospitals, sanitary regulations, and criminal investigations, e.g., postmortems, etc.); and the War Department itself (for matters concerning military hospitals including Qasr al-ʿAini, appointment of doctors and pharmacists to various regiments, etc.).

Incoming (Warid)—code: "S/3/206." These are six registers covering the same period and offering the other side of the correspondence, although the documents are only summaries of the letters actually received.

Registers of the Department of Civil Affairs: Referred to as L/1

This department had various names: first *Diwan al-Khidiwi*, then *Diwan Katkhoda*, then *Diwan Muhafazat Masr*. These registers number 178 of around 500 letters each and cover the period between A.H. 1271 and 1296, i.e., A.D. 1854 to 1878. They are also extremely useful, since they include correspondence among various government agencies concerned with civilian medicine, especially urban sanitation, and the Civilian Hospital in Azbakiyya, which is where the School of Midwives was located.

Registers of the Department of Health Inspection of Cairo, Referred to by the Code M/5

This is called in Arabic *Taftish Sihhat al-Mahrusa*. They have sixteen registers covering the period between A.H. 1266 and 1297, i.e., A.D. 1849 to 1878, with considerable gaps, unfortunately. This contains valuable information regarding the ten "Health Offices" that were established in the various "arrondissements" (*tumns*) of Cairo, vaccination against smallpox, female doctors, street accidents, and urban sanitation.

Registers of the Cairo Police Department, Zabtiyyat Masr, Referred to by the Code L/2/6

These are numerous, but the relevant ones seem to be those subtitled *Qalam Daʿawa* i.e., Unit of [Investigation of] Cases. These are fourteen register covering the period from A.H. 1294 to 1297, i.e., from A.D July 1877 to December 1879. These are also very valuable, since they occasionally record cases of murder or suspected murder, so by necessity report postmortems.

Registers of the Supreme Court, Majlis al-Ahkam, Referred to by the Code S/7/10

These are a total of 318 registers covering the period from A.H. 1274 to 1306, i.e., A.D. 1857 to 1889. These were some of the most informative records of the legal system, as they belong to a Court that was considered the highest in the land. Its records deal with criminal, commercial, and administrative cases. Numerous cases concerning medical malpractice as well as administrative disputes within the medical establishment were dealt with by that body.

The Records of the Syrian Campaign, Referred to as "Sham"

These are fifty-nine boxes in all, containing invaluable information about the campaign (1831–40), including all medical matters, e.g., accounts of medical checkups in the various regiments, condition of the field hospitals in Syria, and so forth.

NOTES

This paper has earlier been presented at conferences in Philadelphia, Paris, and New York. I would like to thank Lila Abu-Lughod, Sabah Ghandour, Tim Mitchell, and Marlène Shamay for providing me with the rich opportunities to present the paper and receive comments on it. For their insightful criticisms I would like to thank Lila Abu-Lughod, Partha Chatterjee, Marwa Elshakry, Peter Gran, Uday Mehta, Tim Mitchell, Anne Marie Moulin, Omnia Shakry, and Jeannie Sowers. Most of the archival work that this paper relied on was done over a period of two years in the National Archives of Egypt, and I would like to warmly thank the officials there for their continued assistance and warm friendship that continues to make working there exciting and pleasurable. My special thanks go to Madam Sawsan Abdel-Ghani and Mr. Ibrahim Fathalla who spare no efforts to make researchers feel that they are part of one "large family."

1. F. M. Sandwith, "The History of Kasr-el-Ainy," *Records of the Egyptian Government School of Medicine* 1 (1901): 11.

2. Al-Shayyal lists fifty-six books in medical and veterinary science that were translated during Mehmed Ali's reign alone; these were exceeded in number only by military books (sixty-four). Jamal al-Din al-Shayyal, *Tarikh al-tarjama wa'l-haya al-thaqafiyya fi ʿasr Muhammad ʿAli* (Cairo: n.p., 1951), p. 38 of the appendix.

3. LaVerne Kuhnke, *Lives at Risk: Public Health in Nineteenth Century Egypt* (Berkeley and Los Angeles: University of California Press, 1990), p. 123.

4. Ibid., p. 122.

5. See, for example, Jean Towler and Joan Bramall, *Midwives in History and Society* (London: Croom Helm, 1986), pp. 99–146, and Jean Donnison, *Midwives and Medical Men: A History of the Struggle for the Control of Childbirth* (London: Historical Publications, 1988), pp. 72–93.

6. Sir William Robert Wilde, *A Narrative of a Voyage to Medeira, Teneriffe, and along the Shores of the Mediterranean* (Dublin, 1844), pp. 234–35.

7. Victor Schoelcher, *L'Egypte en 1845* (Paris, 1846), pp. 44–45.

8. Amira el-Azhary Sonbol, *The Creation of a Medical Profession in Egypt, 1800–1922* (New York: Syracuse University Press, 1991), p. 45.

9. Leila Ahmed, *Women and Gender in Islam* (New Haven: Yale University Press, 1992), p. 135.

10. Nada Tomiche, "The Situation of Egyptian Women in the First Half of the Nineteenth Century," in *Beginnings of Modernization in the Middle East*, ed. William R.

Polk and Richard L. Chambers (Chicago: University of Chicago Press, 1968), pp. 183–84.

11. A.W.C. Lindsay, *Letters from Egypt, Edom, and the Holy Land* (London: Henry Colborn, 1838), 1:34.

12. For a discussion of how Mehmed Ali staged the encounter with foreign visitors, see Khaled Fahmy, *All the Pasha's Men: Mehmed Ali, His Army and the Founding of Modern Egypt* (Cambridge: Cambridge University Press, 1997), pp. 1–8.

13. John Bowring, "Report on Egypt and Candia," *Parliamentary Papers, Reports from Commissioners* 21 (1840): 146.

14. S/3/122/2 (Jihadiyya no. 437), doc. no. 389, p. 163, on 25 Jamadi al-Awwal 1263/November 11, 1846.

15. L/1/5/1 (Muhafazat Masr), doc. no. 9, pp. 17, 32, on 16 Rabiʿ al-Awwal 1276/October 23, 1859.

16. S/3/122/2 (Jihadiyya no. 437), doc. no. 46, p. 49, on 29 Dhu al-Qiʿda 1262/November 18, 1846.

17. Wilde, *A Narrative of a Voyage*, pp. 234–35.

18. Even in his own time the pasha had a reputation for giving too many interviews and making too many announcements; see the Austrian internuncio's remark that "the pasha has not always the virtue of silence and simulation," quoted in M. Sabri, *L'empire égyptien sous Mohamed-Ali et la question d'Orient (1811–1849)* (Paris: Paul Geuthner, 1930), p. 142.

19. Bowring, "Report on Egypt and Candia," p. 146.

20. Ahmad al-Rashidi, trans., *Diya' al-nayyerin fi mudawat al-ʿaynayn* (Cairo: Bulaq, 1840), pp. 3–4.

21. Ahmad al-Rashidi, trans., *Kitab al-wilada* (Cairo: Bulaq, 1842).

22. See Henry Dodwell, *The Founder of Modern Egypt* (Cambridge: Cambridge University Press, 1931), where this idea runs throughout the book and is mentioned explicitly in the conclusion.

23. See, for example, Édouard Driault, *Mohamed Ali et Napoleon (1807–1814)* (Cairo: Royal Egyptian Geographic Society, 1825).

24. The latest example is Afaf Lutfi al-Sayyid Marsot, *Egypt in the Reign of Muhammad Ali* (Cambridge: Cambridge University Press, 1984).

25. Ahmad ʿIzzat ʿAbdel-Karim, *Tarikh al-taʿlim fi ʿasr Muhammad ʿAli* (Cairo: al-Nahda al-Misriyya, 1938), p. 266.

26. Sonbol, *Creation of a Medical Profession*, p. 21.

27. For a brief review of the history of these two epidemics in Egypt in the early nineteenth century, see Kuhnke, *Lives at Risk*, pp. 49–57, 75–78.

28. For Mehmed Ali's concern about the insufficiency of Egypt's manpower to satisfy his military needs, see Fahmy, *All the Pasha's Men*, pp. 50, 92.

29. Kuhnke, *Lives at Risk*, p. 129.

30. Daniel Panzac, "The Population of Egypt in the Nineteenth Century," *Asian and African Studies* 21 (1987): 18.

31. Amin Sami, *Taqwim al-Nil* (Cairo: Dar al-Kutub, 1928), 2:278, letter dated 5 Jamadi al-Awwal 1234/March 2, 1819.

32. S/1/50/5 (Maʿiyya Saniyya, Turki, no. 14), doc. no. 413, and Katkhoda 1/101, both on 26 Dhu al-Qiʿda 1239/July 24, 1824. Each was given a monthly salary of five

hundred piasters (around £5): ibid., doc. no. 419 on 29 Dhu al-Qiʿda 1239/July 27, 1824.

33. S/1/47/7 (Maʿiyya Saniyya, Turki, no. 17), doc. no. 216, on 27 Muharram 1241/ September 12, 1825.

34. In his *Memoires* Clot Bey claims that thanks only to him vaccination was introduced in Egypt. It is obvious from the above-mentioned accounts that this was not the case; Antoine-Barthélemy Clot, *Memoires*, ed. Jacques Tagher (Cairo: I.F.A.O., 1949), p. 157.

35. Kuhnke, *Lives at Risk*, p. 123. Clot was given the honorific title of "Bey" in 1832 after he managed to control the cholera epidemic of that year.

36. This is the famous "public dancer" immortalized by Flaubert in his travel notes on Egypt; see Gustave Flaubert, *Flaubert in Egypt, a Sensibility on Tour*, ed. and trans. Francis Steegmuller (Chicago: Academy Chicago Press, 1979), pp. 113–20.

37. These were female impersonators who often danced in the streets, before houses, and in the courtyards of certain mansions on various occasions; Edward W. Lane, *An Account of the Manners and Customs of the Modern Egyptians* (London: Ward, Lock, 1890), pp. 351, 467.

38. A. B. Clot Bey, *Aperçu général sur l'Égypte* (Paris: Fortin, Masson, 1840), 1:336.

39. James Augustus St. John, *Egypt and Mohammed-Ali* (London: Longman, 1834), 2:176.

40. Ibid., p. 265.

41. On the first major outbreak of syphilis in Europe toward the end of the fifteenth century and its connection to Italian wars of 1494–1559, see William McNeill, *Plagues and Peoples* (New York: Doubleday, 1977), p. 193; and on the spread of syphilis by Napoleon's armies, see John Elting, *Swords around a Throne: Napoleon's Grande Armée* (London: Macmillan, 1988), pp. 294 ff.

42. *Al-Waqa'iʿ al-Misriyya*, no. 334, on December 29, 1831, quoted in Kuhnke, *Lives at Risk*, p. 135.

43. See Sham 1/27, on 20 Jamadi al-Thani 1247/November 26, 1831, on patients being sent to the Abu-Zaʿbal Hospital; and Sham 2/54, on 7 Rajab 1247/December 12, 1831; and Sham 2/88, on 23 Rajab 1247/December 28, 1831, on their being sent to the hospital in Alexandria. In all these cases patients were transported by ship.

44. Sham 3/101, on 10 Shaʿban 1247/14 January 1832.

45. S/5/51/2 (Sijillat ʿAbdin), doc. no. 62, on 30 Shawwal 1247/April 1, 1832.

46. For examples of these preprinted reports, see Sham 7/78, on 11 Muharram 1248/June 11, 1832, and Sham 10/150, on 17 Rabiʿ al-Awwal 1248/August 14, 1832.

47. A. B. Clot Bey, *Risala min Mashurat al-Sihha ila hukama' al-Jihadiyya* (A treatise from the Health Council to the physicians of the army) (Cairo: Matbaʿat Diwan al-Jihadiyya, 1835).

48. *Qanun al-dakhiliyya* (Regulations for barracks and camps) (Cairo: Matbaʿat Diwan al-Jihadiyya, A.H. 1250/A.D. 1834–35), art. 273, p. 52.

49. S/1/48/4 (Maʿiyya Saniyya, Turki), doc. no. 594 on 20 Jamadi al-Awwal 1250/ September 24, 1834. This was a case of two European officers, a pharmacist and a cartographer, who had "a dancer and a singer" in their tents at night. The pasha's

language in this letter is particularly harsh and categorical in forbidding prostitutes to live near army camps.

50. Awamir lil-Jihadiyya 1/10, on 6 Safar 1246/July 27, 1830. This was a case of a certain Osman Agha who had taken a twenty-four-hour leave but came back five days later. When the matter was investigated, he was discovered to have spent his time in a brothel. He was expelled from service altogether.

51. Judith Tucker, *Women in Nineteenth-Century Egypt* (Cambridge: Cambridge University Press, 1985), p. 136.

52. Sham 1/27, on 4 Jamadi al-Thani 1247/November 10, 1831.

53. Bowring, "Report on Egypt and Candia," p. 6.

54. Michael Lewis, *The Social History of the Navy* (London: George Allen and Unwin, 1960), p. 282.

55. Clot Bey, *Risala*, sec. 2, art. 1, p. 6.

56. Ibid., art. 4, p. 6.

57. S/3/122/2 (Jihadiyya no. 437), doc. no. 189, p. 182, on 17 Jamadi al-Awwal 1263/June 2, 1847.

58. Ibid., doc. no. 212, p. 195, on 4 Rajab 1263/July 18, 1847.

59. Ibid., doc. no. 143, p. 169, on 7 Jamadi al-Thani 1263/May 23, 1847.

60. Filib Jallad, ed., *Qamus al-idara wa al-qada'* (Dictionary of administration and justice) (Alexandria, 1890–92), 3:1217, Ministry of Interior Ordinance dated November 11, 1882.

61. M/1/1 (Diwan Isbitalia no. 431), doc. no. 82, p. 18, on 15 Shawwal 1260/ November 11, 1844.

62. On Mehmed Ali's reluctance to spread primary education, see Fahmy, *All the Pasha's Men*, pp. 282–83.

63. She was punished with two hundred lashes of the whip: S/6/2/1 (al-Jamʿiyya al-Haqqaniyya), doc. no. 5, p. 52, on 7 Shawwal 1264/September 6, 1848.

64. Naguib Mahfouz, *The History of Medical Education in Egypt* (Cairo: Government Press, 1935), p. 71.

65. Founded by the Mamluk Sultan al-Mansur Qala'un in 683/1284, this was one of Cairo's chief hospitals that served the urban poor, although it is now believed to have been insufficient for the city's population. For its history and development and ultimate decline in the eighteenth century, see the valuable description by the Turkish traveler Evliya Çelebi in his *Seyahatnamesi*, vol. 10, Misir, Sudan, Habeş (1672–80), (Istanbul: Devlet Basimevi, 1938), chap. 35; and for the condition of the hospital at the time of the French Expedition, see *Description de l'Egypte*, 2d ed., (Paris, 1822), vol. 18, pt. 2, pp. 318 ff.

66. Clot Bey, *Memoires*, p. 321.

67. Kuhnke, *Lives at Risk*, p. 127.

68. M/1/1/ (Diwan Isbitalia no. 431), doc. no. 195, p. 23, on 27 Shawwal 1260/ November 10, 1844; and ibid., doc. no. 182, pp. 40–41, on 16 Dhu al-Hijja 1260/ November 27, 1844.

69. S/3/122/5 (Jihadiyya no. 442), doc. no. 30, pp. 46, 48, on 28 Dhu al-Qiʿda 1264/ October 27, 1848.

70. I could find only a handful of petitions from girls to join the school; the first is from a ten-year-old French girl, called Justine, who was an "orphan with no family or

relatives [but] who is healthy and suitable for the school": S/3/122/2 (Jihadiyya no. 437), doc. no. 66, p. 58, on 21 Dhu al-Hijja 1262/December 11, 1846. See also the case of the girl called Nafisa who was healthy and literate and who requested to join of her own free will: ibid., doc. no. 216, p. 195, on 8 Rajab 1263/June 22, 1847.

71. S/3/122/8 (Jihadiyya no. 450), doc. no. 1, p. 2, on 22 Safar 1276/September 21, 1859.

72. S/11/8/4 (al-Majlis al-Khususi no. 66) decree no. 16, pp. 14–15, on 18 Dhu al-Hijja 1279/June 6, 1863.

73. Sandwith, "History of Kasr-el-Ainy," p. 18.

74. See her account of her trip to, and stay in, Egypt in *Souvenirs d'une fille du peuple, ou la Saint-simonienne en Egypte* (Paris: François Maspero, 1978).

75. M/1/1 (Diwan Isbitalia no. 431), doc. no. 105, p. 23, on 27 Shawwal 1260/ November 10, 1844. It is not clear why al-Nahrawi was chosen for the job. He was not in charge of obstetrics in Qasr al-ʿAini School; rather, the school's chief of obstetrics was Ahmad al-Rashidi, whom we have met earlier (see nn. 20 and 21 above), and who had published a book on the subject, *Bahjat al-ru'sa' fi amrad al-nisa'* (Cairo: Bulaq, 1844). Al-Nahrawi, on the other hand, had translated a book on general anatomy, *Al-tashrih al-ʿam* (Cairo: Bulaq, 1845). In 1857 he was appointed as chief physician of Minya Province: S/3/122 (Jihadiyya no. 444), doc. no. 75, p. 14, on 23 Shaʿban 1273/ April 19, 1857.

76. S/3/122/4 (Jihadiyya no. 440), doc. no. 48, p. 50, on 8 Dhu al-Qiʿda 1263/October 18, 1847, and ibid., doc. no. 120, p. 94, on 12 Rabiʿ al-Awwal 1264/February 17, 1848. On her arrival in Cairo and the exam she administered to the students soon after she assumed her new post, see ibid., doc. no. 87, p. 74, on 26 Muharram 1264/January 4, 1848; and on the dispute about the cost of her lodgings in the Asteria Hotel (probably in Azbakiyya) and who was to pay it, see ibid., doc. no. 129, pp. 101, 106, on 23 Rabiʿ al-Awwal 1264/February 28, 1848.

77. *Al-Waqa'iʿ al-Misriyya*, no. 46, on January 5, 1847, pp. 1–2, quoted in Kuhnke, *Lives at Risk*, p. 128.

78. There are numerous letters concerning this remarkable figure; on her appointment as chief instructor, see S/3/122/9 (Jihadiyya no. 452), doc. no. 235, p. 44, on 26 Dhu al-Qiʿda/July 19, 1857; on her competence, see L/1/5/2 (Muhafazat Masr no. 185), doc. no. 15, p. 40, on 16 Rabiʿ al-Thani 1277/November 1, 1860, and L/1/20/5 (Muhafazat Masr 1043), case no. 24, pp. 137–38, on 8 Shawwal 1277/April 19, 1861.

79. S/11/8/4 (al-Majlis al-Khususi no. 66), decree no. 16, pp. 14–15, on 18 Dhu al-Qiʿda 1279/May 6, 1863.

80. L/1/4/1 (Muhafazat Masr), doc. no. 22, p. 68, on 22 Dhu al-Qiʿda 1280/March 31, 1864.

81. Kuhnke, *Lives at Risk*, p. 142. Kuhnke's information is all derived from *al-Waqa'iʿ*.

82. I could find no document stating clearly the number of *daya*s; the following documents, however, might give an idea of their approximate number. The number of *daya*s registered (most probably in Cairo alone) in 1851 was 565: M/5/1 (Taftish Sihhat al-Mahrusa), doc. no. 126, p. 62, on 25 Rabiʿ al-Thani 1267/February 28, 1851; in 1860 six hundred certificates were printed for the *daya*s in Alexandria: L/1/5/1 (Muhafazat

Masr), doc. no. 7, p. 56, on 21 Jamadi al-Thani 1276/January 16, 1860; in late 1859 there was an order to print four thousand certificates for *daya*s all over Egypt: ibid., doc. no. 38, p. 65, on 3 Jamadi al-Thani 1276/December 28, 1859.

83. Kuhnke, *Lives at Risk*, pp. 129–30.

84. See the explicit regulations issued to one *daya*, Hana' bint Hassan al-Damanhuri, ordering her to report to the *hakima* of the *tumn* of Bab al-Sha'riyya: L/1/5/11 (Muhafazat Masr no. 209), doc. no. 10, p. 37, on 22 Jamadi al-Thani 1286/September 30, 1869. See also the case of a *daya* who not only did not report a difficult, and ultimately fatal, delivery to the relevant *hakima* but violated the law by burying the stillborn baby in the courtyard of the house with the assistance of the baby's father; both were to be punished "according to the regulations": M/5/1 (Taftish Sihhat al-Mahrusa), doc. no. 133, p. 58, on 28 Rabi' al-Thani 1267/March 3, 1851.

85. L/2/31/1, doc. no. 175, p. 124, on 28 Shawwal 1296/October 16, 1879.

86. M/5/1 (Taftish Sihhat al-Mahrusa), doc. no. 20, p. 7, on 16 Dhu al-Hijja 1266/ October 19, 1850.

87. There are numerous letters to that effect; see, for example, M/5/1 (Taftish Sihhat al-Mahrusa), doc. no. 191, p. 74, on 11 Jamadi al-Thani 1267/April 13, 1851.

88. Again, there are several letters to that effect; see, for example, L/1/5/1 (Muhafazat Masr), doc. no. 6, p. 27, on 11 Rabi' al-Awwal 1276/September 27, 1860.

89. L/1/5/1 (Muhafazat Masr), doc. no. 38, p. 65, on 3 Jamadi al-Awwal 1276/ December 28, 1859. For the wording of one such certificate, see L/1/5/1, doc. no. 12, p. 31, on 23 Rabi' al-Awwal 1276/October 20, 1859.

90. M/5/1 (Taftish Sihhat al-Mahrusa), doc. no. 118, p. 57, on 8 Rabi' al-Thani 1267/February 20, 1851.

91. L/1/5/1 (Muhafazat Masr), doc. no. 24, p. 38, on 6 Rabi' al-Thani 1276/November 2, 1859

92. L/2/31/1, doc. no. 44, p. 42, on 14 Sha'ban 1296/August 4, 1879.

93. L/2/31/1, doc. no. 96, p. 119, on 29 Shawwal 1296/October 17, 1879.

94. S/3/122/4 (Jihadiyya no. 440), doc. no. 212, p. 218, on 2 Ramadan 1264/August 2, 1848.

95. M/5/1 (Taftish Sihhat al-Mahrusa), doc. no. 4, p. 1, on 11 Dhu al-Qi'da 1266/ September 18, 1850.

96. M/4/1 (old number: Taftish al-Sihha no. 165), doc. no. 28, p. 22, on 24 Safar 1266/January 10, 1850.

97. M/5/1 (Taftish Sihhat al-Mahrusa), doc. no. 3, p. 1, on 9 Dhu al-Qi'da 1266/ September 16, 1850.

98. S/3/122/2 (Jihadiyya no. 437), doc. no. 150, pp. 72–73, on 12 Muharram 1263/ January 1, 1847.

99. Ibid., doc. no. 155, p. 74, on 12 Muharram 1263/January 1, 1847.

100. Ibid., doc. no. 39, p. 38, on 21 Dhu al-Qi'da 1262/October 11, 1846.

101. The documents regarding this matter are numerous; see, for example, S/3/122/2 (Jihadiyya no. 437), doc. no. 51, p. 75, on 11 Muharram 1263/December 30, 1846, concerning the relationship between the Shura and the *Diwan al-Khidiwi*; and S/3/122/ 4 (Jihadiyya no. 440), doc. no. 23, p. 34, on 3 Dhu al-Qi'da 1263/October 13, 1847, concerning disputes with the Madaris regarding how best to run the Qasr al-'Aini medical school.

102. S/3/122/2 (Jihadiyya no. 437), doc. no. 120, pp. 106–7, on 4 Rabi⁽ al-Awwal 1263/February 20, 1847.

103. See, for example, the interesting letter in which he was complaining of a report published in the *Waqa'i⁽* which stated that a cow had given birth in a village in Upper Egypt to a calf with a human head. He said that this report should never have been allowed to be published because of the disturbances it triggered. He explained that as a result of similar tales, both men and women had been accused of bestiality in the past. He also accused the deputy governor of Upper Egypt, who "insofar as he believed such rumors must be demented and out of his mind": S/3/122/2 (Jihadiyya no. 437), doc. no. 194, p. 182, on 18 Jamadi al-Thani/June 4, 1847.

104. S/3/122/4 (Jihadiyya no. 440), doc. no. 45, p. 44, on 7 Dhu al-Qi⁽da 1263/ November 16, 1847.

105. It should be remembered that the initial group of students were black slaves.

106. L/2/6/2 (Zabtiyyat Masr), case no. 199, pp. 176–78, on 22 Dhu al-Qi⁽da 1294/ November 28, 1877.

107. S/7/10/121 (Majlis al-Ahkam no. 441), case no. 441, on 23 Dhu al-Qi⁽da 1295/ November 19, 1878.

108. S/3/122/6 (Jihadiyya no. 444), doc. no. 133, p. 25, on 28 Dhu al-Qi⁽da 1273/ July 21, 1857.

109. L/2/31/1 (Zabtiyyat Masr), doc. no. 282, p. 67, on 8 Ramadan 1296/August 26, 1879.

110. See the interesting correspondence between the Cairo Police Commissioner, the *Zabit Bey*, and the Shura concerning the complaints from religious men regarding the delays in burials during the cholera epidemic of 1848 and the *hakima*s' responsibility for this: S/3/122/4 (Jihadiyya no. 440), doc. no. 206, p. 222, on 26 Sha⁽ban 1264/July 28, 1848, from the Shura to *Zabit Bey*; S/3/206/3 (Jihadiyya no. 441), doc. no. 1151, p. 121, on 29 Sha⁽ban 1264/July 31, 1848, from *Zabit Bey* to the Shura; and S/3/122/4 (Jihadiyya no. 440), doc. no. 214, p. 226, on 29 Sha⁽ban 1264/July 31, 1848 answering the previous letter.

111. S/7/10/8 (Majlis al-Ahkam no. 670), case no. 74, pp. 125–27, on 11 Rabi⁽ al-Awwal 1276/October 8, 1859.

112. L/2/6/3 (Zabtiyyat Masr), case no. 251, pp. 196–99, on 1 Rabi⁽ al-Awwal 1295/ March 5, 1878.

113. L/2/6/2 (Zabtiyyat Masr), case no. 221, pp. 200–201, on 26 Dhu al-Qi⁽da 1294/ December 3, 1877.

114. L/2/6/3 (Zabtiyyat Masr), case no. 107, pp. 83–84, on 24 Muharram 1295/ January 28, 1878.

115. S/7/10/18 (Majlis al-Ahkam), case no. 556, pp. 181–82, on 24 Ramadan 1280/ March 2, 1864. *Iplikhane* literally means a spinning mill, but in nineteenth-century Cairo it referred to a women's prison. It was located in Bulaq; see S/7/10/3 (Majlis al-Ahkam no. 665), case no. 326, p. 41, on 17 Rabi⁽ al-Thani 1275/November 24, 1858.

116. S/7/10/18 (Majlis al-Ahkam), case no. 410, pp. 100–101, on 4 Sha⁽ban 1280/ January 14, 1864.

117. See the letter from the *Taftish* to *Diwan Khidiwi* in which this is explicitly stated: M/5/1 (Taftish Sihhat al-Mahrusa no. 163), doc. no. 1, p. 1, on 5 Dhu al-Qi⁽da 1266/September 12, 1850.

118. There are numerous examples of these marriage requests; see, for example, S/3/122/2 (Jihadiyya no. 437), doc. no. 95, p. 90, on 4 Safar 1263/January 22, 1847.

119. S/3/122/4 (Jihadiyya no. 440), doc. no. 212, p. 195, on 27 Rajab 1264/June 29, 1848.

120. S/3/122/2 (Jihadiyya no. 437), doc. no. 121, pp. 124 and 135, on 13 Rabiᶜ al-Thani 1263/March 31, 1847.

121. Ibid., doc. no. 128, pp. 138 and 146, on 7 Jamadi al-Awwal 1263/April 23, 1847.

CHAPTER 2

ʿA'isha Taymur's Tears and the Critique of the Modernist and the Feminist Discourses on Nineteenth-Century Egypt

MERVAT HATEM

ʿA'ISHA TAYMUR IN FEMINIST AND MODERNIST DISCOURSES

Early feminist writers and modernist historians have attached social importance to ʿA'isha Taymur's emergence as one of the leading women poets of
nineteenth-century Egypt. One feminist writer described her as the "avant-
garde of feminist awakening" (*taliʿat al-yaqaza al-nisawiyya*).[1] A modernist
historian gave her the parallel distinction of being a member of "the avant-
garde of social and literary renaissance [during the age of Ismail]" (*taliʿat
al-nahda al-ijtimaʿiyya wa al-adabiyya*).[2]

Following in the footsteps of these early writers, contemporary theorists
have taken to including ʿA'isha Taymur in their discussions of the changing
status of women in nineteenth-century Egypt. While all have highlighted the
same set of biographical facts, they have constructed different narratives on the
source and the meaning of the change in gender roles during this period. Consider, for example, the following modernist formulation of Taymur's life:

> ʿA'isha al-Taymuriya and Warda al-Yazji wrote and distributed poetry and tales
> in the late nineteenth century. They were brought up in liberal families and they
> had fathers who supported their learning. These men, disregarding gender "rules,"
> foiled their wives' efforts to produce ladies of the needle rather than women of the
> pen. The fathers brought in special tutors and encouraged their daughters' literary
> inclinations. In this environment, the girls were allowed to develop and express
> alternative perspectives on their society until they were ready to be married and
> then they were expected to conform.[3]

In the above, the authors present Taymur as the product of a liberal/modern
family whose father supported women's learning. The father disregarded and/
or rebelled against the prevailing gendered patriarchal rules, "foiling" the conservative desire of his wife to raise a lady of the needle, not the pen. Not only

did he encourage his daughter's aspirations, but he also hired tutors to guide her literary studies. As a result, ʿAʾisha Taymur developed an unconventional perspective on her society at least until she was married.

In another modernist-feminist formulation, reference to ʿAʾisha Taymur appears as part of the political and social history of the upper and the ruling classes. The following offers a good summary of the argument.

> The openness toward women's study of European subjects was reflected in the practices of the upper classes. Muhammed ʿAli's daughters and their retinues received instruction from European tutors as well as the traditional instruction in Arabic and religion. Upper-class families followed suit, though employing teachers for daughters was evidently a sporadic rather than a routine practice. ʿAʾisha Taymur (1840–1902), a distinguished poet and a member of the Turkish-Egyptian upper class, received an education, despite her mother's opposition, because of her own persistence and her father's support.[4]

Here, women's openness to the study of European subjects is seen as the key to change in gender roles within the upper class. The ascent to power of a new modernizing ruler and enlightened elites within his circle provided support for the important practice of hiring European as well as local tutors for the education of their daughters. Upper-class families sporadically followed suit. In the discussion of how ʿAʾisha Taymur became a distinguished poet, her mother's opposition and her father's support are again asserted. Unlike the previous modernist formulation where she was totally determined by her liberal family, in this second formulation ʿAʾisha's own persistence is underlined, and the result is a more feminist narrative where her agency is recognized in the discussion of the social dynamics of change.

In the above discursive formulations, the modernization of nineteenth-century Egypt is identified with the emergence of enlightened patriarchs, modernizing upper-class elites, and liberal families. These were the central actors in ʿAʾisha Taymur's biography. She rose to fame because of their support, not in spite of it. Modernity is identified with the rejection of women's feminine/domestic roles and the support of their education. The latter presumably transformed their gender roles and increased their options. The women who rebelled against the old domestic roles, like the young ʿAʾisha, were agents of change, and those who did not, like her mother, were its traditional opponents.

With the exception of the detailed biography of Taymur written by the feminist writer Mayy Ziyada, most discussions of Taymur's life focus on her childhood experiences. They are conspicuously silent on how the adult Taymur reconciled her private roles as mother and wife with her new interests, and what sacrifices she had to make to secure her standing as a prominent poet. Most narratives jump from her childhood years and her father's support for her desire for literary education to her triumphant rise as a distinguished poet in later years. In making this leap, authors generally assert faith in the continuation of Egyptian modernity and its enlightened elites without discussing the specific details that contributed to her emergence as a mature poet two decades later. According to this narrative, Taymur's rebellion against tradition and her embrace of modern aspirations were rewarded by widespread acclaim and recognition. In conclusion, the reader is led to believe that modernity delivered on its promise to its protégée.

In what follows, I want to present a different reading of Taymur's experiences based on a balanced discussion and reconstruction of the childhood experiences, which, according to the feminist and modernist discourses, significantly influenced her development as a poet. In addition, I want to discuss the adult experiences on which those discourses are silent and which underline the important roles played by Taymur's daughter, Tawhida, and her female tutors in assisting in and then completing her literary training: experiences that were crucial for her rise to prominence. In this new reading, the dominant masculine narratives, which highlight the power of men and pay secondary or little attention to the contributions made by women in initiating and sustaining the gender-role change, are challenged, and the foundation is laid for a different discourse on the meaning of the change to women. In the conclusion, I discuss how this different reading may help us understand why the new roles Taymur embraced were problematic and presented women with serious dilemmas and conflicts.

TOWARD THE DECENTERING OF THE MASCULINE READING OF TAYMUR'S CHILDHOOD EXPERIENCES

'A'isha Taymur was born in 1840 into the affluent aristocratic class, which had a history of providing private instruction to their female children.[5] In the 1800s her father's grandparents, who were from Turkey and Kurdish Mosul, found their way to Egypt, where they made their name and fortune as soldiers and clerks.[6] As Turkic members of the bureaucracy, they became members of the Egyptian aristocracy.

Taymur's mother was a freed Circassian slave.[7] Up until 1877 when slavery was abolished, many members of the Egyptian aristocracy married white slaves from the Caucusus to maintain their distinct ethnic roots. These slave women were freed once they bore their masters' children.

'A'isha was the eldest of three girls her mother bore her father, Ismail Taymur. She had a brother, who was born much later, one year before her father's death in 1872.[8] As a result, this household was unusually preoccupied with its female children. Initially, in the absence of sons, Taymur's father became actively involved in the affairs of his daughters. Not only did he know about their different interests, but he eventually played an important role in ʿAʾisha's struggle with her mother to add literary training to the roster of feminine occupations she learned as a young girl. This is how ʿAʾisha described this struggle:

> When my mind was ready to develop . . . , my mother, the goddess of compassion and virtue and the treasure of knowledge and experience, brought the tools of weaving and embroidery and exerted herself in teaching me. She explained things clearly and cleverly, but I was not receptive. I was not willing to improve in the feminine occupations. I used to flee from her like a prey seeking to escape the net.
>
> [At the same time], I used to look forward to attending the gatherings of prominent writers without any awkwardness. I found the sound of the pen on paper to be the most beautiful, and I became convinced that membership in that profession was the most abundant blessing. To satisfy my longing, I would collect any sheets of paper and small pens. Then, I would go someplace away from all and imitate the writers as they scribbled. Hearing that sound was very enjoyable. When my mother would find me out, she would scold me and threaten me. This only increased my rejection of embroidery and did not improve my skills.[9]

In the above passage, Taymur described two types of gendered learning that she was exposed to as a young girl. Taymur's mother took on the task of initiating her into the feminine occupations of embroidery and weaving. Through them, girls learned discipline and concentration in childhood. Because Taymur showed very little interest and skill in this type of learning, which was socially valued by her class, conflict broke out between mother and daughter.

Behind her lack of interest in the feminine occupations was her exposure, at a young age, to a different kind of learning. Taymur's experiences suggest that sexual segregation within upper-class families did not begin until children were somewhat older. Taymur mingled freely, at the age of nine or ten,[10] with men from within and outside the family in the literary gatherings that took place at her father's house. This type of learning was associated with maleness and was more glamorous. It was formal and literary. When she developed an interest in this type of learning, she was given to understand that embroidery and weaving were the important skills young aristocratic girls were expected to acquire, and that writing and reading were not.

As the struggle with her mother continued over her lack of interest in feminine education, her father eventually became involved in the conflict, and this had significant implications for the delineation of what his other two daughters were to learn. The negotiations between mother and daughter and between husband and wife on what was to be done offer a complex account of how husbands and wives negotiated changes in the patriarchal rules of Egypt's sexually segregated system. Here is ʿAʾisha's description of this process:

Even though I was genuinely inclined to [literate] learning, I also tried to get my mother's approval. But I continued to dislike the feminine occupations. I used to go out to the reception hall (*slamlik*), past the writers who were there to listen to their melodious verse. My mother—may God rest her in the heavenly gardens—was hurt by my actions. She would reprimand, threaten, warn, and promise to punish. She also appealed to me with friendly promises of jewelry and pretty costumes.

[Finally], my father reasoned with her, quoting the Turkish poet who said: "The heart is not led, through force, to the desired path. So do not torment another soul if you can spare it!" He also cautioned: "Beware of breaking the heart of this young girl and tainting her purity with violence. If our daughter is inclined to the pen and paper, do not obstruct her desire."

"Let us share our daughters: You take 'Afat and give me 'Asmat [another of 'A'isha's names]. If I make a writer out of 'Asmat, then this will bring me mercy after my death." My father then said: "Come with me 'Asmat. Starting tomorrow I will bring you two instructors who will teach you Turkish, Persian, *fiqh* (jurisprudence), and Arabic grammar. Do well in your studies and follow what I instruct you to do, and beware of making me ashamed before your mother."[11]

In this account, the behavior of both mother and daughter did not fit the docile or submissive character of traditional femininity. The daughter resisted her mother's effort to train and socialize her into the feminine role, and the mother was similarly unyielding to the wishes of her husband. It is clear that the patriarch did not exercise autocratic control over his women and children. Instead, he reasoned with his wife and his daughter in an attempt to find a solution. In this account, persuasion and consent were clearly more efficient ways to run the household.

Because feminist writers and modernist historians made a great deal of the mother's opposition to change and the father's support of it, it is important to closely examine the motives of mother and father in what was an unfolding struggle. First, despite the conflict between mother and daughter, Taymur never suggested that her mother was a bad or indifferent caretaker. The latter's opposition to change seems to have derived from concern for her daughter's future ability to demonstrate her feminine skills. Inadequate training in these skills spelled future social criticism for both mother and daughter. While the mother's reaction to her daughter's desire for change was obviously a conservative one, it also reflected an understanding of how patriarchal systems worked. In contrast to her daughter's naive conception of what the issues were (a liking for literature and a distaste for embroidery), the mother's opposition might be read as a recognition that the change her daughter desired needed the patriarch's sanction. Otherwise, the rebellion of a daughter, no matter how special, could be met harshly by both the father and the family's immediate social circles. In discouraging her daughter, she might be seen as protecting her from both and also testing the father's willingness to go along with the change.

While the socialization of young girls was clearly the established responsibility of the mother, and a father did not usually intervene between mother and daughter, the mother's unsuccessful use of various means of coaxing and coercion was a clear invitation for the father to decide what to do about this unexpected development. In response, he proceeded to share with his wife the wisdom of introducing limited changes in some rules for the purpose of maintaining the important ones. Given the failure of the coercive measures, the father argued that it was important to minimize the disruptive impact of their daughter's rebellion. By making an exception in her case, they would be able to ensure that her "purity" was preserved, and that the socialization of their other daughters proceeded as planned.

In ʿAʾisha's account, the father seems to have been apprehensive that the prolonged confrontation between mother and daughter would lead to something more ominous than his daughter's literacy. He explicitly told his wife that in dealing harshly with their daughter's unusual interests, she might drive her to a more serious challenge of the rules—that is, to some action that would taint her (sexual) purity. This stood as the more threatening prospect: a small rebellion could be aggravated into a more serious break with patriarchal rules. In response, he suggested that they accept what was a more tolerable change and in this way avoid a more significant one.

Most analysts have paid little attention to the importance of the mother's cooperation for ʿAʾisha's success in her new endeavors. The mother's continued opposition or disapproval could have subverted the efforts of father and daughter to proceed with the new type of learning, which was time-consuming. There is no mention of either in ʿAʾisha's accounts. The mother's willingness to go along with the change facilitated ʿAʾisha's pursuit of her new studies and ended her rebellious phase without inciting any further challenge of existing patriarchal rules.

In negotiating the change in feminine rules with his wife, Taymur's father referred to a nineteenth-century Islamic precept that educating one's daughter will be rewarded by mercy from God after death. Here, Islam was represented as encouraging parents to educate their daughters. It is also clear that a woman writer was not an unheard-of phenomenon in Egyptian society at that time. There were at least three well-known literary women, who acted as tutors and/ or poets/writers. The adult Taymur called upon some of them to tutor her in poetic meter and Arabic grammar.

Interestingly enough, the father commissioned two male tutors who instructed his daughter in Turkish, Persian, *fiqh*, and finally Arabic grammer. The ranking of importance given to different languages represented both the older indigenous ideal of learning within the aristocracy and the particular history of Taymur's family. Turkish was the spoken and written language of the aristocracy. Persian was added because of the father's Kurdish roots. Arabic was to be taught as a third language. The father's recruitment of male tutors, not female ones, to assist his daughter in the intensive program of learning he designed supports the contention that the existing rules of sexual segregation were flexible: such families as Taymur's utilized elderly male teachers to provide safe education for their female children. The study of *fiqh* represented a novel addition to the Islamic ideal of education given to upper-class girls.[12] It most probably emphasized the learning of social and future marital obligations of young girls within the upper classes. It provided another means by which the father ensured his daughter's socialization into the patriarchal norms that stressed female virtue and responsibilities.

In exchange for assisting ʿA'isha in her new area of interest, the father asked her to "do well in your lessons, follow my instructions, and make sure that I am not shamed before your mother."[13] In accepting, ʿA'isha promised to "obey him, do her best to gain his trust and realize his hopes."[14] Lest the reader miss what the father had in mind, ʿA'isha provided valuable information. When she began to read and then write love poetry, her father frequently criticized and discouraged her. He suggested that "if she read much of this type of poetry, it might lead her to neglect other lessons."[15] In a practical attempt to steer her in a different direction, he referred to the popular Ottoman literary ideal that good poems should be written in three languages.[16] If they were not, then one could not possibly enjoy them.[17] In this context, the father used this ideal to insist that she concentrate on the linguistic aspect of her learning at the expense of the expression of feelings he deemed undesirable.

Our understanding of the father and his motives is not complete unless we highlight the fact that he had three daughters and no sons during this period. With one daughter showing interest in what would have been the proper education of a son, the father could have taken some solace in this unexpected turn of events. The mother, most probably, recognized her husband's longing for a son in the support he was giving to ʿA'isha's education. The attention the father gave to ʿA'isha and the use of the family resources to give her a literary education established her status as a surrogate son.

As for the liberal and/or feminist credentials of the father, any claim he might have to such attributes is clearly contradicted by his support of feminine education for his second daughter, ʿAfat. In the negotiations with his wife, he suggested that she continue ʿAfat's training in traditional feminine skills while he offered ʿA'isha a literary education. It is clear from this arrangement that he was not opposed to feminine education and/or particularly committed to a different type of education for all his daughters. He did not have any problem with ʿAfat's getting a feminine education and did not insist that she follow in her sister's footsteps. This was not just a negotiating technique he employed to convince his wife to go along. It was ʿAʾisha's rebellion that forced the issue to begin with, and before that there is no evidence of his support of unconventional education for his daughters. When ʿAʾisha's rebellion unfolded, it took both parents by surprise. When he intervened, it was out of apprehension that this could escalate into something more serious. In response, he devised a pragmatic strategy, making it clear that he was not committed to extending this literary education to his other daughters. In short, he was not a supporter of new gender roles for his daughters. He isolated ʿAʾisha's education from that of the others and thereby addressed some of his own emotional needs, the needs of one of his daughters, and those of his wife.

In the reconstruction above, the complex motives of mother and father provide an alternative explanation of how the change in the social definition of femininity, represented by Taymur's novel education, was negotiated. In understanding the initial struggle between mother and daughter, one should not discount the effort by this mother, who was a former slave, to shield her daughter from social censure. One should also not overlook the importance of the mother's cooperation and support in ʿAʾisha's successful pursuit of her literary interests. This, along with the father's different type of support for his daughter's education spurred by his fear that her stance might be a prelude to a more serious rebellion, explains how change was contained within existing patriarchal norms.

At the same time, the availability of this new type of education for young girls did not have the revolutionary implication construed by the modernist feminists and historians. Even though Taymur did well in her literary studies, this stage, with its unique experiences for a young aristocratic girl, ended with her marriage several years later.[18] Marriage, domestic responsibilities, and children made it difficult for her to pursue these literary interests. Moving into this new phase of her life concluded her modest challenge of patriarchal rules regarding what young girls should and should not learn.

A FEMININE READING OF TAYMUR'S ADULT YEARS: BREAKING THE SILENCE ON WOMEN'S CONTRIBUTIONS TO CHANGE

The second stage of ʿAʾisha Taymur's struggle against the prevailing patriarchal rules of her time concerned the equally serious need to reconcile her literary ambitions and the wifely/motherly preoccupations of an adult woman. Taymur's childhood education ended when she got married at a young age. Marriage brought on domestic responsibilities and motherhood. For the next decade, Taymur's personal and familial history was not very different from that of her contemporaries. It is not clear how many children she had. In her poems, she discusses two of her children to whom she was particularly close: her eldest, a daughter, and her youngest, a son. Both were supporters of her literary interests. There was also another son, whose accomplishments she extolled in a poem, and at least one other daughter as well.

Taymur was clearly attached to and proud of her eldest daughter, Tawhida, who was an exceptional young girl by the standards of the time. This is how she described her.

> After ten years [of marriage], the first fruit of my heart, Tawhida, who is part of my self and the spirit of my joy, reached the age of nine. I enjoyed watching her spending her days, from morning till noon, between the pens and the ink bottles, and during the rest of the day and evening, she wove the most beautiful crafts. I prayed for her success, feeling my own sadness regarding what I had missed when I was her age and was repulsed by these activities.
>
> When my daughter was twelve years of age, she began to serve her mother and father. In addition, she managed the household, including all of the servants and the dependents. It was then that I was able to find spaces [zwaya] of relaxation.[19]
>
> At this point, it occurred to me to resume what I had missed as a youngster— learning poetic meters. I brought a woman instructor to teach me. . . . But she passed away six months later. My daughter, who had attended these lessons, was able because of her youth and sharp intellect to excel in this art more than I did.[20]

The above suggests the development of at least two new definitions of femininity represented by mother and daughter. Tawhida embodied a more expansive definition of femininity, which took equal delight in the learning of languages and the feminine crafts. In contrast, Taymur represented a femininity that was more masculine in its repudiation of the feminine and its crafts. It assumed relative disengagement from the domestic. In the quotation above, she likens her approach to literary training to a Sufi's retreat to a *zawya*. This was an isolated place removed from all distractions where one devoted oneself to considering one's connection to God. In Taymur's case, Tawhida created such a place within the household by eliminating the domestic distractions that would interfere with her mother's literary training. Taymur the poet, like a Sufi, assumed that she needed time for introspection and some detachment from her surroundings. This meant that her mastery of the tools of the literary craft was achieved through the repression of her gender difference, temporarily suspending her caretaking functions vis-à-vis her husband and children. The death of her husband during this period eliminated marital responsibilities as a primary occupation.

Taymur's experience during both her childhood and the early years of her marriage was based on the assumption of conflict between domestic and non-domestic preoccupations. It delineated a conflicted femininity that pitted women's gendered roles as primary caretakers against the masculine character of their new interests and occupations. It yielded dichotomous definitions of women's private and public interests that were difficult to integrate. Taymur's life was filled with examples of the disintegrative nature of these definitions. In her childhood years, she was brought up as a substitute son, not a young daughter, learning literary writing, not the feminine occupations. Once she was married, her literary interests were repressed by the feminine definitions of wife and mother. Finally, her desire to resume literary training depended on her success in splitting off her feminine functions and transferring them to another female, her daughter. Those who did not have the means to secure or to pay for female assistance could not possibly succeed in these new public roles.

Even Tawhida's early and happy juxtaposition of interests in the feminine and the masculine/literary occupations did not withstand the test of time or adulthood. Owing to her mother's unfulfilled literary ambition, she became saddled with the domestic duties that her mother abdicated. This put an end to her own literary interests and ambitions. It created a competitive dynamic among women whereby the interests of some could be achieved only through the sacrifice of the similar needs of others.

With the arrangement between mother and daughter in place, Taymur recruited three women instructors to help her polish her literary skills. In addition to the older tutor who passed away after six months, she hired Fatima al-Azhariyya and Setita al-Tablawiyya to teach her Arabic grammar and poetic meter.[21] Under their guidance, she began to compose long verse compositions and the lighter literary form of *zajal*.

Who were these women, and what kind of positions did they occupy in a sexually segregated system that has been defined by the modernists as incapable of changing and/or extending to women the rights to education and work that established the revolutionary credentials of modernity? The first, as her title indicates, attended al-Azhar, Egypt's most learned religious institution. During that period, older and/or handicapped women, especially the blind, could attend its religious and language courses.[22] Both groups of women used their knowledge (especially grammar) to make an independent living for themselves. They taught these subjects to other women of the middle and aristocratic classes.[23] This suggests that within the sexually segregated system of the time, age and physical handicap were seen as having a defeminizing effect that entitled some women to move among different households and to gain entry into some masculine occupations. Age and handicap also provided them with some protection from the advances of their male colleagues. Whether al-Azhar awarded these students the same formal degrees as were given to their male counterparts is not known.[24]

The second of Taymur's tutors was skilled in poetic meter. Her working-class title/name, Tablawiyya, literally means "percussions." It is not clear where she acquired her literary skills. Finally, Khadija al-Maghribiyya, who was Taymur's contemporary had competed with male poets of her time and outwitted her critics.[25] Huda Sha'rawi described al-Maghribiyya as ugly.[26] In her case, too, a "handicap" gave her greater freedom and some access to literary circles.

The three working women discussed in this section represent what was an existing subgroup of women in the sexually segregated society of the time: women who not only knew how to read and write but also possessed literary/religious/language skills that they used to earn a living in the public arena, outside of their households. These middle-class women were ahead of their aristocratic counterparts, who were secluded in their harems, in gaining a foothold in the religious and literary arenas. Their age, physical handicap, or homely looks served to explain their interest in and access to the more masculine occupations. In other words, nineteenth-century Egyptian society was beginning to ponder the gendered meaning of some of these changing roles. In one view, women who played these roles were considered to have a dubious femininity. In becoming tutors, poets, and religious scholars, women were warned that they risked losing their femininity and becoming masculine.[27] Their social milieu continued to stress the irreconcilability of masculinity and femininity. Taymur challenged prevailing views and their assumptions. As a young (approximately thirty years old) married woman and a mother who also had literary interests, she was undermining many of the old understandings of why women took on some nondomestic activities. Her literary interests did not provide her with means of employment. She wrote for pleasure and in exchange for public recognition.

Taymur's own venture into the public domain during the period from 1872 to 1878 was most probably influenced by the modernizing tendencies of the new ruler, *khedive* Ismail(1863–79). Under his rule, modernization accelerated.[28] A clear emphasis on Western mannerisms, values, and roles emerged. This had a mixed effect on Taymur. On the one hand, it encouraged her to take on the new role of court translator. On the other, the new role capitalized on her unique familiarity with Persian to serve Egypt's relations with other Middle Eastern countries. While this new role was hidden from public view because it was enacted within the royal court, it took Taymur out of her household. She described it in the following passage. "Her royal highness . . . the mother of *khedive* Ismail, invited me to the palace whenever the relatives of the Persian king visited. . . . I stayed with them during these visits, entertained them, and inquired about their customs and their ethics."[29]

During these visits, Taymur acted as court translator and companion to royal female guests from Persia. In addition to entertaining them, she sought to learn more about their culture. The idea of deploying her language skills in the service of the *khedive* and his guests was clearly new. It resulted in frequent absences from the family. This explains how signs of Tawhida's deteriorating health escaped her. Tawhida had also kept these signs secret so as not to distract her mother from her new preoccupations. Taymur's belated discovery of her daughter's illness and her frantic recruitment of numerous physicians[30] failed to rescue Tawhida. She died at the age of eighteen.

Taymur's reaction to the loss was both unusual and instructive. She burned most of her Turkish and Arabic poems and all the Persian ones written during this period. She explained that she found these Persian poems in Tawhida's folder and that she burned them to mirror the burning of her heart at the loss. She may also have been acting on the unconscious realization that it was her visits with the royal Persian guests to the Egyptian court that had taken her away from home and delayed her discovery of Tawhida's failing health. With most of her poetic production destroyed, she proceeded to actively mourn her daughter for seven years: crying her eyes out and developing eye disease in the process. During this period, the only poetry she produced was a long grieving poem in the memory of Tawhida.

In these acts of mourning, she seemed to acknowledge that her daughter's life was the price she had paid for pursuing the masculine ideal of literary study and taking on the new role of court translator. In both of these occupations, there was no place for maternal responsibility and/or a daughter's dependence on her mother for caretaking. What Tawhida's death brought home was the fatal conflict between a traditional female gender role (women's primary responsibility for children) and the way literary production and public activities outside the household assumed well-bounded individuals—men—who were not involved in taking care of others. In training as a (male) poet would and eventually taking an interest in nondomestic activities outside the home, Taymur had to dissociate herself from mothering as a primary occupation. Tawhida's demise underlined the human cost of these decisions and activities. It provoked enormous guilt feelings that were a response to her perceived abandonment of motherly responsiblilties. To be a "good mother," Taymur would have had to sacrifice her literary ambitions, subordinating her social and emotional needs to those of others. This would have been a difficult decision, considering her early and poignant struggles to pursue these interests and dreams.

In fact, the burning of the poems she produced during this period represented not the repudiation of poetry per se but that of the individualistic/masculine character of her training, which indirectly contributed to the demise of her daughter. As part of her mourning, she wrote a long elegy connecting the literary and the maternal aspects of her self, whose separation had had tragic consequences. Curiously, the elegy represents an old Arabic literary form that recognizes women's gender difference (their emotional connectedness to others) as giving them particular skills in the poetic expression of loss of loved ones. The seventh-century al-Khansa', one of the pre-Islamic and early Muslim women poets, wrote one of the best-known elegies in Arabic poetry mourning the death of her brothers in battle. This poem established the elegy as a respected form of female poetic expression. It recognized women's central public role in formalized grief.[31] It was this poetic tradition that Taymur fell back on as she attempted to integrate the different parts of her wounded self.

CONCLUSION

The feminist and the modernist discourses that represented Taymur as an exemplar of the progressive character of the new society and its gender roles offered ideological formulations of the change. They exaggerated the importance of her father's support, offered an unsympathetic discussion of her mother's role, and maintained silence on the contributions made by her mother, daughter, and female tutors to the completion of her literary education and training. The result was a masculine formulation that generally devalued women and ignored their contribution to the initiation and sustenance of social change.

The above-mentioned discourses were masculine in yet another way. Their valuation of the new roles of poet and court translator was premised on the repudiation of traditional feminine work, whether embroidery or domestic and motherly responsibilities. For example, their discussions rested on the assumption that literary education was superior to embroidery. Yet it was understood that literary work, presented as part of her childhood education, would not be Taymur's primary occupation. It ended with adulthood (i.e., marriage), when she was expected to resume the less valued feminine roles of wife and mother wherein she took care of the needs of husband and children. Here, gender difference was associated with caretaking, the privileging of others' needs, and the imposition of conscious limits on women's (noncaretaking) desires and aspirations. It was only the latter activities that were socially recognized and valued.

It is not surprising that the feminist and the modernist discourses did not valorize the time that Taymur spent as a full-time wife and mother. In fact, both narratives jump over this period to discuss her emergence as a poet, which both considered her most important accomplishment. Because Taymur learned this repudiation of femininity during her childhood initiation into literary learning, she did not hesitate to transfer her domestic responsibilities to her daughter as a means of freeing herself to pursue her literary ambitions. The loss of her young daughter served as a reminder of the human cost of this repudiation of femininity and women's caretaking functions. The burning of most of her poetry followed by her seven years of tears mourning her daughter's death represented a strong condemnation of the devaluation of women's caretaking and the promotion of their nondomestic roles, as well as her perceived complicity in both.

It is also clear that the social definitions of women's old and new gender roles simultaneously privileged the needs of men as husbands/fathers and presented their social experiences as a model for ambitious women. This elevated masculinity as the prized role for both men and women. Through the status of surrogate sons and/or honorary males, women gained some of the social recognition given to men. For the most part, these limited gains did not challenge the patriarchal social reality in which all women were expected to be, above all else, adult caretakers of men and children. This left very little time for literary interests and put real limits on the ability of women to excel in occupations of which it was presumed that men, who were free of domestic responsibility and were looked after by women, were the legitimate members. It also left men without any involvement in domestic and caretaking activities.

It is hard to view this arrangement as extending equality and liberty to women. The homologizing logic of this system (which denied the importance of women's nurturing and caretaking roles and in the process elevated the masculine experience to universal heights)[32] meant that women could claim new interests and options only within the very narrow definitions of masculine social roles and patterns of behavior. They were free only to choose to be like men. If they made this choice, they had to deny their gender difference and consent to its continued social devaluation.

NOTES

1. Mayy Ziyada, "Katiba tuqadim shaʿira" (A writer introduces a poet), in *Hilyat al-tiraz: Diwan ʿA'isha al-Taymuriyya* (Best in its class: The collected poems of ʿA'isha al-Taymuriyya) (Cairo: Dar al-Katib al-ʿArabi, 1952), p. 34.

2. ʿAbd al-Rahman al-Rafiʿi, *ʿAsr Ismaʿil* (The age of Ismail) (Cairo: Dar al-Maʿarif, 1987), 1:299.

3. Margot Badran and Miriam Cooke, introduction to *Opening the Gates: A Century of Arab Feminist Writing*, ed. Margot Badran and Miriam Cooke (Bloomington: Indiana University Press, 1990), p. xxx.

4. Leila Ahmed, *Women and Gender in Islam* (New Haven: Yale University Press, 1992), p. 135.

5. Jonathan P. Berkey, "Women and Islamic Education in the Mamluk Period," in *Women in Middle East History*, ed. Nikki Keddie and Beth Baron (New Haven: Yale University Press, 1991), p. 145.

6. Ahmad Kamal Zadah, "Jiddati: ʿArd wa tahlil" (My grandmother: Review and analysis), in *Hilyat al-tiraz*, p. 16.

7. Ziyada, "Katiba tuqadim shaʿira," p. 56.

8. Ibid.

9. ʿA'isha Taymur, *Nataʿij al-ahwal fi al-aqwal wa al-afʿal* (The results of circumstances in statements and deeds) (Cairo: Matbaʿat Muhammad Afandi Mustafa, 1887), pp. 2–3.

10. This age is an approximate one, which I arrived at by relying on Taymur's assertions concerning when her own daughter started learning other languages and feminine occupations. One can assume that Taymur initiated her daughter into these types of learning at the same age that she undertook them. See Ziyada, "Katiba tuqadim sha'ira," p. 68.

11. Ibid., p. 64.

12. I am indebted to Denise Spellberg for this particular insight and its significance.

13. Ziyada, "Katiba tuqadim sha'ira," p. 61.

14. Ibid., p. 65.

15. Ibid.

16. I am grateful to Jane Hathaway for pointing out the popularity of this Ottoman literary ideal.

17. Ibid.

18. Bint al-Shati' mentioned that she was married at the age of fifteen. See Bint al-Shati', "Al-Sha'ira" (The poet), in *Hilyat al-tiraz*, p. 27.

19. Ziyada, "Katiba tuqadim sha'ira," p. 68.

20. Ibid., p. 69.

21. Ibid., p. 71.

22. *Qissat al-Azhar: Rihab al-'ilm wa al-din* (The story of al-Azhar: The arena of knowledge and religion) (Cairo: Dar al-Hilal, 1973), pp. 21, 191.

23. Ibid., p. 21.

24. Duriya Shafiq, *Al-Mar'a al-Misriyya*, pp. 91–92.

25. Ziyada, "Katiba tuqadim sha'ira," p. 82; Huda Sha'rawi, *Mudhakarat ra'idat al-mar'a al-'Arabiyya* (The memoirs of the pioneer of Arab women) (Cairo: Dar al-Hilal, 1981), p. 45.

26. Sha'rawi, *Muhdhkarat ra'idat al-mar'a al-'Arabiyya*, p. 46.

27. Ziyada, "Katiba tuqadim sha'ira," p. 62.

28. 'Abd al-Rahman al-Rafi'i, *'Asr Isma'il*, 1:201.

29. Ibid., p. 78.

30. Ziyada, "Katiba tuqadim sha'ira," p. 74.

31. Denise Spellberg was also helpful in underlining this point in a discussion of how the new roles took on old forms.

32. Adriana Cavarero, "Equality and Sexual Difference: Amnesia in Political Thought," in *Beyond Equality and Difference*, ed. Gisela Bock and Susan James (London: Routledge, 1992), p. 39.

Part Two

MOTHERS, WIVES, AND CITIZENS:
THE TURN OF THE CENTURY

CHAPTER 3

Crafting an Educated Housewife in Iran

AFSANEH NAJMABADI

SEVERAL recent writings on women in the turn-of-the-century Middle East have noted the centrality of motherhood and wifehood, particularly their regulation through textbooks of domestic sciences, to the discussions of the notion of "woman" in this period.[1] Whether it is argued that women themselves used this modernization and scientization to improve their status in society, or that the process contained and frustrated the possible feminist potentials of women's awakening, or even that the scientization was a disciplinary and regulatory process that crafted a modern womanhood in contradistinction to a traditional one, these arguments do not adequately deal with the significant shifts that concepts of motherhood and wifehood had gone through to produce this discourse in the first place.

If the well-known argument for women's education—that educated women made better mothers and wives—sounds very traditional and, given our late-twentieth-century sensibilities, reads as a reinforcement of women's old professions, this disappointment perhaps arises from lack of attention to what important shifts in "mother" and "wife" constituted the subtext of that argument.[2] In Persian texts, these shifts in meaning from premodern to modern normative concepts reconfigured woman from "house" (*manzil*) to "manager of the house" (*mudabbir-i manzil*). They were closely linked to the educational debates of the last decades of the nineteenth century and the first decades of the twentieth. The modern educational regimes, deeply gendered from the start, were central to the production of the woman of modernity through particular regulatory and emancipatory impulses that I will review in this essay. Moreover, I hope to demonstrate that these two seemingly conflictive impulses in fact enabled each other's work. For woman, the emancipatory possibilities of modernity and its disciplinary "technologies" were mutually productive.

FROM "HOUSE" TO "MANAGER OF THE HOUSE"

Premodern normative concepts of wife and mother can be read through Persian books of ethics that were aimed at producing a perfect Muslim man, as man of God, man of the household, and man of the polis.[3] Although these books vary, there are a number of common points that are at the center of my concern here:

that the father, not his wife, was the manager of the household (*mudabbir-i manzil*) and in charge of the discipline and education of the children (sons, more specifically), and that the biological mother was not necessarily and at times not preferably the nurturer and caretaker of the child.[4] These texts were male-authored; moreover, the reader was assumed to be male, and in the section on discipline and management (*siasat va tadbir*) of the household, he was addressed as the head of the household, as the managing owner of property, wives, children, servants, and slaves. The first function (regulation of property) had not only textual priority over the other three; in fact, the other three seem to have been at the service of the first: "The motive for taking a wife should be twofold, the preservation of property and the quest of progeny; it should not be at the instigation of appetite or for any other purpose."[5] The man was given advice on who constituted a good wife ("The best of wives is the wife adorned with intelligence, piety, continence, shrewdness, modesty, tenderness, a loving disposition, control of her tongue, obedience to her husband, self-devotion in his service and a preference for his pleasure, gravity, and the respect of her own family").[6] He was also advised on how to regulate and rule his wives: "Once the bond of union is effected between husband and wife, the husband's procedure in ruling his wife should be along three lines: to inspire awe, to show favor, and to occupy her mind."[7]

Similarly, the section on children was directed to the man.[8] It was the father, not the mother, who was in charge of a child's upbringing. He was the one who named him, chose a wet nurse, and was responsible for his physical and mental development.[9]

Not a nurturer and an educator—like the later mother of late-nineteenth-century Persian texts on women and education of the nation—the motherhood depicted in these treatises resides in the first place in the womb. Although the mother is given a secondary nurturing role in much of the premodern literature on parenting, her primary contribution is to provide the vessel of the womb for conception and prebirth nurturing of the fetus.[10]

Indeed, some of the reformist critical literature of the nineteenth century continued to treat mothering in apparently similar terms. Mirza Aqa Khan Kirmani (1853/54–96), one of the most important critical intellectuals of nineteenth-century Iran, wrote in *Sad khatabah* (One hundred discourses) of five schools in which "every individual man gains his ethics and perfects his temperament and character. The first of these schools is the womb of the mother where the fetus gains the fundamentals of his ethics and acquires those character traits and attitudes that during the term of pregnancy were in the mother, innately or as acquired character. If, for instance, the mother is mean and jealous, whether she was innately so or became so, undoubtedly this character trait will inhere in that fetus."[11] If she was scared of something, had bad or good dreams, or became ill, this experience, Kirmani argued, would be transmitted to the fetus.

The second school was the family. Every suckling child was trained according to the manners and ethics of his family, the closest among them his mother.[12] This was the only place that Kirmani wrote of the mother as an educator for the child, after which he returned to emphasizing the influences of the womb. For instance, he argued that the reason Iranian children were ugly and ill-statured was because at the time of conception the father had not approached the mother with desire and happiness.[13]

Kirmani argued at great length that the first school, the womb of the mother, was the most important and most influential. What traits of temperament and manners entered into the fetus's blood was very difficult to change. It was for this reason that one had to be considerate toward women and have regard for their rights. He argued that when the time came for people to address their oppressors and complain, the son would seek his rights against the father who had failed to take him to school to learn sciences and skills and techniques and crafts and manners and ways of humanity. In contrast, the fetus in the mother's womb would ask why she had taken it to mourning sessions and cried so much for the dead *imam*s and their relatives, instead of taking care of it in happiness and kindness.[14] Notably, Kirmani suggested that the wife would interrogate the husband about why he had not treated her as a companion and helpmeet, why he had made her dumb, deaf, and blind, deprived her of all rights of humanity, and buried her alive in a house, forcing her to take refuge in tricks and guile. The husband, on the other hand, would complain that the wife, instead of being a companion in life, had ruined his life with trickery.[15]

Despite some similarities between Kirmani's nineteenth-century *Sad khatabah* and a premodern text like Tusi's thirteenth-century *Akhlaq-i Nasiri*, these works differ vastly. Whereas Tusi wrote as a Muslim philosopher for other Muslims and was concerned with the production of the perfect Muslim man, the author of *Sad khatabah* spoke of himself as an Iranian (*man-i Irani*),[16] concerned with the sorry state of the Iranian nation (*millat-i Iran*). He considered his ideal reader to be not a Muslim man in search of this-worldly and otherworldly perfection but an Iranian man concerned with the fate of Iran.[17] The perfect man had changed from a Muslim believer to an Iranian citizen.

The continuities and discontinuities of Kirmani's concept of mother and wife with Tusi's are worth pointing out. To envisage the womb not simply as a vessel but as a school (*maktab*) imputed all the disciplinary and regulatory functions of school to the womb. Not only did the bearer of the womb regulate the character of the fetus, but now the regulatory process turned back upon the womb/woman. National formation began with the womb. If differently constructed Iranians were to be produced, woman as potential mother needed to be regulated and reconstructed. But the new notion of schooling also heralded new rights: because of the womb's central importance, "one needs to pay special attention to and care for women and their rights so that children will not become ill-tempered and bad-natured."[18] In Iran, however, Kirmani argued, "women are deprived of all rights of humanity and are forbidden the pleasures of life. . . . Iranian women are treated as lower than animals; nay, they are less valued than the dogs of Europe and the cats of cemeteries."[19]

Thus in Kirmani's rearticulation of premodern wisdom, the womb became the ground at once for regulatory practices toward women and for awarding women particular rights. This double movement, combining disciplinary techniques and emancipatory promises, becomes a general feature in the re-thinking of gender in the Iranian modernist imagination. I will discuss its workings on several levels later in this essay, but here I want to point out the enabling dynamic of this double movement. It is by no means the case that the two strands of this movement simply contradicted and frustrated one an-other. Rather, the disciplinary and emancipatory moments enabled each other's work; in this particular case, a newly envisaged womb produced the regulatory and emancipatory drives at once in order to produce children worthy of modernity.

Woman was also reconfigured as wife: she was to be man's companion in life. Kirmani argued at length against gender segregation and against the veil, which in his opinion not only failed to guarantee a woman's chastity but con-stituted a severe hindrance to her belonging to humanity and her attainment of education and knowledge. It had reduced half of the Iranian people to a para-lyzed, enchained state of ignorance with no ability to render any service to society. Rules of segregation also deprived men of the beneficial effects of socializing with women. Kirmani held these restrictions responsible for ped-erasty in Iran.[20] Moreover, he argued that men and women married without having known or even seen each other and thus began their married life, more often than not, with dislike—if not hatred— from the first night of marriage when they would finally set eyes upon each other.[21]

In another work, *Hasht bihisht*, most likely coauthored with Shaykh Ahmad Ruhi around 1892 as an explication of Babi religion, Kirmani had expressed similar but more radical views.[22] The authors of *Hasht bihisht* argued strongly against parents' forcing their children to particular choices of spouse, and for the need of men and women to choose their own mates willingly and get to know each other for several years during their engagement. They also spoke of the equality of women and men in the pleasures, benefits, and rights of mar-riage, and of the necessity that women be educated in all sciences, skills, crafts, and ethical matters. They argued for the removal of the veil, but at the same time, to prevent sin, evil, and fornication, they prohibited women from talking to men who were strangers to them.[23] They emphasized women's comprehen-sive equality with men and recommended that men include women as their left hand in all activities so that both hands could work equally. Furthermore, they linked the social lot of women, through motherhood, to the fate of humanity. In other words, motherhood became a mediating term between two concepts central to modernity: progress and women's rights. "Women's *hijab* (veil) and *tura* (laced face cover), their segregation from men, and their loss of all rights of humanity such that they are not even counted among human beings cause great corruption in the world of humanity, because this delicate kind constitutes children's early education. They are the teachers in the household and the fountainhead of all progress for humanity."[24]

This argument differentiates a modernist work such as *Hasht bihisht* from earlier books of advice and ethics. Instead of being part of the household—in fact, sometimes collapsed into the household and referred to as the household (*manzil*)—and subject to the man's management, woman has become the manager of household affairs and the educator of children.[25] Moreover, Kirmani and Ruhi continued to press their argument to full equality of men and women:

> Because of the ill ways men have treated them and have placed them outside the domain of humanity, half of the world of civilization and urbanity has remained unused and without effect. But the world of humanity cannot reach for perfection unless women become equals and partners with men in all affairs and rights; in fact, human traits are much more perfect in women compared to men. . . . in all rights including learning and education, government, inheritance, industries, and commerce women must be equal to men. . . . This decree is for the reform and education of women, to bring them out of the terror house of darkness and ignorance into the open field of the city of humanity and civility. Undoubtedly because of this decree the world of humanity and civility will double in size.[26]

EDUCATIONAL REGIMES

Few, if any, of the nineteenth-century reformers would call for such radical gender parity as Kirmani and Ruhi did. But by the first decade of the twentieth century, in articles in the constitutionalist press, the argument that women should be educated because they were educators of children, companions of men, and half of the nation had gained wide currency and was reiterated as a matter of obvious fact—"like the sun in the middle of the sky."

Hasht bihisht's concept of an ideal educational regime was exceptionally severe: "Children should be taken away from mothers upon birth and taken to a house of education to be brought up under the supervision of skilled teachers and clever women (*zanan-i shatir*) who, in appropriate schools, have studied especially the science of education and upbringing of children."[27] The authors drew on a manufacturing analogy to demonstrate their meaning. Such schools were like a factory that took in as raw material bits of wool and produced delicate fabric.[28] This became a common metaphor even in writings of reformers who did not advocate such a radical break. Schools were often referred to as human-making factories (*karkhanah-'i adam'sazi*), bringing the transformative and regulatory punctuations of modern production onto human beings.

That many writers found this metaphor apt reflects how vastly the concept of education that they were advocating differed from what it sought to replace. The education of men and women in premodern institutional and informal settings of mosques, Qur'anic neighborhood schools, or in the home, could hardly be compared to an orderly regulated manufacturing process.[29]

Not only the educational regime and institutions but the very concept of knowledge was consciously formulated in contradistinction to older concepts of knowledge.[30] In *Sad khatabah*, Kirmani contrasted the concepts of science/knowledge (*ʿilm*) of religious scholars (*ʿulama'*) with that of chemistry, politics, law, political economy, and natural sciences, arguing that "any nation that is more civilized has higher sciences, vaster needs, and higher means."[31]

Whereas in premodern texts knowledge pertained to man's perception of God and his rules,[32] modern knowledge pertained to issues of civilization and progress. The nineteenth-century writers took pains to distinguish their concept from the older "order of things."[33] Zuka' al-Mulk, editor of *Tarbiat* (Education)[34] felt obliged to make this distinction explicit: "If in this newspaper we speak of the weakness of science and the lack of learned men, this has nothing to do with the science of religion and guiding learned men. . . . Undoubtedly religion and faith supersede all else . . . and our learned men . . . are suns in the heaven of truth and stars of the sky of guidance."[35] He then went on to emphasize, however, that "the point is that the order of the day of Resurrection (*nizam-i kar-i muʿad*) depends on the order of making a living (*intizam-i amr-i muʿash*) . . . and of course the country, in order to put in order the affairs of this world, needs arithmetic and geometry and algebra and calculus and analysis and medicine and rules of agriculture and commerce and many other things. For instance, if we want to build a dam or construct a bridge or cure an ill person, would it be correct to go to a learned man of religion?"[36]

Another significant shift was the emergence of a concept of education that had become centered on literacy. The authors of *Hasht bihisht* considered "reading and writing . . . [as] self-evidently the basis for prosperity of any group of people and the key to all progress in the world."[37] Emphasizing literacy as central to the new education, Zuka' al-Mulk wrote, "Whoever cannot read, cannot know, and if he does not know, how can he be a capable person?"[38] This emphasis on reading and writing is related to the shift from a largely oral culture, supplemented with a calligraphic writing tradition, to a print culture.[39] Whereas in the old system of knowledge, it was conceivable that one might become knowledgeable without being literate if one had a powerful and well-trained memory—a cherished quality[40]—the new knowledge could be attained only through reading and writing.[41] Reading now became distinct from reciting—though in many languages such as Persian and Arabic the same word continues to be used for both. Zuka' al-Mulk referred to the ability to read and write as "the key to prosperity and happiness (*kalid-i saʿadat*); nay, it is its elixir (*kimia-yi saʿadat*)."[42] *Kimia-yi saʿadat*, once totally associated with the sciences of religion (the title of the Persian version of Ghazali's *Revival of Religious Sciences* (*Ihya al-ʿulum al-din*) is *Kimia-yi saʿadat*), now had come to be defined as the skill of reading and writing.

It is noteworthy that the nineteenth-century educational treatises, though addressed to men, were not addressed to them as private men, as fathers of the household in their responsibility to educate their sons—as, for instance, *Akhlaq-i Nasiri* had been. Education was now a national concern. It was for the sake of national progress and as a public duty, rather than for individual perfection or as a religious obligation, that the new education was urgently needed. It was thus expected that *the government* would undertake the task. After prophets sent by God to educate people, one writer argued, the task of education fell upon "people in charge and the wise men and kings."[43] The educational duties of the government were to be supplemented by those of private persons of means, not as heads of households but as men of the nation, as citizens: "It is incumbent on any patriot of means and on all powerful lovers of the nation to spread as much as possible these good methods [of education] and to guard the means of universal education (*tarbiat-i ʿammah*)," Mirza Taqi Khan Kashani wrote.[44]

It was within these more general debates on education that girls began to creep in as subjects worthy of being educated. In a significant departure from premodern texts, Kashani's essay, for instance, ended with a section that was addressed to fathers and mothers and called for the education of girls as well as boys: "Teach your children, sons and daughters, science and obedience."[45]

THE DIFFERENCE GENDER MAKES

In addition to their appearance as subjects worthy of education, girls also began to appear next to boys as characters in books designed for the education of the young. A book of parables from 1876 has as many female as male characters in its stories.[46] Designed to highlight good and bad character traits, the stories are thoroughly gendered: those with boys as central characters teach lessons about what character traits were desirable in little boys, and those with female characters construct the desirable character traits for girls. In one parable, Masʿud's New Year's present to his parents is to demonstrate that he can read any text they choose.[47] A frivolous little girl, Kawkab, is disliked by everyone because she is undisciplined and shameless, laughs a great deal for no reason, opens her mouth in front of people and makes awful noises, runs around and pays no attention to others, does not greet people properly, talks nonsense, eavesdrops on others' conversations, and so forth. In contrast, the four-year-old exemplary girl, Khawrshid Khanum, is impeccably obedient and well-mannered. Everyone likes her; she gets up in the morning with her parents without a fuss, dresses herself up, cleans herself, performs her ablutions, and prays. She spends her whole day doing only good things, plays by herself contentedly, does not bother adults, does not meddle, is already in a Qur'anic school and can read the Qur'an and other texts, and does nothing without her mother's permission. The tale ends happily: Kawkab, despite her many defects, is a very smart girl and decides to become friends with Khawrshid Khanum and to learn everything from her. Kawkab reforms and becomes well-liked.[48]

This pattern of moral construction continues throughout the book. Desirable moral traits for boys include being content with life, generosity, not being prone to anger and cruelty, knowing one's manners, being God-fearing and charitable, honesty, and pursuit of sciences and higher education. For girls, they include tidiness, being obedient to one's mother, not hiding anything from one's parents, lack of arrogance, hard work, and learning womanly crafts. One girl, in addition to learning her knitting, sewing, needlework, and embroidery, learns reading, arithmetic, and "the prices of everything." This proves useful since she keeps account of her mother's little sewing and embroidery business. When she loses her mother at the age of eleven, she is already a competent businesswoman and brings one of her aunts to manage household affairs so that she can take care of the business with peace of mind.[49]

Unlike the bulk of the book, which according to the author was a translation/ adaptation from Arabic of an originally French text, the epilogue concerns only young men.[50] It was written by the author himself and titled "On Manners of Talking, Movement, and Eating." In a remarkable cultural shift, the epilogue serves to buttress the gender hierarchies that might have been interrogated by the previous tales. Now the young man is advised to avoid, insofar as is possible, talking to commoners, children, women, and mad or drunk people.[51] He should not walk moving his arms and shoulders, as do women and hermaphrodites.[52] The famous wise man Luqman appears as an interlocutor, advising "his son" not to trust women, not to tell his secrets to women and children, and not to adorn himself as women do.[53] Another figure of wisdom, Abuzarjumihr-i hakim, advises his pupil that what ruins greatness is meanness in rich people, arrogance in ʿulamaʾ, shamelessness in women, and deceit in men.[54] In answer to the question, "Could anyone become fortunate through another person?" he responds, "Man through God, child through father and mother, and wife through a good husband."[55] Thus, through a parallel construction, the wife is placed in the same relation of subordination to her husband as man to God and as children to parents. Despite the epilogue, however, the text is novel for its inclusion of girls as subjects of specific educational attention, unlike the corresponding chapters in *Akhlaq-i Nasiri*, for instance, where the child was evidently, if unstatedly at first, a son.

Other educational texts of the period similarly include girls while clearly marking gender distinctions and hierarchies within that inclusion. *Taʿlim al-atfal* (Teaching children), a teacher's manual on how to teach the alphabet more efficiently through new techniques, has drawings depicting both boys' schools and girls' schools, all pupils properly seated behind desks; however, whereas the boys are all sitting on chairs, the girls are squatting on the floor, behind low desks.[56] After instruction in the alphabet, numerals, and months and years of the zodiac system, a male character, Mirza Muhammad, is used to teach prayers, followed by a female character, Fatima Khanum, to teach fundamentals of religion and the names of the twelve Shi'i Imams.[57] Subsequently, Mirza Muhammad sets an example by becoming a prayer leader for his classmates. Fatima Khanum invites her classmates on a Friday to play with dolls and to sew and "thus they learn the science of housekeeping and the necessary arts."[58] In a second volume, the students are taught poetry, geography, and arithmetic. Notably, there are no girls in the second volume.

The encouragement to include girls in the new educational regime became less ambivalent by the turn of the century. In a cautious statement, Zuka' al-Mulk, after reiterating that the education of children was the key to everything else, noted that this had to start with fathers and sons, but he went on to say that, "God willing, the turn for mothers and daughters to be educated will also come, since experienced scientists and skilled educators have said that the bulk of the education of children is in the hands of mothers. . . . It is evident that daughters like sons need teachers . . . but for now we should pay attention to more urgent matters and reforms."[59] Following this brief remark on daughters' and mothers' education, the paper received and published a piece by no less a personage than Hajji Sadr al-Saltanah, the minister of general welfare (favayid-i 'ammah).[60] After a brief introduction, the author quotes Napoleon to the effect that one must try harder for girls' education than boys', since girls (as future mothers) aid our dear children and lay the foundation for children's education.[61] He continues, "In Europe, girls' schools are separate from and not mixed with boys'. In India, in one of the schools for girls that is built from the charitable deeds of Suhrabji Shahpurji, I saw Zoroastrian girls who shone like stars from the light of science. I went to another school built by Manikji Khawrshidji. Girls were learning crafts and were skilled in sewing." He then expounds on the bad conditions of Iranian women, because they have no literacy skills (savad) and are ignorant of any crafts and arts, whereas even ugly women of Europe are moons in the sky of perfection, because of the holy spirit (ruh al-qudus) of science.[62]

Comparison with Europe also provided an important subtext of Talibuf's Kitab-i Ahmad, one of the most influential books on education in late-nineteenth-century Iran.[63] In the preface, Talibuf speaks as a concerned citizen of Iran. In the book he takes on the voice of a father, tutoring his son, Ahmad. The triple position of citizen/father/tutor allowed Talibuf to write the book not only as a treatise on education but as a modernist text on Iran's sociopolitical problems and how to overcome them. The book was explicitly modeled after Rousseau's Émile. Yet the differences are significant. In the eighth chapter of the first book, the author notes that while in much of the introductory section Ahmad has been echoing Émile's conversations, one must adapt the conditions of the Western Émile (*Imil-i maghribi*) to those of the Eastern Ahmad (*Ahmad-i mashriqi*).[64] The central problem informing the book is not how through a model education to resolve the conflicts between the natural and the social man; rather, it is how to overcome the disparity between the innate giftedness of Iranians and their current state of ignorance and idleness. In other words, how through a scientific education to produce a competent and patriotic citizen. Unlike the solitary Émile, Ahmad has two brothers and two sisters. Through comparison with the experience of the older brother, Mahmud, who has attended the old school system, Talibuf constructs the difference that his proposed educational methods represent: Ahmad is first tutored at home by his father—the narrator of the book—and later, in the second volume, he is sent to one of the new schools. In the third volume, he has already earned an engineering degree and has authored many books. He has become a model scientific citizen. The depiction of the two sisters, Zaynab and Mahrukh, constructs the gender difference. They are childish and playful; at times they are reprimanded by Ahmad for their unbecoming behavior or their ignorance; they are in awe of their smart brother's scope of knowledge. Yet as spectators to Ahmad's various experiments at home—through which he is learning scientific reasoning—they occasionally get to ask a question or offer him a helping hand, confirming his superior knowledge and status while making the point that girls are also eager to learn something. Surprisingly, although at several points Talibuf notes that in "civilized countries" both women and men are educated, there is nothing in these three volumes about the daughters' education.[65] In fact, by the third volume, where Ahmad speaks as an adult model citizen, Mahrukh and Zaynab have totally disappeared. This tension in Talibuf's text is worthy of further consideration. Talibuf presents rather negative judgments about European women and gender relations. He writes with disdain and disapproval of women's wearing low-cut dresses, putting on makeup, and going to dances.[66] The paradox of his noting women's education in "civilized countries" yet not advocating it for Iran perhaps stemmed from this moral anxiety.

EDUCATING EDUCATORS OF THE NATION

The issue of women's education received its first full, detailed attention with the publication in 1900 of a partial translation/adaptation of Qasim Amin's book, *The Liberation of Women*, only a year after its Arabic publication in Cairo.[67] A number of chapters were translated by Yusuf Ashtiani (I'tisam al-Mulk) and published under a significantly different title, *Education of Women* (*Tarbiat-i nisvan*).[68] Amin's status as an Egyptian Muslim thinker served to authorize the publication of the first full-length book in Persian devoted to advocacy of women's education. In his preface, Ashtiani notes that not only had European thinkers composed books on the subject of women's education and its importance, but a group of famous Egyptian writers had also written extensively on women's rights and the necessity of their education.[69] But, he continues, there were still no books in Persian that would uncover the benefits and harms of women's education, and it was for this reason that he has translated a number of the chapters from *The Liberation of Women*. His selectivity is worth noting. Not only is the second chapter, "Women and the Veil," completely eliminated in Ashtiani's adaptation, but the final paragraph of the introductory chapter is changed. Amin wrote,

> Were women's socialization effected in accordance with religious and moral principles, and were the use of the veil terminated at limits familiar in most Islamic schools of belief, then these criticisms would be dropped and our country would benefit from the active participation of all its citizens, men and women, alike.[70]

Ashtiani changes it to the following,

> Provided education of women is carried out according to fundamentals of our solid religion and rules of morals and manners, and with due regard to conditions of *hijab*, we will reach our goal, bitter conditions will be behind us, and sweet days will emerge.[71]

Whether he modified Amin's proposition to avoid the kind of reception this book had received in Egypt, or because this reflected his own stance on the issues of veiling and gender segregation at this time, the selectivity and adaptation, as well as the change in the book's title, point to two important conclusions. First, for him and other Iranian reformers of this period, the central target of reform regarding women's status was women's education. On this there was a strong consensus. Second, no fixed connection existed between the issue of veiling and women's education. While some, such as Mirza Aqa Khan Kirmani, considered the veil and gender segregation as signs of backwardness and impediments to women's progress, other reformers, such as I'tisam al-Mulk and Talibuf, considered the veil and gender segregation customs worthy of respect and preservation.[72] Similarly, in the writings of women on education from the end of the nineteenth century onward, there was no single position on the issue of unveiling among the women who worked for education. Muzayyan al-Saltanah, a tireless educationalist, publisher and editor of one of the most important early women's journals, *Shukufah* (1914–18), vehemently opposed unveiling and wrote in her journal against women's abandonment of *hijab*. At the same time, she published essays and poetry by women such as Shams Kasma'i and Shahnaz Azad known for their alternative views.[73]

For Kirmani and Ashtiani, as much as for Amin, the central conviction was that the "evidence of history confirms and demonstrates that the status of women is inseparably tied to the status of a nation."[74] The progress of the nation was seen as dependent on the progress of women.[75] And if the country's backwardness as compared to Europe could be overcome through the acquisition of sciences and a new kind of education, then the conditions of women could also be improved in a similar move.[76] Women's education was now perceived as the most fundamental step in the nation's quest for civilization. As we come to the first years of the twentieth century, we encounter the argument that women's education should be given higher priority than men's, since from educated women would arise a whole educated nation.

From the very beginning, women's education was seen as distinct from men's education. Once the domain of the man of the polis had expanded into the national community, this man of the nation, unlike the man of *The Nasirean Ethics*, could no longer be expected to be in charge of both national politics (*siasat-i mudun* having become *siasat-i mamlikat*) and management of the household (*tadbir-i manzil*). Woman was now to become his helpmeet, to become the manager of the household (*mudabbir-i manzil*), instead of being subject to his management. Like the transformation of the womb from a vessel to a school, the transformation of woman from house to manager of the house was at once a regulating and an empowering moment. The regulatory and disciplinary regime of modern sciences was to come to bear on woman's daily life activities. Whereas the man was to be educated in the new sciences to be up to the tasks of national politics, economics, and modern industries, the woman was above all to be educated in the science of home management:

> [A] woman cannot run her household well unless she attains a certain amount of intellectual and cultural knowledge. She should learn at least what a man is required to learn up through the primary stage of education. . . . It is important for a woman to be able to read and write, to be able to examine the basis of scientific information, to be familiar with the history of various countries, and to be able to acquire knowledge of the natural sciences and of politics. . . . [A] woman who lacks this upbringing will be unable adequately to carry out her role in society or in the family.[77]

Transformation of the wife from household to manager of the household required the breakup of female homosociality within that space. Whereas previously female homosociality was seen as a threat to male bonding, a disruption of the world of men, of the relation between men and between man and God, now it would pose a threat to the orderly management of the household, which required the wife to regulate her female servant instead of chatting, socializing, and solidarizing with her. This was explicated at some length in the literature that advised women on how to deal with their servants.[78]

Family itself was now reenvisaged. Socially, it became relocated in relation to the national community, rather than in relation to other kin groups and families: "[T]he family is the foundation of a country," and within the family, woman as mother was the foundation. As such "her intellectual development or underdevelopment becomes the primary factor in determining the development or underdevelopment of the country."[79] This reconfiguration gave new meanings to motherhood. A mother was no longer merely the vessel for the growth of the fetus; her nurturing and educating roles became more important and began to overshadow her function as a womb. Mothering came to be defined as nurturing and educating. In fact, she was now to mother the country. Unlike the situation in the Nasirean household, in which the father was fully in charge of the children's upbringing, now the mother acquired the primary responsibility.[80] Maternal ignorance was now seen as the prime reason for troubles of all kinds.[81] Women's education was therefore oriented toward the upbringing of an educated (male) citizenship. This was not a call "for equality of education for men and women," but for "the possibility for boys and girls to have a comparable educational experience throughout the primary stage."[82]

The envisaging of the family as the foundation of the nation, as standing for a building block of the nation, also meant reenvisaging relationships within it. Ignorant women were not only unsuitable as mothers but also unfit as spouses: "An educated man likes order and a systematically arranged home. . . . When a man finds his wife in this ignorant condition, he quickly despises her."[83] In place of the Nasirean awe of wife for husband, in an evident heterosexualization of male homosociality, a sentiment comparable to friendship between men was proposed to constitute the right bond between husband and wife: "Friendship provides us with a good example of the power of true love between individuals."[84] This was yet one more reason for women's education: "A man and woman whose upbringing and education differ cannot experience this type of love."[85]

Unlike the original publication of the Arabic text in 1899, the translation and publication of Amin's book in Persian in 1900 did not become an occasion for public debate on the education and status of women. The publication was well received among reform-minded intellectuals but does not seem to have provoked counterarguments.[86] There were occasional articles that obliquely talked of women's education.[87] More explicitly, a serialized article in the Calcutta-published journal *Habl al-matin* argued extensively along the same lines as Amin's book. It emphasizes women's lack of education as the cause of a nation's decline and misfortune, expresses its regret that "we Muslims have neglected this important matter and have done nothing to educate our women," and asks, "How could any people hope for progress if their women who constitute the first teachers and educators of their children are captives in the realm of ignorance?"[88] A subsequent section gives four reasons why education of women would benefit men: (1) children's education would become perfect because both parents would be working on it, (2) children's gifts would become evident at an earlier stage of life, (3) today's men are educated, but they are stuck with uneducated wives; children thus receive contradictory training and education from their fathers and mothers, which produces problems in their education, and (4) every nation's civilization is dependent on women's and men's education, since men and women need to live and socialize together.[89]

Education of women is also linked in this article to the imperial power of Europeans: "But even in household management women of Europe and America have surpassed those of Asia. A European household gives cause for envy to an Asian king's palace. The good order of household objects and the pleasantness of the rooms . . . competes with the gardens of paradise. . . . Husband and wife, like body and soul, provide each other with comfort of life and happiness of soul. They assist and love each other. . . . Nations that have mothers like European women can conquer other lands and rule over other nations."[90] In the East, however, women are kept ignorant yet expected to fulfill three immense tasks: to keep their husbands happy, educate their children, and manage the house. This is beyond their ability. How can a woman who is ignorant of her tasks and her husband's rights manage to satisfy him, especially if the husband is a man of science and a master of an art? Their pairing is like putting a parrot and a crow in the same cage.[91] Most interestingly, women's role in the house is projected as paralleling that of men in social affairs and national politics. In fact, for man to be able to be the good citizen, woman must be a good household manager: "Woman's role in the management and order of the house and in supervising its income and expenditure is like that of a minister of the land. . . . The well-being of the family and supervision of rights of the people of the household and the general direction of the household belong to the mistress of the house. Men who are in charge of the big affairs of the world cannot spend their valuable time in these small matters."[92]

These discussions do not seem to have produced immediate results in terms of furthering women's education. Three and a half years later, another series of articles in the same journal, entitled "Rights and Liberties of Women," referred to Qasim Amin as a pioneer of women's education and reviewed the attacks against him and the debates of that time in the Egyptian press. It noted the translation of his book by Mirza Yusuf Khan I'tisam al-Mulk into Persian, its publication in Tabriz, and its favorable reception in Iran, expressing regret that in Iran, unlike other Islamic countries, nothing but talk had come of it all.[93]

As in Egypt, as Omnia Shakry shows (chapter 4 in this volume), the conceptual shifts in meaning of "wife" and "mother" found their more immediate effect in projections of a new kind of mother and wife in texts on child rearing. One such text was *Tarbiat-i atfal* (Rearing of children).[94] Whereas there were no assumptions in the premodern texts that the biological mother and the breast-feeder of the child should be one and the same person (in fact, the child was to be entrusted to a wet nurse upon birth), the author of *Tarbiat-i atfal* argues that "a mother who entrusts her child to someone else upon birth has taken away from herself half of the label 'mother' and should thus not be called a mother. What is better and lovelier and more suitable than a mother looking after her own children? But some mothers prefer to leave this job to others and engage in useless leisure activities. This is the result of bad education that these mothers have received from their forebears."[95] The author regrets that mothers are ignorant of motherly skills and promises that if "women, instead of learning useless arts, would spend their time learning how to look after their children, how to dress them with ease and handle them safely, how to feed them to ensure their health, how to exercise them," soon wonderful results would emerge.[96]

While the mother, rather than the father, is now the person addressed in a text on the upbringing of children, the child remains a male child. She is to mother sons of the homeland (*abna'-i vatan*). After some introductory remarks about the relationship between physical and mental health, the author, quoting Montaigne, recommends that children should be kept away from things that would make them female-tempered and turn them into beautiful youth. They should instead become strong young men; if children were brought up in comfort and ease, they would not become men.[97]

The book is composed of three parts: on physical upbringing, mental upbringing, and on (wet) nurses. In chapter 1, we are told that the health of a newborn depends on things prior to birth, such as the state of intercourse between husband and wife, the conditions of marriage, their age, manners, and other qualities. Subsequent chapters give advice to pregnant women on how they should dress, eat, move, wash, and bathe, on the state of their feeling, and on sexual intercourse during pregnancy. Other chapters cover in detail such topics as hygiene of the newborn, effects of cold and heat on the newborn, clothing of the newborn, how to put it to sleep, and feeding the baby (the differences between human milk and that of cow, goat, or donkey, the amount of milk and for how long the baby should be breast-fed, the effect on their milk of what mothers and wet nurses eat, the effect of their menstruation, the effect of sexual intercourse, of pregnancy, of anxiety and nervous conditions on milk, how to tell good and bad milk apart). Five chapters are devoted to arguing why, for the mother, the child, the family, and the nation—and on no less than physiological, emotional, and moral grounds—it is best for the child to be nursed by the mother. The next four chapters cover the qualities of a mother who wants to breast-feed her own baby. Mixed feeding receives a one-page chapter, poor mothers and difficulties of infants in suckling one each, before a concluding chapter brings this long subsection to a close.

Despite such detailed persuasions and exhortations, the author concedes that some mothers may not be able to breast-feed their own infants; in such cases hiring a wet nurse is preferable to artificial feeding. A wet nurse should be brought in, rather than the infant's being sent out. Other chapters cover artificial feeding (a very last resort), bowel movements, urination, perspiration, and monitoring the child's weight, teething, weaning the baby, walking, exercising, and taking the child outdoors, smallpox vaccination and other childhood diseases, and how to deal with a child's death.

Book 2 is devoted to the mental upbringing of the child (*tarbiat-i 'aqlani*). Reiterating the advantages of a child's growing up on mother's milk and father's kindness, instead of being sent away for a couple of years to a village wet nurse, the author emphasizes that even if the child is entrusted to a wet nurse for physical care, the mother must remain in charge of mental care and intellectual development.[98] Again unlike the *Nasirean Ethics*, which assumed that the father was in charge of the child's upbringing, this section of the book is addressed to the mother. A third book discusses the issue of whether children should be brought up with other children or individually. A chapter on crèches for working mothers has been omitted in the translation, the translator notes, since it was not seen as relevant to the conditions of Iran. The translator finally brings the book to a close by reminiscing about his own mother.[99]

The publication of a book of this genre marked an important moment: the moment of entry of the printed words of male authors (a European author mediated through the Iranian translator) and modernist reformers into a domain that had been largely oral and female. Previously, advice on child rearing had been passed orally among women, mothers and daughters, wet nurses and nannies, sisters, female friends, and neighbors. The entry of male-authored texts into this female domain began to regularize mothering practices toward the upbringing of new men, men of the nation.

These early themes, the crafting of a new kind of mother and of a new kind of wife, and the accompanying proposition that the progress of the nation depended on the education of women, were echoed in articles in the constitutionalist press of the first decade of the twentieth century. The following passage from the constitutionalist journal *'Adalat* combines many of the oft-repeated arguments in favor of women's education:

It is evident that the progress and prosperity of every country and nation are dependent in general on science and the knowledge of men and in particular on the education of women. . . . If our women [*pardagian*—the veiled ones] are not educated, how can they take proper care of our newborn who are the hope of our dear homeland? How can they know the correct rules of nursing the child, that is, the three ways of natural nursing, artificial feeding and the proper combination of both? How will they know how many times and how much daily they must feed the child and how to organize the child's sleep time, how to bathe it and keep it tidy and clean? And should it become necessary to entrust these fruits of our hearts to nannies, how will they know what the shape and face and hair and teeth and milk and age and breast of the nanny they choose should be like? How will they know when it is time to wean a child? What proper food to give it? . . . Doesn't a man who is sensitive and thinks dearly about his religion and homeland deserve a companion who shares his grief and comfort? . . . Also if our women continue to be ignorant, how can they manage the affairs of the household? . . . If they know nothing about hygiene, how can they nurse the sick?[100]

It was in the same period that the establishment of new schools for girls gained momentum.[101]

MOTHERS OF THE NATION CLAIMING CITIZENSHIP

By the first decade of the century, women had taken charge of girls' education, wrote tirelessly in the press on female education, encouraged women of means to put their resources into this cause, organized fund-raising events, and provided free schooling for those who could not afford it. The early girls' schools were all established by women and often in their own residences. Many of them faced hostility. Memoirs and letters of some of the women involved provide us with moving accounts of the difficulties they faced in this pioneering work.[102] The issue of women's education became one of the bones of contention between pro- and anticonstitutionalist forces. Shaykh Fazl Allah Nuri (discussed in Sullivan's essay, chapter 6, this volume), a prominent anticonstitutionalist cleric, saw "the opening of schools for women's education and elementary schools for young girls," along with "spread of houses of prostitution," as one of the breaches in Islamic law perpetrated by constitutionalists.[103] This statement was construed as the Shaykh's fatwa against women's education and was used to agitate for the closing down of the new educational establishments. Women educationalists voiced the most articulate defenses of girls' schools in this debate. Addressing Shaykh Fazl Allah Nuri directly, one woman essayist took him to task on his religious credentials. She insisted that her God, unlike his, was just and had not created men and women of different essences such that one deserved the blessings of education and the other was to remain bestial; that the Prophet of her God had made it obligatory for all Muslim men and women to seek education, whereas his God had forbidden women to seek education. She challenged him to name a single woman close to the Prophet who was illiterate or ignorant, and interrogated his right to speak in the name of *shari'a* (Islamic law), going on to defend the structure and curriculum of modern schools over traditional *maktab*s, explaining the benefits of education for women, and eventually concluding that nothing in Islam opposed women's education. Unless he could answer all her arguments, he would have to admit that he had spoken thoughtlessly.[104]

In the women's writings of this period, both the general discourse of progress and civilization and the more particular notion of women's roles as educated mothers, wives, and household managers were employed not only to insist on their right to education but as a jumping-off point for demands for further equality with men: If the backward nation could catch up with European civilized nations through the acquiring of modern sciences and education, as the modernist discourse upheld, the backward woman could catch up with the modern man in a similar move, women authors argued. A female teacher of one of the new girls' schools wrote, "What is the difference between women of Iran and those of Europe except for science? Why is it that women of Europe are on a par with men or are even superior to them?"[105] Connecting the modernist theme of the centrality of science to the progress of nations, a female school principal similarly argued:

> The key to the treasure of prosperity in both worlds ... is science alone. Through science alone humanity can succeed in satisfying its needs and pushing forward its civilization. Its principles of ethical purification, home management, and politics could be based only on science. And solely through science can it protect its honor, property, life, and religion. ... It was through science that they [Europeans] took away Turkistan and the Caucasus from us;[106] it was through the force of science that India, with such glory and with some 260 million inhabitants ... was separated from us. The same with Egypt, Greece, Crete, Sicily, Spain, etc. ... Through science they have swallowed more than half of Iran, the true birthland of ourselves and our forefathers, and they intend to take away the rest. ...
>
> Perhaps some may think that the Europeans are not of our kind, and therefore to think of becoming their equal is impossible. First, this is utterly false. ... Second, even if that were true, what do you say about the Japanese? At least we should follow our Asian sisters, the Japanese, ... in pursuing sciences and acquiring industries. It must be emphasized that educating women is more important than educating men, since the education of men is dependent on education of women and their caretakers. Therefore, you respected women must seriously and with great effort seek sciences and spread knowledge ... so that liberty, equality, and fraternity can be established in our homeland and we too can acquire that civilization and life that the Europeans have.[107]

Claiming oneself as a new kind of mother and wife was the crucial link in these arguments:

> Because of the duties of a woman to mother and educate humanity, the harms of ignorance are a hundredfold worse for them and the advantages of learning a thousand times greater. A learned woman will keep her house clean and orderly, thus making her spouse happy. A learned woman will educate her child according to rules of health and hygiene and wisdom. ... A learned woman will protect her

family relationship and will prevent discord and difference, which is the greatest cause of destruction of family and nation. . . . A learned woman can advise her spouse in some worldly affairs. . . . A learned woman can increase her spouse's happiness when he is happy and console him when he is sad.[108]

Daughters of Shams al-Ma'ali, founders of two schools for girls, explained in a letter to the journal *Iran-i naw* that they had decided to establish these schools so that "in the future, every household is headed by a learned lady who knows well household management, child rearing, sewing, cooking, and cleaning, and from whose breast milk love of homeland will be fed to the infants so that they shall be deserving of service and sacrifice."[109]

The trope of family was sometimes used analogically (the country is like a family), sometimes as a unit that went into the composition of the country ("the prosperity of every city and country is dependent on the order and prosperity of its homes. . . . if there is order and progress in every home, a city will progress and become civilized and wealthy"). Both were put to work in support of women's education: "Progress, prosperity, and the order of every home are dependent upon [a nation's] women. . . . Until women are educated, progress and civilization of the country are impossible."[110]

What has been subsequently categorized as a "discourse of domesticity"— that is, the vast literature on scientific housekeeping, child rearing, and husband keeping that was produced at the turn of the century by both male and female writers—and from a late-twentieth-century viewpoint may seem to have frustrated the perspectives of women's lives and contained their social advance, for women of the early twentieth century provided the very grounds upon which the male domain of modern education could be opened up to women: women needed to be educated in all these sciences of household management in order for families to prosper and for the country to become civilized.[111] Women's assuming the position of the learned (*mudabbir va mudir*) manager and head of the household (*manzil*)—instead of being part of the household subject to the management of the man—far from frustrating the dynamics of women's movement into public life and national recognition provided the empowering basis for it. That this move also produced the later containment of women's drive toward higher education became evident in the 1930s when the issue of university education for women was debated and those opposing it used these arguments against women's admission to universities.[112] But that is a much later episode of the story and for that reason, I would argue, that categorization of the literature which scripted a new concept of woman centered on notions of scientific household management, learned mothering, and educated husband keeping as a discourse of domesticity or cult of domesticity is a misnomer that prevents us from understanding why women embraced these notions in the first place.

The literature on scientific household management achieved its full development in the pages of the women's press. The first women's journal was in fact named *Danish* (Knowledge). Edited by Dr. Kahhal, a woman ophthalmologist with an active practice,[113] it began publication in September 1910, with a banner that read: "This is an ethical journal of the science of housekeeping, child rearing, husband keeping; useful for girls' and women's moral development. It will not say a word on national politics." Many articles were devoted to household management[114] (including discussion of how to manage servants—a topic that occupied an even more prominent place in the pages of Iran's second women's journal, *Shukufah*), husband management,[115] child rearing,[116] and children's health and hygiene.[117]

Though later issues began to run articles on how to look after one's clothes and hair, and information on cosmetics, the emphasis for sustaining one's marriage was put on education.[118] "A girl educated in Europe," praised the "new situation of women." In the old days, she argued, women had no education and had no status in their husband's eyes unless they were young and beautiful; now educated women had many good qualities. One good moral outcome of this situation was that husband and wife now lived together in affection and did not look at other people. What a big mistake it had been when women sought their place in their husband's heart through making up their faces and putting on fancy clothes, instead of paying attention to educating their children and housekeeping. It was in fact knowledge and good qualities that a husband never tired of, not good looks and fancy clothes. She exhorted her dear sisters who were already educated to continue seeking knowledge and not to waste their lives. She urged them to be equal to their husbands, at least in education. They should not think that having pleasant manners and a kind tongue could guarantee his love. A wife should be a friend and companion to her husband; that is, in every work and every matter she should be a help to him. But how could an uneducated wife give help to her husband?[119]

By this time both male and female authors placed higher national priority on girls' education than on boys' education, or even on the development of a body of new law, the issue that had occupied the center of modernist discourse a few decades earlier: "The progress, uplifting, and civilization of every nation, every country, is dependent on three things: first, the education of girls; second, science; third, law. . . . The education of girls, which is the first step for prosperity and the first step for uplifting, is far more important than the other two, since it is girls and women from whom sons and daughters come and by whom they are educated until they are of school age."[120]

As I have already indicated, discussion of these issues was used not to contain and frustrate women's activity but to effect it. For instance, women were told that "if a woman is illiterate, she should pursue literacy immediately, because only if she can read the newspapers will she know everything and be able to communicate effectively with her husband."[121]

Though earlier articles were sometimes addressed to both mothers and nannies, the emphasis was decidedly on biological mothers' nurturing their children and using nannies only as a last resort. An article in the third issue of the journal was devoted to all the physical, moral, and political ills that ensue from entrusting one's child to a nanny.[122] Mothers were told to avoid giving their unique (*yiganah*) child to a stranger (*biganah*) nanny; the child must receive nourishment from the breast of mother's love.[123] Much was made of the goodness of the mother's milk and of the dirty/impure milk of a nanny who lived an unhygienic life. The author described a child whose eyes developed a twisted condition because the nanny had twisted eyes, a Persian prince who drank camel's milk and rode camels all his life because he had been entrusted to an Arab lady in childhood, an honorable lady who was incontinent all her life because her nanny had been so and she had inherited the disability from her,[124] and the foul language that children pick up from their nannies.[125] The article ended with a list of conditions to set and qualities to look for should one have no recourse but to entrust the child to a nanny.[126]

Perhaps even more than *Danish*, the journal *Shukufah*, begun in 1914, was oriented toward production of a new type of mother and envisaged new marital relationships *Shukufah* was edited by Muzayyan al-Saltanah, herself an active educationalist who established three elementary schools and one vocational school for girls during the same period as she was publishing *Shukufah*. She also served as a kind of inspector ("investigative reporter") of girls' schools in Tehran in that period. She would visit schools and write reports in the pages of *Shukufah* about the students and the quality of teaching.

Article after article in the pages of *Shukufah* advised women to forget all the nonsense that their mothers and grandmothers had taught them about how to keep their husbands. To become a woman of modernity was a learning process that demanded an unlearning, a de-constitution, of womanhood.[127] Women were told that they should consider the house their kingdom to run. All the important qualities necessary for running the affairs of a country, such as the basics of humanity, honesty, trustworthiness, hygiene, working hard, valuing time, seeking knowledge, resistance in the face of hardship, avoiding bad manners, were learned in childhood, argued Maliktaj. If there was a woman who taught these to her children, then you knew for certain that the affairs of that country would fare well and the country would advance, and vice versa.[128] Muzayyan al-Saltanah also demonstrated a concern about regularization of schools' curriculum and put great emphasis on schools as the place for ethical and moral development of young girls.[129] Though the journal continued *Danish*'s tradition of publishing series of articles on women's as well as children's health and hygiene, a growing number of articles were concerned with women's moral development, demonstrating a clear anxiety over the direction of changes that were becoming evident in women's social performance.[130]

The new schools were constituted as the social space for development of moral behavior, and for learning the sciences of cooking, sewing, child care, and husband management. A special curriculum was thus developed for the scientization of household affairs (*umur-i baytiyah*); it included courses on home management, education of children, hygiene, fine arts and crafts, and cooking. Textbooks were also produced with this orientation in mind. *Tarbiat al-bunat* (The education of girls), for instance, one of the texts prepared for the new girls' schools, was translated from the French by Mirza ʿAzizallah Khan, with the express intent of its becoming a second-grade textbook. It was published in 1905, and by 1911 it was already into its second printing. The book, subtitled "The Science of Home Management," is organized in six parts (twenty lessons). It begins with a definition of this science, "on which the happiness and prosperity of every family depends,"[131] and goes on to explain why, despite possible popular cynicism, home management is a science and ought to be taught and learned as such. The book ends with a dozen recipes for French soups and other food. It gives examples of positive and negative repercussions for the lives of families with learned versus illiterate housewives, defines the necessary characteristics of a competent housewife as order, competence, and cleanliness, and projects three female character types among housewives. The first is disorderly and careless. Named Lady Pleasure (ʿIshrat Khanum), she is wasteful of her own efforts and her husband's property, and spends her time chatting away with other women of the neighborhood. The second, Lady Agreeable (Bihjat Khanum), strives to be a good housewife, draws upon her traditional know-how to do her best, but is disorderly because she has never properly learned how to run a household. The third, who is held up as an exemplar, knows how to categorize and to label things properly, to keep a budget book, and to organize her time efficiently, and thus is able to finish her chores before her husband and children return home. When they are back, she busies herself with some light sewing, or reading a book, or keeping her husband company. Unlike Lady Pleasure, who spends her time in idle conversation with other women—a disapproved female social activity—the exemplary woman is oriented toward companionship with her husband. Significantly, she is named Lady Chaste (ʿIsmat Khanum), transmitting chastity through the new science to the modern educated woman.[132]

Thus was crafted the new woman: the scientific mother and the companionate wife, the learned woman versed in the sciences of cooking, sewing, and breast-feeding. Of such woman, ministers, state scribes, doctors, and professors would be born, not porters and mean fortune-tellers.[133] She would not only produce better children; she would also prevent her man from behaving badly, "as American women have stopped their men from drinking and obstinacy."[134]

The school curriculum included, in addition to the science of homemaking, lessons on hygiene and the introduction of sports and gymnastics. The desirability of the latter now began to be linked to a critique of veiling. In a graduation address focused on the science of hygiene, Badr al-Dujá Khanum, graduating from the American College for Girls, expressed her regret that because of veiling Iranian women had been deprived in recent centuries of engaging in sports, and thus it was not surprising that most Iranian women were weak and unhealthy.[135]

Later, in the 1920s, we come across a new genre, the rules of etiquette (*adab-i mu'ashirat*): texts of initiation that were designed to teach women how to interact properly with unfamiliar men. Once these were learned, it was imagined that woman would be ready to step into a heterosocial arena without undermining the social and cultural order:

> The words *chastity* and *honor* are not in the vocabulary of creation. A woman is
> not born chaste; she becomes the protector and the policer of her chastity. Until
> women learn the duty of policing and guarding themselves, freedom will create
> irreparable damage for their womanly delicacy and feminine pride. Therefore we
> must teach self-policing. Freedom will follow. . . . In Europe and the free coun-
> tries, in parks and promenades, one rarely sees a man gazing at a woman or a
> woman paying any attention [to a man], unless they have made their chastity and
> honor their means of livelihood. . . . A good policer is a woman who does not
> allow those who are seeking to deceive and use her to utter a single impolite or
> improper word. . . . Once women are shown the ways of policing, that is, the rules
> and etiquette of women's socializing with men, then freedom and sharing life
> between women and men will follow without any hindrance.[136]

I want to emphasize here again the enabling work of two seemingly conflicting notions: one disciplinary, the other emancipatory. It was the moment of "freedom and sharing life" with men that made the self-policing not only a workable but a desirable project for women. And, conversely, the new disciplinary and regulatory practices and concepts defined the acceptable social space for freedom for the modern woman. The success of this double work made her place in the nation possible. She would be ready to become a citizen. In fact it was within the space of the girls' schools that women had already begun to constitute themselves as citizens from the time of the Constitutional Revolution. Following the then popular pattern of forming associations, women formed their own associations, held meetings, and gave fund-raising "garden parties" to raise funds for the government and for girls' schools.[137] Forming such associations had itself become an expression of citizenship. Girls' schools, often private residences of prominent women, were at once places of learning and venues for such meetings. Thus women were constituting at once a new individual self through literacy and a new social self through patriotic (*vatani*) political activities. As "managers of the house," they were beginning to transform "the house" into a social space of citizenship.

Women in these meetings spoke as citizens, as "we Iranians," addressed the general political problems facing the country, and often bemoaned the disadvantages that deprived them of the chance to be of more help to the homeland. Not only did women make a claim to the rights of citizenship, but they sometimes proved their concern as citizens by challenging the ability of men to run the Constitutional regime.[138]

In fact, the first cautious claims to equality made by women were formulated within the educational domain. "I take up the pen to complain greatly about fathers and husbands of Iranian girls. Why do they not know yet that woman and man in this world are like the two wheels of a carriage: they must be equal, neither having any privilege over the other. If one of the two wheels of a carriage is deficient, it will be impossible for it to move," wrote Shahnaz Azad. This precarious claim to equality was immediately modified in these terms: "It should be evident that by equality I mean equality in education and learning of sciences, not in any other matter."[139]

Another woman, Shams Kasma'i was more daring. In a poem sent to *Shukufah* from Ashkabad, she called upon her sisters to educate themselves in order to cure all their deficiencies, to use their power of speech, reason, and rationality to conquer the whole world, to set fire to all superstitions, to tear asunder the veil of oppression, and to prove the equality of their rights with men through their words, their deeds, and all their power.[140]

This poem could well be the first pronouncement of the language of equality of rights, of a new kind of modern feminism, in Iran. The new mother and wife had begun to make a different claim to womanhood. These new claims eventually came to clash with the limits set by the former discourse, as I have pointed out. This clash came to the fore in the context of the new round of "educational debates" of the 1930s. Did women need to go to higher education institutes? Was not the goal of their education to become better mothers and wives? What were they going to do with their higher diplomas then? These arguments were advanced against women's entry to upper grades of high school and later university education. Having been entrapped by the very discourse that had opened up education to them in the first place, women now opted to enlarge their notion of "domestic duties" to mean national service. The new home to whose management they now began to lay a claim was no longer their conjugal household but the national home, Iran. Women's embrace of Riza Shah's agenda in the 1930s can thus be seen as not a "selling out" of women's cause to the increasingly powerful state; rather, Riza Shah's program of constructing the citizen as a servant of the state—*nawkar-i dawlat*—provided the possibility for women to break out of the trap of what can now indeed be named domesticity. They could claim their right to higher education and to many professions in the name of service to the state. Having mothered the nation, they could now serve the state. Again, one can see both disciplinary and emancipatory dynamics in this scenario: appropriation of the notion of servant of the state enabled women to claim their right to higher education and professions while subjecting those rights to regulations, demands, and agendas of the state—a legacy that marked the Iranian women's movement during the Pahlavi era.

NOTES

An earlier draft of this paper benefited from presentations in seminars at Georgetown University and New York University. I would like to thank Yvonne Haddad and Tim Mitchell for providing me with those opportunities. Work on this paper was carried out in 1994–95, during my year as a visiting fellow at the Institute for Advanced Study, Princeton—an occasion that provided me with a unique working environment. Special thanks to Joan W. Scott who made that year intellectually challenging and supportive, and to Lila Abu-Lughod, Elizabeth Frierson, Yvonne Haddad, Mary Poovey, and Tim Mitchell for stimulating conversations and critical comments. I would also like to thank the readers for Princeton University Press for helpful comments.

1. Beth Baron, *The Women's Awakening in Egypt: Culture, Society, and the Press* (New Haven: Yale University Press, 1994); Margot Badran, *Feminists, Islam, and Nation: Gender and the Making of Modern Egypt* (Princeton: Princeton University Press, 1995); Afsaneh Najmabadi, "Veiled Discourse—Unveiled Bodies," *Feminist Studies* 19, no. 3 (Fall 1993): 487–518.

2. See Baron, *Women's Awakening*, p. 67: "An ideology of womanhood emerged from the early women's press that reinforced women's roles as mother, wife, and homemaker." And Badran, *Feminists, Islam, and Nation*, p. 63: "Education for girls was quickly harnessed to the cult of domesticity; it was put to the service of elevating women's family roles, especially that of mother."

3. See, for instance, Nasir al-Din Tusi, *Akhlaq-i Nasiri*, ed. Mujtabá Minuvi and ʿAliriza Haydari (Tehran: Khwarazmi, 1978), a thirteenth-century C.E. text. English translation: Nasir ad-Din Tusi, *The Nasirean Ethics*, trans. G. M. Wickens (London: George Allen & Unwin, 1964); Jalal al-Din Dawwani, *Akhlaq-i Jalali*, a fifteenth-century C.E. text (Lucknow: n.p., 1957); Muhsin Fani Kashmiri, *Akhlaq-i ʿalamara: akhlaq-i muhsini*, ed. Kh. Javidi (Islamabad: Pakistan and Iran Center for Persian Studies, 1983), a seventeenth-century C.E. text. For a discussion of ethics in Islamic premodern writings, see R. Walzer and H.A.R. Gibbs, "Akhlak," *Encyclopaedia of Islam*, 2d ed., pp. 325–29; and F. Rahman, "Aklaq," *Encyclopaedia Iranica*, pp. 719–23. See Avner Gilʿadi, *Children of Islam: Concepts of Childhood in Medieval Muslim Society* (London: Macmillan, 1992), p. 4, on the Greek origins of some of the important ethical, psychological, and pedagogical notions in these texts.

4. A note of clarification is warranted here. Although the books of ethics that I draw upon range from the thirteenth to the seventeenth century, I am not presuming that the discourse on ethics remained unchanged in this period. A study of the historical transformations of the ethical discourse for this period is beyond the scope of this essay, and my arguments here do not depend on it. My use of *The Nasirean Ethics*, for instance,

is a recognition that this text had acquired a "model for imitation" status. Later texts took a great deal, in many cases verbatim reproduction of large sections and arguments, from this text and modeled their rhetorical and formal structures upon it. This does not mean that the discourse, much less child-rearing practices, remained identical. Some of these differences I will note in the text. Beyond these differences, however, it is their common assumptions that concern me here.

5. Tusi, *The Nasirean Ethics*, p. 161, *Akhlaq-i Nasiri*, p. 215; see also Fani Kashmiri, *Akhlaq-i ʿalamara*, p. 127.

6. Tusi, *The Nasirean Ethics*, p. 161, *Akhlaq-i Nasiri*, pp. 215–16; see also Fani Kashmiri, *Akhlaq-i ʿalamara*, p. 128.

7. Tusi, *The Nasirean Ethics*, p. 162; *Akhlaq-i Nasiri*, p. 217. We are also told that "[t]he philosophers have said that a worthy wife will take on the role of mother, friend and mistress." (Tusi, *The Nasirean Ethics*, p. 164; *Akhlaq-i Nasiri*, p. 219.) In *Akhlaq-i ʿalamara*, the third point in the regulation of a wife is significantly different: that the husband should treat his wife's relatives with respect and that he should not, without good cause, hurt her by bringing in another wife: "The relation of man to *manzil* (household? wife?) is like that of heart to body. A man cannot be manager (*mudabbir*) of two *manzil*s, in the same way that one heart cannot be source of life for two bodies." (Fani Kashmiri, *Akhlaq-i ʿalamara*, p. 131.)

8. See Tusi, *The Nasirean Ethics*, pp. 166–67; *Akhlaq-i Nasiri*, p. 222; see also Fani Kashmiri, *Akhlaq-i ʿalamara*, p. 136. Fani Kashmiri prefaced this section by emphasizing that the child was given in trust by God to father and mother and that God held both responsible for the child's upbringing (p. 135). Yet by the end of this paragraph the plural subject becomes singular and masculine (in his recitation of Arabic narratives). He also considered a wet nurse preferable to mother for the care of child (p. 136).

9. Persian does not have distinct pronouns for "he" and "she," and the words used for "child" in these writings, *farzand* and *kudak*, could refer to either a girl or a boy; that is, there is no linguistic sign to designate the child as a boy; I have followed the authors' own later textual disambiguation in using the pronoun "he" to designate the child, since at the end of this section, after all has been said about the child's tutoring, chastisement, encouragement, skills he needs to learn, qualities he needs to acquire, Tusi, for instance, concludes: "So much for the chastisement of children. In the case of daughters, one must employ, in the selfsame manner, whatever is appropriate and fitting to them. They should be brought up to keep close to the house and live in seclusion, cultivating gravity, continence, modesty and the other qualities we have enumerated in the chapter on Wives. They should be prevented from learning to read or write, but allowed to acquire such accomplishments as are commendable in women. When they reach the bounds of maturity they should be joined to one of equal standing." (Tusi, *The Nasirean Ethics*, p. 173; *Akhlaq-i Nasiri*, pp. 229–30.) For a similar close, see Fani Kashmiri, *Akhlaq-i ʿalamara*, p. 141. The textual place of this one paragraph displays the "supplementarity" of "daughter" to "child" in this ethical discourse.

10. Tusi, *The Nasirean Ethics*, p. 179; *Akhlaq-i Nasiri*, pp. 237–38.

11. Mirza Aqa Khan Kirmani, *Sad khatabah*, MS in Edward G. Browne Collection, Cambridge University Library. Sections of *Sad khatabah* concerned with Kirmani's views on women were published in *Nimeye Digar*, no. 9 (Spring 1989): 101–12. Quotation from *Sad khatabah*, p. 126b; in *Nimeye Digar*, p. 103. For Kirmani's life and an

analytical survey of his writings, see Firaydun Adamiyat, *Andishah'ha-yi Mirza Aqa Khan Kirmani* (Mirza Aqa Khan Kirmani's thoughts) (Tehran: Payam, 1978).

12. Kirmani, *Sad khatabah*, p. 127b; in *Nimeye Digar*, p. 103.

13. Kirmani, *Sad khatabah*, p. 156b. The third school was the religion of the people, which explained why Jews, Christians, and Muslims were different in character. The fourth was the government; Kirmani argued that people under oppressive governments developed differently from those under just governments. And finally, the fifth school was the climate and natural circumstances of the land. (*Sad khatabah*, p. 128a; in *Nimeye Digar*, p. 103.)

14. The reference to "mourning sessions" concerns the many shi'ite rituals of mourning the tragic misfortunes of the eleven *imam*s, 'Ali and his male descendants, the most important of which are the Muharram rituals commemorating the battle of Karbala in C.E. 680 in which Husayn and his followers were killed by Yazid's army.

15. Kirmani, *Sad khatabah*, pp. 149b, 150a and b, and 151a.

16. Ibid., p. 95b.

17. On the significance of this shift in self-constitution for the emergence of nineteenth-century Iranian modernism, see Mohamad Tavakoli-Targhi, "The Formation of Two Revolutionary Discourses in Modern Iran: The Constitutional Revolution of 1905–1906 and the Islamic Revolution of 1978–1979" (Ph.D. diss., University of Chicago, 1988).

18. Kirmani, *Sad khatabah*, p. 128b; in *Nimeye Digar*, p. 104.

19. Kirmani, *Sad khatabah*, pp. 128b and 129a; in *Nimeye Digar*, p. 104.

20. The modernist writings on gender also mark the heterosexualization of love. Love in classical Perso-Islamic literature is often male homoerotic. This is reflected not only in the celebration of male-male love couples, such as Mahmud and Ayaz, but also in books of advice with separate chapters on love and marriage, where in the former chapters the beloved is male, and issues of marriage and love, unlike the case in the later modernist discourse, are constructed as belonging to different domains. See, for instance, 'Unsur al-Ma'ali, *Qabusnamah*, ed. Ghulamhusayn Yusufi (Tehran: Jibi, 1974), chap. 14 (pp. 100–106), "On Love," and chap. 26 (pp. 144–46), "On Seeking a Wife." With the heterosexualization of love and the romanticization of marriage, homosexuality came to be viewed as a debased expression of sexual appetite that resulted from sexual segregation and the unavailability of women to men. On modernist judgment of premodern homoerotic love, see Nasrallah Purjavadi, "Badah-'i 'ishq," *Nashr-i danish* 12, no. 2 (February–March 1992): 6–15, where he speaks of the love of Mahmud for Ayaz as "morally the most filthy (*aludah'tarin*) of loves" (p. 8). On similar developments within Turkish modernity, see Deniz Kandiyoti, "Afterword," in this volume.

21. Kirmani, *Sad khatabah*, pp. 135a through 138a; in *Nimeye Digar*, pp. 109–12.

22. Mirza Aqa Khan Kirmani and Shaykh Ahmad Ruhi, *Hasht bihisht* (n.p., n.d.). On the significance of Babism for the emergence of Iranian modernity, see Mangol Bayat, *Mysticism and Dissent: Socioreligious Thought in Qajar Iran* (Syracuse: Syracuse University Press, 1982).

23. Kirmani and Ruhi, *Hasht bihisht*, p. 9. Later in the text, on p. 122, this prohibition is modified: women can talk to strange men, but no more than twenty-eight words, and only when matters of necessity arise.

24. Ibid., p. 121.

25. For a similar shift in turn-of-the-century Lebanon, within the context of the socioeconomic transformations there, see Akram Fouad Khater, "'House' to 'Goddess of the House': Gender, Class, and Silk in Nineteenth-Century Mount Lebanon," *International Journal of Middle East Studies* 28, no. 3 (August 1996): 325–48.

26. Kirmani and Ruhi, *Hasht bihisht*, p. 122. The word "decree" (*hukm*), refers to Babi religious edicts.

27. Ibid., p. 144.

28. Ibid., p. 145.

29. On premodern educational institutions and concepts of knowledge, see Jonathan P. Berkey, *The Transmission of Knowledge in Medieval Cairo: A Social History of Islamic Education* (Princeton: Princeton University Press, 1992). See also his "Women and Islamic Education," in *Women in Middle Eastern History: Shifting Boundaries in Sex and Gender*, ed. Nikki Keddie and Beth Baron (New Haven: Yale University Press, 1991), pp. 143–57, for a discussion of premodern Islamic education of women.

30. My arguments in this essay are greatly influenced by the writings of Mohamad Tavakoli-Targhi. See "Refashioning Iran," *Iranian Studies* 23, nos. 1–4 (1990): 77–101, and "The Formation of Two Revolutionary Discourses." In particular, I take from his writings the importance and meaning of conceptual shifts in notions such as science/knowledge, nation, and politics in nineteenth-century Iran.

31. Kirmani, *Sad khatabah*, pp. 94 through 98; quotation from 97a.

32. See, for instance, Zayn al-Din al-ʿAmili al-Jabaʿi, *Munyat al-Murid* (a sixteenth-century C.E. text), trans. Muhammad Baqir Saʿidi Khurasani (n.p.: Intisharat-i ʿilmiyah Islamiyah, 1950), p. 30, on division of knowledgeable people (*danishmandan*) into three categories: ʿalim bi-allah, ʿalim bi amr-allah, and ʿalim bi-allah and amr-allah.

33. On changes in concepts of *taʿlim* and *tarbiat* as pertains to Egypt, see Timothy Mitchell, *Colonising Egypt* (Cambridge: Cambridge University Press, 1988); Omnia Shakry, "Schooled Mothers and Structured Play: Child Rearing in Turn-of-the-Century Egypt," chap. 4 in this volume. For Morocco, see Dale F. Eickelman, *Knowledge and Power in Morocco: The Education of a Twentieth-Century Notable* (Princeton: Princeton University Press, 1985). See also Margot Badron, "From Consciousness to Activism: Feminist Politics in Early Twentieth Century Egypt," in *Problems of the Middle East in Historical Perspective*, ed. John Spagnolo (London: Macmillan, 1992), pp. 27–48.

34. It began publication in 1896 and was devoted to the idea that the contemporary differences among nations had nothing to do with any innate differences but arose from different educational regimes. ("Opening Remarks [*Aghaz-i sukhan*]," *Tarbiat*, no. 1 [December 17, 1896]: 1–3.) It advocated that "[a]ny nation that sees itself behind any other nation is obligated by requirements of humanity . . . to race after education and to go with its head instead of its feet [that is, to move at top speed] on the path of civilization to catch up with the caravan that has gone ahead of it." (*Tarbiat*, untitled lead article in no. 2 [December 24, 1896]: 1–4; quotation from p. 1).

35. *Tarbiat*, lead article dubbed a parenthetical remark (*jumlah-'i muʿtarizah*) to clarify some points and avoid misunderstandings, in no. 4 (January 7, 1897): 1–4; quotation from p. 1.

36. Ibid., p. 2.

37. Kirmani and Ruhi, *Hasht bihisht*, p. 139.

38. *Tarbiat*, no. 42 (September 30, 1897): 3; in Persian it reads, "*har kah nakhwanad*

chah danad va har kah nadanad chah tavanad?" This represents an extension of the chain between power and knowledge, as expressed in the well-known verse from Firdawsi—"whosoever is knowledgeable, he shall be a capable person" (*tavana buvad har kah dana buvad*)—to link knowledge and reading.

39. See Walter J. Ong, *Orality and Literacy: The Technologizing of the Word* (London: Routledge, 1982).

40. See Mary Carruthers, *Book of Memory: A Study of Memory in Medieval Culture* (Cambridge: Cambridge University Press, 1990).

41. I would like to thank Jonathan Berkey for helpful conversations about this point. Further confirmation appears in the entries in biographical dictionaries on blind scholars, some born blind. See Fedwa Malti-Douglas, "*Mentalités* and Marginality: Blindness and Mamluk Civilization," in *The Islamic World: From Classical to Modern Times*, ed. C. E. Bosworth, Charles Issawi, Roger Savory, and A. L. Udovitch (Princeton: The Darwin Press, 1989), pp. 211–37. See also Dale F. Eickelman, "The Art of Memory: Islamic Education and Its Social Reproduction," in *Comparing Muslim Societies: Knowledge and the State in a World Civilization*, ed. Juan R. I. Cole (Ann Arbor: University of Michigan Press, 1992), pp. 97–132.

42. "On Schools (*Makatib va madaris*)," no. 48 (November 11, 1897): 2.

43. Zhiniral Mirza Taqi Khan Kashani, *Tarbiat: namah'ist dar qavaʿid-i taʿlim va tarbiat-i atfal* (Education: An essay on rules of training and educating children) (Isfahan: Dar al-tabaʿah-'i farhang, 1881), p. 47.

44. Ibid., p. 46.

45. Ibid., p. 61.

46. Mahmud ibn Yusuf, *Ta'dib al-atfal* (n.p., 1876).

47. Ibid., pp. 6–10.

48. Ibid., pp. 11–17.

49. Ibid., pp. 110–19.

50. Ibid., pp. 185–209. Much of the educational writing in Persian from this period on was closely linked with the French educational debates and texts of the time.

51. Ibid., p. 187.

52. Ibid., p. 188.

53. Ibid., pp. 195, 197, and 201.

54. Ibid., pp. 203–4.

55. Ibid., pp. 206–7.

56. Miftah al-Mulk Mahmud, *Taʿlim al-atfal* (Tehran: n.p., 1897), 1:5, 11, 21, 32, 42, and 96; 2:19, 32, 60, 105, and 117. In contrast, a depiction of a Qur'anic school has all the pupils sitting on the floor and the teacher in the act of caning a pupil (2:11).

57. Ibid., 1:68–80 and 95–101.

58. Ibid., pp. 81–94 and 102–6; quotation from p. 105.

59. Untitled lead article, *Tarbiat*, no. 36 (August 19, 1897): 1–4; quotation from pp. 1–2.

60. *Tarbiat*, no. 40 (September 16, 1897): 2–4.

61. Ibid., p. 3.

62. Ibid., pp. 3–4. Comparison between women of Europe and Iranian women, including mention of different educational practices regarding men and women, went back at least to the late eighteenth century, to the travelogues written by Persian-speaking voyagers from India and Iran to Europe. In fact, this "travel literature" constituted

a central medium through which reconceptualizations of gender, including issues of women's education, took place. See Mohamad Tavakoli-Targhi, "Imagining Western Women: Occidentalism and Euro-eroticism," *Radical America* 24, no. 3 (July–September 1990): 73–87.

63. ʿAbd al-Rahim ibn Abu Talib Tabrizi (Talibuf), *Kitab-i Ahmad ya safinah-'i Talibi* (Istanbul: n.p., 1893). A second volume was subsequently published in 1894 (Istanbul: Matbaʿah-'i Khawrshid). A third volume was published under a different title, *Masa'il-i hayat* (Tiflis: Matbaʿah-'i Ghayrat, 1906).

64. Talibuf, *Kitab-i Ahmad*, 1:81.

65. Ibid., p. 72; 2:4.

66. Talibuf, *Masa'il-i hayat*, p. 36.

67. For an English translation, see Qasim Amin, *The Liberation of Women*, trans. Samiha Sidhom Peterson (Cairo: American University in Cairo Press, 1992). There is a large critical literature on Amin's works in English. See, for instance, Leila Ahmed, *Women and Gender in Islam* (New Haven: Yale University Press, 1992); Baron, *Women's Awakening*; Badran, *Feminists, Islam, and Nation*; and essays by Lila Abu-Lughod and Omnia Shakry in this volume (chaps. 4 and 7). Here I am concerned with Amin's text, through its Persian translation, as a document within the educational debates of this time in Iran.

68. Yusuf Ashtiani, trans., *Tarbiat-i nisvan* (Tabriz: Matbaʿah-'i Maʿarif, 1900). A fuller translation was published later, translated by Muhazzib, "under instructions from the Ministry of Education," under the title *Zan va azadi* (Woman and liberty) (Tehran: Chapkhanah-'i markazi, 1937). Muhazzib also translated Amin's *al-Marʿat al-jadida*, "under instructions from the Ministry of Education," under the title *Zan-i imruz* (Today's woman) (Tehran: Chapkhanah-'i markazi, n.d.).

69. Ashtiani, *Tarbiat-i nisvan*, unnumbered initial pages. The titles he lists are: Amin's *Tahrir al-Marʿa, Falsafat al-zuwaj, al-Marʿa fi al-sharq* (Marqus Fahmi, 1894), *al-Marʿa fi qarn al-ʿashrin*, and *al-Marʿa fi al-'usra*.

70. Amin, *The Liberation of Women*, p. 10.

71. Ashtiani, *Tarbiat-i nisvan*, p. 14.

72. For Talibuf's position, see Talibuf, *Kitab-i Ahmad*, 2:11, where the unveiling of women is seen as one of the ill consequences of falling under foreign Christian rule; and p. 34, where he refers to "the good custom of our women's *hijab*" (ʿ*adat-i mamduhah-'i hijab-i 'unas-i ma*).

73. The dichotomous division between traditionalist and modernist positions was consolidated during the Pahlavi period. In the early 1930s, under Riza Shah, all independent women's journals and organizations were replaced by a single state-sponsored organization, Ladies Center (*Kanun-i banuvan*, established in 1935). This was followed by the unveiling order in early 1936. The Ladies Center was officially under the supervision of the Ministry of Education, and schools and Tehran University were the sites where many of the initial unveiling experiments were carried out. It was these later political and cultural developments that consolidated the identity between women's rights and unveiling in the domain of the modern.

74. Ashtiani, *Tarbiat-i nisvan*, p. 12 (Amin, *The Liberation of Women*, p. 6).

75. Ashtiani, *Tarbiat-i nisvan*, p. 69 (Amin, *The Liberation of Women*, p. 75).

76. Ashtiani, *Tarbiat-i nisvan*, p. 63 (Amin, *The Liberation of Women*, pp. 63–64).

77. Ashtiani, *Tarbiat-i nisvan*, pp. 17–18 (Amin, *The Liberation of Women*, p. 12).

78. See, as an example, "The Incurable Pain of Being in the Hands of Ignorant Servants (*Dard-i bi'darman-i giriftari dar dast-i khadamah-'i nadan*)," *Shukufah* 3, no. 9 (April 13, 1915): 2–3.

79. Ashtiani, *Tarbiat-i nisvan*, p. 69 (Amin, *The Liberation of Women*, p. 72).

80. Ashtiani, *Tarbiat-i nisvan*, p. 41 (Amin, *The Liberation of Women*, p. 23).

81. Ashtiani, *Tarbiat-i nisvan*, pp. 47–49 (Amin, *The Liberation of Women*, pp. 26–27).

82. Ashtiani, *Tarbiat-i nisvan*, p. 52 (Amin, *The Liberation of Women*, p. 28).

83. Ashtiani, *Tarbiat-i nisvan*, p. 29 (Amin, *The Liberation of Women*, p. 17).

84. Ashtiani, *Tarbiat-i nisvan*, p. 34 (Amin, *The Liberation of Women*, p. 20).

85. Ashtiani, *Tarbiat-i nisvan*, p. 35 (Amin, *The Liberation of Women*, p. 20).

86. See, for instance, the letter from Talibuf to I'tisam al-Mulk, dated 26 Sha'ban 1318 (December 15, 1900), reprinted in *Bahar*, nos. 9–10 (May–June 1911): 551–52.

87. See, for instance, "On Reforming the Condition of Schools in Iran (*Dar islah-i vaz'-i makatib-i Iran*)," *Parvarish* 1, no. 17 (October 15, 1900): 7–10; 'Abd al-Husayn, "Adventures in Europe (*Mukhatirat-i 'Urupa*)," *Parvarish* 1, no. 21 (November 16, 1900): 2–4; and the editorial essay (untitled) in *Ma'arif* 2, no. 34 (February 27, 1900): 3.

88. "An Essay Devoted to Education of Girls (*Maqalah-'i makhsus dar ta'lim-i 'awrat*)," *Habl al-matin* 9, no. 12 (January 6, 1902): 16.

89. "An Essay Devoted to Education of Girls (*Maqalah-'i makhsus dar ta'lim-i 'awrat*)," *Habl al-matin* 9, no. 16 (February 6, 1902): 5–7.

90. "An Essay Devoted to Education of Girls (*Maqalah 'i makhsus dar ta'lim-i 'awrat*)," *Habl al-matin* 9, no. 17 (February 10, 1902): 15–16; quotation from p. 15.

91. Ibid.

92. Ibid.

93. "Rights and Liberties of Women (*Huquq al-mar'a va hurriyat al-nisvan*)," *Habl al-matin* 12, no. 38 (June 26, 1905): 12–14; no. 39 (July 3, 1905): 20–22; no. 43 (July 31, 1905): 6–7; no. 44 (August 7, 1905): 10–11.

94. Muhammad Tahir ibn Iskandar Mirza ibn 'Abbas Mirza, *Tarbiat-i atfal* (n.p., 1891).

95. Ibid., pp. 5–6. The class implication of this argument is worth noting. Women "of leisured classes" are assumed to engage in giving their enfants to wet nurses. The practice, however, was much more widely in use. Though they did not hire professional wet nurses, women of other classes often breast-fed each other's infants, especially during the illness of a neighbor or a friend.

96. Ibid., pp. 7–8.

97. Ibid., pp. 12–13.

98. Ibid., pp. 234–35.

99. Ibid., p. 264.

100. "A Letter from the City (*Maktub-i shahri*)," *'Adalat* (formerly *Hadid*) 2, no. 19 (November 23, 1906): 5–8. See also Sayyid Husayn, "On the Duties of the Real Teachers of Men, That Is, Women (*Dar farayiz-i murabbian-i haqiqi-i mardan ya'ni nisvan*)," *Hadid* 1, no. 13 (September 21, 1905): 4–6; "The Ill Effects of Ignorance of Mothers (*Vakhamat-i nadani-i madaran*)," *Hadid* 1, no. 15 (October 4, 1905): 2–3. Zia'allah, untitled article, *Hadid* 1, no. 20 (October 10, 1905): 5–6; Muhammad Riza, "Seeking Knowledge Is Incumbent upon Every Muslim Man and Woman (*Talab al-*

ᶜilm faridatun ᶜala kull muslim wa muslima)," *Hadid* 2, no. 13 (September 12, 1906): 1–2; Naᶜmat'allah, "Family Life or Real Happiness (*Hayat-i ᶜa'ilah ya saᶜadat-i haqiqi),"* *ᶜAdalat* 2, no. 43 (April 15, 1907): 8 and no. 44 (April 24, 1907): 5–8; Muᶜavin al-Tujjar, "Letter from a Wise Person (*Maktub-i yaki az khiradmandan),"* *ᶜAdalat* 2, no. 46 (Rabiᶜ al-awwal 1325; May 1907): 7–8; "School for Girls (*Madrasah-'i bunat),"* *Vatan* 1, no. 1 (January 6, 1906): 3–4; "Education of Girls Is the Most Important Precondition of Civilization and Improvement of Ethics (*Tarbiat-i bunat shart-i aᶜzam-i tamaddun va tahzib-i akhlaq ast),"* *Subh-i sadiq* 2, no. 27 (March 8, 1908): 1–2; Vasiq al-Saltanah, "Seeking Knowledge Is Incumbent upon Every Muslim Man and Woman (*Talab al-ᶜilm faridatun ᶜala kull muslim wa muslima),"* *Iran-i naw* 1, no. 56 (November 1, 1909): 4; Munir Mazandarani, "Seeking Knowledge Is Incumbent upon Every Muslim Man and Woman (*Talab al-ᶜilm faridatun ᶜala kull muslim wa muslima),"* *Iran-i naw* 1, no. 91 (December 17, 1909): 1–2.

101. American Presbyterian missionaries had established a girls' school in 'Urumiyah in 1838. Sisters of St. Vincent de Paul opened schools for girls in 1865 in 'Urumiyah, Salmas, Tabriz, and Isfahan, and one in Tehran in 1875. In 1895 the American School for Girls was established in Tehran. Schools for girls were established by various religious denominations of Iran in the last decades of the nineteenth century. Armenian schools for girls were established in Tehran in 1870, in Qazvin in 1889, in Sultanabad in 1900, and in Isfahan in 1903. The first Jewish school for girls in Tehran, *Ittihad (Alians)*, was established in 1898, and in Kirman Zoroastrians established *'Unas-i Jamshidi* in 1902. *Tarbiat-i bunat* was established in 1911 by Baha'is in Tehran. The first Muslim school for girls on the new model is reported to have been established in Chalias near Kirman in 1897, but we know nothing more about this school. This was followed by *Parvarish* in 1903 in the residence of Hasan Rushdiyah with Tubá Rushdiyah (his sister-in-law) as its principal. This school was forced to close down within a short time because of the open hostility it faced. More lasting efforts came on the eve of the Constitutional Revolution (1906–9). *Mukhaddarat* was established in 1905, *Dushizigan* (by Bibi Khanum Astarabadi) and *Hurmatiyah-'i sadat* in 1906, and in 1908 Tubá Azmudah opened *Namus*. The following years witnessed a rapid expansion of such schools in Tehran. Provincial capitals followed suit: *Bunat* was opened in Qazvin in 1908, *Bunat-i Islami* in Rasht in 1911, and *Fatimiyah* in Shiraz in 1920. The information on girls' schools has been extracted from newspaper reports of the period and from the following sources: Ministry of Education, Endowments, and Fine Arts (*Vizarat-i maᶜarif va awqaf va sanayiᶜ-i mustazrifah*), *Qavanin va nizam'namah'ha, ihsa'iyah-'i madaris va makatib, aᶜza' va mustakhdimin* (for 1927), pp. 62, 74, 110, 112, 124, 130, 132, 142, 158, 162; "Brief History of Education (*Tarikhchah-'i maᶜarif*)," pt. 2, in *Taᶜlim va tarbiat* 4, nos. 7–8 (October–November 1934): 459–64; Shams al-Din Rushdiyah, *Savanih-i ᶜumr* (Tehran: Nashr-i Tarikh-i Iran, 1983), p. 148; and Fakhri Qavimi, *Kar'namah-'i zanan-i mashhur-i Iran* (Tehran: Vizarat-i Amuzish va Parvarish, 1973), pp. 128, 131, 142. By 1911, there were 47 schools for girls in Tehran with 2,187 students (compared with 78 for boys with 8,344 students). See Mustafá Mansur al-Saltanah, *Rapurt-i salianah dar bab-i maᶜarif va taᶜlimat-i ᶜumumi: sanah-'i 1328–29* (Tehran: Vizarat-i maᶜarif va favayid-i ᶜammah va awqaf, 1911), appended tables, no page number or table number. For more information on women's education and in particular the establishment of schools, see the forthcoming essays in *Encyclopaedia Iranica* on education.

102. See Qavimi, *Kar'namah*; Badr al-Muluk Bamdad, *Zan-i Irani az inqilab-i mashrutiyat ta inqilab-i sifid*, 2 vols. (Tehran: Ibn Sina, 1968, 1969) for some of these stories. For a contemporary account, see the letter by Bibi (Khanum Astarabadi), "Letter from a Woman (*Maktub-i yiki az nisvan*)," *Tamaddun* 1, no. 15 (May 7, 1907): 2–3. See also Mihrangiz Mallah and Afsaneh Najmabadi, eds., *Bibi Khanum Astarabadi and Khanum Afzal Vaziri* [in Persian] (New York and Bloomington, Ill.: Nigarish va nigarish-i zan, 1996).

103. Huma Rizvani, ed., *Lavayih-i Aqa Shaykh Fazl'allah Nuri* (Tehran: Nashr-i tarikh-i Iran, 1983), pp. 28, and 62. Many other religious leaders, however, such as Hajj Mirza Hadi Dawlatabadi, father of Sadiqah Dawlatabadi (discussed by Sullivan, chap. 6 in this volume), Shaykh Hadi Najmabadi, father of Agha Baygum and Bibi Najmabadi, and Shaykh Muhammad Husayn Yazdi, husband of Safiyah Yazdi, supported the establishment of new schools for girls, and their own female family members were active educationalists.

104. "Essay from a Lady (*Layihah'-i yaki az khavatin*)," *Habl al-matin* (Tehran) 1, no. 105 (September 1, 1907): 4–6. For another protest letter by a group of women, see "Grievance of Association of Women of Tehran to the Respected Association of Students (*Tazallum-i jamaʿat-i nisvan-i Tihran bah anjuman-i muhtaram-i ittihadiyah-'i tullab*)," *Musavat* 1, no. 18 (March 22, 1908): 5–6.

105. "On the Miseries of Women (*Dar bicharigi-yi zanan*)," *Iran-i naw* 3, no. 102 (July 26, 1911): 3.

106. This refers to the tzarist takeover of these provinces in northern Iran in various military campaigns in the first half of the nineteenth century, delineating the contemporary borders of Iran in the north.

107. *Iran-i naw* 1, no. 114 (January 18, 1910): 4.

108. From the speech of one of the students of the Hunar school, on the occasion of the examination of its students, *Iran-i naw* 3, no. 83 (July 3, 1910): 3.

109. *Iran-i naw* 1, no. 19 (September 15, 1909): 3. See also Tayirah, "Letter from an Iranian Lady (*Maktub-i yaki az khanumha-yi Irani*)," *Iran-i naw* 1, no. 17 (September 13, 1909): 2, and her long essay serialized in the same paper, in which she developed similar arguments for women's education: Tayirah, "Essay by a Knowledgeable Lady (*Layihah-'i khanum-i danishmand*)," *Iran-i naw* 1, no. 65 (November 13, 1909): 3; no. 69 (November 18, 1909): 3; no. 78 (November 30, 1909): 2–3; no. 84 (December 8, 1909): 3; no. 92 (December 18, 1909): 3–4.

110. All quotations from Tayirah, "Essay by a Knowledgeable Lady (*Layihah-'i khanum-i danishmand*)," *Iran-i naw* 1, no. 78 (November 30, 1909): 2–3.

111. It is significant that the Persian expressions, constructed in parallel, "house management," "husband management," and "child management" (*khanah'dari, shawhar'dari*, and *bachchah'dari*) were distinct and remain largely so, indicating rather distinct tasks and preoccupations. In other words, a combined construct, such as "housewife" (*zan-i khanah'dar*), was not opted for until recently and even then largely as a statistical category.

112. See Camron Amin, "The Rise of the Professional Woman in the Iranian Press, 1910–1946" (paper presented at the Berkshire Conference of Historians of Women, June 1996), and his "The Attentions of the Great Father: Reza Shah, 'The Woman Question,' and the Iranian Press, 1890–1946" (Ph.D. diss., University of Chicago, 1996).

113. She is often wrongly referred to as the wife of one Dr. Kahhal, based on a reading of *khanum duktur Kahhal* as *khanum-i duktur Kahhal*, perhaps an indication of historians' disbelief that a woman ophthalmologist could have existed.

114. "Household Management (*Khanah'dari*)," *Danish*, no. 1 (September 11, 1910): 4–5; no. 4 (October 22, 1910): 7–8; no. 6 (November 6, 1910): 4–6; no. 8 (November 28, 1910): 8.

115. "Husband Management (*Rasm-i shawhardari*)," *Danish*, no. 1 (September 11, 1910): 5–6; "Husband Management (*Shawhardari*)," no. 7 (November 13 1910): 4–6.

116. "Child Management (*Bachchah'dari*)," *Danish*, no. 10 (December 17, 1910): 2–3.

117. "Children's Hygiene (*Hifz al-sihhah-'i atfal*)," *Danish*, no. 1 (September 11, 1910): 2–3; no. 3 (October 10, 1910): 4–6; no. 4 (October 22, 1910): 2–4; no. 5 (October 31, 1910): 8; no. 8 (November 28, 1910): 2–4; no. 17 (February 4, 1911): 2–3; no. 23 (March 25, 1911): 5–7; no. 25 (April 22, 1911): 5–7; no. 30 (July 20, 1911): 2–4.

118. *Danish*, no. 7 (November 13, 1910): 6–7; no. 8 (November 28, 1910): 7–8; no. 9 (December 10, 1910): 6–7; no. 10 (December 17, 1910): 5–8; no. 17 (February 4, 1911): 3–4; no. 25 (April 22, 1911): 8; no. 26 (May 8, 1911): 4–7.

119. "Letter from a Girl Educated in Europe (*Maktub-i yiki az dukhtarha-yi tarbiat'shudah-'i Yurup*)," *Danish*, no. 27 (May 23, 1911): 2–3.

120. ʿAli Zanjani, "Education of Girls (*Tarbiat-i dukhtaran*)," *Danish*, no. 22 (March 12, 1911): 2–3; quotation from p. 2.

121. "Husband Management (*Rasm-i shawhardari*)," *Danish*, no. 1 (September 11, 1910), p. 6.

122. "Nanny Cannot Be Kinder Than Mother (*Dayah az madar mihraban'tar nimishavad*)," pt. 1, *Danish*, no. 3 (October 10, 1910): 2–4, pt. 2, no. 5 (October 31, 1910): 2–4. Recall that Fani Kashmiri had argued the opposite: that it was preferable to engage a nanny for the care of the child. *Akhlaq-i ʿalamara*, p. 136.

123. "Nanny Cannot Be Kinder Than Mother," pt. 1, p. 2.

124. Ibid., pp. 3–4.

125. Ibid., pt. 2, p. 2.

126. Ibid., pp. 3–4.

127. See, for instance, R.H.M., "Iranian Women's Knowledge: One of the Origins of Our Misfortunes (*Maʿarif zanha-yi Iran: yiki az sarchashmah'ha-yi badbakhti-i ma*)," *Shukufah* 1, no. 9 (May 5, 1913): 1–2; no. 10 (May 26, 1913): 2–3; no. 11 (June 13, 1913): 3; no. 14 (August 27, 1913): 3. "On the Fundamentals of Respected Ladies' Lives (*Dar asas-i zindigi-i khanumha-yi muhtaram*)," *Shukufah* 1, no. 17 (November 4, 1913): 3; 2, no. 18 (November 21, 1913): 4; no. 19 (December 15, 1913): 3; no. 20 (December 25, 1913): 4; no. 23 (February 12, 1914): 3–4.

128. Maliktaj, Untitled article, *Shukufah* 1, no. 4 (February 14, 1913): 2–3; no. 5 (February 28, 1913): 2–3; no. 7 (April 2, 1913): 1; no. 7 (April 2, 1913): 1. For other articles on the importance of educated wives and scientific mothers for the political fate of the country, see N. R. (An Iranian girl), "Learning about the Truth of Matters (*Agahi ya haqiqat-i matlab*)," *Shukufah* 1, no. 6 (March 13, 1913): 2–3; article by principal of elementary school "Hurriyah-'i sadat," "The Green Grass Was Trampled upon by Discord (*Basat-i sabzah lagadkub shud bah pa-yi nifaq*)," *Shukufah* 1, no. 7 (April 2, 1913): 1–2.

129. "What Is a School and What Are Its Qualifications? (*Madrasah chah nam ast va sharayit-i 'u kudam ast?*)," *Shukufah* 1, no. 5 (February 28, 1913): 1–2; no. 7 (April 2, 1913): 2–3; no. 8 (April 20, 1913): 2–3; no. 9 (May 5, 1913): 3; no. 14 (August 27, 1913): 2–3. "Enter the House through Its Entrance (*Fa'idkhalu al-buyut min abwabiha*)," *Shukufah* 1, no. 12 (July 28, 1913): 2–3; no. 14 (August 27, 1913): 1.

130. "Bad Imitation (*Taqlid-i bad*)," article started in issue no. 1 (which I have not been able to find), continued in *Shukufah* 1, no. 5 (February 28, 1913): 3; no. 7 (April 2, 1913): 3. "Who Is a Good Girl? (*Dukhtar-i khub kudam ast?*)," *Shukufah* 1, no. 11 (June 13, 1913): 3. A more detailed analysis of *Shukufah* deserves a separate essay.

131. Mirza ʿAzizallah Khan, *Tarbiat al-bunat* (Tehran: Matbaʿah Khawrshid, 1905), p. 6.

132. Emphasizing the link between the acquisition of modern education and chastity, many of the earliest schools for girls were named appropriately: *Namus* (honor), *ʿIfaf* (chastity), *ʿIsmatiyah* (place of chastity/innocence), *ʿIffatiyah* (place of chastity), and perhaps most tellingly *Hijab* (veil). In other words, education was constructed as a replacement of the physical veil, as protector of honor and chastity. For further discussion of this point, see Najmabadi, "Veiled Discourse."

133. See "On Children's Hygiene (*Dar hifz al-sihhah-'i atfal*)," *Shukufah* 1, no. 17 (November 4, 1913): 1.

134. "On Duties of Real Teachers of Men, That Is, Women (*Dar farayiz-i murabbian-i haqiqi-i mardan yaʿni nisvan*)," *Hadid* 1, no. 13 (September 21, 1905): 4–6.

135. *Iran-i naw* 3, no. 81 (July 1, 1911), p. 3.

136. *Payk-i saʿadat-i nisvan* (a women's journal published in the northern provincial capital city Rasht, under the editorship of a woman, Rushanak Nawʿdust) 1, no. 1 (October 7, 1927): 8. See also the article titled "Chastity," in the same journal, 1, no. 6 (September 1928): 168–74. Other journals of the same period, such as *Iranshahr*, *Farangistan*, and *Nahid* had similar articles in their women's columns.

137. For a discussion of these women's activities, see Janet Afary, "On the Origins of Feminism in Early Twentieth-Century Iran," *Journal of Women's History* 1, no. 2 (Fall 1989): 65–87; Bamdad, *Zan-i Irani*; Mangol Bayat-Philipp, "Women and Revolution in Iran, 1905–11," in *Women in the Muslim World*, ed. Lois Beck and Nikki Keddie (Cambridge: Harvard University Press, 1978), pp. 295–308; Rushanak Mansur, "Women's Images in the Constitutionalist Press (*Chihrah-'i zan dar jarayid-i mashrutiyat*)," *Nimeye Digar*, no. 1 (Spring 1984): 11–30; ʿAbd al-Husayn Nahid, *Zanan-i Iran dar junbish-i mashrutah* (Saarbrucken: Nuvid, 1989); Afsaneh Najmabadi, "*Zanha-yi millat*: Women or Wives of the Nation?" *Iranian Studies* 26, nos. 1–2 (Winter–Spring 1993): 51–71; Homa Nategh, "The Woman Question in Some of the Writings of the Left from the Constitutional Movement to the Era of Riza Khan (*Mas'alah-'i zan dar barkhi az mudavvanat-i chap az nihzat-i mashrutah ta ʿasr-i Riza Khan*)," *Zaman-i naw* 1 (November 1983): 8–17, 27; Eliz Sanasarian, *The Women's Rights Movement in Iran* (New York: Praeger, 1982).

138. For a discussion of these points, see Najmabadi, "*Zanha-yi millat*."

139. *Shukufah* 4, no. 4 (January 20, 1916): 2–3.

140. *Shukufah* 4, no. 8 (April 2, 1916): 8–9.

CHAPTER 4

Schooled Mothers and Structured Play:
Child Rearing in Turn-of-the-Century Egypt

OMNIA SHAKRY

THIS ESSAY attempts to explore some of the conjunctures and disjunctures between European colonial and metropolitan discourses and indigenous modernizing and nationalist discourses on women and mothering in turn-of-the-century Egypt. Tracing the proliferation of debates on motherhood and proper child rearing through a number of scientific-literary and religious journals, I will attempt to elaborate the changing conception of the "good mother" and proper mothering as situated within the contemporaneous discourses of domesticity.[1] I will be analyzing what Dipesh Chakrabarty has recently referred to as "*public* narratives of the nature of social life in the family."[2] Such narratives crystallized into a normative and didactic discourse that helped to re-create and redefine the parameters of what was considered ideal in conceptions of motherhood, child rearing, and domesticity within a colonial context.

A fundamental shift, I will argue, occurred at the turn of the century in which mothers came to be responsible for the physical, moral, and intellectual development of children within the nexus of a nascent nationalist discourse.[3] With the onset of a "modernizing" discourse, the emphasis shifts in a number of ways toward the problematization of *tarbiya*[4] (upbringing, education) and its recasting along scientific lines according to modern, hygienic, and rational principles for developing "productive members of society." As child rearing became localized within the realm of motherhood, its aim became the creation and cultivation of new types of children "acclimated to physical, mental, and moral work" and imbued with an ethic of industry and economy. This discursive shift and elaboration of a new notion of motherhood occurred at a juncture of colonial-hygienic discourse in which the onus would be placed on the competence of the Egyptian mother, with a consequent policy of encouraging the "rational upbringing of children" through private philanthropic and governmental organizations.

Motherhood, as taken up within the context of colonialism, was fundamental to the constitution of national identity and entailed the formation of a series of discursive practices that demarcated women as both a "locus of the country's backwardness" and a sphere of transformation to be reconstituted and raised up onto the plane of enlightened rationality.[5] As such, it figures centrally in turn-of-the-century modernizing discourse and was essential to the nationalist project. Thus the focus on proper rational and scientific mothering is situated within both the colonial discourse on motherhood and the nationalist discourse on modernity.

Within the Egyptian colonial setting, untutored "ignorant" mothers were problematized by both colonial administrators and indigenous modernizing reformers as particularly unsuited for the preparation of a new generation. Those who asserted their unsuitability held up the example of an advanced and scientific European pedagogy to corroborate their argument, pointing to the relationship between proper mothering and the progress of the nation. Parallel European metropole discourses on mothering and the nation, aimed primarily at the lower classes, positioned women analogously as markers of progress and backwardness, but the concern for motherhood was often couched in terms of an imperial imperative, essential for the preservation of a national and cultural ascendancy and a concomitant concern with physical and racial degeneration.[6]

Moreover, discussions on proper mothering, in both the metropole and colony, intersected with philanthropic movements geared toward a pedagogy of the lower classes. Such discursive practices sought to isolate "internal others" (metropole lumpenproletariat; working-class mothers in both metropole and colony; poor whites in the colonies) and will be analyzed as an attempt to reconstitute motherhood along middle-class lines of rational-economic and scientific-hygienic domesticity and child rearing, serving both to efface and to recast class differences under the rubric of an "ideal mother." This helped to consolidate a bourgeois family form.[7]

The conjunctures between colonial and nationalist discourse on women are truly striking, and thus I hope to show that Egyptian discussions of motherhood need to be situated within the context of both colonial and anticolonial nationalist discourses on modernity. I attempt to draw attention to these continuities, focusing specifically upon the ways in which the colonial and nationalist projects intersected with issues related to gender and class. Analyzing views from both the liberal secular-nationalist and Islamist press, I attempt to highlight the common set of assumptions shared by both about the nature of mothering, child rearing, the progress of the nation, and the backwardness of Egyptians.

I also argue, however, that it would be wrong to presume that anticolonial nationalist discourses on motherhood, and in particular those of the Islamists, were merely parasitic upon colonial or European discourses. Crucial to the discourse of *tarbiya* was the indigenous concept of *adab*, entailing a complex of valued dispositions (intellectual, moral, and social), appropriate norms of behavior, comportment, and bodily habitus.[8] Further, the formation of the

new "private sphere" within the Egyptian setting was fashioned within the
parameters of a historically constituted Islamic discursive tradition. Both
Westernized modernizing reformers and Islamist reformers situated their own
projects as a defense of true Islam and a critique of *taqlid* (or blind imitation
of customs and traditions). In particular, the advocacy of Islamic reform in the
sphere of education and *tarbiya* on the part of the thinkers in the *salafiyya*
movement was rooted in a desire for a national nonsecular modernity, producing a fundamental difference between the colonial and nationalist discourses
on modernity.[9]

Islamist reformers were able to draw upon resources indigenous to the Islamic discursive tradition that emphasized the proper pedagogy for children,
the cultivation of the body, and the moral education of the self as essential for
the constitution of a rightly guided Islamic community. Such norms of pedagogy were complementary, and not antithetical, to the modernist disciplining
of the body and rationalization of the household.

"THE MEN OF TOMORROW AND THE MOTHERS OF THE FUTURE"

The colonial project was marked by the intensive generation and elaboration
of modes of knowledge production that would seek to contribute to the *moral
and material* improvement of the native population. The discourse of uplifting
an entire population onto a higher plane of material and moral well-being
intersected with colonial representations and constructions of gender and segregation. Women, perceived as sequestered beings isolated from the machinery of "society," could be demarcated as "the locus of the country's backwardness" and would come to be instrumental in practices aimed at "social and
political discipline."[10] Colonial policy sought to "penetrate that 'inaccessible'
space . . . and thus commence . . . to 'work from the inside out.' "[11]

As Gayatri Spivak has pointed out, "imperialism's image as the establisher
of the good society is marked by the espousal of woman as the object of
protection from her own kind."[12] The particular interplay between British
colonial discourse on Islam and women (with its rhetorical fetishization of
the veil, seclusion, and polygamy), in which colonial discourse constructed
the subject "woman" as a category to be isolated and penetrated, articulated
with anticolonial nationalist discourse on that very same terrain.[13] I will begin,
then, with the earl of Cromer as I take *Modern Egypt* to be a hallmark text
of the colonial period, laying the foundations for much of the later colonial
discourse on the condition of women and the general standard of living of
the Egyptian people. As Cromer elaborates, "The position of women in Egypt,
and in Mohammedan countries generally, is, therefore, a fatal obstacle to
the attainment of that elevation of thought and character which should accom-

pany the introduction of European civilisation, if that civilisation is to produce its full measure of beneficial effect. The obvious remedy would appear to be to educate the women."[14] In fact, female education was perceived as one of the main contributions to the "moral and material" improvement of the Egyptians that the British had been able to achieve.[15] Yet Cromer is quick to qualify his statement.

> It, of course, remains an open question whether, when Egyptian women are educated, they will exercise a healthy and elevating influence over the men. . . . If it can be once admitted that no good moral results will accrue from female education in Egypt, then indeed, the reformer will despair of the cause of Egyptian education generally in the highest sense of the word. . . . [T]his much is well-nigh certain—that the reformer may instruct, may explain, he may argue, he may devise the most ingenious methods for the moral and material improvement of the people . . . but unless he proves himself able, not only to educate, but to elevate the Egyptian woman, he will never succeed in affording the Egyptian man . . . the only European education which is worthy of Europe.[16]

The colonial civilizing project, thus postulated, stood or fell with its ability to permeate and reconstruct the domain of women. These very same themes of the moral and material improvement of the Egyptian woman reverberate throughout nationalist discourse, which would later come to construct women as serving a productive function, as bearers of the nation and its children, essential for the development of a generation of morally upright, intellectually developed, and productive citizens.

Partha Chatterjee's discussion of Bengali Hindu anticolonial nationalist discourse has pointed to its situating of the "women's question" in an inner domain of spirituality, localized within the home and embodied by the feminine, enabling nationalist discourse to construct a cultural essence distinct from that of the West.[17] Thus he states,

> [N]ationalism did in fact provide an answer to the new social and cultural problems concerning the position of women in "modern" society, and . . . this answer was posited not on an identity but on a difference with the perceived forms of cultural modernity in the West. . . . [T]he relative unimportance of the women's question in the last decades of the nineteenth century is to be explained not by the fact that it had been censored out of the reform agenda or overtaken by more pressing and emotive issues of political struggle. The reason lies in nationalism's success in situating the "women's question" in an inner domain of sovereignty, far removed from the arena of political contest of the state.[18]

The case of Egypt highlights, I think, some of the dangers of generalizing across colonial or postcolonial histories. The "women's question" in Egypt clearly linked both the moral and material domains and articulated in complex ways with colonial discourse. Although Egyptian nationalist discourse clearly sought to uphold women as a source of cultural integrity, it also localized them as an arena for the social, political, and cultural progress of the nation. That is to say, the advancement of the nation in the "material" fields of law, administration, economy, and statecraft[19] was positioned in such a way that progress for the *umma*, or community, could not be achieved independently of progress in the domain of women, and more specifically mothers.

It is thus useful to view the positions women were placed in by colonial and nationalist discursive formations, as an articulatory practice that sought to reconstruct women, by protecting, advancing, or developing them, as *both* a domain of culture (Chatterjee's inner domain) and progress (outer domain). Nationalist discourse continuously situated women as the mothers of the (social and political) men of the future. The localization of proper and rational mothering as integral both to woman's primary definition and to the production of the nation was essential to such a process. This double "ideological work of gender" localized women as backward and ignorant but simultaneously delineated them as a sphere of transformation. It required both a positing of mothering as a naturalized and universal function of women and an assertion that Egyptian mothers were particularly unsuited for the preparation of the new generation.

In 1911 Shibli Shumayyil, a medical doctor who practiced and taught in Egypt, underscored the importance of motherhood in the creation and progress of a nation in an article entitled "Men of Tomorrow."[20] Shumayyil was particularly focused upon science as part of a rational universal faith and was concerned with issues of public health, hygiene, and welfare in Egypt. He states,

> If you want to know the future of a country, look to their children, for they are the results of the past and the mark of the future. Look to their health, their *tarbiya*, and their education, from the time that they are a fetus in their mother's womb until the day they are born and raised in their mother's lap, until the day they leave the schools and are added to society as productive members. For it is on the basis of their health and plenitude that the community (*umma*) develops, and on the strength of their education and upbringing that its prosperity and success are achieved.[21]

In fact, a theme that threads through the turn-of-the-century literature in Egypt is the need to create a "generation of mothers" who would be able to care for the well-being of their children and hence secure the well-being and advancement of the family and the nation.[22] Beth Baron has analyzed the discourse on mothers, morality, and nationalism, pointing to the ways in which "the women's question" was taken up in tandem with the "Egyptian question" by male authors, as well as female authors in the women's press at the turn of the century.[23] In contrast to Bengal, where Chatterjee has argued that the "women's question" disappeared with the rise of nationalist politics, the Egyptian nationalist movement took up the two questions simultaneously. Women's participation in anticolonial nationalist struggle was consistently framed in terms of their role as mothers of the nation. Liberal nationalists were eager to promote women's "progress" along the lines suggested by Qasim Amin.

Salama Musa, an intellectual and women's advocate, stated, "In those years there were two subjects that we used to discuss more than anything else, as they concerned the whole of Egyptian society. They were the English occupation, and Qasim Amin's movement for the liberation of women."[24] Ahmed Lutfi al-Sayyid, the editor of the nationalist newspaper of the *Umma* party, *Al-Jarida*, was equally involved in the "emancipation of women" and the reform of Egypt's current educational practices. As Albert Hourani states, al-Sayyid viewed education as the "only effective means to national maturity and real independence . . . even more important than the education given in the schools was that given in the family. 'The welfare of the family is the welfare of the nation' and the problem of the Egyptian family was at the heart of the problem of Egypt."[25] Within the nexus of anticolonial nationalist struggle, then, mothering took on a supplemented value: that of inculcating nationalist virtues in the face of colonial oppression.

Much of the discourse on the education of women and the importance of child rearing was gleaned from Qasim Amin's core text *The Liberation of Women* (*Tahrir al-mar'a*), published in 1899. Amin, known for advocating "women's liberation" through education, the removal of the veil, and an end to seclusion, emphasized the importance of civilizing women in order to enable them to provide the proper "physical, intellectual, and moral upbringing" for their children, and hence to ensure the progress of the nation.[26] A brief discussion of Amin is useful because of the extent to which the arguments he puts forth on child rearing resonate in the later *tarbiya* literature.

Amin inextricably links the development and progress of the nation to the condition of women, a link that is forged precisely by women's ability to properly raise a generation of children. Indeed, this is how differences between nations are to be understood, for "we cannot consider traditions to be the same in a civilized nation as in an ignorant, barbaric one, because the behavior of every individual in a society is appropriate to the intellectual abilities of that society and to the method by which its children are brought up . . . [The] evidence of history confirms and demonstrates that the status of women is inseparably tied to the status of a nation."[27] Amin is quite keen to point out that "the inferiority of Egyptians is a consequence of their deprivation from this early education. An Egyptian child grows like a weed. . . ."[28] One of the points that he consistently underscores is the importance of mothering for the formation of "adult men."[29]

Amin begins a discussion titled "Women and the Nation" with an overview of European global hegemony, linking it to Darwinian theories of natural selection and survival of the fittest. How, according to Amin, can Egyptians

"preserve their existence," "strive toward security and survival," and "gain
control over [their] own wealth"—how can "the land . . . justifiably belong to
its inhabitants rather than to strangers"—in the face of this battle? It is, indeed,
"those intangible intellectual and education capabilities that are central to
every other type of power." As such, for a nation to survive in the face of this
form of competition, it must be "concerned with the structure of its families,
for the family is the foundation of a country. Consequently, since the mother
is the foundation of the family, her intellectual development or underdevelopment becomes the primary factor in determining the development or underdevelopment of the country."[30]

Amin's central concern lay with the proper cultivation of mothers who
would be able to create the necessary "men of the future." And indeed, the
expressions "the men of tomorrow and the mothers of the future" (*rijal al-
ghad wa ummahat al-mustaqbal*)[31] surface repeatedly in the *tarbiya* literature
and signal the interconnections between motherhood and national progress.

EMPIRE IS ROOTED IN THE HOME

And some day, perhaps, the future mothers of the
nation will be taught and trained in vital matters, vital
for mothers and therefore for babies and empires.
(Caleb Saleeby)[32]

How intimate is the connexion which exists between
the women of England, and the moral character maintained by this country in the scale of nations.
(Sara Ellis)[33]

Homi Bhabha has recently provided a useful theoretical venue from which
to conceptualize the complex workings of national identity formation. Pointing to the "ambivalence that haunts the idea of the nation," he suggests that
we evoke the ambivalent encoding of national subjects as objects of a nationalist pedagogy and subjects of a performative signification that re-creates
the nation-people as subjects of a coherent national culture and life. By paying
attention to the ways in which cultural and political identity is negotiated
through the partial fixation of meanings, especially within the marginal
spaces of national identity, he suggests ways in which the fractal nature of
nationalist discourse may be opened up for analysis. The double movement of
encoding what lies inside the nation but is also exterior to it (e.g., working
class women, peasantry) as well as the Other outside (colonized, colonizing
Others) allows us to see the multiple and fractal constitution of colonial and
metropolitan national identity as formed against the multiple sites and boundaries of an Other.[34]

Discourses on mothering in both the metropole and the colony were integral to just such a process of the constitution of national identity. In what discursive field were the discourses on motherhood and the nation structured in the metropole? Linda Colley has discussed the construction of British identity during the eighteenth and nineteenth centuries in terms of the "forging" of an identity not "because of an integration and homogenization of disparate cultures. Instead, Britishness was superimposed over an array of internal differences in response to contact with the Other, and above all, in response to conflict with the Other."[35]

How were women in particular situated within the discursive field of British national identity? Anna Davin has discussed the redefinition of women's roles in early-twentieth-century Britain and provides a useful contiguous narrative of the discourse on mothering in the colonial metropole. Davin elaborates upon the ways in which the emergent ideology of motherhood and domesticity and the burgeoning of official and private activity centered upon public health, domestic hygiene, and child welfare during the first decade of the 1900s, and how these intersected with issues of class and imperial domination. The concern for proper mothering was often couched in terms of national and imperial interests, and a concern for racial degeneration. Children were posited as "citizens of tomorrow" and a "national asset" upon which "the future of the country and empire" depended.[36] Consequently, concern over the (white) British population's birthrate intensified. Fears about depopulation mushroomed and the focus turned to women and mothers as a site of the reproduction of the nation and the maintenance of racial health and purity. Women became "mothers of the race."

At this juncture of empire building, then, the sound condition of women and children was posited as essential for the future of England. The production of a nation healthy "in body and mind" was localized in motherhood as mothers became responsible for the physical development and character formation of children. The elevation of motherhood was linked to the production and preparation of the next generation as both an imperial and a domestic (social) obligation. Dr. Caleb Saleeby, a chief proponent of maternalism and eugenics in the early twentieth century, quite clearly illustrates many of these intersections between race, empire, nation, and motherhood. In discussing the complementary campaigns of maternalism and eugenics, Saleeby states in his characteristically polemical style,

We are about to discover that the true politics is domestics, since there is no wealth but life and life begins at home. We are going to have the right life born, and we are going to take care of it when it is born. . . . We propose to rebuild the living foundations of empire. To this end we shall preach a new imperialism . . . demanding that over all her [England's] legislative chambers there be carved the more than golden words, "There is no Wealth but Life."[37]

His views on politics and domestics are clearly delineated. He states that "[t]he history of nations is determined not on the battlefield but in the nursery, and the battalions which give lasting victory are the battalions of babies. The politics of the future will be domestics."[38] Raising the level of maternal hygiene, sanitation, and education became important because "empire is rooted at home." Mothers were cast as builders and preservers of state and empire and hence also as repositories of national identity. Indeed, "parenthood necessarily takes its place as the supreme factor of national destiny . . . true patriotism must therefore concern itself with the conditions and the quality of parenthood. . . . "[39] His was a "eugenic patriotism."[40]

Saleeby laments what he perceives to be the inordinate attention paid to the logistics of empire at the expense of the cultivation of race culture. "Today our historians and politicians think in terms of regiments and tariffs . . . the time will come when they must think in terms of babies and motherhood. We must think in such terms too if we wish Great Britain to be much longer great."[41] One of the questions that obsessed him was why empires and imperial peoples degenerate. While acknowledging the importance of an accumulated heritage of knowledge, art, and power, Saleeby emphasized that the maintenance of empire depended on the upkeep of the race.

> If the race degenerates . . . the time will come when its heritage is too much for it. . . . If an Empire has been built the degenerate race cannot sustain it. *There is no wealth but life: and if the quality of the life fails, neither battleships nor libraries nor symphonies nor anything else will save a nation.* Empires and civilisations, then, have fallen, despite the strength and magnitude of the superstructure, because the foundations decayed. . . . Acquired progress will not compensate for racial or inherent decadence. If the race is going down, it will not compensate to add another colony to your empire; on the contrary the bigger the empire the stronger must be the race. [42]

Ann Stoler has pointed to the importance of maintaining the European family and bourgeois respectability to the consolidation of the boundaries of rule in the colonies.[43] Early-twentieth-century eugenics discourse in metropole France, England, and Germany emphasized the importance of European women of good stock as a source of national vitality and hence glorified the "cult of motherhood" while simultaneously placing it under scientific scrutiny.[44] Stoler discusses the transplanting of eugenics discourse and its principles in the colonies, "which pronounced what kind of people should represent Dutch or French rule, how they should bring up their children, and with whom they should socialize . . . [A] common discourse was mapped out onto different immediate exigencies of empire as variations on a gender-specific theme exalting motherhood and domesticity."[45]

Part of the "imperial imperatives" of colonial women was the upholding of European middle-class morality and the concomitant stress upon the cultivation of hygienic and economic domestic science, cleanliness, and moral upbringing. Although the focus on women's domestic and maternal roles, and particularly child rearing, was linked to metropole concerns of national welfare, the colonial situation initiated highly specific issues regarding motherhood and reproduction, such as anxieties about racial purity, degeneracy, sterility, and enervation in the colonies.[46]

Metropole discourses, then, cast motherhood as an imperial imperative, essential for the preservation of national and cultural ascendancy. Proper child rearing thus became a point of condensation for a series of discourses on nationhood, race, culture, and civility. Within the Egyptian colonial setting, untutored "ignorant" mothers were problematized, and motherhood was posited as a locus of national backwardness, in contrast to the scientificity of European methods of child rearing. In the context of colonialism, among both colonized and colonizing nations, mothers were positioned as repositories of national identity, as well as markers of national progress or backwardness.

I turn now to a more detailed discussion of the prescriptive literature on child rearing in order to demonstrate how it was recast as a rational and scientific practice of women essential for modernity. Such scientific specifications, in both the metropole and the colony, entailed an idealization of middle-class norms. Further, in the case of Egypt, these discussions often set up explicit contrasts between local and foreign child-rearing practices, in order to provide a critique of "traditional" Egyptian pedagogy. The similarities between Egyptian and British metropolitan nationalist discourse both on the importance of mothering for the nation and on maternal ignorance are truly striking.

SCIENTIFIC CHILD REARING

How exactly were Egyptian women to become suitable "mothers of the future"? Baron has addressed the new discourses of domesticity[47] and child rearing that arose at the turn of the century.[48] Pointing to the tendency in the medieval literature to address issues of child rearing and the proper moral and religious training of children to the father, a point elaborated by Najmabadi in this volume (chapter 3), Baron notes the shift in the late nineteenth century "in focus and audience from the father to the mother as the central figure in shaping the child . . . [and as] a critical influence on the child's early life."[49] A proliferation of pedagogical-didactic treatises and articles appeared, discussing aspects of mothering ranging from proper health care for pregnant women to the importance of breast-feeding and the denigration of wet nurses.[50] Perhaps more significant, "[t]he importance of the endeavor [motherhood] was the theme taken up by the new tarbiya literature, which instructed women on raising and socializing their children. . . . Taken together the literature argued that child raising was no longer a job to be delegated to servants or relatives.

Mothers were directed to spend more time with their children, closely super-vising their health and development."[51] Indeed, in *The New Woman*, Qasim Amin points explicitly to his omission of "the father's role in bringing up children. This is not an oversight but a recognition of the fact that the central figure in this activity is the mother."[52]

The specificity of this period's prescriptive literature, in both metropole and colony, marks the era as one concerned with the demarcation and constitution of autonomous spheres of domesticity, child rearing, and schooling, as well as the intensive pedagogy and instruction felt necessary for the construction of those spheres along the axes of modernity. That is to say, the discourses of domesticity and child rearing required a series of discursive practices that con-structed them as such, as well as a problematization that defined them in their present state as inefficient, irrational, and unproductive, and hence impedi-ments to national progress. The emphasis on proper scientific and rational mothering was thus positioned in terms of the progress of the nation, conceptu-alized in terms of the health, wealth, and vitality of the population.[53] Through proper mothering, women could be integrated into the "fabric of the nation" in the most productive manner possible.

Most relevant to our discussion is the privileging of the child and the medi-calization of the family, as Michel Foucault has discussed, as a result of which the correct management of childhood became a nodal point in eighteenth-century Europe. The family emerged as "a dense, saturated, permanent contin-uous physical environment which envelops, maintains and develops the child's body." The nexus of obligations—and Foucault here confines his dis-cussion to obligations of a physical kind (e.g., hygiene)—came to bind parents and children alike, turning the family into a "localized pedagogical apparatus," an agent of medicalization focused on the health of children. "The healthy, clean, fit body, [and] a purified, cleansed, aerated domestic space" figure prom-inently in the formation of the modern family.[54] We will have reason later to question Foucault's emphasis upon the disciplinization of the family as an individualizing (rather than, say, communal) technology of selfhood.

In nineteenth-century Europe, as the call for proper "mothers of the next generation" was being made, a didactic discourse emerged directed toward the working classes. The problem of childbearing and childrearing was localized and attributed to the "ignorance" of working-class mothers, who were faulted for their inability to teach children disciplined habits. Such maternal ignorance was often blamed for faulty hygiene and neglect of children as discussions of infant mortality and child welfare gained popularity, and justified reforms such as physical education, feeding schoolchildren, and providing food, clean milk, hygiene, and cookery classes for girls and mothers.[55]

Education and pedagogy for working-class mothers sought to address this maternal ignorance in nutrition, diet, and sanitation through lectures, pam-phlets, manuals, infant consultations, health visitors, and ladies' sanitary associations.[56] These associations helped set a middle-class standard of hygiene. Schools were often crucial to the attempt to transform working-class life by instilling an ideology of domesticity and the habits of discipline.[57] These forms of pedagogy helped disseminate a middle-class ideal of motherhood and domesticity as a national duty. They constructed divergences from the domestic ideal of middle-class family life as moral and psychological deficiencies, thereby serving as an eraser of class markers.[58] The overriding importance of motherhood and the consolidation of the bourgeois family and form, with mother as child-rearer and home-keeper, thus linked the health and wealth of the nation and intersected with the maintenance of empire and the changing conditions of production under industrial capitalism.[59]

The elaboration of this new conception of child rearing, conceived now as a full-time occupation of mothers, along with the perception of childhood as a critical stage of life requiring its own norms and practices, marks an important moment in the consolidation of a bourgeois domestic sphere in Egypt. To constitute the Egyptian family as modern would require both its rationalization and disciplinization. Juan Cole has discussed feminism in turn-of-the-century Egypt as reflective of indigenous transformations related to the differential impact of Egypt's integration into the world market on the upper-middle and lower-middle classes.[60] He argues that feminism was more ideologically suited to the needs of the upper-middle classes, as it served to bolster the transition from the lavish aristocratic lifestyle of the Turco-Circassian elite to the more rationalized ideal of the European bourgeoisie—an ideal fit for the new agrarian capitalist class.

For our purposes, Cole's elaboration of the very class-specific nature of feminism in Egypt is key. It points to the extent to which an idealized bourgeois private sphere related to class-specific concerns (e.g., seclusion, veiling, child rearing by nannies rather than mothers), reflected attitudes toward European values, and addressed the new role of the Ottoman-Egyptian elite at the turn of the century. Amin himself, it should be recalled, situated his reforms as applicable to the upper classes, as rural and lower-class women did not have the same restrictions.[61]

Discursive practices parallel to those in Europe surrounding motherhood were widespread among the Egyptian upper and middle classes within the colonial setting. For instance, faulting what he perceives as an "exaggerated" belief in fate as preordaining both virtue and corruption, Qasim Amin points to the interaction between heredity and environment, especially the stimulation of the senses that shape the child's disposition.[62] Amin targets the same image as was dwelt on by colonial administrators and travelers: ignorant, superstitious mothers, unaware of the proper rules of hygiene, who will be unable to mold children properly. These themes recur in the prescriptive literature on child rearing I discuss below. A child's upbringing, we are told, hinges upon a mother's ability to imbue a child's personality with good qualities.

Ignorant mothers, on the other hand, simply allow their children to do whatever they please and to observe immoral actions that may lead to corrupt habits; they neglect their children's cleanliness, encourage them to be lazy, and raise them to have superstitious beliefs in charms, evil spirits, and *jinn*.[63] It is precisely Egyptian mothers' refusal to shape their children's personality according to proper conceptions of what is hygienic, moral, and industrious that Amin is critiquing.

As we have seen, then, with Qasim Amin, the criticism leveled against Egyptian mothers related both to their ignorance of the rules of health, hygiene, and *adab* and to their pernicious inculcation of superstitious beliefs in the minds of their children. Shibli Shumayyil similarly encodes the cultural evolution of nations through a social Darwinian discussion of mothering, echoing many of the complaints that Amin had articulated.

> Mothers are the first and foremost factor to influence children, and their influence is far greater than that of the father. . . . What the child learns from the mother in the way of natural inclinations, habits, manners, and rational thought is most influential, and nothing thereafter exceeds its influence regardless of its strength. Imagine, then, a mother who does not know the rules of hygiene or manners (*adab*) . . . , is ignorant of science, and knows nothing but superstitions and common sayings that corrupt her mind. She might, for example, leave her child dirty to avert the evil eye, or teach her children to fear . . . ghouls and spirits! After she nurtures him with this milk of ignorance, she then leaves him with a wet nurse, who does not favor the child or treat him kindly in any way. . . . Can you imagine the state of this poor child's health, morals, and mind? Imagine the difference when this child meets another whose mother is in the vanguard in terms of what develops her mind, is polite and familiar with all the rules of proper, scientific manners (*adab*), and whose nobility derives from her simplicity in life, her *tarbiya*, and her cleanliness. She does not have superstitious beliefs that she plants in her child's head until his ideas are corrupt; rather, her *tarbiya* leaves his reason free and unfettered by ignorance and superstition. She cares for his health, his bodily cleanliness, his clothing, food, and drink, and allows for sufficient air in his room. Judging between these two children will be as easy as judging between the two mothers, and this difference is further evidenced in differences between nations. Thus will we find there are differences between the children of various nations, by which the civilized nations emerge victorious.[64]

Shumayyil's discussion of mothering not only encodes a logic of progress and civilization but also serves to localize the development of nations within a domestic space. The home in general, and mothers in particular, are demarcated as the locus of social disorder—expressed as ignorance, superstition, immorality, or lack of hygiene.

A final example is provided by Saleh Effendi Hamdi Hammad in an excerpt taken from his book *For the Sake of Life* (*Fi sabil al-hayat*) and reprinted in

Al-Hilal in 1907.[65] In the piece, entitled "Proper Child Rearing," he distinguishes among three types of *tarbiya* that correlate with three phases of life and socialization.[66] His typology illustrates the compartmentalization that modern socialization was thought to need in order to be effective:

> [N]atural or physical *tarbiya* (*al-tarbiya al-taba'iyya*): this is the *tarbiya* of bodies with a view to all the necessary health measures encompassing proper food and drink, clothing, rest, and physical exercise, because the strength of the body is one of the most important ways to develop and strengthen the mental faculties and to spiritualize the self. . . . The second type is mental or rational *tarbiya* (*al-tarbiya al-'aqliyya*), which entails the use of science and information in order to develop the mental faculties; this is usually acquired in schools and libraries, although it benefits greatly from the proper environment. . . . The third type of *tarbiya* is moral *tarbiya* (*al-tarbiya al-adabiyya*) . . . if a person's actions are not built on the principles and components of morality . . . then it follows that we will not find these righteous characteristics in him and that he will increase in evil and will be a negative force in society.[67]

These three "schools" of *tarbiya*, as Hammad refers to them, have three corollaries in the child's phases of socialization: the family in which the child is brought up, the school in which the child learns the necessary principles of science and knowledge, and the society in which he lives.

Representations of backward mothers and unhealthy children served to prop up a bourgeois ideal of motherhood and rationalize a series of pedagogical and philanthropic interventions that placed women and children within a nexus of regulatory and supervisory controls. Such controls, however, were never purely repressive. Rather, they functioned as positive injunctions defining what a good Egyptian mother should be—if she were to care for the health and welfare of her children and, by extension, the nation.

SCHOOLED MOTHERS AND STRUCTURED PLAY

As stated earlier, nineteenth-century Europe was the site of a series of reform movements that sought to isolate and problematize the care children were receiving and provide them with more "stimulating environments." Foremost among these movements was the kindergarten and day-care movement in imperial Germany. Articles in *Al-Hilal* and *Al-Muqtataf* often described the European kindergarten movements as models to be emulated. Both journals usually carried columns giving practical advice and tips for mothers and housewives on child rearing and household management.[68] Many of the pieces discussed developments in these fields in other contexts, primarily Anglo-American and European. For instance, two published in the November 1903 issue of *Al-Hilal* dealt with the importance of kindergartens or some form of structured play for children.[69] One of the articles described the German kindergarten movement, as developed by Froebel. Pointing to Froebel's discovery that the development and health of plants was most influenced by their early stages of care, and to his later application of the principle to humans, the author is careful to show the earlier European origins of the idea. From Pestalozzi in the late eighteenth century onward, with the development of "play schools" or "schools for infants," we are told, the importance of mothers' proper upbringing of children in their first years of life was acknowledged, and particularly the inadequate care that poor mothers provided for their children.[70] Froebel's project, the article continues, differed from these earlier movements in that

> its purpose is to raise children such that they are acclimated to physical, mental, and moral work in this world, without exposing their health or mind to any harm. In his observation and monitoring of children's nature, Froebel noticed that physical activity is of the utmost importance, followed by mental activity, as may be seen in a comparison between an unresponsive child and a child who actively responds to and engages with his environment. . . . What we may conclude from all of this is that children must be trained in whatever cultivates their talents and refines their morals but does not tax their minds or tire their bodies. This is why Froebel developed lessons on the principles of play and music in which children may be comfortable and be educated from the ages of two to six. . . . It did not take long for the results of these schools to be visible and to popularize themselves all over Europe and the United States, and there can be no doubt that [this movement] has greatly affected the bodies and minds of [these nations'] people.[71]

The articles highlight the European origins of play schools or schools for infants and, more important, try to show the connection between the exercizing of children's bodies and minds and the development or advancement of European nations.

This last point is forcefully made in a March 1913 piece in *Al-Muqtataf* entitled "Child Rearing." The article begins with a discussion of infant mortality. "Every child's death," we are told, "deprives the nation of a man or woman in the future." After acknowledging the infant's particular susceptibility to illness, the article asserts that more than half of all infant deaths may be attributed to "the ignorance and negligence of mothers."[72] Citing European progress in reducing infant mortality, the article refers specifically to the decreased rate of infant death in Paris following the recent opening of institutes for the instruction of mothers (*ma'ahid li-irshad al-ummahat*) in the proper sanitation, hygiene, and nutrition of infants. Supervised by doctors and run by nannies, the schools required mothers to come once a week to hear lectures and advice to mothers on proper child rearing, and they supervised and carefully monitored the progress of children (weight, general health, cleanliness). The two factors considered most important in child care were cleanliness and sanitation. Mothers were advised to bathe their children daily in the morning, and with respect to nutrition the doctor would specify the type and amount of food mothers should give their children. After diatribes against swaddling and artificial feeding, the article ends with some basics of child care: "a child must be exposed to light and air, and must be assigned specific times for feeding, sleeping, and bathing every day. His cleanliness must be cared for as well as everything he eats or comes in contact with. He must be allowed space for movement, in order for his body to develop properly."[73]

TOWARD AN ETHIC OF ECONOMY

One of the trends in the *tarbiya* literature was to encourage mothers to care for their own children, thus consolidating and maintaining both class and cultural divisions. Servants were often vilified as corrupting morals with their ignorance and bad character and indeed even destroying the possibility of building noble character traits in children, a discourse that widened the gap between children raised by nannies and those raised by their mothers.[74]

Similar discourses emerged that called into question both the lower classes' ability to care for children, owing to harsh environments, and the extravagance of the upper classes, who produced indolent, slovenly, and unproductive children unaware of the importance of an ethic of economy or labor. Both types of argument attempted to inculcate an ethic of rational child rearing, guided by industry and economy. In a 1905 piece entitled "The Woman and Household Chores," the editor cites an article published in a nineteenth-century American magazine in which the author discusses the degradation of women and their children's health. The quotations selected are indicative of contemporary anxieties perceived to be plaguing the upper-class Egyptian household:

> [S]he stated, "there is no cure for this deterioration except for avoiding the dangers that threaten the nation by teaching women household chores. Just as our ancestors taught their women, so must we teach them cooking and baking and train them to raise their children and to pay attention to household care and management," and then she described the wealthy woman and said, "How can the [wealthy] woman who is concerned only with extravagance and beautification properly raise her children, when she is distracted from them by taking care of herself, and she simply hands them over to nannies, because she considers nothing but herself important?" And much of that statement is applicable to us.[75]

The focus on upper-class women's ability to participate in domestic management and to raise their children properly had become a contentious issue.

Labiba Hashim, discussed in more detail below, was also quick to fault the wealthy for leaving the care of their children to servants, warning that they would not be able to create men and women of the future. Excess lavishness, she argued in her 1911 lectures, lead to the cultivation of selfishness, slovenliness, and laziness. She continued, "When parents know how to . . . instill the proper attitudes and tendencies toward work, economy, uprightness, and modesty, they will find their children one day serious men who will work toward the betterment of themselves and humanity and be loyal to the nation, and well-mannered cultured women who will be able to raise their children according to the proper rules of *adab* and be proud of them."[76] Industry and economy were perceived as among the most important habits to inculcate for all classes. In a 1903 piece giving "advice to the children of the wealthy," the author, Ahmed Hafez, warns against the phenomenon of

> wealthy children who detest work and consider humans created for food, drink, and the enjoyment of the pleasures of the body. . . . They are in grave error and have exposed themselves to the dangers of the self (*nafs*). . . . Their parents have also endangered their wealth, for if they die and leave the wealth that they have created, with great effort, to their sons who do not understand the meaning of earning, they will surely squander all that their parents have worked for. If they do lose their wealth, it would have been better had they been born poor, for the poor at least have their strength and health, which is the capital of the poor. . . . The only solution, then, is to provide them with knowledge and develop their rational faculties, which would fortify their future. Knowledge . . . is the only true inheritance; money is only a supplement. . . . Isn't the wise thing for parents to do, then, to teach and train their children, for money will be useless if the child cannot use it wisely. Indeed, an ignorant wealthy person would be better off had he been born poor. If, however, the wealthy child is left with wealth and developed reason, he will be a most useful person.[77]

Similarly, a 1908 entry under the rubric of "Household Management," a column that appeared regularly in *Al-Muqtataf*, entitled "Child Rearing according to the Principle of Economy," attempts to communicate the importance of raising children with an ethic of economy:

> [I]f you compare the differences among people in terms of their industry and economy, you will find that [this aspect of character] harks back to whether they were raised with an ethic of economy in their childhood. Those raised on economy, even if their parents are wealthy, will know the value of money and will not waste it, and will understand the value of time, health, and labor. . . . Those raised on improvidence, even if their parents are poor, or who do not know the value of time, health, and labor, will live an idle and indolent life and will leave this world without having made any impact.[78]

The article then continues to emphasize the necessity of teaching children, especially of the wealthy, the value of labor and the necessity of *tarbiya* and education regardless of individual or familial wealth. America is held up as an example of a country in which emphasis is placed upon teaching children the value of labor, and an anecdotal illustration is given about teaching children the value of money and of saving through a system of chores in the home performed in exchange for small wages. This applies equally for boys and girls since "the girl who is taught to help her mother in the home will be a judicious wife able to run her household." But "the most important principles to inculcate in children are industry and economy."[79]

Educating mothers in scientific child rearing and the importance of an ethic of economy was part and parcel of the nineteenth-century transformation of *tarbiya*. This entailed the modernist demarcation of the "public" and the "private" into separate spheres and related to new conceptions of the space of the household, as separate from politics, economy, and statecraft. Women, now conceived of as "mothers of the future," were integral to the construction of the home as a rationalized space of order and cleanliness now referred to as *tadbir al-manzil*. At the same time, proper child rearing was inserted into a larger framework of modern education and schooling.

Child rearing came to be understood as a public responsibility, essential for the constitution of morally upright, productive, efficient citizens of the nation. The demands of "this world" necessitated the creation and cultivation of new types of children "acclimated to physical, mental, and moral work" and imbued with an ethic of industry and economy. The home was meant to provide the groundwork for a national future by preparing children for citizenship and, ultimately, the nation for modernity.

THE IGNORANCE OF MOTHERS

In what follows I would like to juxtapose two sets of discussions on child rearing in order to illustrate the extent to which feminist authors in the liberal-secular press and the Islamist press shared a common set of assumptions about the nature of mothering, child rearing, the progress of the nation, and the backwardness of the Egyptians. Despite the very real differences in these discoures, I want to highlight the extent to which women were similarly localized as a sphere of backwardness and defined as individuals who *were* to be uplifted. Nevertheless, the two sets of discussions differed substantively regarding the manner in which this uplifting should be done and the impetus behind the reform of the family in the first place.[80]

After discussing a series of lectures given by Labiba Hashim at the Egyptian University in 1911, I will turn to the writings of Malak Hifni Nassif. I do this not with the intent of effacing the important differences between writers such as Nassif who explicitly situate their reforms within an Islamic discursive tradition, and others who do not, a point to which I return later. Rather, it is to illustrate how a fundamental shift occurred at the turn of the century that affected a wide range of thinkers.

Labiba Hashim, a Syrian editor and writer who migrated to Egypt at the turn of the century, was a prominent member of the women's press and edited the journal *Young Woman of the East* (*Fatat al-sharq*) from 1906 to 1939. A member of the Women's Educational Alliance, she was active in both women's and educational reform.[81] Hashim begins her lectures on child rearing, published later as *Kitab fi al-tarbiya*, by emphasizing the importance of proper child rearing for the country, as this is the principle manner in which useful and contributing members of society are produced. Nevertheless, she faults contemporary mothers for doing little to facilitate this process, despite the best of intentions and personal character traits.

> [Good intentions and character traits] are not enough for knowing how to care for the health of our children and the stimulation of their minds. *Tarbiya* is a wide field of knowledge, and it is not adequate for child-rearers to be of sound constitution and morals; they must learn the knowledge necessary for the proper upbringing of children until they earn the right to care for children who will be the men and women of the future.[82]

Unfortunately, according to Hashim, the difficulty of learning the science of *tarbiya* had led many men and women to simply leave the task of child rearing to governesses or teachers, in contrast to the response of Europeans and Americans of the era who "treat it [child rearing] as more than a science, and so their nations have advanced and their peoples progressed astonishingly while we still remain ignorant of the rules of *tarbiya* . . . and we do not teach parents how to raise their children."[83]

Hashim praises recent attempts in Egypt to reform schools but states that this in no way absolves parents, especially mothers, of the responsibilities of child rearing. Iterating the contemporary theme that the early years of childhood are the most essential for the development of the intellect, she states,

> The mother is more essential to the proper development of the child, and *tarbiya* is mostly in her hands. There is no doubt that the early years are those in which the child's reason is formed and in which he is most susceptible to habituation and external influences. It is therefore a grave oppression for a mother to be ignorant of the rules of *tarbiya* since she will raise her child according to whatever is in her mind of corrupt principles and ill beliefs, which will be impossible to remove later.[84]

In a rhetorical trope quite common to the *tarbiya* literature, and seen above in Qasim Amin, Hashim asks us to imagine a child whose mother is steeped in ignorance and engages in all types of superstitious practices, forcing her child to wear amulets and leaving him dirty to avert the evil eye. This child, we are told, will remain unaffected by the entire process of schooling. And even if the child is from a wealthy family, "he will be no better than ignorant illiterates or lowly vagrants."[85]

The central problem of Egypt, then, according to Hashim, is the "ignorance of mothers of the principles of hygiene." Hashim even cites studies on the rate of infant death (Egypt's is among the highest) and explains that infant mortality may be correlated with the backwardness of a nation.[86] Mothers, whether ignorant or educated, are ignorant of the process of child rearing and know nothing of the rules of health, hygiene, and manners. Thus she states, "This is what called me to *tarbiya* as a topic of research, in order that we [may] find ways to improve *tarbiya* by teaching girls in schools the rules of health, hygiene, and *adab* in preparation for the day that they will become mothers, and in order for them to recognize their duties as parents. In this way our society may advance and reform itself through a generalization of proper *tarbiya*."[87] "*Tarbiya*," Hashim explains, "is a science that entails the inculcation of the good virtues in the child and the removal of evil germs." It is a two-pronged process of physical *tarbiya* (*tarbiya badaniyya*) and the training of the child's disposition (*tahdhib al-ʿaqida*), in contrast to the common pattern in which children of the fellahin and those of the intelligentsia are raised to develop only one of the two principles.[88] Hashim's emphasis on the unitary nature of *tarbiya* for all classes, and the equal implication of the upper classes and fellahin alike in ignorant child rearing practices, highlights the extent to which the ideology of motherhood being promulgated entailed its embourgeoisement.

Malak Hifni Nassif, or "Searcher in the Desert" (Bahithat al-Badiya) as she was then known, was quite concerned in both her lectures and her articles with the reform of *tarbiya* and education. Nassif, who graduated from Saniyya Teacher Training College, was active as a teacher, writer, and lecturer. Many of her articles appeared in *Al-Jarida*, the newspaper of the nationalist *Umma* party during the first and second decades of the twentieth century.[89] Strident in her critique of both current child rearing practices in the home and contemporary schooling for girls, she advocated the dual reform of the home and female education. For Nassif, girls who were not offered the opportunity of schooling were unjustly deprived, but at the same time schools could not be deemed solely responsible for the "retrogression of females," as the mere fact of sending girls to school was insufficient for the process of *tarbiya*. In fact, she feared that many of the benefits, like orderliness, that would be obtained from the education of girls and could be usefully applied to the home, would be corrupted by a poor home environment. This was especially the fault of "ignorant" mothers. Nassif recounts a story told to her by a schoolmistress regarding the "filthiness" of her female students. She uses this as a paradigmatic example of the "vast difference" between the English mother and her Egyptian counterpart with respect to their knowledge of the rules of *tarbiya*.[90]

In a lecture in which she discussed the importance of female education and work outside the home, Nassif clearly points out the ill effects of female ignorance. "We know that the deficiencies of our primary *tarbiya* and that of our young peers is no doubt related to the ignorance of our mothers. . . . and the home will have its own specific impact regardless of the effort expended by schools on educating and disciplining (*tahdhib*) minds and morals."[91] She saw *tarbiya* and education as inextricably linked, faulting those who would wish to separate the two. Further, it was not knowledge that ruined the morals of girls, but faulty or insufficient *tarbiya* (*al-tarbiya al-naqisa*). "The home is the edifice upon which *tarbiya* should be built, and if homes are not appropriate for the improvement of the *tarbiya* of our children, then we should work for their reform." Nassif argued that it would be simply wrong to blame schools, for though they have an influence upon *tarbiya*, the flaw is in the family (*al-ʿayb fi al-usra*).[92]

How did Nassif view the purpose of the *tarbiya* of girls generally, and Egyptians in particular? Proper *tarbiya* should aim to make women useful members of the body politic and should prepare them for their roles as wives and mothers. It is clear that the form of female education she was advocating related to the practicalities of what were perceived as gendered differences in nature, tasks, and futures. For instance, girls needed to be educated sentimentally, to pity the poor and less fortunate; they also needed to be physically trained in order not to succumb to any of the illnesses currently afflicting educated girls (poor sight, infertility, and the like). Nassif found the problem of poor physical health among educated girls particularly troubling, as it endangered their reproductive capacities as well as the health of the new generation. A decrease in births among the educated would be especially harmful, as it would negate any possible future benefit accrued from mothers who knew the rules of hygiene, whose children would inevitably be better cared for in health and manners. Girls also needed to be educated practically in the skills of household management, and Nassif suggests the incorporation of a practical household training component into their education.[93]

Nassif was often solicited for advice to women about improving or uplifting themselves. She recommended such innovations as compulsory primary education for all classes of girls; opening schools for girls at the primary and secondary level; teaching religion in girls' schools; having at least one Egyptian woman overseer in each girls' school, her task being to supervise the morals of girls and, in particular, their adherence to the fundamentals of religion.[94] Unlike Hashim, however, Nassif was concerned primarily with the inculcation of the proper moral and religious virtues in schoolgirls. Thus her specific proposals for topics of instruction included the following: teaching girls proper religion, that is, Qur'an and sunna; teaching household management at both the practical and the intellectual levels; and teaching hygiene. Further reforms proposed were to expand schools for female nurses; to establish dispensaries and hospitals in every district, with medical lectures for the sick; and to teach mothers about their own and their children's well-being and cleanliness, especially in light of mothers' ignorance of the rules of hygiene. Teaching Egyptian women practical arts such as sewing, embroidery, and the principles of child rearing also lay at the root of Nassif's reforms—reforms that would free them from reliance on foreign women.[95]

In a lecture in which she compares Western and Egyptian women, Nassif expounds on this last point more explicitly, going through all the phases of womanhood from the moment when the female child is born, to infancy, then adolescence, and marriage (including household economics and management, morals, and customs), and finally the role of motherhood. In comparison to their Western counterparts, Nassif finds Egyptian women sorely lacking in the ability to care for their own children. Whereas Western women nurse and clean their own children, in Egypt the upper classes consider breast-feeding a shame and hire nursemaids and servants. Egyptian mothers are also negligent about their children's health. Indeed, she argues, "there is the greatest difference between our pallid-colored rude-tongued child and the healthy-bodied and well-raised (*muhadhib bi'l-tarbiya*) Western child. There is nothing lovelier than to see him in the mornings and evenings greet his parents or excuse himself or thank someone." Western children, we are told, learn to please their parents and are never beaten. Egyptians, however, have two equally pernicious methods of *tarbiya*: either a rigorous and harsh discipline or a lax pampering. Further, Nassif compares Western and Egyptian children in terms of their exposure to natural sites and the "special equipment" used to facilitate their development and structure their play. Simply put, "Western women have advanced stages beyond us in both their knowledge and their work, even though we are no less intelligent than they."[96]

In a review of *Al-Nisa'iyyat*, a collection of articles published by Nassif in *Al-Jarida*, Rashid Rida takes the opportunity to emphasize the importance of educational reform in Egypt, especially in light of changing social conditions, but is careful to point out and critique the increased Westernization of education. Taking other male writers on "the women's question" as a point of contrast to Nassif, he praises her writings on women for avoiding two pitfalls—excessive theoreticism and slavish imitation of foreigners. The strength of Nassif's approach, rather, lay in its foundation in religion and practical experience and its concern for the benefit of the Egyptian woman.[97]

Nassif's mobilization of Western women and mothers in her critique of Egyptian child-rearing practices functioned within a complex set of assumptions about the backwardness of Egypt—in particular, as it related to the education and advancement of its women. This is not at all to imply that Nassif ever advocated wholesale Westernizing reforms or even that her reformist impulse was rooted solely in a comparative vein rather than in an indigenous tradition of Islamic reform or critique. Rather, it is simply to highlight what Partha Chatterjee has explicated in terms of the double bind in which anticolonial nationalist thought finds itself. Nationalist discourse, to constitute itself as nationalist, must "demonstrate the falsity of the colonial claim that the backward peoples were culturally incapable of ruling themselves in the conditions of the modern world. Nationalism denied the alleged inferiority of the colonized people; it also asserted that a backward nation could 'modernize' itself while retaining its cultural identity. It thus produced a discourse in which, even as it challenged the colonial claim to political domination, it also accepted the very intellectual premises of 'modernity' [i.e., the theoretical framework of post-Enlightenment rational thought] on which colonial domination was based."[98]

THE REASONS FOR OUR BACKWARDNESS

Are we to conclude from the preceding discussion that nationalist discourses on motherhood were merely derivative of colonial or European discourses? As Dipesh Chakrabarty has argued, the creation of a domestic sphere in colonial Bengal confronted resistances that refused to align along the bourgeois public-private axis. Pointing to other configurations of self and community, he elucidates the construction of bourgeois domesticity in colonial Bengal as hinged upon two fundamental strategies of exclusion: the rejection of companionate marriage (denial of the bourgeois private) and of the secular historical construction of time by an invocation of collective memory (denial of historical time). Both were linked to an explicit rejection and reformulation of the Western rhetoric and teleology of freedom. Chakrabarty is careful to assert that this is not to be interpreted as yet another example of India's incomplete, failed, or inadequate transition to modernity. Rather, it should be understood as a voice of ambivalence.[99]

Indeed, much the same could be said of the Egyptian setting, where the formulation of a modern "private" sphere was articulated in tandem with an explicitly nonsecular conception of proper pedagogy. Even Westernized modernizing reformers like Qasim Amin or the turn-of-the-century feminists, such as Huda Sha'rawi and Malak Hifni Nassif, situated their own projects as a defense of Islam and a critique of *taqlid*.[100] Their projects were often conceptualized as an illustration that "true Islam"—that is, Islam unadulterated by "traditional" accretions, such as superstitious practices—was entirely compatible with modernity. Thus they were engaged in a complex dialogue with colonial discourse, which had posited Islam as the locus classicus for both the backwardness of the nation and the subordination and oppression of its women. The articulation, then, of an anticolonial nationalist modernity with colonial discourse, as Chatterjee has argued, lay within the same discursive field.

The case of child rearing is instructive. Virtually all the educational reformers used the West as a form of contrast to "our backwardness." Such an internalization of notions of backwardness implied along with it the adaptation of a unilinear, progressive, and secular concept of historical time. How did these reformers seek to explain Egypt's backwardness within this teleological framework? For the colonized intelligentsia the concept of the potential educability of backward peoples, rather than an innate inferiority, served as a point of entry into progressivist debates. Education, then, formed a nodal point around which a series of reformist polemics were framed. In particular, it was women's inadequate education and the lack of a proper science of *tarbiya* that were targeted as impediments to national progress. Mothers were deemed "ignorant" of the principles of modern child care, and explicit contrasts were set up against a scientific European pedagogy, both to explicate the "reasons for our backwardness" and to point the way to a modern postcolonial nationalist future. Indigenous modernizing reformers, women's philanthropic and feminist organizations, and colonial administrators were all implicated in this project.

Qasim Amin, for instance, attributed great importance to the role of mothers in *tarbiya* and was quite critical of what he perceived to be Egyptian society's neglect of women's role in child rearing and its "animalistic" emphasis on childbearing. For Amin, the backwardness of Egypt was in large part attributable to the inadequate attention paid to *tarbiya*. He states,

> I believe that the time has come to base our upbringing on correct, sound scientific principles. We should aim for an upbringing that produces superior men with sound judgement and knowledge. They should be able to combine education, good manners, knowledge and work. It should be an upbringing that can rescue us from the shortcomings that foreigners hurl at us everyday, in every tongue. All these short-comings . . . are products of one phenomenon—our inadequate process of upbringing. All Egyptians involved in the formulation of various theories believe that a proper upbringing is the only medicine for this disease. This pertinent viewpoint is widespread, found in books, newspapers and at discussions held at social and intellectual gatherings. It is even accurate to state that this viewpoint has become popular opinion. It has produced the shared feeling among people that the country's future depends upon its methods of upbringing.[101]

An anonymous article, printed in *Al-Hilal* shortly after the publication of Amin's book, entitled "The Nation Is the Fabric of Its Mothers and Thus We Must Educate Girls," attempts to argue along similar lines:

> Those who have studied the reasons for the backwardness of our country have found ignorance to be the primary cause and have encouraged the generalization of knowledge, but have limited their discussion to boys, whereas women should be the primary concern since they are the foundation for society and no society whose mothers are ignorant and know only their room, home, and family will ever succeed. . . . How can we entrust to women in such a state [of backwardness] the upbringing of our children, the men of the future? Children are constituted as their mothers wish, and if we do not raise the level of mothers, we will not raise the level of children, unless we cultivate them [mothers] with proper knowledge.[102]

Saleh Effendi Hamdi Hammad, quoted earlier, echoed many of the themes found in Qasim Amin. Here, the degenerate household was posited as the locus of ignorance and the reason for the immaturity of Egyptian civilization. In his 1907 piece entitled "Proper Child Rearing" he asserts,

> If we look closely and critically at our national condition and the organization of our affairs in order to determine the degree to which these necessary principles have been applied, and hence our level of civilization, we will find that we have not achieved a state of maturity and advancement with respect to the principles of *tarbiya*. . . . The *tarbiya* in the household and family is in a degenerate state. Unfortunately, in our part of the world concern and care for the health of children and their proper *tarbiya* is nonexistent among mothers and fathers. Both are immersed in ignorance; they do not care for the proper feeding, cleanliness, health, and morals of their children. . . . We deny them [children] the right to a proper *tarbiya* and, therefore, ourselves and our society the right to the men of tomorrow and the mothers of the future.[103]

Despite the seeming consensus indicated by the quotations selected above, there remained important differences between the Westernizing reforms advocated by someone such as Qasim Amin and the suggestions made by the contributors to *Al-Manar* I discuss below. Within the terms of the debate used by Islamists, a clear distinction was to be made between modernity, or modernization, and Westernization. Arguing from within an Islamic discursive tradition, they presented moral and religious pedagogy geared toward the inculcation of virtues and bodily dispositions as an integral part of the process of *tarbiya*. Further, the overarching framework within which the disciplinization of the child's body and the rationalization of the home were to occur was a *communal* conception of this-worldly, rightly guided ethical being. Finally, Islamists subscribed to a nonsecular concept of historical time—framing reform (*islah*) as a project of renewal (*tajdid*) in the face of the decline and digression of the Muslim world from the true path of Islam. I turn now to a discussion of the journal *Al-Manar* and its views on the reform of *tarbiya*, with its explicit critique of Westernization, as articulated in the first decade of the twentieth century.

AL-MANAR AND THE CRITIQUE OF WESTERN CIVILIZATION[104]

In a 1911 conference devoted to developing an agenda for educational reform (*islah al-tarbiya wa al-taʿlim*), many of the usual concerns found in the journal *Al-Manar* were expressed in the form of programmatic statements. Among the reforms called for were religious instruction in schools, compulsory primary education, the inclusion in curricula of several practical forms of knowledge (agriculture, mechanical engineering, and the like), the publication of a book, or compendium, of morals ("comprehensible enough for the masses"), evening literacy classes, and village education. Bahithat al-Badiya, who also attended the conference, suggested reforms similar to those mentioned above. These included expanding schools for nurses, teaching women medicine, and establishing girl's schools, with instruction in sewing, embroidery, general household management, and child rearing.[105]

This programmatic agenda highlights several features that characterized the reformist impulse of the journal. I want to focus on the intense dissatisfaction expressed with current educational and child rearing practices. This was framed in terms of a desire to place Egypt solidly on a trajectory of progress (conceptualized in terms of an Egyptian backwardness in contradistinction to an advanced European path of modernity), and, more important, in terms of a specifically Islamic conception of the reasons for the decline of nations and communities. From the perspective of Albert Hourani, Islamic thinkers such as Jamal al-Din al-Afghani, Muhammad ʿAbduh, and Rashid Rida all begin from the question "Why are Muslim countries backward in every aspect of civilization?" and formulate their religious and secular reforms in accordance with a modernizing and Westernizing impulse. However, there are other ways to view these thinkers.

The *salafiyya* reforms can be seen instead as part of an Islamic discursive tradition and the attempt to formulate an Islamic modern. Talal Asad has defined an Islamic discursive tradition as a "tradition of Muslim discourse that addresses itself to conceptions of the Islamic past and future with reference to an Islamic practice in the present."[106] That is to say, it is a historically constituted and evolving argument about the goods that constitute the tradition, extended both historically through time and geographically through space. It entails modes of argumentation and reasoning internal to the tradition, as well as embodied practices.[107]

Crucial to the concept of Islamic reform is a mode of historical consciousness that includes a conception of the decline (*inhitat*) and reform (*islah*), renewal (*tajdid*), or revivification (*ihya'*) of the moral, religious, and political sciences. John Voll has provided a useful overview of the historical continuity in the themes of *islah* and *tajdid* in Islamic history.[108] At the core of these concepts is a return to the fundamentals of religion (*usul al-din*) and the core texts of the Qur'an and hadith. The concept of *islah* refers to reform but also embodies a conception of rightly guided moral and ethical behavior and aims to increase the righteousness of the *umma*. The concept of *tajdid*, or revival, refers to renewal of the authentic Islamic spirit and also embodies a moral-ethical dimension. These modes of reform, then, need not depend upon a unilinear progressive concept of historical time insofar as their referent is the perfect model existent in revelation. At the same time *tajdid-islah* does not lie outside the realm of historically constituted human experience. Although inspired by the first centuries of Islam, Islamist reformers do not aspire to re-create it. Further, though the standards that inspire *tajdid-islah* are constant, the specific nature of the reforms does reflect historical specificities of time and place.[109]

More specifically, nineteenth-century Islamic reformers drew upon and continued many of the themes of the eighteenth-century Islamic renewal movements.[110] These were characterized by a critique of current orthodoxy and the reformulation of an Islamic intellectual orthodoxy to counteract what was perceived as moral decline. Themes common to the eighteenth-century reform movements that recur in the nineteenth century were the call for a return to the Qur'an and sunna of earlier generations as the basis for Islamic law; a revival of hadith studies (*'ilm al-hadith*); a rejection of *taqlid* (blind imitation of customs and tradition, and especially of the legal schools of thought); a critique of certain forms of popular religion, as well as superstitious or un-Islamic practices; and a reassertion of *ijtihad*, or independent legal interpretation.[111]

Thus the concepts of *tajdid-islah* represent a radical mode of critique indigenous to the Islamic discursive tradition, although the contexts in which they are mobilized and the crises to which they respond are historically specific. For the nineteenth-century Muslim reformers, the crisis was that of colonialism. The nature and context of the reforms and the fact that at the turn of the century the Muslim intelligentsia were responding to colonial allegations of Muslim stagnation are, of course, crucial. The distinction I want to make, however, is between defining the call to reform the state of Muslim society as rooted in a Westernizing impulse and understanding it as a genuine attempt from within the Islamic tradition to formulate an Islamic modernity, within the context of a historically specific and newly constituted constellation of power relations.

Reading through the multitude of articles in *Al-Manar* on the reasons for the rise of European nations and the decline and colonization of the East, one gets the distinct impression that thinkers were attempting to make sense of a nexus of sociopolitical relations of subjugation and domination in which the Arab Muslim East was perceived as backward. But the reasons for that backwardness were related not only to a technological or industrial retrogression but to a *digression* from the true path of Islam. Hence there was a call for a revivification of the core texts and arguments of the Islamic discursive tradition. Although appropriating the concepts of progress and retrogression, Islamists redefined them within the terms of the Islamic tradition, as revival (*tajdid*) and decline (*inhitat*) or digression (*inhiraf*), superimposing a moral dimension onto both. Further, through the reformation of the household, and *tarbiya* in particular, the East could reclaim its glorious past, freed from the constraints of Turkish backwardness and decay, as well as European colonization. Central to this argument was the critique of *taqlid*, or blind imitation, of both indigenous and European customs and mores.

The fact that the reforms proposed are modern should not at all be surprising, unless of course one simplistically bifurcates tradition and modernity. One should see this Islamic modernism, rather, as indicative of the reforms' position of interiority both to the historically constituted Islamic discursive tradition and to the project of modernity. Muhammad ʿAbduh and his disciples' advocacy of Islamic reform in the sphere of education (al-tarbiya wa al-taʿlim), as elsewhere, was not an "invented tradition" of an Islamic modernity that operated as a mere ruse, or a cloak for a modernizing impulse.[112] It must be recognized as rooted in a genuine sense of belonging to a tradition, combined with a desire for a national nonsecular modernity.

Further, as Asad has pointed out, crucial to the Islamic discursive tradition are embodied practices. That is, "prescribed moral-religious capabilities, which involve the cultivation of certain bodily attitudes (including emotions), the disciplined cultivation of habits, aspirations, and desires," and which necessitate correct, apt, and effective performance. They are "practical rules and principles aimed at developing a distinctive set of virtues (articulated by din [religion])."[113] Nineteenth-century Islamist reformers, then, were able to draw upon an indigenous body of thought and writing from within the tradition that specifically addressed proper pedagogy for children; this entailed the cultivation of the body, the disciplining of the self, the formation of moral character, the inculcation of the virtues, and correct conduct—all to be embodied in practice.

Hence the modernist focus on hygiene and the cultivation and disciplinization of the body (tarbiyat al-jasad) was not antithetical to Islamic discourse at the turn of the century but was in fact complementary to it. The larger framework within which the disciplinization of the child's body and the rationalization of the home were to occur, however, was a concept of rightly guided moral and ethical practice, to ensure both the salvation of the child's soul and the upholding of a this-worldly communal norm of ethical being. Thus the conception of the child's self-actualization was understood not in terms of the liberal ideal of the sovereign, autonomous, and self-constituted subject. Rather, actualization—understood as the cultivation of religious sentiments, the inculcation of the moral virtues, and the formation of disciplined souls and bodies—could occur only under the aegis of the collective subject (i.e., the community). The aim of this disciplinization, as well as the product, was to be irreducibly different from that of the West. Instead of self-mastery and freedom, the ideals posited were rightly guided ethical being and ethical knowhow, to be achieved within the Muslim umma.[114]

For the turn-of-the-century Islamists, the techniques of the self to be inculcated in children through a proper religious pedagogy were inconceivable once divorced from communal norms of ethical being.[115] The cultivation of bodies, minds, and selves (tarbiyat al-jasad, al-ʿaql wa al-nafs) was to be undertaken in accordance with the public good and modeled on the religious virtues. The inculcation of the virtues in the self was intended explicitly to serve the renaissance of the umma. European pedagogies that endorsed a cultivation of the self disarticulated from religious instruction, based on science and utilitarian logic alone, were singled out in *Al-Manar* for critique. The entire process of *tarbiya* itself would be rendered nonsensical in the absence of religion as a guiding principle for the cultivation of the virtues. In a 1912 lecture reprinted in *Al-Manar*, the appropriate modular forms that *tarbiya* was to assume were delineated as follows: the *tarbiya* of nations (*tarbiyat al-ummam*), the *tarbiya* of households and mothers (*tarbiyat al-buyut wa al-ummahat*), that of selves by selves (*tarbiyat al-mar' li-nafsu*), the cultivation of the virtues and religious *tarbiya* (*al-fadila wa al-tarbiya al-diniyya*), and the *tarbiya* of the will (*tarbiyat al-irada*).[116]

Questions centered on whether a *tarbiya* could be found that would combine religion and nationalism, and whether this existed in Egyptian schools, in religious, secular, or European pedagogy.[117] The issue of education for girls was particularly sensitive. *Al-Manar* was virulent in its critique of the practice of sending girls to foreign schools run primarily by Europeans. Realizing that this was done partly because of the Egyptian neglect of women's upbringing (*ihmal tarbiyat al-mar'a*), they asked whether girls taught in foreign schools would learn the manners, morals, principles, and forms of worship (*'ibadat*) of their religion. They would not, asserted the critics; rather, they would leave the schools Christianized or Westernized, neither Muslim nor Egyptian, leading to discord in their marital households.[118]

What, then, was the real purpose of female education? To prepare women for household management (*tadbir al-manzil*) and child rearing (*tarbiyat al-awlad*). Which merely rendered moot the question of how foreign schools could provide a solid foundation for the family if they estranged girls from the manners, customs, and morals of their religion and nation. Government schools, too, taught girls along Western lines, and in fact all schools in Egypt could be said to be unsuitable for the proper *tarbiya* of girls. All of this boded ill for women's future ability to raise their own children and care for their households. The call needed to be made for a radical revamping of Egyptian educational and pedagogical practices, before corrupt influences spread throughout all social classes in the nation.[119]

Again and again, *tarbiya* and education were asserted as the cornerstones upon which the prosperity of the nation should be built, as the marker of the progress and advancement (or backwardness) of all nations. *Tarbiya* was conceived of as an art—that of raising children properly from their infancy until the time when they could work and become productive members of their society. *Al-Manar* asserted that although many had realized the urgent need for reform, very little action had been taken. Even worse, people had come to believe that teaching foreign languages or European laws was sufficient, as it prepared people for government jobs, never realizing that such a self-interested approach was diametrically opposed to the interests of the nation. It was suggested that students obtain a grounding in the fundamental principles of religion (*'ilm usul al-din*), which included a knowledge of the forms of worship and the prescribed norms of Muslim conduct (*'ibadat; 'ilm fiqh al-halal wa al-haram*) and the study of disciplining morals and reforming manners (*'ilm tahdhib al-akhlaq wa islah al-'adat*). The latter required a knowledge of philosophical reasoning and psychology, sociology (*'ilm al-ijtima'*) (the study of peoples, civilizations and their characters, manners and customs),[120] geography, history, political economy, household management (especially relevant for girls, as it would be their occupation and they were currently ignorant of it), accounting, languages, hygiene, and public health.[121]

By 1912, it could be claimed that no one could question the need for reform in *tarbiya* and education, as the call was being made all over the Muslim world, even at al-Azhar, the prestigious center of religious learning. In a lecture given by Rashid Rida, the decline of Muslim nations is bemoaned, the crisis seen as spanning language, religion, morals, and manners. In asking what kind of *tarbiya* Muslims needed to reform their morals, and what kind of education would refine their reason, the Islamic intellegentsia of *Al-Manar* sought to ground the renaissance of Islamic nations in the articles and principles of the Islamic faith. Moreover, such a grounding needed to be aligned with the modern concerns of an ordered household and proper child rearing if the East were to "catch up" with European advancements in scientific pedagogy and education.[122]

Such concerns, then, were applicable to child rearing as well as to education. For instance, a favorable description of a book on *tarbiya* by Dr. 'Abd al-'Aziz Effendi Nazmi, which *Al-Manar* urged its readers to purchase, claimed that "it is apparent that no mother can do without a knowledge of the rules of hygiene with respect to such matters." The text itself was written specifically with an audience of mothers in mind. In fact, each of the chapters was presented as an actual lecture to mothers. The chapter topics are instructive: the importance of breast-feeding; the rules of breast-feeding; the infant's bed and bedroom; the rules of psychological health (*sihat al-nafs*); infant weaning and nutrition; the infant's clothing; bodily cleanliness and the child's play; proper care of wounds; children's exercise; and the development of their intelligence.[123]

Often the neglect of household *tarbiya* as an object of study and reform was lamented. The critique of contemporary child-rearing practices was aimed against both those who left their children to do as they pleased according to their whims and caprices, and those "Westernized among us . . . who have taken on foreign nannies who teach children their language and raise them according to the customs of their lands (*'adat aqwamihim*)."[124]

The call for the total and systematic reorganization of both child-rearing practices and schooling, however, was cast not in terms of an imitation of Western practices and institutions but in terms of the cyclical time of the decline and rise of nations and peoples, as Ibn Khaldun and others had taught. Especially salient, as *Al-Manar* points out, was the tradition of Islamic reformism, with a lineage including Abu Hamid al-Ghazali, Abu Bakr al-ʿArabi al-Maghribi, Zakariyah al-Ansari, and, of course, Jamal al-Din al-Afghani. Such a renaissance (*nuhud*) was perceived as the means by which the circulation of an illness in the body politic could be remedied, and the glorious past of Islam be restored through the reform of education.[125]

Similarly, in a sermon (*khutba*) given in 1912 the upbringing of homes (*tarbiyat al-buyut*) is posited as the foundation of all that may be built subsequently, and it is mothers who bear the primary burden of this role. "How will this matter be dealt with when our women are ignorant of everything related to *tarbiya*—all forms of knowledge, and religious and secular manners (*adab*)? . . . A national upbringing cannot proceed unless we teach women what it is necessary for them to know in order to raise their children." Again, Muslims who imitate foreigners, or allow their children to be raised by foreign nannies, are berated. The construction of the argument itself is intriguing and relates, in part, to the growing interest in the new social sciences. The assumption that women's foreign upbringing would result in the complete transformation of Egyptian society along the lines of the West is asserted to be a gross misunderstanding of sociology, of the characters of nations (as anyone who had read Le Bon would surely know), and an error in the science of *tarbiya*. What would result, in effect, would be the decimation of national character, not the creation of a society like those of the West. Women, then, ought to be taught in the language, customs, morals, and religion of their own country, and they should also learn the science of child rearing and household management, the rules of health and hygiene, accounting, and a rudimentary knowledge of history and geography. Here, the critique of European nannies is made more forcefully. "Many of the wealthy use European nannies, who teach the children a language, morals, and manners that are not their own—resulting in children who will be formed so as to become incommensurate with their mothers. Yes, those who are raised by foreign women will be more refined in contemporary social manners and cleanliness than others . . . but what we are calling for is a *tarbiya* with which we can be a vibrant and united nation, as other civilized nations are, but we cannot achieve this through imitational Westernization."[126]

CONCLUSION

In discussing the discourses on motherhood in the context of colonialism, I have put forth several arguments. First, that Egyptian discussions of motherhood need to be situated within the context of both colonial and anticolonial nationalist discourses on modernity. As Lila Abu-Lughod points out in her introduction to this volume, the "women's question" interacted in complex ways with modernity and postcoloniality—gender figured centrally in anticolonial nationalist resolutions to problems of national backwardness and how best to become modern. Within the Egyptian colonial setting the discourses on mothering were integral to the constitution of a national identity, with women positioned as markers of national backwardness. Mothers were deemed "ignorant" of the principles of modern child care, and their ability to function as proper mothers of citizens of the modern nation was questioned. Explicit contrasts were thus set up between Egyptian child rearing and a scientific European pedagogy, both to explicate the "reasons for our backwardness" and to point the way to a modern postcolonial nationalist future.

Second, I argued that the specific manner in which women were to be "remade" entailed the constitution of a private sphere of bourgeois domesticity, with motherhood recast as a rational, scientific, and hygienic vocation of women. Such a project often attempted to erase and recast class differences by consolidating an "ideal mother" modeled along middle-class lines. Further, to reconstitute the Egyptian family as both national and modern, the new discourses of child rearing aimed to cultivate new types of children—physically, mentally, and morally fit, industrious and productive citizens.

More important, however, I also argued that one should not presume that anticolonial nationalist discourses on motherhood were merely derivative of colonial or European discourses. Indeed, the formation of a "private sphere" within the Egyptian setting was often articulated from within the parameters of nonsecular conceptions of proper pedagogy. Whether Westernized modernizers or Islamist reformers, thinkers situated their own projects as a defense of Islam and an illustration that "true Islam" was not antithetical to modernity. Such assertions arose in a complex dialogue with colonial discourse, which had posited Islam as the reason for the backwardness of Muslim nations.

Thinkers of the *salafiyya* movement, in particular, explicitly situated their reforms within an Islamic discursive tradition and a national nonsecular project of modernity. Islamists framed their projects within a nonsecular concept of historical time and drew upon an indigenous tradition of moral and religious pedagogy geared toward the cultivation of the body, the disciplinization of the self, and the formation of moral character. Hence the modernist focus on health, hygiene, and the cultivation and disciplinization of the body was not antithetical to Islamic discourse at the turn of the century but complementary to it. The larger framework within which the disciplinization of the child's body and the rationalization of the home were to occur, however, was a concept of rightly guided moral and ethical practice. The child's actualization, understood as the cultivation of religious sentiments, the inculcation of the moral virtues, and the formation of disciplined souls and bodies, could occur only within the framework of the community (*umma*). The aim of this disciplinization, as well as the product, was to be irreducibly different from that of the West.

Rather than view the Egyptian experience as merely a bad copy of a supposedly uniform and coherent European model of modernity, we can explore the ways in which cultural translations and hybridizations sought to negotiate ~~~~ speaking positions from which the national modern could be formulated.[127] If we are to construct the beginnings of what Gyan Prakash has referred to as a "critique of the colonial genealogy of the discourse of modernity," we must come to understand not only the ways in which colonialism was constitutive of European modernity but also the ways in which modernity, and its concomitant regime of power/knowledge, was refashioned, renegotiated, and rendered intelligible in non-European contexts. As postcolonial critiques often remind us, the signification of the modern as such requires its articulation with the nonmodern Other; it must be authorized as such, and that process of authorization is itself fractured.[128] The "women's question" in Egypt is a perfect illustration of how a local nationalist discourse articulated in very complex ways with colonial discourse, seeking to situate itself as *both* modern and Islamic. It was an ambivalent articulation of identity and difference with the West.

NOTES

For her encouragement, insightful comments, and criticisms on earlier versions of this paper I am especially grateful to Lila Abu-Lughod. Participants in her spring 1995 Gender Politics seminar provided helpful comments on an earlier draft. Samira Haj, Gananath Obeyesekere, Robert Tignor, and the anonymous reviewers at Princeton University Press also provided helpful feedback on earlier versions. Special thanks to Marwa Shakry for her support, criticisms, and patient editing.

1. The main sources drawn upon are journal articles from *Al-Hilal, Al-Muqtataf,* and *Al-Manar* (with the proliferation of articles on child rearing from 1890 to 1920); Qasim Amin's core text on women, *Tahrir al-mar'a* (*The Liberation of Women*); as well as classic colonial texts, such as the earl of Cromer's *Modern Egypt. Al-Hilal* (1892) founded by Jurji Zaydan, and one of the most widely circulated Middle Eastern periodicals at the time, and *Al-Muqtataf* (1876), founded by Ya'qub Sarruf and Faris Nimr, were both Lebanese-Egyptian (literary-scientific-cultural) journals, decidedly secular in tone, that advocated Westernizing reforms. *Al-Manar* was founded in 1898 by Rashid Rida, a disciple of Muhammad 'Abduh, as a journal of religious interpretation (*tafsir*) and philosophy, as well as social criticism. I do not wish to bifurcate *Al-Hilal* and *Al-Muqtataf*, on the one hand, and *Al-Manar*, on the other, as "modernist" versus "traditionalist." I see all three as decisively modern and reformist, but whereas *Al-Manar* belongs to and situates itself with respect to an Islamic tradition, the other two do not.

2. Dipesh Chakrabarty, "The Difference-Deferral of a Colonial Modernity: Public Debates on Domesticity in British Bengal," in *Subaltern Studies* VIII, ed. David Arnold and David Hardiman (Delhi: Oxford University Press, 1994), pp. 50–88; quotation p. 52.

3. Previous notions of child rearing, it seems, were geared primarily toward the moral development of the child and were conceptualized in terms of notions of moral

being and personhood, as in medieval texts such as al-Ghazali's *Ihya' 'ulum al-din* and al-Jawziyya's *Tuhfat al-mawdud fi ahkam al-mawlud*. It would be beyond the scope of the present study to trace the shift that is presupposed to have occurred during the nineteenth century; I can merely suggest what earlier notions of child rearing may have entailed. See Avner Gil'adi, *Children of Islam: Concepts of Childhood in Medieval Muslim Society* (New York: St. Martin's Press, 1992).

4. Timothy Mitchell has discussed the shift that occurred in the use of the term *tarbiya* (education). "The word *tartib*, meaning such things as 'arrangement (into ranks)', 'organisation', 'discipline', 'rule', 'regulation' (hence even 'government') was replaced in the field of learning by the like-sounding word *tarbiya*. Until perhaps the last third of the nineteenth century *tarbiya* had meant simply 'to breed' or 'to cultivate,' referring, as in English, to anything that should be helped to grow—the cotton crop, cattle, or the morals of children. It came to mean 'education,' the new field of practices developed in the last third of the century." Timothy Mitchell, *Colonising Egypt* (Cambridge: Cambridge University Press, 1988), p. 88. It is this new constellation of practices, with respect to the education and rearing of children, and by extension the fostering of community and nation, that I am trying to trace. For an insightful discussion of transformations in the process of education and Qur'anic schooling in nineteenth- and twentieth-century Yemeni pedagogy, see Brinkley Messick, *The Calligraphic State: Textual Domination and History in a Muslim Society* (Berkeley and Los Angeles: University of California Press, 1993), especially chaps. 4 and 5.

5. Mitchell, *Colonising Egypt*, p. 113.

6. Anna Davin, "Imperialism and Motherhood," *History Workshop* 5 (1978): 9–65; Anne McClintock, *Imperial Leather: Race, Class and Gender in the Colonial Contest* (New York and London: Routledge, 1995); Ann Stoler, *Race and the Education of Desire: Foucault's History of Sexuality and the Colonial Order of Things* (Durham, N.C.: Duke University Press, 1995), and "Carnal Knowledge and Imperial Power: Gender, Race, and Morality in Colonial Asia," in *Gender at the Crossroads of Knowledge: Feminist Anthropology in the Postmodern Era*, ed. Micaela di Leonardo (Berkeley and Los Angeles: University of California Press, 1991), pp. 51–101.

7. See Davin, "Imperialism and Motherhood"; Ute Frevert, "The Civilizing Tendency of Hygiene: Working-Class Women under Medical Control in Imperial Germany," in *German Women in the Nineteenth Century: A Social History*, ed. John Fout (New York: Holmes and Meier, 1984), pp. 320–44; Anita Levy, *Other Women: the Writing of Class, Race and Gender, 1832–1898* (Princeton: Princeton University Press, 1991); Mary Poovey, *Uneven Developments: The Ideological Work of Gender in Mid-Victorian England* (Chicago: University of Chicago Press, 1988).

8. Messick, *The Calligraphic State*, pp. 77–79. The activities denoted by the verbal noun *ta'dib* (to educate, discipline, punish) and its corollary process of *tahdhib* (to instruct, correct, train, educate, culture) were meant to ensure the formation of a child endowed with good breeding, manners, decency, morals, decorum, etiquette, and civility.

9. The *salafiyya* reformers were a group of Islamic thinkers centered on the thought and writing of al-Sayyid Jamal al-Din al-Afghani (1838–97) and Muhammad 'Abduh (1849–1905), who formed the critical mass of the late-nineteenth- and early-twentieth-century Islamic reform and revival movement. Their ideas on educational reform and in particular those espoused by Rashid Rida, 'Abduh's disciple, in the journal *Al-Manar*

are discussed at length below. For a general background, see Charles Adams, *Islam and Modernism in Egypt* (London: Oxford University Press, 1933), and Albert Hourani, *Arabic Thought in the Liberal Age 1789–1939* (Cambridge: Cambridge University Press, 1983).

10. Mitchell, *Colonising Egypt*, pp. 111–13.

11. Ibid., p. 112.

12. Gayatri Chakravorty Spivak, "Can the Subaltern Speak?" in *Marxism and the Interpretation of Culture*, ed. Cary Nelson and Lawrence Grossberg (Urbana: University of Illinois Press, 1988), pp. 271–313; quotation p. 299.

13. Partha Chatterjee, *Nationalist Thought and the Colonial World: A Derivative Discourse?* (London: Zed Books, 1986); *The Nation and Its Fragments: Colonial and Postcolonial Histories* (Princeton: Princeton University Press, 1993).

14. The earl of Cromer, *Modern Egypt*, 2 vols. (New York: Macmillan, 1908), 2:539.

15. As Harry Boyle, Cromer's Oriental secretary, states, "It is difficult to exaggerate the benefits which will accrue to the country at large when the unwholesome—and frequently degrading—associations of the old harem life give place to the healthy and elevating influence of a generation of mothers, keenly alive to the responsibilities as regards the moral training and welfare of their children." Clara Boyle, *Boyle of Cairo: A Diplomatist's Adventures in the Middle East* (Kendal: Titus Wilson and Son, 1905; reprint, 1965), p. 56; cf. Mitchell, *Colonising Egypt*, p. 112.

16. Cromer, *Modern Egypt*, 2:540–42.

17. Chatterjee, *The Nation and Its Fragments*, pp. 116–34.

18. Ibid., p. 117.

19. Chatterjee's outer domain, ibid., p. 26.

20. On Shumayyil, see Hourani, *Arabic Thought in the Liberal Age*, pp. 248–53.

21. Shibli Shumayyil, "Rijal al-ghad wa al-tarbiya al-madrasiyya," *Al-Hilal* 19, no. 7 (April 1911): 413–18; quotation p. 413.

22. The recent literature on women, motherhood, and the nation is vast; see, for example, *Woman-Nation-State*, ed. Nira Yuval-Davis and Floya Anthias (London: Macmillan, 1989); *Mothers of a New World: Maternalist Politics and the Origins of Welfare States*, ed. Seth Koven and Sonya Michel (London: Routledge, 1993). On Egypt, see Mitchell, *Colonising Egypt*, pp. 111–13; Beth Baron, "Mothers, Morality, and Nationalism in Pre-1919 Egypt," in *The Origins of Arab Nationalism*, ed. Rashid Khalidi et al. (New York: Columbia University Press, 1991), pp. 271–88, "The Construction of National Honor in Egypt," *Gender and History* 5, no. 2 (Summer 1993): 244–55, and *The Women's Awakening in Egypt: Culture, Society and the Press* (New Haven: Yale University Press, 1994); Leila Ahmed, *Women and Gender in Islam* (New Haven: Yale University Press, 1992), chaps. 7–10; Thomas Philipp, "Feminism and Nationalist Politics in Egypt," in *Women in the Muslim World*, ed. Lois Beck and Nikkie Keddie (Cambridge: Harvard University Press, 1978), pp. 277–94. See also Meredith Borthwick, *The Changing Role of Women in Bengal 1849–1905* (Princeton: Princeton University Press, 1984), especially chap. 5, for a discussion of the changing conception of motherhood in colonial Bengal and the proliferation of mother-oriented and child-care manuals from the 1860s onward. For critical discussions on the discourses of motherhood and domesticity in colonial Bengal, see Pradip Kumar Bose, "Sons of the Nation: Child Rearing in the New Family," in *Texts of Power: Emerging*

Disciplines in Colonial Bengal, ed. Partha Chatterjee (Minneapolis and London: University of Minnesota Press, 1995), pp. 118–44; Chakrabarty, "The Difference-Deferral of a Colonial Modernity"; and Samita Sen, "Motherhood and Mothercraft: Gender and Nationalism in Bengal," *Gender and History* 5, no. 2 (Summer 1993): 231–43. On Iran, see Afsaneh Najmabadi,"*Zanha-yi millat*: Women or Wives of the Nation," *Iranian Studies* 26, nos. 1–2 (Winter–Spring 1993): 51–71.

23. Baron, "Mothers, Morality, and Nationalism," and *The Women's Awakening in Egypt.*

24. As cited in Baron, "Mothers, Morality, and Nationalism," p. 276.

25. Hourani, *Arabic Thought in the Liberal Age,* pp. 181–82.

26. On Qasim Amin, see Mitchell, *Colonising Egypt,* pp. 112–13; Hourani, *Arabic Thought in the Liberal Age,* pp. 164–70; and Ahmed, *Women and Gender in Islam,* pp. 144–68.

27. Qasim Amin, *The Liberation of Women* (1899), trans. Samiha Sidhom Peterson (Cairo: American University in Cairo Press, 1992), pp. 5–6.

28. Qasim Amin, *The New Woman* (1900), trans. Samiha Sidhom Peterson (Cairo: American University in Cairo Press, 1995), p. 60.

29. "We have forgotten that an adult man is a product of his mother's influence during childhood. I wish that men would understand the importance of this complete tie between a man and his mother. It is the crux of everything that I have written in this book, and I repeat: it is impossible to have successful men unless their mothers prepare them for success. This is the worthwhile goal that civilization has entrusted to the women of our era. Women carry out these heavy responsibilities in all the civilized countries of the world, bearing children then molding them into adults." Amin, *The Liberation of Women,* p. 71.

30. Ibid., pp. 64, 72.

31. See, for instance, Saleh Hamdi Hammad, "Al-Tarbiya al-sahiha," *Al-Hilal* 15, no. 6 (March 1907): 371–73.

32. Caleb Saleeby, *The Progress of Eugenics* (London: Funk and Wagnalls, 1914), p. 79.

33. As cited in Linda Colley, *Britons: Forging the Nation 1707–1837* (New Haven and London: Yale University Press, 1992), p. 276.

34. Homi K. Bhabha, "DissemiNation: Time, Narrative, and the Margins of the Modern Nation," in *Nation and Narration,* ed. Homi K. Bhabha (London and New York: Routledge, 1990), pp. 291–322.

35. Colley, *Britons,* p. 6. Colley deals more directly with the question of Otherness in her article "Britishness and Otherness," in which she questions the dearth of scholarly attention paid to the constitution of British identity against the Other. She points to the need for attending to the dynamics that obtained between "Britishness" and the wider context of the "external" empire, rather than the Four Nations (or "white" empire) model so widely focused upon. The salience of Otherness, particularly after 1783, so Colley argues, emerged out of the incorporation of difference (religious, linguistic, racial) into empire and the export of "internal" others (Irish, Scottish) in large numbers to the colonies, practices that enabled a sense of British selfhood in relation to these colonized Others. See Linda Colley, "Britishness and Otherness: An Argument," *Journal of British Studies* 31 (1992): 309–29.

36. Davin, "Imperialism and Motherhood," p. 10.

37. Caleb Saleeby, *Parenthood and Race Culture: An Outline of Eugenics* (New York: Moffat, Yard and Company, 1910), p. 38.

38. As cited by Davin, "Imperialism and Motherhood," p. 29.

39. Saleeby, *Parenthood and Race Culture*, p. 164.

40. Saleeby, *The Progress of Eugenics*, p. 108.

41. Saleeby, *Parenthood and Race Culture*, p. 313.

42. Ibid., p. 304; emphasis in original.

43. See Stoler, "Carnal Knowledge and Imperial Power"; *Race and the Education of Desire*, chap. 5; and "A Sentimental Education: Native Servants and the Cultivation of European Children in the Netherlands Indies," in *Fantasizing the Feminine: Sex and Death in Indonesia*, ed. Laurie Sears (Durham, N.C.: Duke University Press, 1995), pp. 71–91, in which she deals more specifically with the focus upon proper child rearing and education in the colonial context and the education of sentiments as a strategy for preserving racial and class boundaries in the Netherlands East Indies. Such colonial concerns included assaults on native mothers and nursemaids as corrupting or contaminating influences on children's morality, as well as attempts to inculcate appropriate psychological dispositions and national-cultural attachments, thereby defining motherhood as a full-time occupation. On the idea of an *internal frontier* and the politics of exclusion, see her "Sexual Affronts and Racial Frontiers: European Identities and the Cultural Politics of Exclusion in Colonial Southeast Asia," *Comparative Studies in Society and History* 34, no. 2 (July 1992): 514–51.

44. Stoler, "Carnal Knowledge and Imperial Power," pp. 71–73.

45. Ibid., pp. 73–74.

46. Ibid.

47. The discourses of domesticity entailed the elaboration of women's role as primarily involved in the domestic sphere in keeping with the rational, efficient, and productive ordering and "economic" management of the household. Baron discusses the inauguration of the terms "mistress of the house" (*rabbat al-dar*) and "household management" (*tadbir al-manzil*), as well as the manuals that popularized them. Baron, *The Women's Awakening in Egypt*, pp. 155–58. The specificity of the prescriptive literature, although reminiscent of medieval conduct literature, differs in both the audience addressed and the explicit topos of domesticity, which had only recently been elaborated as a domain of women. Marilyn Booth's discussion of domesticity and women's biographies is particularly illustrative of the intersections among nationalist discourse, bourgeois familial identity formation, and the privileging of the maternal-domestic role concomitant with its inscription as modern. See Marilyn Booth, "'May Her Likes Be Multiplied': 'Famous Women' Biography and Gendered Prescriptions in Egypt 1892–1935," *Signs* 22, no. 4 (1997): 827–90.

48. Baron, *The Women's Awakening in Egypt*.

49. Ibid., pp. 158–59.

50. Ibid., pp. 159–61; Margot Badran, *Feminists, Islam, and Nation: Gender and the Making of Modern Egypt* (Princeton: Princeton University Press, 1995), pp. 61–65.

51. Baron, *The Women's Awakening in Egypt*, p. 163.

52. Amin, *The New Woman*, p. 51.

53. Michel Foucault has situated the emergence of the health and the physical well-being of population in the eighteenth century as an essential objective of political power

within what he terms the governmentalization of the state. The emergence of governmentality, he argues, entailed a shift in modes of governance in which the family no longer served as a model of government and sovereignty was no longer conceived of as the management of the household. Instead, population became the ultimate end of government, inaugurating the instrumentalization of the family. Foucault discusses this "power over life"—a dual process of optimizing the strength of the population and its constituent subjects while simultaneously rendering them more governable—as a fundamental site for the deployment of modern power. For Foucault's elaboration of governmentality, bio-power, and the political investment of the individual body and the body politic, see Michel Foucault, *The History of Sexuality*, vol. 1, *An Introduction*, trans. R. Hurley (New York: Vintage/Random House, 1978); "The Politics of Health in the Eighteenth Century," in *Power/Knowledge: Selected Interviews 1972–1977*, trans. C. Gordon (New York: Pantheon Books, 1980), pp. 166–82; "Governmentality," in *The Foucault Effect: Studies in Governmentality*, ed. G. Burchell, C. Gordon, and P. Miller (Chicago: University of Chicago Press, 1991), pp. 87–104; and "The Political Technology of Individuals"in *Technologies of the Self: A Seminar with Michel Foucault*, ed. L. Martin, H. Gutman, and P. Hutton (Amherst: University of Massachussetts Press, 1988), pp. 145–62.

54. Foucault, "The Politics of Health in the Eighteenth Century."

55. Davin, "Imperialism and Motherhood," p. 16; cf. Colley, *Britons*, pp. 240–41.

56. Davin, "Imperialism and Motherhood," 24–28. Ute Frevert has discussed what she terms the "civilizing tendency of hygiene," a medico-hygienic pedagogy directed primarily toward working-class women in imperial Germany. By the early twentieth century pedagogy was institutionalized through baby-care centers, often run by women or welfare organizations, which problematized working-class mothers' abilities in household management as well as child care and laid an emphasis on "rational child care." Frevert analyzes the medicalization and hygienic civilization of the working classes as part of the wider attempt at normalizing and maximizing the economic rationality and efficiency, as well as the health, and therefore labor vitality, of the working classes, through their "adoption of middle-class values and habits and the[ir] . . . mental integration into capitalist society and economy." Frevert, "The Civilizing Tendency of Hygiene," p. 321.

57. Davin, "Imperialism and Motherhood," pp. 36–43.

58. Ibid., p. 53. Mary Poovey has discussed the "ideological work of gender" in terms of its fractured and uneven development across subject positions of class, race, and gender, showing how the consolidation of the idealized image of the domestic woman within midcentury Victorian bourgeois ideology served to depoliticize class relations. Poovey, *Uneven Developments*. Anita Levy has also looked at Victorian middle-class intellectuals' representations of "disorder in the house of the poor" as a means by which the middle class attempted to secure its hegemony: by "representing *what it was was not*, the middle class defined *what it was* and so secured its corporate identity," as well as enmeshing working-class families within "a machinery of governance exterior to them." Such representations coded social and economic information in moral and hygienic terms, focusing upon the family, along with the individual self, as a locus of social disorder, and consolidating the ideal of the healthy middle-class body within the confines of a new domestic space. Levy, *Other Women*, chap. 2; quotation p. 24.

59. Davin, "Imperialism and Motherhood," pp. 55–56. On the nature of the transition to the modern bourgeois family, new conceptions of childhood and child rearing, and their relation to the development of bourgeois individualism, private property, and industrial capitalism in the European context, see Phillipe Ariès, *Centuries of Childhood: A Social History of Family Life* (New York: Alfred Knopf, 1962); Leonore Davidoff and Catherine Hall, *Family Fortunes: Men and Women of the English Middle Class 1780–1850* (Chicago: University of Chicago Press, 1987); Friedrich Engels, *The Origins of the Family, Private Property and the State* (New York: International Publishers, 1884; reprint, 1972); Edward Shorter, *The Making of the Modern Family* (New York: Basic Books, 1977), and Eli Zaretsky, *Capitalism, the Family and Personal Life* (New York: Harper and Row, 1978). Taken together, this literature points to the coeval development of socialized production under capitalism, the development of private property, and the emergence of the nuclear family and household as a single isolated and seemingly independent unit. The family came to be characterized by a domestic ideology, the idealization of the familial role for women (especially child rearing), companionate marriage, and the "invention of childhood" as a stage requiring a specific form of pedagogy and education. Zaretsky, in particular, argues that the family must be understood as part and parcel of the development of a capitalist mode of production, and bourgeois familial ideology as constitutive of the demarcation of the family as apparently autonomous and separate from the "economy" and "production."

60. Juan Cole, "Feminism, Class, and Islam in Turn-of-the-Century Egypt," *International Journal of Middle East Studies* 13 (1981): 387–407. Cole focuses on the antithetical positions on feminism taken up by the upper-middle class (as embodied by Amin) and the lower-middle class or petite bourgeoisie (as embodied by Talʿat Harb), relating the latter's refusal to take up the injunction to "emancipate women" to a differential class positioning and a more negative attitude toward European values.

61. See, for example, Amin, *The Liberation of Women*, p. 50.

62. Ibid., pp. 23–25. For a sense of what other conceptions of mothering, some of which Amin is critiquing, may have been, see Lila Abu-Lughod's discussion of perceptions of mothering and child rearing among the Awlad ʿAli Bedouin, in "The Marriage of Feminism and Islamism in Egypt: Selective Repudiation as a Dynamic of Postcolonial Cultural Politics," chap. 7 in this volume; and *Writing Women's Worlds: Bedouin Stories* (Berkeley and Los Angeles: University of California Press, 1993), especially chap. 3.

63. Amin, *The Liberation of Women*, pp. 26–27.

64. Shumayyil, "Rijal al-ghad wa al-tarbiya al-madrasiyya," pp. 413–14.

65. Hammad had translated Fénelon's *L'éducation des filles* as *Tarbiyat al-banat* (Cairo: Matbaʿat Madrasat Walidat ʿAbbas al-Awwal, 1909) and John Stuart Blackie's *On Self Culture, Intellectual, Physical and Moral* as *Tarbiyat al-nafs bi'l-nafs* (Cairo: Matbaʿat Madrasat Walidat ʿAbbas al-Awwal, 1906); see Mitchell, *Colonising Egypt*, p. 198 n. 53.

66. Hammad, "Al-Tarbiya al-sahiha," pp. 371–73.

67. Ibid., p. 371.

68. The columns often contained a wealth of miscellaneous information. For example, *akhbar ʿilmiyya (*scientific news*)* contained entries on topics as varied as fear of

cats, the increased population of Germanic peoples, schools in Japan, trees, the wireless telephone, types of food, and the prevention of cancer. See "Akhbar ʿilmiyya," *Al-Hilal* 14, no. 1 (October 1905): 49–55.

69. "Kindergarten aw riyadat al-atfal," *Al-Hilal* 12, no. 3 (November 1903): 76–77; "Falsafat al-laʿb," *Al-Hilal* 12, no. 3 (November 1903): 91–92.

70. "Kindergarten aw riyadat al-atfal," pp. 76–77.

71. Ibid., p. 77

72. "Bab tadbir al-manzil: tarbiyat al-atfal,"*Al-Muqtataf* 42, no. 3 (March 1913): 294–95.

73. Ibid., p. 295.

74. For similar discourses in the colonial East Indies, see Stoler, "A Sentimental Education" and *Race and the Education of Desire*, chap. 5.

75. "Al-Marʾa wa ashghal al-manzil," *Al-Hilal* 14, no. 1 (October 1905): 51–52.

76. Labiba Hashim, "Al-Tarbiya," *Al-Muqtataf* 38, no. 3 (March 1911): 274–81; quotation p. 281.

77. Ahmed Hafez, "Nasiha li-abnaʾ al-aghniyaʾ," *Al-Hilal* 12, no. 5 (December 1903): 153–54.

78. "Bab tadbir al-manzil: tarbiyat al-awlad ʿala al-iqtisad," *Al-Muqtataf* 33, no. 3 (March 1908): 255–56; quotation p. 255.

79. Ibid., p. 256.

80. Leila Ahmed has recently discussed Qasim Amin, and other Westernized modernizing reformers in Egypt, in terms of their class position within the colonial formation and subsequent reproduction of colonial discourse on women. However, her presentation of Amin as an example of an androcentric, patriarchal individual who internalized orientalist and colonial discourse and simply rearticulated it "in native, upper-middle class voice" elides certain similarities (women as a sphere of backwardness) and occludes certain differences (the role of religious pedagogy) between the modernizing reformers she speaks of and what she refers to as "indigenous feminists," such as Malak Hifni Nassif. This is, in part, what I am trying to address in this subsection. See Ahmed, *Women and Gender in Islam*, p. 162.

81. Baron, *The Women's Awakening in Egypt*, pp. 26–27, 179.

82. Hashim, "Al-Tarbiya," p. 274.

83. Ibid., p. 274.

84. Ibid., p. 275.

85. Ibid., p. 276.

86. Ibid., p. 277.

87. Ibid., p. 278.

88. Ibid., p. 277.

89. On Nassif, see Ahmed, *Women and Gender in Islam*, chapter 9; and Hoda al-Sadda, "Malak Hifni Nassif: halqa mafquda min tarikh al-hayat," *Hajar: Kitab al-Marʾa* 2 (1994): 109–19.

90. Bahithat al-Badiya, "Tarbiyat al-banat fi al-bayt wa al-manzil," in *Al-Nisaʾiyyat: majmuʿat maqalat nushirat fi al-jarida fi mawduʿ al-marʾa al-misriyya*, 2 vols. (Cairo: Matbaʿat Al-Jarida, 1910), 1:18–21.

91. Bahithat al-Badiya, "Khutba fi nadi hizb al-umma," in *Al-Nisaʾiyyat*, 1:104.

92. Ibid., pp. 95–118.

93. Bahithat al-Badiya, "Muhadara fi tarbiyat al-banat," in *Athar Bahithat al-Badiya: Malik Hifni Nassif 1886–1918*, ed. Majd al-Din Hifni Nassif (Cairo: Wizarat al-thaqafa wa al-irshad al-qawmi, al-mu'asasa al-misriyya al-ʿamma li'l-ta'lif wa al-tarjama wa al-tibaʿa wa al-nashr, 1962), pp. 136–42.

94. This was perceived as especially important, as most of these schools had foreign teachers, ignorant of the manners and customs of the country, leaving the girls with no one to correct any errors they made in religion or mores. Nassif asks us to imagine them as they leave the schools, with a *tarbiya* that would differ from their husband's—a potential source of marital tension. Cf. the discussions in *Al-Manar* cited below.

95. Bahithat al-Badiya, "Ashar wasa'il li-tarqiyat al-mar'a al-misriyya," in *Athar Bahithat al-Badiya*, pp. 124–29; Bahithat al-Badiya, "Khutba fi nadi hizb al-umma," in *Al-Nisa'iyyat*, 1:95–118.

96. Bahithat al-Badiya, "Khutba fi al-muqarinitayn bayn al-mar'a al-misriyya wa al-mar'a al-gharbiyya,"in *Al-Nisa'iyyat*, 1:118–42.

97. Rashid Rida, "*Al-Nisa'iyyat*," *Al-Manar* 14, no. 1 (1911): 71–73.

98. Chatterjee, *Nationalist Thought and the Colonial World*, p. 30.

99. Dipesh Chakrabarty, "Postcoloniality and the Artifice of History: Who Speaks for 'Indian' Pasts?" *Representations* 37, no. 4 (Winter 1992): 1–26.

100. Indeed, it could be argued that for Amin even to enter the debate on women he had to mobilize the idiom of the Islamic discursive tradition as a legitimating framework; on Amin's appropriation of Muhammad ʿAbduh, see Ahmed, *Women and Gender in Islam*, p. 270 n. 16. For a discussion of the debates surrounding Amin as refracted through *Al-Manar*, see the reviews of *Al-Mar'a al-jadida* in *Al-Manar* 3, no. 32 (1901): 750–54, and *Al-Manar* 4, no. 1 (1901): 26–34.

101. Amin, *The Liberation of Women*, p. 28.

102. "Al-Umma nasij al-ummahat faʿalayna taʿlim al-banat," *Al-Hilal* 16, no. 4 (January 1908): 239–43; quotation pp. 240, 242.

103. Hammad, "Al-Tarbiya al-sahiha," pp. 371–73.

104. For a discussion of *Al-Manar* and Rashid Rida's positioning within the *salafiyya* movement, see Adams, *Islam and Modernism*, pp. 177–204; Hamid Enayat, *Modern Islamic Political Thought* (Austin: University of Texas Press, 1982), pp. 68–83; and Hourani, *Arabic Thought in the Liberal Age*, pp. 222–44.

105. "Al-Mu'tamar al-misri: al-tarbiya wa al-taʿlim," *Al-Manar* 14, no. 6 (1911): 457–60.

106. Talal Asad, "The Idea of An Anthropology of Islam," (Washington D.C.: Center for Contemporary Arab Studies Occasional Papers, Georgetown University, 1986); quotation p. 14.

107. Asad's conceptualization of an Islamic discursive tradition is based upon Alasdair MacIntyre and must be distinguished from any concept of an "invented" tradition. MacIntyre conceives of a living tradition as "an historically extended, socially embodied argument, and an argument precisely in part about the goods which constitute that tradition . . . [T]he history of a practice in our time is generally and characteristically embedded in and made intelligible in terms of a larger and longer history of the tradition through which the practice in the present form is conveyed to us. . . . Living traditions, just because they continue a not-yet-completed narrative, confront a future whose determinate and determinable character, so far as it possesses any, derives from the past." MacIntyre's notion of a tradition is inextricably linked to a conception of

virtues and practices that presuppose the individual's situatedness within a (moral) community. It is this form of membership, constituted through a historical and social identity, that renders your present identity as bearer of a tradition. See Alasdair MacIntyre, *After Virtue: A Study in Moral Theory*, 2d ed. (Notre Dame, Ind.: University of Notre Dame Press, 1984), chaps. 14 and 15; quotation pp. 222–23.

108. John Voll, "Renewal and Reform in Islamic History," in *Voices of Resurgent Islam*, ed. J. Esposito (New York and Oxford: Oxford University Press, 1983), pp. 32–47. The renewalist tradition, according to Voll, is marked by three continuing themes: the call for a return to or strict application of the Qur'an and sunna of the Prophet (often targeting popular religion, the orthodox Islamic establishment, and the innovations of non-Islamic ideas and practices—*bid'a*); the assertion of the right to *ijtihad* in this application, rather than a reliance upon *taqlid* (*ijtihad* is to be understood not as simply an individual intellectual exercise but as a legitimizing basis from which to pose a critique of existing conditions and institutions in society, a way to challenge communal consensus, *ijma'*); and the reaffirmation of the authenticity and uniqueness of the Qur'anic experience in contrast to other Islamic modes of synthesis. For a useful discussion of *ijtihad*, see Wael Hallaq, "Was the Gate of *Ijtihad* Closed?" *International Journal of Middle East Studies* 16 (1984): 3–41.

109. Thus, as Voll states, "it is an effort of socio-moral construction or reconstruction making use of a normative standard found in the Qur'an and the Sunna of the Prophet. This standard is independent from the changing historical conditions and specific contexts and it is available as a criterion to be used by renewers as a standard for judging the value of existing conditions and institutions." Voll, "Renewal and Reform in Islamic History," p. 35.

110. See Samira Haj, *Reconfiguring Tradition: Islamic Reform, Rationality and Modernity*, forthcoming. I am grateful for her clarification on the continuity of the eighteenth- and nineteenth-century themes of Islamic reform and the attempt to formulate an Islamic modern.

111. The names most commonly associated with the eighteenth-century Islamic reform movement are Muhammad Ibn 'Abd al-Wahhab (1703–87), Muhammad Ibn 'Ali al-Shawkani (1759–1834), Shah Wali Allah (1702–62), and 'Uthman Ibn Fudi (1754–1817). See Daniel Brown, "The Emergence of Modern Challenges to Tradition," in *Rethinking Tradition in Modern Islamic Thought* (Oxford: Cambridge University Press, 1995), pp. 21–42; Ahmad Dallal, "The Origins and Objectives of Islamic Revivalist Thought, 1750–1850," *Journal of the American Oriental Society* 113, no. 3 (1993): 341–59, and Fazlur Rahman, *Islam*, (Weidenfeld and London: William Clowes and Sons, 1966), chaps. 12 and 13.

112. The most powerful critique of such oppositions, specifically as they relate to the Islamic tradition, is Talal Asad's "The Idea of an Anthropology of Islam," in which he critiques the post-Enlightenment bifurcation of tradition (religion) and modernity (reason), arguing against interpretations that posit traditions as somehow spurious, as "fictions of the present, reactions to the forces of modernity—[suggesting] that in contemporary conditions of crisis, tradition in the Muslim world is a weapon, a ruse, a defense against a threatening world, that it is an old cloak for new aspirations and borrowed styles of behavior," p. 15. See also his *Genealogies of Religion* (Baltimore: Johns Hopkins University Press, 1993), chap. 6, and Haj, *Reconfiguring Tradition*.

113. Talal Asad, "Modern Power and the Reconfiguration of Religious Traditions. Interview by Saba Mahmood," *Stanford Humanities Review* 5, no. 1 (1995): 1–16; quotation pp. 12–13. For an interesting use of Bourdieu's notion of bodily hexis and bodily manifestations as "master symbols of differences between [Victorian and Muslim] pedagogies" in the context of colonial and Egyptian discourses on indigenous pedagogy, Muslim body ritual, and education, see Gregory Starrett, "The Hexis of Interpretation: Islam and the Body in the Egyptian Popular School," *American Ethnologist* 22, no. 4 (1995): 953–69. Marcel Mauss provides a more useful conception of bodily practices as techniques of the body—which entail a habitus implying education rather than imitation, acquired abilities, faculty, apt performance, and craft. Such techniques are both effective and tradition-informed. "Man's first and most natural technical object, and at the same time technical means is his body." The techniques of the body, then, are culturally specific and historically constituted, and they entail a basic education of the body. See Marcel Mauss, "Techniques of the Body," in *Incorporations*, ed. Jonathan Crary and Sanford Kwinter (New York: Zone Books, 1992), pp. 455–77.

114. A noteworthy medieval example is Abu Hamid al-Ghazali's core text *Ihya' ʿulum al-din* (The revivification of the religious sciences), which includes a discussion of the proper guidance for children during the early stages of life and with respect to the improvement of their morals and *adab* (see vol. 3, "Kitab riyadat al-nafs wa tahdhib al-akhlaq wa muʿalajat amrad al-qalb," "bayan al-tariq fi riyadat al-subyan fi awwal nushu'ihim wa wajh tahdhibihim wa tahsin akhlaqihim." Ghazali's discussion is noteworthy in several respects: first, pedagogy is understood as primarily a moral education—one that creates dispositions and is therefore crucial in the formation of the child's character. Its main purpose is to ensure the salvation of the child's soul, and parental responsibility for the child's education is to be understood as a religious duty. Its orientation, then, is spiritually eschatological. That is, this-worldly, rightly guided practice is oriented to the hereafter. Second, Ghazali's conception of the modes of training appropriate for children before the age of discernment (*tamyiz*) is one of *taʿwid* (or, roughly, habituation) and entails the disciplining of the body and the cultivation of the senses in order to inculcate the appropriate dispositions toward good deeds, morally upright behavior, religious practice, moderation in the sensory stimulation, instincts, and pleasures of the body (food, drink, sleep) and revulsion toward evil deeds and morally reprehensible actions. The process of *ta'dib* was to be developed by the cultivation of shame and shyness and the elaboration of the faculty of distinction or discernment (*tamyiz*). It was to entail the regulation of the child's environment as well as specific instruction in religious obligations. Among the qualities desired were obedience to parents, humility, moderation, generosity, decency, and modesty. Children were to be taught to avoid lying, envy, gossip, garrulousness, boasting, and laziness. See al-Imam Abu Hamid Muhammad al-Ghazali, *Ihya' ʿulum al-din* (1097–1109) (Cairo: Matbaʿat al-Istiqama, 1965), pp. 72–74.

115. My discussion of techniques of the self is reminiscent of the Foucauldian concept of technologies of the self, which he defines as "modes of training and modification of individuals, not only in the obvious sense of acquiring skills but also in the sense of acquiring certain attitudes" and concerned with the specific modalities by which individual subjectivities and dispositions are constituted by techniques of self-management. For Foucault it is the interface between technologies of the self and technologies

of power (or the objectivizing of the subject) that constitutes governmentality. Foucault's historical explication of technologies of the self is, however, marred by a curious subordination of the ways in which selves monitor selves within a positive economy of truth in relation to others, be it through relations of authority or community. How technologies of the self relate to the social body and body politic is crucial to the understanding of the mechanisms of power that help selves to constitute selves. See Foucault, *Technologies of the Self*, pp. 16–49; quotation p. 18.

116. "Al-Tarbiya wa wajh al-haja ilayha wa taqsimiha: wa al-kalam ʿala tarbiyat al-ummum wa al-islam, wa al-tarbiya al-diniyya wa al-islam, wa tarbiyat al-irada," *Al-Manar* 15, no. 8 (1912): 567–86.

117. See "Al-Tarbiya al-sahiha wa al-taʿlim wa al-islah," *Al-Manar* 14, no. 3 (1911): 181–82.

118. Of course, the critique applied to more than the education of girls. In a critique of current educational practices, the article attacks both private and governmental institutions, the former for profiteering motives and the latter for fostering education as merely an avenue for jobs. The thrust of the critique hinges on the aims of this type of education, which merely fosters personal self-interest and materialist interests and, in the case of Europeanized institutions, has led to the enslavement and servitude of people to the chimera of freedom (*tawahum al-huriyya*). Indeed, the pernicious effect of Western influences and slavish imitation of Western mores was said to have led to the corruption of *tarbiya*. It was argued that students left these schools as Europeans, no longer Muslim or Eastern. Further, their European *tarbiya* led them to become contemptuous of their ancestors (*salaf*) and to worship all things foreign, all in the name of civilization (*al-madaniyya*). Their adoration of foreign civilization (*ghururihim b'ism al-madaniyya al-ifrinjiyya*) corrupts the nation, while they claim to be reformers. Nonethless, Rida does not deny the need for European manufactures, knowledge, and practical arts. Such adaptations, however, were to proceed in tandem with the preservation of language, customs, religion, and *shariʿa*. See "Fatihat al-sana al-sabbʿiat ʿashar," *Al-Manar* 17, no. 1 (1913): 1–11.

119. "Tarbiyat al-banat," *Al-Manar* 1, no. 23 (1898): 436–38; "Al-Madaris wa al-tarbiya wa al-taʿlim," *Al-Manar* 14, no. 4 (1911): 293–95.

120. It would seem to be precisely the type of sociology, or social science, popular in fin-de-siècle France, and in particular that of Gustave Le Bon, whose *Les lois psychologiques de l'évolution des peuples* was translated into Arabic by Ahmad Fathi Zaghlul, as *Sirr tatawwur al-ummam*. Zaghlul also translated the immensely popular *A quoi tient la supériorité des Anglo-Saxons?* by Edward Demolins, translated as *Sirr taqaddum al-inklis al-saksuniyyin*; see Mitchell, *Colonising Egypt*, pp. 110–11, 122–24, 200 n. 112. Other popular translated works were Edmond Demolins, *L'éducation nouvelle*, translated as *Al-Tarbiya al-haditha* by Hassan Tawfiq al-Dijni (Cairo: Matbaʿat Misr, 1901), and Gustave Le Bon's *Psychologie de l'éducation* (Paris: Flammarion, 1904), translated as *Ruh al-tarbiya*, by Taha Husayn (Cairo: Dar al-Hilal, 1922). Several installments of the latter appeared in *Al-Hilal* in 1923. Le Bon's influence could be felt strongly even in less Westernized journals, such as *Al-Manar*. For a discussion of the influence of Le Bon on turn-of-the-century political thought among the Egyptian bourgeoisie, see Mitchell, *Colonising Egypt*, pp. 122–25, and p. 201 n. 112 for other Arabic translations of Le Bon's work.

121. "Ma la bud minu," *Al-Manar* 1, no. 30 (1898): 567–74.

122. "Al-Khutba al-ra'isiyya: hajatuna ila islah al-tarbiya wa al-taʿlim," *Al-Manar* 15, no. 5 (1912): 336–41.

123. "Kitab tarbiyat al-atfal," *Al-Manar* 6, no. 19 (1903): 754.

124. "Al-Khutba al-ra'isiyya," *Al-Manar*, p. 338.

125. Ibid., p. 340.

126. "Al-Tarbiya wa wajh al-haja ilayha wa taqsimiha," *Al-Manar*, pp. 572–73.

127. See Chakrabarty, "The Difference-Deferral of a Colonial Modernity."

128. Homi K. Bhabha, *The Location of Culture* (London and New York: Routledge, 1994); Gyan Prakash, "Subaltern Studies as Postcolonial Criticism," *American Historical Review* 99, no. 5 (1994): 1475–90.

CHAPTER 5

The Egyptian Lives of Jeanne d'Arc

MARILYN BOOTH

IF YOU WERE a consumer of women's magazines in Egypt, 1922, you might well pick up an issue of the *Magazine of the Women's Awakening*. You would immediately encounter two framing declarations on the magazine's front cover: "Awaken your women, and your nations will live"; and "Nations are made by men, and men by mothers." If you were reading the November 1922 issue, you would find, a few pages in, a regular if short-lived series, *Shams al-tarikh* (The sun of history), and beneath it in smaller letters you would read, "An excerpt from the history lessons that Professor Shaykh Mukhtar Yunus delivers to the pupils of the Government Secondary Girls' School in Hilmiyya al-Jadida, Cairo."[1] You might be quickly caught up in the solemnity of the lesson, for it opens in the tones of a Friday mosque sermon.

> Some of those whom God created in the image of humankind think Woman unfit
> for momentous deeds. By your Lord! those people are prone to error, and mis-
> taken is their vision. Throughout history [Woman] has refuted their view, proving
> them to be on the wrong track. Here is a fragrant image for you: a short life history
> of a young woman. Aged men whom earthly life had made senile were incapable
> of doing what she did. For in 1429 the English beseiged Orléans. A peasant girl
> came forth to rescue it, one sprouted from the earth of Domrémy. . . . With great
> effort she won over the hearts of the naive and gained the favor of Charles VII,
> after he and more than one of his ministers had mocked her. Yet such derision was
> in line with the "women's awakening" in France at that time.[2]

Mukhtar Yunus's two-page biographical sketch of Jeanne d'Arc appeared some nine months after Britain's unilateral announcement of Egypt's independence, a first formal step for Egypt out of colonial rule, but one that left Britain in control of financial, military, and foreign affairs. Published in a milieu of nationalist, anti-imperialist activism, this "short life history of a young woman" was anything but remote from contemporaneous struggles to define a nationalist agenda for an Egypt that would be modern and independent. Jeanne's life as narrated by the shaykh addressed an urgent question: How must inherited notions of a gendered and classed division of labor shift if the envisioned nation was to emerge?

If by 1922 you had become an avid follower of the early women's press in Egypt, you would know that this narrative of Jeanne d'Arc's life was one of hundreds of biographical sketches of women published in the women's periodicals that appeared in Egypt from 1892 on, as well as in biographical dictionaries of notable women. And this life narrative might especially pique your interest, for of all those "Famous Women" profiled in women's magazines in Egypt before 1940, Jeanne d'Arc appeared more frequently than any other. Jeanne as biographical subject drew more treatments than even popular subjects that were closer to home: Safiyya Zaghlul ("Mother of the Nation," spouse of nationalist leader Saʿd Zaghlul); Turkish feminist politician Halide Edip; Pharaoh Nitocris; Arab warrior Khawla bint al-Azwar; militant Queen Zenobia of ancient Palmyra; early-twentieth-century Egyptian feminist commentator Malak Hifni Nasif. Jeanne d'Arc took the spotlight more often than any other non-Arab or non-Muslim subject of biography in these magazines, too, including often-featured subjects like Russian monarch Catherine the Great, Indian writer and nationalist activist Sarujini Naidu, French novelist George Sand, and American astronomer Maria Mitchell.

This essay responds to the obvious question: Why Jeanne? There is no single answer to this question but rather a cluster of images. Together, they suggest that Jeanne's persona, rewritten in Egypt by editors, regular magazine contributors, and readers writing in, could symbolize identities of immediate import to competing agendas and local struggles of the time. Jeanne could represent the anti-imperialist activist in the service of a nation in formation; the devout believer who puts personal faith into action on behalf of the nation; the peasant as crucial in the national struggle; the young woman as having to reconcile duty to nation with duty to family. In fact, Jeanne's encapsulation of the very struggle between different loyalties and identities, rather than simply her ability to represent those loyalties, is a key to Jeanne's popularity. The image of Jeanne could be used to hierarchize (if ambiguously) the relationships among these loyalties, to give primacy to one definition of community over another, or to offer a dramatic transcendence of potentially fractured loyalties. My reading of biographies of Jeanne d'Arc published in Egypt between 1879 and 1939 explores how Jeanne fit into local agendas—initially a proto-feminist one but increasingly a liberal nationalist and anti-imperialist one that demanded a unificatory narrative of nationalist strength which would incorporate and subsume all classes and both genders in the cause. Second, I examine the emphases and rhetoric in these texts that constructed a Jeanne suitable for local consumption, emphases that simultaneously furthered liberal nationalist agendas on the politics of religious identity and gender. Third, I look at how the politics of gender and nation intersected with the fact of Jeanne's Westernness: for biographers in Egypt territorialized and domesticated this icon of Western nationalisms, feminisms, and subnational resistances to national hegemonies, but also questioned the extent to which she could be remade as "local."

In her study of representations of the female in European modernities, Rita Felski has noted that narratives of modernity diverge according to "the gender of their exemplary subjects."[3] In Egypt, biographies of "Famous Women" in the early women's press, in the dominant press, and in biographical compendia of notable women were abundant—and are important—because they constructed a complex narrative of modernity that put female heroines at the center. These texts explored the implications for women of visions of modernity that were shaping and shaped by interrelated discourses of nationalism, anti-imperialism, pedagogy, and economic development in Egypt from the late nineteenth century on. Because biography could make an epistemological claim on its readers that fiction—highly suspect at the time—could not, narratives of women's lives enacted the particulars of an imagined gendered modernity that countered the dominant narrative of the modern—in Egypt as elsewhere—as masculine. As the two banner statements from the *Magazine of the Women's Awakening* advise, this was a narrative that articulated the domestic as a modern space encapsulating "woman." But, unlike much of the polemics around the women question in Egypt at this time, biography posed (upper- and middle-class) women's modernity as a fluid space (to a point) of movement and transference between the domestic and the public. In other words, a feminine modernity could be proposed as the space between the magazine's juxtaposed epigraphs and Yunus's biography of Jeanne d'Arc. As Felski reminds us, (European) women activists' own appropriations of public space, of roles heretofore reserved for men (at least normatively), cannot be ignored as factors in the construction(s) of European modernities.[4] The same is true for Arab women activists; in Egypt, discursive constructions of the domestic have to be investigated in the context of elite women's movement into public space (an arena that nonelite women had not had the luxury of avoiding, even if they occupied a very different sort of public space).[5]

How were these narratives elucidated by, and constitutive of, the lives of women and girls in Egypt at the time? If biography was performative in the sense of providing a possible set of responses to and critiques of available gendered models of the modern, how did it intersect with the nondiscursive experiences of its readers (who were a small subset of the Egyptian populace indeed)? While this is an enormous question that one essay cannot fully address, it must be recognized at least that this was a time of great change and transition in the lives of some women and men. The established boundaries of gendered experience within Egypt's urban middle and upper classes were changing on the ground, as the political elite broadened from a land-based aristocracy to include an emerging professional class, and as rapid urbanization and industrial development were changing the geographic distribution and class composition of the population. Nationalist programs that had begun to emerge in the late nineteenth century had been influenced by Egyptian intellectuals' long acquaintance with the social organization of European societies. Girls of the elite were going to school, and they and their elders were agitating for young women to enter Cairo University, to enter the professions, to study overseas.

Thirty years before, women in Egypt and elsewhere in the Arabic-speaking world had begun publishing magazines for a female readership. They had begun forming new kinds of organizations, from charitable projects to study circles, that allowed intellectual exchange and encouraged the formation of new social networks. These activities were the province of women of means and leisure, although female professionals working for a living gradually took on leading roles. Women of all classes—aristocrats and early professional women, women of the peasantry and emerging proletariat—were visible as participants in the nationalist demonstrations of 1919, the spontaneous, nation-wide response to Britain's banishment of Egypt's nationalist leaders. Elite women's participation in public politics spurred the founding of the Egyptian Feminist Union, the first explicitly feminist organization in Egypt. The publication of Yunus's overtly didactic biography of Jeanne d'Arc preceded by five months the founding meeting of the EFU.[6]

At a time when Egyptian nationalisms and feminisms were taking shape, the question of siting women in an envisioned postcolonial nation was an urgent and controversial one, involving critical appropriations and rejections of models from outside the Arab world. There was no single nationalist or feminist answer to the question of women's place(s) but rather a multiplicity of ideological and activist offerings. To get inside this multiplicity requires close attention to specific historically grounded discourses of the time. Unpacking the genre of women's biography gives us not a straightforward map of the discursive production of "women" in a particular series of historical moments but something more like a maze. It forces us to recognize the multilayered and seemingly internally contradictory nature of the politics of gender, nation, and class, as intellectuals in Egypt searched for answers to the pressing problems they saw their *watan*—as both "homeland" and "nation"—facing. It compels us to recognize that modernity, as it was being produced in Egypt, could hold both perils and benefits for women (of certain socioeconomic strata, at least). Moreover, it demands that we confront the complex ways in which thinkers in Egypt deployed "foreign" discourses. Scholars of Muslim-majority societies who have taken gender as the pivotal axis for historical study have tended to simplify and binarize the fraught issue of "Western" versus "indigenous" sources for the ideological and social construction of gender in those societies in the modern period. In fact, the genre of "Famous Women" biographies contests this simplistic view even as it suggests the importance of class as a modality that represses aspects of (imperialized) experience in the interests of capturing the right to represent local ideals of gendered behavior. Jeanne d'Arc, epitome of Western politico-ideological histories, malleable symbol of how gender might (and might not) inflect contests over the definition of national identities, is one splendid if startling focus for these questions as they were playing out in Egypt.

What a late-twentieth-century reader finds contradictory in these texts may not have looked contradictory at the time. Insistent on the imperative of reading texts according to how they might have been read by their first readers, I prefer to read these biographies in their (cross-cultural) historical context without providing a "resolution" to the conflicting messages within. Rather, I want to emphasize the possibility of conflict as significant and productive in itself, as an open-ended series of dialectics that might have produced different resolutions for different groups of people. For texts may carry contradictory messages according to the particular axes of power against which they are read.[7] The Egyptian lives of Jeanne d'Arc exemplify the appropriation of a single figure by competing identities and ideological interests, a leitmotif in Jeanne d'Arc's posthumous history in the West.

Most of the nineteen biographical sketches of Jeanne that I discuss here are clustered in the first thirty years of the twentieth century, as are a few biographies of other women that invoke Jeanne as exemplary.[8] Throughout, I consider the emergence of Jeanne in Egypt in the context of her contemporaneous image in France and the United States, two likely if not always direct sources for writers in Egypt.[9] For Jeanne's popularity in Arabic coincided not only with a crucial political period in Egypt but also with heightened political exploitation of her image in Europe and the "Joan of Arc vogue" in the United States. The Jeanne d'Arc rage was fueled by the propaganda needs of World War I; by the immediate postwar efforts of those who wanted the commemoration of Jeanne to become simultaneous—indeed, synonymous—with the French nation's celebration of itself; by Jeanne's canonization, fortuitously occurring in 1920; and by the five-hundredth anniversaries of her moment of glory (1429) and her death (1431). The memorials these moments produced provided a culmination to "the cult of Jeanne." Indeed, writing in 1931 on Jeanne's memorialization in stone, Agnes Kendrick Gray enthused that not only was she kept alive in Orléans, Lorraine, and Rouen but "she is remembered in the uttermost parts of the earth."[10] Gray may not have had Cairo in mind, but in Egypt, biographies of Jeanne from the early 1930s paraded Jeanne's commemorations for local readers, as they had lauded her canonization a decade before (as much in Muslim- as in Christian-edited magazines).

To suggest the dialectic of local usefulness, local suitability, and local appropriation of "the Western" that shapes these texts as I outlined above, I begin by introducing the "Famous Women" genre in which the Jeanne biographies are situated, and briefly I delineate the construction of Jeanne in two nineteenth-century compendia of women's biography, for they offer grounds for a potentially feminist reading of female heroism as a legitimate, indeed crucial, part of public politics and as an act historically grounded and collectively situated. Next, I trace Jeanne's sharpening image as resistance leader, shaped by shifts in the local political scene. Tracing two other facets of her image important to political discourse at the time—Jeanne as peasant and as young woman—I suggest that feminist readings of Jeanne were shaped by, and then uneasily submerged in, the imperatives of an emerging anticolonialist and postcolonial nationalism that had to clarify the gender boundaries of a nation in formation. In sum, I propose that Jeanne as local hero—as a symbol of community—was an ambivalent but appropriate figure for readers' and writers' attention in Egypt. Her image as a performance of femininity raises questions: Could the astounding events of Jeanne's life, constructed in Egyptian magazines, be truly domesticated for the consumption of Egypt's growing (if still tiny) population of literate girls and women? Where did Jeanne sit, between a feminist consciousness that had taken root in the late nineteenth century among a few upper-class women, and nationalist programs that recognized the need for women's symbolic and on-the-ground participation in nation formation but preferred to ignore the implications of this for social organization along patriarchal lines? Where to place Jeanne within a post-1919 organized feminism that wanted to support but not subordinate itself to the nationalist imperative, in a postwar context shaped locally by Wilsonian declarations of self-determination juxtaposed with the quashing of nationalist hopes by Great Britain and the enormous popular response thereto? Where did Jeanne belong in the struggle to define a collective identity based on the various possibilities that a pharaonic, early Christian, Muslim, and (much later) Arab nationalist and anticolonialist heritage posed?

Since the age of Christine de Pisan (1364–1430), Jeanne has been appropriated by Western feminists (in act when not yet in name) as a woman who openly transgressed all the gendered boundaries of her society.[11] Feminists among Jeanne's local biographers gestured toward this image while carefully framing it in locally acceptable terms that sometimes traced and sometimes buried the questions Jeanne's history still bears, and the power it holds. These texts remind us how polyvalent, creative, and local are feminist acts and meanings (even when they appear to be "borrowed"), as they articulate with other agendas and grow out of specific historical moments.

A CANON OF NOTABLE WOMEN

Women's magazines for readers of Arabic and biographical dictionaries of *and by* women first appeared in Egypt. They were produced by women who had emigrated from Greater Syria and then by Egyptians. While these magazines circulated outside Egypt, and while "Famous Women" would appear in magazines founded elsewhere (like the Damascus-based *New Woman*), Egypt was the major site of production and is my focus here.

Biographies of notable women caught on quickly as a regular magazine feature. They appeared in sixteen out of twenty magazines published 1892–1939 that I have been able to examine.[12] Editors usually offered these one-half-page to eight-page profiles one to an issue, in series under the rubric "Famous Women" (*Shahirat al-nisa'*) or a near equivalent. If these biographies were entertaining, and if they pointedly offered a protofeminist genealogy of notable women, such were not the only reasons they flooded the women's press. The "Famous Women" narratives filled a need for exemplary texts that constructed (competing) images of the ideal female citizen at a time when femininity and citizenship were subject to debate. Where should one's loyalties lie? How should the gendered subject express and fight for them?

Unlike some of the polemics on the women question in the press and in treatises motivated by the national question, biographies of women proposed models of womanhood through concrete, historically attested example. But their concreteness produced narratives of womanhood that might challenge the rhetoric framing the life story. For example, in 1914 *The Fair Sex* (*al-Jins al-latif*, founded 1908) lauded French balloonist Sophie Blanchard (d. 1819) as a fine spouse, for she was an untiring support to her husband's adventurous schemes and a careful caretaker of dwindling family finances. Yet with dramatic flair this text also narrated her own exploits in the air. Did schoolgirls pick up the overt message of domesticity's centrality, or did they dream rather of afternoons piloting a balloon to great acclaim? Biography offered an unstable composite image of "perfect" womanhood.

Nancy Armstrong has argued that the centrality of the English novel to the definition of a modern subjectivity constructed first as female (and therefore to shifting the whole socioeconomic basis of English political history) rests partly on the "pleasures of literature," on texts that could shape "moral hegemony ... largely through consent rather than coercion."[13] Like novels in England, biography in Egypt could offer a positive and pleasurable guide to conduct, a mode of thinking about female subjectivity that disguised even as it constructed the centrality of gender to histories of political institutions. Narratives of women's lives might echo and shape the hopes and changing experiences of women editors, writers, and readers. For the women who produced and consumed biographical dictionaries and magazines, these texts operated to construct a collective autobiography of possible future lives.[14] Not at all univocal in what they prescribed and proscribed, these texts were remarkably consistent over time and across a range of publications in marking past (and ongoing) lives of notable women not as extraordinary but as repeatable.[15] They were models that the new (bourgeois, urban) woman might ignore at her peril. The "Famous Women" biographies were part of a larger conduct literature. In Foucauldian terms, they were one cultural technology that could shape ideas about self and community among a targeted group of girls and women. That schoolgirls first heard of Jeanne d'Arc in history class, and that these lectures moved to journals produced for schoolgirls, among others, suggests that teachers and editors recognized biography's didactic potential.

The founding of more than twenty magazines for and about women by 1914, and fourteen more by 1935, suggests strong interest on the part of writers and editors in capturing a growing female readership, although some magazines were directed as much or even more to men—notably, *Woman in Islam*, founded in 1901 by Ibrahim Ramzi, the contributors to which were also men. Yet most journals featuring biography were largely produced by women and aimed rhetorically at a female audience, although men were welcomed as contributors and readers. Prominent examples (all of which published biographies of Jeanne d'Arc) are Labiba Hashim's *Fatat al-sharq* (Young woman of the East, 1906–39); Balsam ʿAbd al-Malik's *Majallat al-marʾa al-Misriyya* (The Egyptian woman's magazine, 1920–39); Ruza Antun's *Majallat al-sayyidat wa al-banat* (The ladies' and girls' magazine, 1903–4)—where Ruza's brother Antun supplied the "Famous Women"—and *Fatat al-Nil* (Young woman of the Nile, 1913–15).[16]

Gender was not the only marker of difference in the "women's press."[17] Many founder-editors, especially in the early period, were Ottoman Syrian ("Shami") immigrants to Egypt, most of them Christians. A few editors and writers, such as Balsam ʿAbd al-Malik, were Egyptian Coptic Christians. Not surprisingly, different emphases surfaced: ʿAbd al-Malik stressed cross-religious national unity and Coptic contributions to nation building. Most of the Egyptian Muslim editors focused on Islam as the basis of a new society, although in the context of competing Egyptian nationalisms and a vocal Islamic reformist movement, this meant different things to different people. The Syrian Christian editors emphasized shared regional or "Arab" interests, celebrating Arab Muslim women as exemplars for Arabs while mostly ignoring non-Arab Muslims, and were muted, if not silent, on separatist Egyptian nationalism in its several faces, eschewing both criticism and praise (although they lauded Egyptian women through biography). The upper echelons of this community were conversant with European societies, to say the least, and Syrians were often accused of being pro-British, not without cause, although for many this was a cultural identification more than a matter of strict political allegiances. Yet in spite of different percentages of Muslim-versus-Christian or Arab-versus-European subjects, the biographies they published were remarkably similar in focus. That Jeanne d'Arc was featured in journals run by Copts, Egyptian Muslims, and Syrian Christians (as well as in a Syrian Muslim's biographical compendium) suggests both the power and mutability of her image and the permeability of ethnic, religious, and political boundaries when it came to the writing of exemplary lives in Egypt.[18]

Yet as they expose the exuberantly inconsistent rhetoric of women's magazines—the variety of outlook within individual magazines as well as among them—the "Famous Women" texts remind one that inconsistency and multiplicity might push the boundaries of women's expectations for themselves. Natalie Zemon Davis has argued that in early modern France, images of "disorderly" and "uncommon" women could both solidify and undermine the social status quo, and that "[p]lay with the exceptional woman-on-top, the virtuous virago, was . . . a resource for feminist reflection on women's capacities." Among such figures was Jeanne d'Arc. "By the early eighteenth century," says Davis, " speculation about virtuous Amazons could be used not only to praise the wise rule of contemporary lawful queens . . . but also to hint at the possibility of a wider role of citizenship for women."[19] In Egypt, life narratives of Jeanne and many other "uncommon women" played a similar role, sanctioning nationalist agendas for state construction while encouraging women to think beyond existing limits—but not too far beyond.

JEANNE IN THE CANON

In France, the United States, and elsewhere early in this century, Jeanne was a powerful symbol of national identity combining tropes of purity and exclusivity, of the necessary crystallization of an idea of nation against a defined other. Martha Hanna has shown the centrality and tractability of the symbolic Jeanne in the political contestations of early-twentieth-century France, and especially in the campaign of the royalist opposition group Action française against the Third Republic.[20] Yet during World War I, the Action deferred to the national crisis, and Jeanne became a symbol of national resistance and reconciliation—and also, ironically, of French-British unity against the Germans. In the United States, it was Jeanne's declaration as "Venerable" in 1894 that sparked "an adulation which lasted for over three decades," as "American periodicals . . . cause[d] Joan of Arc's name to become a familiar household word." It may well have been some of these periodicals from which writers in Egypt obtained their material. For Americans, it was Jeanne's life story, her qualities of "courage, truth, purity, gentleness, and beauty," the romantic possibilities of her image, that popularized her and shaped the presentation of and response to wildly successful treatments like Mary Hartwell Catherwood's fiction *The Days of Jeanne d'Arc*, serialized in 1897 and published in book form immediately thereafter. Interest in Jeanne in Egypt coincided with these moments, and with an outpouring of publications in Europe and North America, scholarly and popular, on Jeanne.[21] Yet the path of cultural translation, of how Jeanne's story traveled to Egypt, remains obscure, for (in the best tradition of Jehannic lore) this was not a path of carefully constructed academic stepping-stones but one of popular-journalistic traversings, of memory, fascination, and romance.

THE EARLIEST BIOGRAPHIES

In Egypt Jeanne's history first appeared in two collections of women's biography authored by women. Zaynab Fawwaz's (ca. 1850–1914) *Scattered Pearls on the Classes of Mistresses of Seclusion* came out in 1894, two years after the launching of the first Arabic women's magazine, the *Young Woman*, and the same year Jeanne was declared Venerable. (In the *Young Woman*'s opening editorial, founder-editor Hind Nawfal had named Jeanne as one foremother to emulate.)[22] One of Fawwaz's few contemporary subjects (and Hind Nawfal's mother), Maryam al-Nahhas (1856–1888) was the first female to write a biographical dictionary of women in Arabic. Her *Fine Woman's Exhibition of Biographies of Famous Women* (1879) never made it into print beyond a prototype of the first volume. Unlike Fawwaz's 552-page work, what al-Nahhas saw into print consisted of a slim sixteen pages, whatever the original manuscript might have been. Yet at least five of the closely printed pages were taken up by a biography of Jeanne d'Arc.[23]

Fawwaz's compendium provided material for, and perhaps inspiration to, women's magazines, most obviously the long-running *Young Woman of the East*.[24] This was not the first journal to feature "Famous Women," for they had appeared in the *Young Woman* and other magazines of the 1890s, but it popularized biographical sketches as a monthly first-page feature that prefaced opinion pieces on the women question; articles on child rearing, home management, cooking, and personal grooming; and fiction. Fawwaz's authorship was not always attributed, but her work was significant in setting up a canon of "Famous Women" to feature.[25]

Fawwaz and al-Nahhas had behind them an august Arabic tradition. The respectability of biography may have attracted them and the editors of women's magazines.[26] Since the third century A.H. (ninth C.E.), biographical dictionaries covering "classes" or generations of eminent individuals had provided an index of Muslim elites and had served the crucial function of testing the legitimacy of oral transmitters of the Prophet's acts and words. From this there emerged an exemplary cast that modern-day writers of didactic biography could exploit. Women had been subjects in medieval male-authored collections, and material for life histories of women abounded in multigeneric literary compendia. But to be the female author of a biographical dictionary of women, and to include non-Muslim and non-Arab women, was unprecedented.[27]

Although Fawwaz patterned her entries on the rhetorical contours of earlier biographical practice, her use of conventional formulas gestured toward an exemplarity that exceeded the boundaries of accepted gender roles for the old and even the newly emerging urban elites. This was consistent with her essays in the general press, attacking commentaries that misrepresented, to Fawwaz, women's social experience, their abilities and needs.

Fawwaz's life history of Jeanne d'Arc begins with a physical portrait. Although we have no evidence of the historical Jeanne's appearance, European iconography had constructed a physical presence that Fawwaz drew upon.[28] In a culture where upper- and middle-class women's hair was covered, and usually their faces as well (although that was already changing among Syrian Christian women like those of the al-Nahhas family),[29] such physicality of description might seem startling. Fawwaz's mention of long hair attracted later biographers. Was this image of femininity displayed meant as a veiled criticism of *hijab* (veiling and seclusion)? Or as an unmistakable marker of the feminine that readers could not ignore? Or were Fawwaz and others simply reproducing European images? Of course, those images displayed bodies from full-figured to Twiggy-like, hairstyles from short and blonde to long and dark, garb from a no-nonsense tunic and armor to a flowing skirt or a gold-worked gown.[30] That writers in Egypt invariably chose long, uncovered hair and "pure" white attire for Jeanne might have arisen from a mission to emphasize the feminine as visible yet, when visible, uncorruptible.

Fawwaz, who refers autobiographically to seclusion's constraining effect in her preface to *Scattered Pearls*,[31] possibly sketched the image of Jeanne's dark tresses as a pointed comment. Certainly, Jeanne's physicality depicted in Fawwaz's words communicated a publicly visible female presence. Yet it is a cautious visibility: Fawwaz's portrait of Jeanne echoes a terminology and ideal of feminine beauty common in Arabic (male-scripted) belletristic and biographical tradition. More important, for Fawwaz physical features articulate a moral countenance, a metaphoric function in line with premodern Arabic biography writing and with other portraits in Fawwaz's dictionary: "Jeanne d'Arc . . . was a French girl who was clear [or: pure] of complexion, slender of build, deep-black of eye, with coal-black hair falling over her shoulders. Visible on her comely countenance were qualities of bashfulness and gentle sweetness, while her features gave indication of resolve, aspiration, and self-possession."[32] Not only would later biographies of Jeanne reiterate this cluster of characteristics; throughout the "Famous Women" genre, this was the core of the ideal woman: bashful and resolute, sweet and self-possessed, mild and highly ambitious. Such a mix of traits was necessary for the dynamic yet self-effacing female presence that many in Egypt, women and men, saw as underwriting their vision of national progress. Indeed, this image could be seen to embrace the contradictory faces of modernity for women in Egypt.

Yet Fawwaz's version was not so self-effacing. For the heroine-appropriate characteristics that mark Jeanne precede a portrait of dynamism, public performance, and vocality, questioning the "bashfulness" of the heroine's demeanor. "How often she mounted her horse and raced ahead [or: competed] when it was not saddled or bridled, out of boldness and chivalry. She was possessed of eloquent speech whose good sense was plain, of deeds based on rectitude, soundness, and utility."[33] Fawwaz employs traditional Arabic literary imagery and Qur'anic diction to pose a profile of the active, utterly visible woman who crosses socially sanctioned gender boundaries (without benefit of saddle or bridle!).

Al-Nahhas, writing earlier, eschewed the reliance on medieval Arabic biography's rhetorical contours that allowed Fawwaz, fifteen years later, to highlight women's visibility through the ages and simultaneously to subvert conservative notions of women's place. What al-Nahhas chose to elucidate via Jeanne was a women's history of public activism, another kind of visibility crucial to the formation of local feminisms. Packing in names of notable women, she summoned an ongoing collective history of female achievement and evoked the power of famous female lives to motivate young girls: "Jeanne recalled what she had heard about women famous for courage (*basala*) and audacious initiative (*iqdam*) who had saved their countries from destruction, such as the women of Bohemia who had borne arms and defended their homeland's honor."[34] Al-Nahhas cements this sense of linkage two pages later, characterizing Jeanne herself with *basala* and *iqdam*, "through which the French were able to expel the English from the country they had taken over and of which they had nearly proclaimed Henry VI king."[35] Given credit for the final expulsion of the English years after her death, Jeanne's action and qualities echo exactly those of the "women of Bohemia."

Notions of community and linkage were crucial in the construction of a collective exemplary image of womanhood through the medium of "Famous Women." Yet the specific content of "community" varied, especially as time passed. Biographies furthered notions of community as female, crossing boundaries of chronology and culture. But increasingly, and especially in the 1920s and 1930s, they also defined "community" as national or regional. This is evident in the Jeanne d'Arc biographies, and it is inseparable from the growing imperative of nationalist anti-imperialist resistance to Great Britain. If al-Nahhas's and Fawwaz's pre-twentieth-century representations of Jeanne privileged the image of the uncompromisingly visible and publicly active woman, they set the stage for her inscription as nationalist heroine in later biographies.

JEANNE D'ARC IN THE SERVICE OF THE NATION

Marina Warner dates Jeanne's transformation into a French national heroine as beginning in the sixteenth century, along with her rebirth as "romantic heroine," removed from the fearsome implications of the previously dominant image of Jeanne as Amazon. Yet it was in the late nineteenth century that she became a "serious political symbol" of unity and national optimism, an embodiment of prevailing European concepts of nationalism.[36]

In Egypt as in France and the United States, in the first decades of the twentieth century Jeanne was coming to represent for some an ideal of national unity, collective vigor based on selfless individual initiative, and community resistance to external aggressors. If in France she stood at the symbolic center of the struggle between monarchism and republicanism, in Egypt she embodied the urgency of a popular response to imperialist force, a response that could (for a time) work with constitutional monarchism. The period of these texts' appearance was that in which the vocabulary of nation and anti-imperialism became so semantically full that popular songs and poetry needed only to mention a few key words to rouse popular sentiment.[37]

The pre-1919 biographies of Jeanne in Egypt treated the English with relative forbearance. Fawwaz, al-Nahhas, an 1895 biography in the mainstream monthly the *Crescent*, and the *Women's and Girls' Magazine*'s 1903 sketch all inclined to dispassionate description of Jeanne's political context.[38] Even so, traditional metaphors and rhetorical patterns, intermittently punctuating the text, called attention to a context of uneven and implacable struggle. For example, Fawwaz selectively utilized rhymed and rhythmic prose (*saj'*), since the Qur'an (and perhaps before) a marker of linguistic and literary superiority but one that was now moving out of favor as writers sought more direct means of communication, especially in the press. The sparseness of Fawwaz's *saj'* gave it added semantic effect, for it highlighted a certain motif: "France was on the edge of a pit of flame, as the English with their wars made her taste humiliating woe mixed with shame."[39] The *Crescent* used a worn literary conceit (which could have been borrowed from European texts) that took on fresh resonance when it was "the claws of the English" from which Jeanne had to rescue France.[40] *Young Woman of the East*'s 1911 biography proposed a motif popular in later texts: Jeanne's death was a "black stain on the English" that history had preserved.[41]

With the second wave of women's journals, founded in the early 1920s mostly by Egyptians rather than immigrant Syrians, Jeanne appeared in full nationalist garb bedecked with dazzling anti-British trimmings. Surely this was a product of both changing times and the changing constitution of the women's press.[42] Ironically, this was the period when some women and men were rejecting the use of Western models for Arab women. In December 1919, the *Fair Sex*, edited by Malaka Sa'd, a Copt, announced a shift in editorial policy toward "Famous Women." Recapitulating the strategy of featuring (white) European and American women as historically necessary, it spelled out changing tactics of biography production in a context of self-justification and assertion against "the West":

> We promised ourselves almost from the magazine's founding to open [each issue] by speaking of lives of individual ladies who had become famous in the West through their beneficial deeds . . . and had made their own lives exalted examples to those growing to adulthood after them. From our Western sisters, we hoped, Eastern women would elicit that which would make our souls strive for the heights and yearn to awaken.
>
> Some years passed, and we began taking pride in our own dear ladies who . . . had taken it upon themselves to labor with the pickax of honor, planting seeds of greatness in their young. Now it is our due to take pride in Eastern women generally, and Egyptian women in particular, for among them have emerged [women] far greater than the famous Western women. We love to bring out the truth and to encourage our Egyptian sisters; this compels us to no longer restrict ourselves to histories of famous European women. From now on we will strive to tell many histories of ancient Egyptian queens and Eastern women geniuses. Let them be a visible example to today's rising young women, who spare no effort for Egypt's emergence and success.[43]

Such a declaration reminds us that 1919, the high point of popular resistance to Britain's imperial presence, was a pivotal point in Egyptians' and other Arabs' formation of a collective identity. Yet such rhetoric was not followed in practice, for in the women's magazines (including the *Fair Sex*) Western biographical subjects continued to appear, and this was as true of Egyptian-run as of Syrian-run publications. In fact, the 1920s saw the publication of nine biographies of Jeanne. Clearly her credentials were transferable.

The first postwar biography of Jeanne in Egypt appeared in *Young Woman of Young Egypt*. Founded in April 1921 by Emily ʿAbd al-Masih, a Copt, it played up cross-religious unity—as its stable of authors, not limited to Copts, confirmed. Its third issue featured "Jeanne d'Arc: Young Woman of Orléans," by Zaynab Sadiq (a Muslim). Here, the diction of imperialist blight has sharpened: the English "plunder and pillage." "Ruin and destruction" spur Jeanne to action. "Zeal" (*hamas*) guides Jeanne more than divine voices do, and *hamas* can have a secular political connotation as much as a religious one. No subtle treatment here of the outcome, either: "[Jeanne] gave the English the worst sort of defeat."[44]

This diction prepares the ground for a telling anachronism that first appears in a biography published later that year; for from the 1920s on, repeated anachronisms lace the rhetoric that frames Jeanne's life. In the *Women's Awakening* it is not the English but the British army that Jeanne faces! This is a startling usage: there were no "British" until nearly three centuries after Jeanne. It becomes even more conspicuous for its siting in a traditional metaphor heard in the *Crescent*'s biography of a quarter-century before: "That girl it was," says Mustafa Bahij, "who rescued France (her dear homeland) from the claws of the powerful British army. It was practically trampling her country underfoot[45] with its horses' hooves and piercing city walls with the force of its projectiles and its strength of assault" (or, "its cockiness"!). When Bahij says Jeanne went to the dauphin "after crossing 150 leagues . . . through regions crammed with the *dababat* of the English and surrounded by trickery and frightening things," it is tempting in light of his evocation of "the British army" to read *dababat* not as medieval catapults but as a modern semantic reincarnation: tanks.[46]

Biographies of the 1920s modify and embellish earlier motifs. Yunus's "History Lesson" of 1922, quoted at the beginning of this essay, echoed Bahij on the English, even though otherwise the two biographies were very different. Yunus went one step further, referring to "the settler-colonialists" from whom Jeanne freed Orléans.[47] In 1925 a biography in the secular nationalist *Magazine of the Egyptian Woman* yokes Bahij's diction to Yunus's: "she had to cross 150 leagues through regions packed with the settler-colonialist English and surrounded by trickery and dangers." This text reinforces the equation of "English" and "colonialist" by incorporating anti-imperialist rhetoric prevalent at the time in popular speeches, poems, and songs. Charles VII asks Jeanne, "How can I part from the one who has saved France from capture, slavery, and servitude?"[48]

It is difficult not to see the political turmoil of early-twentieth-century Egypt in these biographies—not just in the characterization of the "rapacious enemy" but in a representation of domestic politics.[49] Charles VII is portrayed not only as weak but as "living a life of degradation and apathy in his court, surrounded by a retinue with no concern but to eat and drink. It never occurred to them to think about France as it was perishing and suffering the evil of punishment."[50] While this echoed the image of Charles VII dominant in European Jeanne legends, it is easily read as an acceptably veiled comment on the internal politics of resistance in Egypt. Disaffection with Egypt's Sultan (later King) Fu'ad had been openly expressed in 1919 through broadsides and colloquial poetry. Through the 1920s the same attitude obtained: "Fu'ad's failure to assume a strong nationalist stance in the face of British control (as well as his propensity for good living *à la européene*) had made him an object of scornful indifference to much of the local populace, and a source of despair to the nationalist leadership."[51]

FAITH, THE NATION, AND A TRAGIC END

In the West Jeanne had become more a secular than a religious symbol, infused with the romantic conception of nature as defining goodness and conferring grace.[52] This may have been as true for the religious establishment as for the proponents of a romantic nationalism; scholars have suggested that Jeanne was canonized in 1920 "not for her visions or her exploits in the name of the faith but for her exemplary life."[53] Moreover, in the context of post-Enlightenment rationalism in Europe the nature of Jeanne's "voices" was problematic—were they of divine, external provenance, or were they the product of Jeanne's inner imaginings? Finally, Jeanne's story posed a challenge to religiously defined authoritarianism because by highlighting the role of the French bishopry in Jeanne's trial and execution, writers could attack the established church as a bigoted, reactionary force in French history and could highlight its class interests against those of the bourgeoisie and peasantry. In many European treatments, Jeanne's own religiosity was muted in her usefulness as a populist, anticlerical symbol.

Thus to highlight Jeanne as a *religious* icon posed a departure from contemporary Western iconography.[54] But for writers in Egypt, Jeanne's mission as divine suited a milieu where obedience was unquestioningly a matter of submission to divine law. Of even greater salience was the notion of religiosity as providing an unassailable sanction and source of energy for nationalist action. For example, *Morals of the Young Woman*'s 1926 life of Jeanne confirmed the bond between divine sanction and nation, repeating the imagery of blood/ patriotism conflated: "God foreordained a girl in whose veins the blood of patriotism ran hotly."[55] This anchors the finale's call to arms: "Truly the way of God is the way of the nation. Whosoever dies for the sake of the nation indeed has died in the way of God."[56]

For liberal nationalist thinkers in Egypt, "secularity" presumed that individuals had a religious identity and a sense of community based on religion, but that such a sense could be subordinated to identity as a member of a territorially defined nation.[57] This view presumed the coexistence of different religions under a single deity—and under a single state. While earlier biographies in Egypt had spoken of Jeanne's mission as divinely appointed, it was in the early 1920s that readers would find God and nation coupled: "In her heart she bore unflagging faith and firmness. She strove for the nation's sake until God inscribed a mighty victory for her and she scattered her enemies completely."[58] A dramatic finale to this biography invoked that cross-culturally captivating image of Jeanne as heroine of the oppressed:

> God knows she was innocent . . . but what does the weak, wronged one do before tyrannical powers? . . . How fervid the moan of the wronged, innocent ones, as it ascends to the heavens to affirm the glory of the soul, the greatness of the spirit. It inscribes an everlasting document, witness to humanity's wrongdoing, its tyranny to and enslavement of weak brothers. . . . The sharp curses the weak bring down on the tyrannical strong are the sole power in the hands of the weak. O that the tyrannical oppressor listen to the moan of the anxious, to the wail of the wronged! When the fires rose, Jeanne entered. She began to murmur, to say unintelligible things, to supplicate her tortured nation with an agony that made her harsh, hard-hearted enemies weep.[59]

Here, the text links the sanction of the divine to the moral inevitability of the triumph of the weak. In the context of hopes wrought locally by Woodrow Wilson's postwar declaration of the right of self-determination, nation-right was literally sacred.

Irene Fenoglio-Abd El Aal has noted that religion was assumed unquestioningly as the grounding of the ethical domain and of nationalism in (some) 1920s Egyptian women's magazines. For the *Magazine of the Women's Awakening* this was an Islamic grounding; for the *Egyptian Woman's Magazine*, it was a "more discreet," unspecified religious basis.[60] In either case, writers in Egypt accepted without question that Jeanne took her cues from divinely inspired visions. For it was convenient indeed that divine sanction could legitimate both nationalist struggle and women's visible participation therein.

What message might Jeanne's tragic end, not at all muted in these biographies, offer to young women in Egypt? That they must ultimately sacrifice their own interests to those of the nation elided the question of what their own interests might be. Jeanne's individuality and her anguish disappear beneath the glory of her sacrifice, as she supplicates not God but her "tortured nation." Putting community above self was a goal to be constantly borne in mind, and the confluence of national need and religious obligation emerged in a diction whose religious overtones could hardly be overlooked: "Is there anything more awesome than sacrifice!—the sacrifice of evanescent matter for the sake of the eternal nation's pleasing prosperity."[61] In these biographies, Jeanne is sacrificed not because she is a female out of bounds, but because she is a successful anti-imperialist who awakens her "nation" to action.

If Jeanne's image(s) encapsulated unresolved tensions between individual and community identity, definitions of proper gendered comportment and national duty that marked the liberatory discourses of the time, there was another crucial element to her embodiment of the nation for readers in Egypt. The biographical subject of the "Famous Women" genre was almost invariably aristocratic, elite, or from a European (and increasingly local) middle class: these were the women whose lives were to be emulated, just as these were the readers whom magazine editors envisioned. But the Jeanne biographies, taking a potent symbol of national strength as their focus, had to take account of a world beyond that of an emerging national(ist) bourgeoisie. They did so in terms that harnessed that world to an Egyptian liberal (bourgeois) nationalist program.

CLASS AND NATION: THE PEASANT AS NATIONALIST ICON

If class was generally unspoken as a marker of ideal womanhood in the "Famous Women" texts, it was nonetheless articulated in the choice of biographical subjects and the life pattern constructed as that of the "ideal woman."[62] Of course, as middle-class women began to populate the professional working stratum in the early twentieth century, biographies of middle-class Egyptian women became more numerous in magazines catering to them, such as *Magazine of the Women's Awakening* and the *Egyptian Women's Magazine*. European middle-class women notable for public and especially intellectual achievements, or alternatively (or simultaneously!) for their woman-behind-the-man roles, had been profiled all along. Women outside this socioeconomic range rarely appeared. The image of the ideal female citizen was to be constructed on a bourgeois ideal of national unity. When a working-class woman did appear, almost invariably the motif of individual effort on behalf of the nation framed her. This gave the subject significance. It allowed her to be a subject.[63] And it narrowed the differentiation between her and her upper-class compatriots.

Warner claims that one element of Jeanne d'Arc's attractiveness as icon was that she was above class. She exemplified prophecy as "a career open to talents," and, as peasant, she fit the revolutionary ideal of nobility conferred by merit rather than by birth.[64] And by the late nineteenth century, in the embrace of romantic nationalism in Europe the child-peasant overshadowed other available images of Jeanne.[65] But in the Egyptian context Jeanne's utility was not so much in occluding class as in incorporating it into a nationalist ideology, not quite the same thing. Jeanne offered an impeccable representation of the peasant as pillar of the nation. And if this image was borrowed, that did not mute its resonance on the Egyptian scene.

Jeanne's village origins are not dwelt upon in the earliest biographies from Egypt. It is the flood of biographies in the 1920s that celebrate Jeanne as peasant—biographies that appear in Egyptian-run magazines, at a time when Egyptian nationalism was heavily imbued with a "salt-of-the-earth" romanticism. They are the same biographies, by and large, that highlight resistance to "the British" as colonizers.

Yunus, writing in 1922, is the first to label Jeanne a *fatat fallaha*, a "peasant girl, grown from the earth of Domrémy, fleeing from her father the shepherd."[66] This precedent occurs in a narrative that explicitly exemplifies a "universal" lesson—historically attested, teleologically inevitable, the author suggests—about ignoring women's abilities: "This fine woman was burned in the Rouen marketplace. About fifty years later people realized her worth and filled the French air with statues of her. For people had come to understand woman's status, to comprehend that she might surpass man. Perhaps a woman could even lead men. For every nation that diminishes the value of its women courts speedy ruin."[67] Yunus ties this in to the fortunes of the nation. That the *fallaha* label first occurs here signals the urgency of representing the peasant as well as the female in such a way as to foster the formation of an ethos of national, "classless" unity.

Jeanne's childhood provides a narrative of pastoral that romanticized the peasantry in line with the prevailing liberal nationalist discourse. For the *Egyptian Women's Magazine* in 1925, "[Jeanne's] childhood was naive and pure, as is the case for offspring of herdsmen who know nothing of this life but fresh air, light, freedom, and their songs, which they chant standing next to their quiet livestock."[68] Jeanne's family did indeed make a living from their own livestock. The family was not wealthy, but they had a solid economic base, and Jeanne's father may have held official posts in Domrémy.[69] He was hardly the "herdsman" of these sketches, a figure that perhaps reflects an urban, nationalist bourgeois perception of rural society.[70] The unsullied goodness of the Ideal Peasant is yoked to the "true national sentiment" Jeanne embodies.[71]

That the stalwart, close-to-nature peasant and the courageous nationalist leader could merge in one figure on horseback accentuated the topos of the *fallah(a)* as backbone of the nation. This was an image dear to the hearts of many nationalist intellectuals, often urbanites who looked back nostalgically to rural roots. Muhammad Haykal, from a prominent, well-off, urbanized family that of course retained its rural landowning base, gave himself the pseudonym "An Egyptian Fallah" when he published his novel *Zaynab: Manazir wa-akhlaq rifiyya* (Zaynab: Rural scenes and manners) in 1913.[72] This classic of romantic nationalism constructed the peasant most strikingly in the title character. Zaynab is victim both of constraints imposed on females in her milieu and of class-based injustice. Perhaps the trodden-upon Zaynab could metamorphose into a positive heroine in the figure of Jeanne d'Arc, an image more akin to the heroic *fallaha*-as-Egypt works of the sculptor and national hero Mahmud Mukhtar. At the same time, Jeanne was helpfully distant. Celebrating her peasant origins did not require attending to the conditions of life that peasants in Egypt endured.

Just as in France Jeanne could come to represent the nation, in Egypt she could represent the perfect nationalist product of a concern with "uplifting" the peasant and "training" women—all for the betterment of the nation. She stood for individual initiative, the primacy of national duty and the incorporation of religious loyalties therein, the necessity of sacrifice for the nation, and the virtue of the rural populace.

If Jeanne embodied Egyptian nationalist ideals effectively, in the terms of local gender politics she could be constructed as unthreatening. Her assumption of a "male" role could be glossed as anomalous even as it underlined the lengths to which the loyal "citizen," male or female, might go in the interests of the nation. Jeanne's femaleness featured prominently in these texts. It made her exemplary. But it was not necessarily Jeanne as public figure alone that was to be emulated. The same biographies that emphasized Jeanne's peasant origins and privileged the diction of anti-imperialist nationalism tended to

feature the domestic, nurturing Jeanne. For an active public woman must return to the hearth. The domestic had to frame the rest—even if highlighting
women's other pursuits implicitly questioned motherhood and home management as privileged or all-consuming identities.

THE FAMILY: NATIONALIST FATHER, NURTURING MOTHER

The "Famous Women" biographies continually construct images of family
and parental roles as central to the self-fulfillment and sense of duty (familial/
national) of the ideal modern woman. The family grouping presented in biography is insistently nuclear, as in the conduct literature aimed at women that
publishers in Egypt were offering.[73] This was consonant with liberal nationalist analyses of how women as the core of a well-defined family unit were
to advance national development. It was not only the "Famous Woman"
who provided the model but also her parents. The Jeanne biographies were
no exception.

The ideal father for a "Famous Woman" was that ubiquitous figure in liberal
male nationalist discourse of the time, the supportive liberal father who actively sought his daughter's education.[74] The villain was the one who resisted,
vocally and by erecting obstacles in the way of his daughter's professional
desires. Jacques d'Arc, an ambiguous enough figure in "Jehannic Studies," is
not a neutral figure in these texts. By and large he appears as villain: an obstacle to Jeanne's desires, he is also a foil that highlights her determination. For
Fawwaz, Jeanne's "father showed her harshness and violence to the point
where she would flee"—an echo of Fawwaz's attacks on the treatment of girls
in her essays in the press.[75] For the *Morning*, Jacques's alleged bad treatment
contrasted with Jeanne's goodness: when five-year-old (*sic*) Jeanne's father
heard she was having visions, "he beat her until she was forced to flee, to work
as a servant with a widow who owned a hostel. There she appeared an exemplar of the chaste, active, serious girl."[76]

By the mid-1930s, though, the family rather than just the father takes center
stage. An ideal image of the nuclear family—complete with a clearly defined
gendered division of labor—permeates a 1938 biography in the *Festival*: "It
was her three brothers who helped her father in tilling the soil and tending the
livestock. As for Jeanne and her sisters, they took care of the housework,
mended the clothes, did needlework, and so forth."[77] Here, the ideal female
subsumes the ideal peasant girl, out tending her family's flocks. Within this
image of the nuclear family, Jeanne's father appears as a good-hearted man
who cared for his children, who opposed Jeanne out of concern rather than
fixed ideas of a girl's place.

In the "Famous Women" texts collectively, mothers—both mothers of biographical subjects and subjects themselves—got plaudits as conscientious par-

ents for whom motherhood ("training" the offspring) was central. Yet, consciously or not, such mothers prepared daughters for more than one kind of work and more than one avenue to self-fulfillment.[78] The power of the image of the educating mother emerges in *Al-Mahrajan*'s biography of Jeanne. Having disposed of the father, the author declares, "His wife Isabella cared for [the children] and taught them how to read and write."[79] The specificity of this description, its consonance with liberal nationalist views of women's role as educator of future nationalists (and also with the programs of early feminists), stands out against Jeanne's known history: while by the end of her life she was able to sign her name, she probably had at most only "some rudimentary writing ability," and her mother was almost certainly illiterate.[80]

AFTER THE BATTLE: THE HEROINE AS HOMEBODY

Jeanne's insertion into the domestic follows a dominant rhetorical practice in the "Famous Women" genre: these biographies construct domesticity as the anchor of female existence, but an anchor with many ropes. Through the 1930s the perfect nationalist woman as portrayed in biography combines informed domesticity with work outside the home that is constructed as unthreatening to a strictly gendered division of labor. Moreover, most (but not all) types of work approvingly portrayed presume a certain class identity by assuming achievable levels of education, leisure, and independent income: charity work, teaching, writing.[81] These texts also celebrate full-time wives and mothers of nationalists: raising a nationalist son (*sic*) is the quintessential female nationalist act. But as I have already suggested, these portraits are subject to competing interpretations. That domesticity was placed at the center made possible the argument for other lives.[82]

The Jeanne texts demonstrate how biography could convey an ambiguous message to Egyptian schoolgirls, for Jeanne's life fit uncomfortably at best into a narrative of domesticity and clearly defined gender roles. Jeanne's apparent rejection of a domestic life (through her acts, if not her words), her insistent virginity, her visibility, and her cross-dressing contradict the message of domesticity's centrality.[83] How was her image reconciled with it?

The attributes that mark Jeanne from one biography to another echo those that characterize other "Famous Women": determination, intelligence, boldness, integrity, steadfastness. Her image contrasts repeatedly with that of Charles VII as vacillating and fearful. Adversity and opposition intensify her will to act, as when she meets only "scorn and indifference" from "the commander of the French armies, because of the grossness of his nature, the harshness of his heart, and his arrogance; but she could not be budged."[84] Her sterling qualities overwhelm all else and defuse resistance to her acts: "Even her enemies mourned her for her steadfastness and courage . . . and admitted she was the best of maidens in character and religion."[85] Such qualities become exemplary markers of the feminine, as when the *Egyptian Woman's Magazine* inserts a generalizing declaration into its biography of the Maid of Orléans: "and woman is resolute if she determines so to be."[86]

These narratives highlighted Jeanne's visibility. Yet, if Jeanne as historical figure was in the limelight, Egyptian biographies characterized her as uninterested in public fame and celebration. Jeanne's alleged dismissal of Charles's planned banquet after the victory at Orléans, for instance, illustrated simultaneously her seriousness, her selflessness, and her modesty: "The king invited her to a feast but she refused, saying it was a time for effort and determination, not for revelry and gratification."[87] Modesty implied simplicity, too: her attested love of finery[88] never appears in these texts. (This silence supported the media's widespread, fervid warnings of a purported increase in ostentatious women, especially those consuming European fashions.)

As in contemporaneous European representations of Jeanne, her masculine dress is glossed as battlefield necessity. The possibility of a more abiding interest in cross-dressing does not arise.[89] Her masculine demeanor, moreover, is offset by an emphasis on her flowing hair and the whiteness (purity!) of her garb—a different way of expressing the same message, perhaps, as is conveyed by European paintings of Jeanne in armor and flowing skirt.[90]

These biographies articulate a concept of femininity shaped by national duty—and national duty as shaped by a concept of feminine action. Jeanne, domesticated, counters the "masculine" aspects of her public heroism and reifies the division of "public" and "private" into "masculine" and "feminine."[91] Jeanne at home in Egypt constructs an image of acceptable feminine action consistent with dominant motifs in the "Famous Women" genre, notably women's activism as selfless and community-oriented. A trajectory of emergence from and return to the home defines the enterprise. Such constructions uphold an essentialist view of women's nature yoked to nationalism as domestic duty: "[Jeanne] breathed into [the army] her patriotism and zeal so their hearts were set on fire. How beautiful is the holy striving of woman, how innocent her fidelity. She is loyal to her nation as she is to her child; she loves her country as she loves flowers and sweet basil. She has no greedy ambitions: it cannot be said that she has incentives, as certain men do, for her love of the nation. No: she loves it because she sees this as her duty."[92]

The message schoolgirl readers were to receive inscribed definite boundaries around women's public activism. For example, an oft-repeated motif was Jeanne's desire to return home after the crowning at Rheims: "Today I have fulfilled all I promised to do for your victory, so free me and I shall return to my father, that I may watch the livestock and spin wool in conformity to the ways of the house in which I was raised." Yet Jeanne's desire to return home communicates an ambiguous message: for she does not return.[93]

The Egyptian Jeanne (like many other "Famous Women") shows sensibilities these biographers define as feminine. She did not kill with her own hands, they stress, a point on which she insisted during her condemnation trial (1431).[94] Biographies celebrate her nurturing capacity: for the *Crescent* only "caring for the poor" lifted her low spirits in the uncertain time after Charles's coronation.[95] For Sadiq, "[Jeanne's] compassion meant she did not fail to bind the wounds of the stricken enemies."[96] In the transcripts of Jeanne's trials, witnesses talked of her occupation with the poor of her environs, and she herself spoke of her distress at seeing blood flow.[97] But what writers in Egypt emphasized was compassion as a marker of the feminine more than as a sign of intense piety and virtue.

The Egyptian Jeanne's pointedly feminized nationalist role reaches its rhetorical height in Saniyya Zuhayr's 1933 biography in the *Egyptian Woman's Magazine*. Zuhayr couples her essentialist blueprint of complementary gender roles with a high-romantic image of Jeanne: "With her femininity and tenderness woman is able to do what the strongest, most courageous men cannot, for in that gentleness and tenderness resides a magic that pierces to the depths of [people's] hearts, giving them whatever stamp the woman desires and wills."[98] Jeanne fits the mold: watching her father's sheep "imprinted her with that gentleness and softness. She became famous in her environs for her purity and her compassion for the sick and poor."[99] News of war stirred up "sympathy and mournfulness" in young Jeanne. Her description echoes romantic-era images of Jeanne popular in the West (and earlier treatments in Egypt), for "she wore the garb of soldiers but no helmet. Her beautiful hair ran freely on her shoulders, bound by a white band, so that she was distinguishable among the soldiers."[100] Jeanne's actions as constructed in these texts conform to this "feminine" image: she was "respected" and "worshiped" by the soldiers and "did not intervene in their technical movements but rather left that to the commander, Dunois. She limited herself to urging on (*ighra'*) the troops [by telling them] God was with them."[101] Here, Zuhayr follows a European thematics of Jeanne evident from the earliest sources, but one from which Jeanne's legend as constructed by popular collective memory in the West diverges. It is most likely that Jeanne did not "lead" the troops in terms of being the military commander in charge. However, it seems unlikely that her role was limited to that of "urging on." Contemporary and later sources attest that commanders sought her judgment on tactics, and that she was indeed in the thick of battle: "in the matter of war she was very expert," testified the duc d'Alençon at her rehabilitation trial, "in the management of the lance as in the drawing up of the army in battle order and in preparing the artillery. And at that all marvelled."[102] Zuhayr emphasizes a battlefield role that feminizes Jeanne's image according to prevailing constructions of nationalist femininity in Egypt that were themselves constructed partly out of nineteenth-century European gender ideologies. At the same time, this role fits nicely into the high Arabic tradition, wherein it is a commonplace that pre-Islamic and early Muslim women frequented the battlefields—to encourage and shame "their men" into action.[103]

Zuhayr insistently denies any threat that Jeanne as symbol might pose to received notions of gender boundaries: "when the battle [at Orléans] ended, her feminine characteristics returned to her. She wept at the blood and the slain she saw and the moaning of the wounded she heard."[104] These boundaries had shifted substantially by the 1930s, when this text appeared. Perhaps Zuhayr's insistence was comforting to some, dubiously nostalgic to others.

COMMUNITY AND COMMUNITIES

The Jeanne biographies gave urgency to the question of whether Egyptian national identity and the formation of feminist discourses could depend on models appropriated from the West. While Jeanne could serve as a faultless anti-imperialist heroine and exemplar, some editors were uncomfortable with the level of decontextualization that Jeanne as exemplar demanded. I have already noted that as nationalist resistance to Great Britain came to permeate Egyptian society, anxiety about using Western subjects pervaded the "Famous Women" sketches. If exemplary biography constructed a female community that superseded national and ethnic boundaries, and if it occluded power asymmetries between colonizer and colonized, a discourse that *interrogated* notions of community often framed individual "Famous Women," including Jeanne d'Arc. Mobilizing a theme common in nationalist and reformist discourses, this approach voiced admiration for what (aristocratic and middle-class) women of the West had achieved, as it articulated a critical position on European and North American societies and asserted local pride and identity defined against that collective Other.

The "Famous Women" biographies complicate the issue of intellectual Arab women's attitudes toward European women. They challenge scholarship that has constructed a binary "Westernized versus vernacular" framework for the study of Arab feminisms especially in Egypt.[105] For if some biographies repressed links between liberal ideologies of gender and imperialist practices by celebrating European women whose achievements had advanced their nations' expansionist objectives, others questioned the narrative of colonial superiority by showing "their women" as subject to the same restraints as "ours" (this could foreground a class alliance, too). Through narrative, biographies rejected the notion of the colonized subject's innate inferiority by privileging commonalities of experience and differing social conditions. They asserted local histories against imported ones, resisting the subsumption of Egypt into a historical narrative written by the colonizers.

Twice, *Young Woman of the East* profiled an anonymous "Young Woman of Qaraqish [a town in Libya]." The first time was in 1912, the year after the

Italians had invaded Libya, generating impassioned sympathy, concern, and anxiety in Egypt.[106] According to Margot Badran, the war "propelled Egyptian women into collective action," relief work to support the Libyans.[107] The second version came out in 1919 during the most intense period yet of nation-wide anti-British action in Egypt, and at a time when the Libyan resistance was pushing the Italians to the coast.[108] In both cases the narrative celebrated Libyan popular resistance to Italian imperialist desire and pointedly noted the cross-gender (but highly differentiated) nature of this resistance: "the women show no less courage [than the men] in the thick of the fray, for they follow their men and encourage them. They don't fear the sound of heavy guns."[109] This approving description echoed the same gendered battlefield function at-tested in medieval biographies for pre-Islamic and early Muslim women and intertextually articulated in Zuhayr's biography of Jeanne. Utilizing this mate-rial, editors celebrated women's presence on the battlefield, but here *Young Woman of the East* went further: the exhortatory role is named as equal in activism and courage to men's fighting role. The profile constructed a village heroine who led "sons of her people" into battle, who was wounded but "re-mained courageous" and upright.[110] The Young Woman of Qaraqish bore an uncanny resemblance to Jeanne d'Arc.

Indeed, European journalists had been calling this young woman "the sec-ond Jeanne d'Arc," said *Young Woman of the East* (1912). But this European media labeling was an unacceptable frame for the heroine's life story. "*We* believe this courage coming from Arab girls to be nothing strange among us. So we should name her Khawla [bint al-Azwar, a famous early Muslim war-rior, another popular "Famous Woman"]." Instead of relying on European sources, the text quoted at length from an essay on the Libyan heroine published by Turkish writer Fatima ʿAliyya in the Istanbul press.[111] ʿAliyya elaborates on the "Khawla" theme by enumerating (with some exaggeration) Muslim women once prominent in military conflict. Her choice of example is strategic: these women fought the crusaders.

> The French have Jeanne d'Arc. Just one, but they never forget her. Yet the pages of our history overflow with reports of our daughters whose courage raised them to the ranks of heroes. Can we add this woman's name to those of her forebears?
>
> When the crusader armies attacked Aleppo, Hanifa—daughter of al-Malik al-ʿAdil, ruler of Egypt, and niece of the famous Salah al-Din al-Ayyubi [Saladin]—led an army to defend her homeland. She gave the enemy huge losses and the worst sort of defeat, making [the army] retreat. The one who defeated King Louis, or St. Louis, in the battle of Mansura was Shajarat al-Durr, leader of an army.[112]

The effect is to construct a collective resistance to a European naming of Arab/Muslim/colonized experience, and simultaneously to chastise a community for ignoring its own historical precedents. ʿAliyya's rhetoric overwhelms the sin-gularity of Jeanne d'Arc by asserting a numerical superiority of "local" fighting women. In the end, this resistance—and this gendered collectivity—embrace an urban Turkish Muslim (ʿAliyya); a Syrian Christian resident in Egypt (Labiba Hashim, *Young Woman of the East*'s founder-editor and biographical columnist); a rural Libyan Muslim (the young woman of Qaraqish); an early Arab heroine from the Arabian peninsula (Khawla); and two medieval Muslim women leaders (ʿAliyya's heroines Hanifa and Shajarat al-Durr).[113]

The 1919 version omits ʿAliyya's text. And instead of "the second Jeanne d'Arc," the heroine is "the Arab Jeanne d'Arc." No discomfort with the borrowed label? Perhaps now it was enough to change the modifier. This gave the subject a regionwide collective identity and implied Arab solidarity against European colonialisms, subordinating the heroic European figure to a politics of anti-imperialism.[114]

The construction of both commonality and separate histories in "Famous Women" narratives contests the long-standing assertion that feminist agendas in the Arab world (most work has centered on Egypt) were entirely of Western origin. To argue that liberal feminist programs were uncritically Westernist—or that nationalist and feminist treatments of the women question were wholly derivative of colonial discourse—ascribes an inaccurate passivity to local debates and fails to appreciate the complex uses of Westernizing discourses. Quite literally, writers used and contested Western images in the service of their own agendas.[115]

The complexity of this position is beautifully illustrated by the *Magazine of the Women's Awakening*'s 1926 biography of Zakiyya ʿAbd al-Hamid Sulayman, daughter of a prominent Bedouin. The biography narrated Zakiyya's career, from study in England to educational leadership as a trainer of teachers and founder of schools, a high bureaucrat in the Egyptian government. Anecdotes from Zakiyya's student life construct a powerful model:

> An English[-nationality] teacher was explaining the life history of Jeanne d'Arc to her class. When she reached the point of [Jeanne's] rout of the English, [Zakiyya] clapped her hands without even being aware of it, so taken was she by the idea of heroism. When [the teacher] came to how that courage was consumed by fire, tears came from [Zakiyya's] eyes—the most eloquent possible expression of her innermost being; and then she shouted, "Let the English leave our country!" The teacher was astonished and said to her in a tone full of insinuation, "You are still Egyptian?" [Zakiyya] answered her without a pause, "This eternal [source of] pride will always be mine."[116]

This passage challenges a common complaint in the Egyptian press of the time: that Egyptian girls abroad were losing their Egyptianness. At the same time, it aligns biographer and subject with a strong anti-imperialist stance, and it implies that individual goals and nationalist ones need not be in conflict. Moreover, the text illustrates the didactic potential of biography in the training of a female elite. Jeanne as exemplar turns Zakiyya into exemplar.

A CONCLUSION

Jeanne's presence in Egypt exploited her European personae. Egyptian nationalist and feminist agendas intersected conveniently with changing European images of Jeanne: from available iconography, authors in Egypt chose what they found useful. These texts mirrored the contours of the romantic humanist inscription of Jeanne dominant in nineteenth-century France. Jeanne as peasant, Jeanne as symbol of a strong and independent nation, Jeanne as an example to women—all found their way into Egypt. What did not appear was the skeptical, rationalist strain in European polemics on Jeanne, the romantic notion of inner inspiration as opposed to external, divine direction, or the relative lack of interest in Jeanne as religious icon in a turn-of-the-century America shaped by the ideology of Protestantism.[117]

Above all, the iconography of Jeanne in Egypt exploited her potential as a figure of anti-imperialist struggle who embodied a liberal nationalist program. For in a single persona she could combine the tropes of unificatory nationalism (rendering temporarily unproblematic, if not invisible, the divisions of gender, region, class, and even religious identity), women's active social participation as crucial to successful nationhood, and the struggle of minority groups for justice against fearsome odds. She was the female leader contesting gender oppression in her own life to act on behalf of a community. She was Maude Gonne, "the Irish Joan of Arc"; Christabel Pankhurst, the "Warrior Maiden"; Ida B. Wells, a "Joan of Arc" model for an African-American girl; Ann Northrup on horseback in the New York City 1996 Gay and Lesbian Pride March.[118] In a nation like Egypt demanding freedom from European colonial rule, writers turned Jeanne's image against its Western origins, exploiting a potent Western cultural symbol as a visible sign of East-West encounter, a tragic yet inevitably triumphant struggle of weak against strong.

Clearly, these biographical sketches do show change over time, even as they exhibit continuity of theme. Early feminists tended to emphasize community as female, while those most concerned with a nationalist agenda, or a regional Arab struggle for autonomy against the Ottomans and the Europeans alike, stressed community as ethnic or national, downplaying differences of gender, religion, and territorial loyalty. For Fawwaz, who frequently contributed essays to the mainstream press on women's need for independent employment possibilities and greater mobility, as well as ripostes to those who highlighted gender differences as natural and immutable, Jeanne was above all the model of a publicly active woman who could transgress received gender boundaries when necessary, and who commanded respect for her public work. Such emphases grew more muted over time as a politics that defined women first and foremost as the educated and educating mother, the modern domestic woman, became paramount (and, argues Badran, as reformist nationalists' interest in an alliance with feminists plummeted after the 1922 "independence").[119] This image had to contend with Jeanne as anti-imperialist heroine, as the articulation of an anti-British nationalism grew increasingly urgent.

Fighting "British imperialism," Jeanne could stand for a national resistance that highlighted women and the peasantry, foregrounded selflessness and sacrifice as the duty of women and peasants, and helped define nation as inclusive while romanticizing the terms of that inclusiveness. Impeccable in her saintly aura, Jeanne could embody a gendered nationalist identity simultaneously militant and domesticated.

The extent to which any of Jeanne's Egyptian lives were "feminist" and "Arab" depends entirely on the immediate context of production and discourse in which they surfaced. This context is itself responsive to the complexity of defining identities against discursive and material onslaughts on Egyptian society, personal and communal seductions from within and without, and modes of defining nation and society that were fiercely local and self-consciously modern. Moreover, these texts (and the "Famous Women" biographies collectively) suggested through their ordering of priorities and attributes that to be a (happy) new woman was not necessarily to celebrate the public and the modern unequivocally. Lila Abu-Lughod warns us in her introduction to this volume that "[t]he tricky task . . . is how to be suspicious of modernity's progressive claims of emancipation and critical of its social and cultural operations and yet appreciate the forms of energy, possibility, even power that aspects of it might have enabled, especially for women." It was no less tricky for women and men in Egypt then. If highlighting biographical subjects as paragons of domesticity could be a defensive act against public lives for women, equally this could suggest that "real women" had used constructions of domesticity to expand their lives in ways that gave them satisfaction. The move between territories of the home and community space could be justified in terms of national need.

In Egypt as elsewhere, Jeanne's image invites attention to intersections of national and sexual politics, and how the female body resides at the very center of political contestation, where "culture appears as a struggle among various political factions to possess its most valued signs and symbols."[120] In Egypt as elsewhere, Jeanne's femaleness provided a point of interrogation as much as an image of accepted, unquestioned heroism. That Jeanne could be appropriated at all in Egypt reminds us how unpredictable may be the interactions of nationalist, anti-imperialist, and pro-Western discourses; but also of the power of that common confluence of the national and the sexual, the female body as emblematic of the nation. The equivocal nature of Jeanne's image for Egyptians reminds us that, as Eve Sedgewick has said, "it may be that there exists for nations, as for genders, simply no normal way to partake of the categorical definitiveness of the national, no single kind of 'other' of what a nation is to which all can ... be definitionally opposed."[121] At the same time, Jeanne's story defined as "categorical other" the imperialist presence of Great Britain and reminded readers of the enormity of the empire's reach, geographically and historically.

Perhaps Jeanne's popularity in Egypt during the period of nationalist struggle was sustained by her "anti-British" aura. Yet, as I have tried to show, it arose from a convenient cluster of characteristics that narratives of her life could foreground, and from the power of her image to explore and resolve the troubled relationships between the communities she could represent—above all, the conflicted relationship between emerging feminism and nationalism. The rhetorical power of her image in these texts underlines my argument that women's biography worked to stabilize a model of womanhood appropriate to the demands of an emerging ethos of nationalist state construction. Yet narratives of a life could break open the socially sanctioned boundaries of female experience, potentially destabilizing any fixed image of "womanhood." As subjects of biography, not only Jeanne but an admirer of Jeanne could accomplish this, as the biography of Zakiyya ʿAbd al-Hamid Sulayman, English-trained daughter of a Bedouin, shows. Zakiyya's zeal is firmly nationalist and is not linked explicitly to imagining possibilities for her own life. As some writers of biography sought to direct women's energies toward "national needs," women and girls could read off a message of self-determination, individual as well as collective. That Zakiyya had a high-profile public career when this biography appeared could not have escaped the notice of its readers.

In 1937, the Egyptian Woman's Magazine called Jeanne d'Arc "an aberrant exemplar to her kind."[122] This captures perfectly the double-edged prescriptive potential of the "Famous Women" biographies as performances of a gendered and colonized modernity. Jeanne, "aberrant" and "exemplar," could mark out more than one future for imaginative schoolgirls in early-twentieth-century Egypt.

APPENDIX

I. Chronological List of Biographies of Jeanne d'Arc in Egypt, 1879–1938

Al-Nahhas, Maryam. "Jan Dark." In Maryam ibnat Jibra'il Nasrallah al-Nahhas, qarinat Nasim Nawfal al-Tarabulsiyya al-Suriyya, *Mithal li-kitab Maʿrad al-hasna' fi tarajim mashahir al-nisa'*. Alexandria: Matbaʿat Jaridat Misr, 1879. Pp. ?[7]–11.

Fawwaz, Zaynab. "Jan Dark." In Zaynab bint ʿAli al-Fawwaz al-ʿAmili, *Kitab al-Durr al-manthur fi tabaqat rabbat al-khudur*. Cairo/Bulaq: Al-Matbaʿa al-Amiriyya, A.H. 1312 [1894 C.E.]. Pp. 122–24.

"Jan Dark, fatat Urliyan." [Ser. Ashhar al-hawadith wa-a'zam al-rijal.] *Al-Hilal* 4, no. 4 (October 1895): 121–28; 4, no. 5 (November 1895): 166–68.

"Jan Dark: fatat anqadhat watanaha bi'l-harb." [Ser. Ashhar al-nisa'.] *Majallat al-sayyidat wa al-banat* 1, no. 2 (May 1903): 37–39.

"Jan Dark." [Ser. Shahirat al-nisa'.] *Fatat al-sharq* 5, no. 4 (January 1911): 121–23.

"Ikram katiba Muslima li'l-qadisa Jan Dark." *Al-Mashriq* 19, no. 2 (February 1921): 108–14.

Sadiq, Zaynab. "Jan Dark, fatat Urliyan." *Fatat Misr al-fatat* 1, no. 3 (June 1921): 109–11.

Bahij, Mustafa. "Jan Dark." *Majallat al-nahda al-nisa'iyya* 1, no. 5 (December 1921): 120–21.

Yunus, Muhammad Mukhtar. "Jan Dark 'la pusil' fi al-qarn al-khamis 'ashara." [Ser. Shams al-tarikh 2.] *Majallat al-nahda al-nisa'iyya* 2, no. 4 (November 1922): 104–5.

"Jan Dark." [Ser. Shahirat al-nisa'.] *Majallat al-mar'a al-Misriyya* 6, no. 5 (May 1925): 271–73.

"Jan Dark, aw al-fatat al-shahira." *Adab al-fatat* 1, no. 5 (May 1926): 97–99.

Nur, Hasan Muhammad. "Jan Dark." *Majallat al-nahda al-nisa'iyya* 4, no. 12 (November 1926): 405–6.

"Jan Dark." *Al-'Arusa* 225 (May 22, 1929): 3–4.

Zuhayr, Saniyya. "Jan Dark munqidhat faransa." [Ser. Min al-tarikh.] *Majallat al-mar'a al-Misriyya* 14, nos. 3–4 (March–April 1933): 99–101.

"Jan Dark." *Shahirat nisa' al-tarikh fi'l-sharq [wa-fi] al-gharb ma'a 20 qissat ghuram li-ashhar al-'ashiqat fi al-tarikh.* [Malhaq riwa'i li-jaridat *Al-Sabah*.] [Cairo]: Matba'at Al-Sabah, n.d. [early 1930s]. Pp. 14–15.

"The Heroine Joan of Arc." *Al-Majalla al-sanawiyya li-madrasat al-Amira Fawziyya al-thanawiyya li'l-banat.* [English Section.] 2 (1934): 4.

"'Uzmat al-wataniyya al-haqqa, aw Jan Dark." *Majallat al-mar'a al-Misriyya* 18, no. 3 (March 1937): 81–84.

Musa, Ahmad Sadiq. "Butulat Faransa fi saha'if ra'i'a min tarikh Faransa: al-Munqidha." *Al-Mahrajan* 2, no. 12 (June 1938): 65–71.

II. Other Texts Mentioning Jeanne

"A haqqan ahraqat Jan Dark?" *Ruz al-Yusuf* 1, no. 3 (November 9, 1925): 7.

"Fatat Qaraqish." [Ser. Shahirat al-nisa'.] *Fatat al-sharq* 6, no. 10 (July 1912): 361–63. Attributed to *Al-Ittihad al-'Uthmani*.

"Jan Dar [*sic*] al-'arabiyya." [Ser. Shahirat al-nisa'.] *Fatat al-sharq* 14, no. 2 (November 1919): 41–42.

"Karistin di Bizan." [Ser. Shahirat al-nisa'.] *Fatat al-sharq* 6, no. 4 (January 1912): 121–23. Attributed to *Al-Raqib*.

"Al-Nabigha al-Misriyya al-Anisa Zakiyya 'Abd al-Hamid Sulayman." *Majallat al-nahda al-nisa'iyya* 4, no. 12 [48] (November 1926): 412–14.

Al-Sirinjawi, 'Abd al-Fattah. "Batalat al-tarikh." *Majallat al-mar'a al-Misriyya* 8, no. 1 (January 1927): 51–53.

NOTES

I want to thank the National Endowment for the Humanities Research Fellowship Program and the Ford Foundation (Cairo) MERC Program, for supporting research that contributed to this essay. For comments and suggestions, I am grateful to Lila Abu-Lughod, Don Crummey, Ken Cuno, Natalie Zemon Davis, Alice Deck, Kevin Doak, Blair Kling, Kathryn Oberdeck, David Prochaska, Cynthia Radding, Mohammed Tavakoli, Mary Christina Wilson, and Paul Zeleza. And I thank my children, Paul and Carrie Cuno-Booth, who endured many stories and much haranguing about "that woman knight"—and who have given me still more versions of her life to contemplate.

1. This was the Madrasat al-banat al-thanawiyya al-amiriyya bi'l-Hilmiyya al-Jadida, Cairo, one of the earliest state secondary schools for girls, upgraded from elementary school status. It was not until the early 1920s that state secondary education for girls existed. See Margot Badran, *Feminists, Islam, and Nation: Gender and the Making of Modern Egypt* (Princeton: Princeton University Press, 1995), pp. 142–43; Beth Baron, *The Women's Awakening in Egypt: Culture, Society, and the Press* (New Haven and London: Yale University Press, 1994), p. 129.

2. Muhammad Mukhtar Yunus, "Jan Dark 'la pusil' [*sic*; Fr. *la pucelle*] fi al-qarn al-khamis ʿashara," *Majallat al-nahda al-nisaʾiyya* 2, no. 4 (1922): 104 5; quotation p. 104. Quotation marks in original.

3. Rita Felski, *The Gender of Modernity* (Cambridge and London: Harvard University Press, 1995), p. 4.

4. Ibid., pp. 18–19.

5. The basic study on nonelite women in Egypt is Judith Tucker, *Women in Nineteenth-Century Egypt* (Cambridge: Cambridge University Press, 1985). My argument on contextualizing the discourse of domesticity is developed in Marilyn Booth, " 'May Her Likes Be Multiplied': 'Famous Women' Biography and Gendered Prescription in Egypt, 1892–1935," *Signs* 22, no. 4 (1997): 827–90.

6. On the histories of these institutions, see, in addition to the works cited in n. 1, Ijlal Khalifa, *Al-Haraka al-nisaʾiyya al-haditha* (Cairo: Al-Matbaʿa al-ʿArabiyya al-Haditha, 1974); Latifa Salim, *Al-Marʾa al-Misriyya wa al-taghyir al-ijtimaʿi* (Cairo: GEBO, 1984); Amal al-Subki, *Al-Haraka al-nisaʾiyya fi Misr bayna al-thawratayni, 1919 wa 1952* (Cairo: GEBO, 1986).

7. In trying to articulate my own politics of reading, I am indebted especially to the observations of Mary Poovey, Rita Felski, and Nancy Armstrong, in explaining their own expectations and desires as readers. See Mary Poovey, *Uneven Developments: The Ideological Work of Gender in Mid-Victorian England* (Chicago: University of Chicago Press, 1988); Felski, *The Gender of Modernity*; and Nancy Armstrong, *Desire and Domestic Fiction: A Political History of the Novel* (Oxford: Oxford University Press, 1987). My preference for the concept "axes of power" follows Felski's (*The Gender of Modernity*, p. 32).

8. After the 1930s notable women's biographies became less frequent in women's magazines in Egypt. See Marilyn Booth, *May Her Likes Be Multiplied: Biography, Prescription, and Gender Politics in Egypt* (Berkeley and Los Angeles: University of California Press, forthcoming), chap. 7. Moreover, space constraints preclude discus-

sion of later biographies of Jeanne d'Arc: one in Munira Thabit's journal *Al-Amal* (1952); three in "Famous Women" compendia of the same decade, Sufi ʿAbdallah's *Nisa' muharabat* (1951), Mubarak Ibrahim's *Nisa' shahirat* (1952), and Anwar al-Jundi's *Shahirat al-nisa'* (1958); and the latest text I have located—also the sole full-length biography of Jeanne in Arabic I have found—ʿAbd al-Latif Muhammad al-Dumyati, *Jan Dark: ʿard wa tahlil wa taʿqib* (Cairo: Matbaʿat al-Dar al-Misriyya liʾl-Tabaʿa wa al-Nashr wa al-Tawziʾ), 1966. I discuss these in Booth, *May Her Likes Be Multiplied.*

9. It is quite possible also that writers relied on material in Turkish—for example, in women's magazines published in Istanbul. Yet many editors were familiar with European languages and publications. For a discussion of this see Booth, *May Her Likes Be Multiplied*, chap. 1.

10. Agnes Kendrick Gray, "Jeanne d'Arc after Five Hundred Years," *American Magazine of Art* (American Federation of Arts) 22 (1931): 369.

11. On de Pisan as an early feminist theorist, see Joan Kelly, "Early Feminist Theory and the *Querelle des Femmes*, 1400–1789," in *Women, History, and Theory: The Essays of Joan Kelly* (Chicago and London: University of Chicago Press, 1984), pp. 65–109.

12. This and the next few paragraphs summarize my detailed analysis of this material in "May Her Likes Be Multiplied." My findings in that essay are based on 450 biographical sketches in periodicals, as well as biographical compendia.

13. Armstrong, *Desire and Domestic Fiction*, p. 16. She borrows the phrase "pleasures of literature" from Robert and Maria Edgeworth, late-eighteenth-century writers on the educational needs of girls.

14. For more detail see Booth, "May Her Likes Be Multiplied." I am indebted to feminist scholars who, studying women's life narratives, first emphasized this auto/biographical symbiosis, now a commonplace notion. I single out for mention the work of Liz Stanley, the Personal Narratives Group at the University of Minnesota, and the contributors to Bella Brodzki and Celeste Schenck, *Life/Lines: Theorizing Women's Autobiography* (Ithaca: Cornell University Press, 1988).

15. The term "repeatable women" comes from Afsaneh Najmabadi, in her "Comments. Women, Culture, Nation: Egyptian Moments" (symposium held at New York University, April 7, 1995), discussing my work.

16. On this press before 1920, see Baron, *The Women's Awakening*, and Ijlal Khalifa, "Al-Sahafa al-nisa'iyya fi Misr, 1919–1939" (M.A. diss., Cairo University, 1966), introduction. For the later period, see Khalifa, cited above, and "Al-Sahafa al-nisa'iyya fi Misr, 1940–1965" (Ph.D. diss., Cairo University, 1970). See also Irene Fenoglio-Abd El Aal, *Défense et illustration de l'Egyptienne: Aux débouts d'une expression féminine* (Cairo: Centre d'Etudes et de Documentation Economique, Juridique et Sociale, 1988).

17. In "*Woman in Islam*: Men and the 'Women's Press' in Turn-of-the-Century Cairo" (unpublished MS, 1997), I argue for an approach that analyzes male authorship in the women's press as a (re)writing of masculinities. See also Booth, *May Her Likes Be Multiplied*, chap. 6.

18. Most of these texts are unsigned and hence by convention the responsibility of the editor(s). (A higher percentage of the Jeanne d'Arc biographies than of the sample as a whole are attributed to specific contributors). This quasi-anonymity makes it impossible to ascertain definitively the ethnic or national origins, the gender, and the religion of the actual "author." But I am more concerned in the larger study of which

this essay is a part with the production of texts within specific publication contexts than with individual "authorship." On authorship and intertextuality in the "Famous Women" genre, see Booth, "May Her Likes Be Multiplied," pp. 845–46.

19. Natalie Zemon Davis, "Women on Top," in Natalie Zemon Davis, *Society and Culture in Early Modern France: Eight Essays* (Stanford: Stanford University Press, 1975), pp. 131, 133, 144.

20. Martha Hanna, "Iconology and Ideology in the Idiom of the Action française, 1908–1931," *French Historical Studies* 14, no. 2 (1985): 215–39. I am indebted to Natalie Zemon Davis for directing me to this essay.

21. Ann Bleigh Powers, "The Joan of Arc Vogue in America, 1894–1929," *American Society Legion of Honor Magazine* 49, no. 3 (1978): 177, 178, 180, illus. 179. The period saw "the Joan works of some thirty American authors" (180).

22. Hind Nawfal, "Iydah wa iltimas wa istimsah," *Al-Fatat* 1, no. 1 (1892): 3. Nawfal's trio of famous women includes Hypatia and al-Khansa', intimating a history of foremothers that crosses boundaries of ethnicity, nation, and religion. She also mentions female pharaohs as a source of pride, implying a shared identity with Egyptian women. An abridged version of this article translated by Beth Baron appears in Margot Badran and Miriam Cooke, eds., *Opening the Gates: A Century of Arab Feminist Writing* (London: Virago; Bloomington and Indianapolis: Indiana University Press, 1990), pp. 217–19.

23. The first six pages following the frontispiece are missing in the University of Cairo copy, the sole one I have located. Maryam ibnat Jabra'il Nasrallah al-Nahhas qarinat Nasim Nawfal, al-Tarabulsiyya al-Suriyya, *Mithal li-kitab ma'rad al-hasna' fi tarajim mashahir al-nisa'* (Alexandria: Matba'at Jaridat Misr, 1879). *Al-Hasna'* as an epithet signifies "the beautiful woman." Yet as the feminine form of the adjective meaning "good" or "excellent" it connotes qualities not limited to the physical, as I have tried to convey in my translation.

Page 7 begins in the middle of the political context that probably is the first section of the Jeanne d'Arc biography. It seems likely that this was the first biography to follow that of Princess Jasham. It is followed by biographies of Catherine I of Russia and Layla bt. Hudhayfa b. Shaddad. A second volume alluded to by Fawwaz never appeared (Zaynab bint 'Ali Fawwaz al-'Amili, *Al-Durr al-manthur fi tabaqat rabbat al-khudur* [Cairo/Bulaq: Al-Matba'a al-Amiriyya, A.H. 1312 (1894 C.E.)], pp. 515–16). Fawwaz says that al-Nahhas began working on this "general book to revive the mention of the girls of her gentle kind [sex]" in 1873. Fawwaz described it as containing "biographies of famous women, alive and dead, arranged after the fashion of European dictionaries" (*Al-Durr*, p. 515).

24. *Fatat al-sharq* ran from 1906 to 1939. On its use of Fawwaz, see Marilyn Booth, "Exemplary Lives, Feminist Aspirations: Zaynab Fawwaz and the Arabic Biographical Tradition," *Journal of Arabic Literature* 26 (1995): 141–44. I am writing a book on Fawwaz and gender politics in Egypt and the Levant.

25. This is suggested not only by Hashim's obvious (and occasionally attributed) reliance on Fawwaz but also by the presence in several magazines of women who might have not been the most obvious choices but who are also featured in *Al-Durr* such as flyer Sophie Blanchard (on whom, see Booth, "May Her Likes Be Multiplied," pp. 877–78).

26. See Booth, "Exemplary Lives," p. 122; Marilyn Booth, "Biography and Femi-

nist Rhetoric in Early Twentieth-Century Egypt: Mayy Ziyada's Studies of Three Women's Lives," *Journal of Women's History* 3, no. 1 (1991): 40, 58 n. 6.

27. On historically attested women in premodern Arabic literary and religious works, see Hilary Kilpatrick, "Some Late ʿAbbasid and Mamluk Books about Women: A Literary Historical Approach," *Arabica* 42 (1995): 56–78; Fatima Mernissi, *The Forgotten Queens of Islam*, trans. Mary Jo Lakeland (Cambridge, Eng.: Polity Press, 1993); Ruth Roded, *Women in Islamic Biographical Collections: From Ibn Saʿd to Who's Who* (Boulder, Colo.: Lynn Reiner, 1994); D. A. Spellberg, *Politics, Gender, and the Islamic Past: The Legacy of ʿA'isha bint Abi Bakr* (New York: Columbia University Press, 1994); Barbara Stowasser, *Women in the Qur'an, Traditions, and Interpretation* (Oxford and New York: Oxford University Press, 1994); Marilyn Booth, "Women's Biographies and Political Agendas: Who's Who in Islamic History" (review essay), *Gender and History* 8, no. 1 (Spring 1996): 133–37; and Booth, "Exemplary Women."

28. Marina Warner, *Joan of Arc: The Image of Female Heroism* (New York: Knopf, 1981), pp. 33–43; also Bonnie S. Anderson and Judith P. Zinnser, *A History of Their Own: Women in Europe from Prehistory to the Present*, vol. 1 (New York: Harper and Row, 1988), pp. 153, 476 n. 9. Warner shows that in Europe Jeanne had to be given a physical presence through writing and the visual monuments erected to her memory. "Beauty" was a sign of Jeanne's virtue (*Joan of Arc*, p. 37). With the post-Renaissance rewriting of Jeanne from Amazon to romantic heroine a feminine physicality was given especial prominence (pp. 213–14).

29. Nadia Farag, "*Al-Muqtataf*, 1876–1900: A Study of the Influence of Victorian Thought on Modern Arabic Thought" (D. Phil. diss., Oxford University, 1969); Beth Baron, "Unveiling in Early Twentieth-Century Egypt: Practical and Symbolic Considerations," *Middle Eastern Studies* 25 (1989): 370–86. Margot Badran has long emphasized that veiling was not in itself a primary issue for early feminists but was of greater concern to male nationalists, who saw it as a sign of "backwardness" and therefore of shame. See *Feminists, Islam, and Nation*, pp. 23–24.

30. In Maurice Boutet de Monvel's popular 1896 children's biography, Jeanne's long light-brown hair became a short cap as soon as she defined her mission. Maurice Boutet de Monvel, *Joan of Arc*, introduced and translation edited by Gerald Gottleib, (New York: Pierpont Morgan Library and Viking Press, 1980). Warner mentions long hair as an emerging motif and sign of Jeanne's beauty (*Joan of Arc*, pp. 213–14).

31. Booth, "Exemplary Lives," p. 128.

32. Fawwaz, *Al-Durr*, p. 122.

33. Ibid.

34. Al-Nahhas, *Mithal*, p. 7. Several names of individual fighting women follow this statement.

35. Ibid., p. 9.

36. Warner, *Joan of Arc*, pp. 213–17; pp. 236–38.

37. I make this claim based on my knowledge of dialect poetry (including sung poetry) in the 1920s.

38. Nawfal, *Mithal*, pp. 7, 9–10; Fawwaz, *Al-Durr*, pp. 122–23; "Jan Dark, fatat Urliyan," *Al-Hilal* 4, no. 4 (1895): 123–24; *** [Farah Antun], "Jan Dark, fatat an-qadhat watanaha bi'l-harb," *Majallat al-sayyidat wa al-banat* 1, no. 2 (1903): 37–38. *Al-Hilal* devotes more space proportionately to the political scene than to Jeanne's life

history, as contrasted with the women's magazines and biographical dictionaries. This is in line with a tendency in the "general-interest" magazines *Al-Hilal* and *Al-Muqtataf* to subordinate life histories of women to intellectual and/or cultural trends to which the subject can be linked (Booth, "May Her Likes Be Multiplied," pp. 863–65).

39. Fawwaz, *Al-Durr*, p. 122. When the English saw Jeanne all in white, on her white horse and grasping her white banner, says Fawwaz, "they fled from before her like donkeys in fright, from thralldom taking flight" (p. 123).

40. "Jan Dark," *Al-Hilal*, p. 125. The next year Mark Twain's mock-memoir of Jeanne appeared; the narrator, Sieur Louis de Conte, used a similar metaphor: "[f]or more than three quarters of a century the English fangs had been bedded in [France's] flesh. . . . " (Jean François Alden [Mark Twain], *Personal Recollections of Joan of Arc, by the Sieur Louis de Conte (Her Page and Secretary), Freely Translated Out of the Ancient French into Modern English from the Original Unpublished Manuscript in the National Archives of France* [New York: Harper and Brothers, 1896], p. 6).

41. This is the sole biography of Jeanne I have located from this decade, not a good one for the press in Egypt. With increasing paper shortages and other economic hardships, political uncertainties wrought by World War I, and military law and censorship, the teens saw the closure of many periodicals, including most of the first wave of women's journals (Baron, *The Women's Awakening*, p. 34).

42. It may also have articulated feminists' struggle to maintain visibility for the issue of women's place in the context of urgent anti-imperialist activism.

43. "Shahirat al-nisa'," *Al-Jins al-latif* 12, no. 3 (1919): 81–82. In fact, three years before, *Al-Jins al-latif* had featured two premodern Arab Muslim women, singer Fadl al-Madaniyya and poet Layla al-Ukhayliyya; pre-Islamic poet Amina bint ʿUtayba had appeared previously. But the emphasis was more pronounced in the 1920 volume, which featured ʿAʾisha bint Abi Bakr, spouse of Muhammad, the founder of Islam; Fatima al-Nabawiyya, Muhammad's granddaughter; and de facto ruler Sitt al-Mulk. These women are prominent in Islamic history. The reference to ancient Egyptian queens indicated another popular subject group of "Famous Women," especially in the 1920s when Egyptian nationalists were emphasizing Egypt's pre-Arab past as a marker of a distinct national identity (Booth, *May Her Likes Be Multiplied*, chap. 7).

44. Zaynab Sadiq, "Jan Dark, fatat Urliyan," *Fatat Misr al-fatat* 1, no. 3 (1921): 109; p. 109; p. 109; p. 110.

45. The verb also means "to treat with humiliation."

46. Mustafa Bahij, "Jan Dark," *Majallat al-nahda al-nisaʾiyya* 1, no. 5 (1921): 121. This is one of many instances of Bahij's close but inexact echoing of Fawwaz. The latter says that Jeanne "had to traverse 150 leagues of territory saturated by the English and encompassed by sly trickery *(makara)(Al-Durr*, p. 122). Bahij adds the *dababat*.

47. Yunus, "Jan Dark 'la pusil,' " p. 105.

48. "Jan Dark," *Majallat al-marʾa al-Misriyya* 6, no. 5 (1925): 271; p. 272.

49. "Jan Dark," *Al-ʿArusa*, no. 225 (1929): 3. Cf. Hanna, "Iconology," pp. 219–21, 234–37, on the thinly veiled political messages produced by the Action française's use of Jeanne.

50. "Jan Dark," *Al-ʿArusa*, p. 3. The religious overtones of "suffering the evil of punishment" were surely not lost on readers.

51. Marilyn Booth, *Bayram al-Tunisi's Egypt: Social Criticism and Narrative Strategies* (Reading, Eng.: Ithaca Books, 1990), p. 58.

52. Warner, *Joan of Arc*, pp. 239–42.

53. Anderson and Zinnser, *A History of Their Own*, p. 160; see also p. 213; Warner, *Joan of Arc*, pp. 240–45.

54. A few biographies note that "the French sold Jeanne to the English," but the English are the ultimate villains throughout this set of texts. In general the trial and execution are not portrayed as the work of a French ecclesiastical institution aligned with the English. Rather, they are forthrightly "a blotch on the pages of English history," "a mark of shame on the brow of imperialism." Ahmad Sadiq Musa, "Butulat Faransa fi saha'if ra'i‘a min tarikh Faransa: al-munqidha," *Al-Mahrajan* 2, no. 12 (1938): 71; "Jan Dark," *Shahirat nisa' al-tarikh fi al-sharq [wa fi] al-gharb ma‘a 20 qissat ghuram li-ashhar al-‘ashiqat fi al-tarikh*, Malhaq riwa'i li-jaridat *al-Sabah* ([Cairo]: Matba‘at al-Sabah, n.d. [early 1930s], p. 15). Sadiq puts more blame on the French: after jealousy broke out among the French army commanders (perhaps an implicit reference to the difficulty of being a female in Jeanne's position), "her situation deteriorated, her star descended, and they [the French] left her a prisoner in enemy hands" ("Jan Dark, fatat Urliyan," p. 11). Yunus says that the "people of Burgundy took her prisoner and sold her to the English, an act of treachery on their part toward their country, and a crime against a loyal girl" ("Jan Dark 'la pusil,'" p. 105). But he deploys this to stress that this "crime" occurred only because Jeanne transgressed accepted gender boundaries.

55. "Jan Dark, aw al-fatat al-shahira," *Adab al-fatat* 1, no. 5 (1926): 97. And France is "her beloved *watan*" (p. 98).

56. Ibid., p. 99.

57. To use the term "liberal nationalist" in the context of postcolonial theorizing on the nation invites objections based on the slippage between nationalist praxis in nations contesting European imperial control and the European underpinnings of "classical liberalism." This debate lies beyond the scope of the present essay, but since these thinkers defined themselves literally as working within (their own understandings of) European liberalism, the term is a valid one to use. The basic text on this issue remains Albert Hourani, *Arabic Thought in the Liberal Age, 1798–1939*, rev. ed. (Cambridge: Cambridge University Press, 1983); more recent scholarship has explored its implications.

58. "Jan Dark," *Majallat al-mar'a al-Misriyya*, p. 272.

59. Ibid., p. 273.

60. Fenoglio-Abd El Aal, *Défense et illustration*, pp. 95–96, 119.

61. "‘Uzmat al-wataniyya al-haqqa," p. 81.

62. See my analysis of *al-Fatat*'s biography of Maria Theodorovna in "May Her Likes Be Multiplied," pp. 872–74.

63. With a fortunate choice of adjective whose double meaning resonates, Haylana ‘Abd al-Malik, a Coptic merchant in Tanta, is called "the noble/self-made (‘isamiyya) woman, the only Egyptian woman who has worked in trade and succeeded in it to an extent that makes one rejoice." She grew up in Tanta, illiterate, "her only legacy a fiery soul and a strong will." Description of how she supported the local peasantry by single-handedly raising the price of cotton precedes a declaration that she did her share for the nationalist movement by opening her storehouse to the followers of Sa‘d Zaghlul for their rallies ("Haylana ‘Abd al-Malik," *Majallat al-mar'a al-Misriyya* 5, no. 6 [1924]:

324. This biography is also useful to the magazine in emphasizing Copts' contribution to the nation as well as highlighting the subject's contributions to the Coptic community: she "fought against injustices done to Copts [in Tanta].") Austrian labor activist Adelheid Popp (1869–1939) is another working-class subject; she is lauded for helping other working-class women (Hasib al-Hakim, "Min al-kukh ila al-barlaman: Madam Bawb," *Majallat al-mar'a al-Misriyya* 8, no. 3 [1927]: 117–21).

A biography dramatically rendered of one Alice Ayres (d. 1885), described as a domestic servant of a member of the English bourgeoisie, says that the subject "sacrificed her life in good faith to save those who were not her kin." The biography opens with a homily valorizing woman's self-sacrifice for her community—whether it be defined by family or nation ('Iffat Sultan, "Al-Tadhiya: Alis Ayirs: fatat injiliziyya basila," *al-Jins al-latif* 7, no. 8 [1915]: 265–69; quotation p. 265). Similar themes are sounded in a rare profile of an "ordinary Egyptian," "Al-Sitt Umm Muhammad" (*Majallat al-mar'a al-Misriyya* 7, no. 5 [1926]: 267.) The clearest indication of a class orientation on the part of the editors/writers comes in statements such as that closing a biography of Catherine I of Russia: "She was one of the most honorable and refined women, despite her base origins and the obscurity of her lineage." ("Katirina al-ula imbiraturat Rusiya," *Fatat al-sharq* 3, no. 2 [1908]: 41–43; quotation p. 43). At the same time, it should be kept in mind that phrases such as this draw upon the conventional diction of classical biographical dictionaries and pinpoint the elite bias of this genre.

64. Warner, *Joan of Arc*, p. 97; p. 246.

65. Ibid., chap. 12. Boutet de Monvel's biography is suffused with images of children and emphasizes Jeanne as child/peasant (*Joan of Arc*).

66. Yunus, "Jan Dark 'la pusil,'" p. 104.

67. Ibid., p. 105.

68. "Jan Dark," *Majallat al-mar'a al-Misriyya*, p. 271.

69. Warner calls her father "dean" of the village (*Joan of Arc*, p. 58). "In 1423 Joan's father was the villager who signed the agreement with the leader of a band of soldiers, a yearly fee levied on each household paid so that there would be no pillaging" (Anderson and Zinnser, *A History of Their Own*, p. 116). It is clear from witnesses at the time that the family was propertied but not wealthy and was respected by the villagers as "honest and decent farmers and true Catholics of good repute." See Régine Pernoud, *Joan of Arc by Herself and Her Witnesses*, trans. Edward Hyams (New York: Stein and Day, 1966; reissued, Lanham: Scarborough, 1982), pp. 16–20; quotation p. 17.

70. These texts conflate "herdsman" and "peasant," which are not the same thing, nor are their roles conflated in the context of Egypt's ecology and society.

71. For *Adab al-fatat* (1926), Jeanne is a "young shepherdess, of fine physical constitution and nature, living the life of those villagers, free of artificiality" ("Jan Dark," p. 97). For others, she simply "tends her father's flocks" ("Jan Dark," *al-'Arusa*, 3). See also Saniyya Zuhayr, "Jan Dark munqidhat faransa," *Majallat al-mar'a al-Misriyya* 14, nos. 3–4 (1933): 99–101: "The work she did was watching her father's livestock" (p. 99).

72. His primary motive, however, may have been to conceal his identity, for the dubious image of a fiction writer was not consonant with his career as lawyer. In later editions his name appeared on the title page. See Roger Allen, *The Arabic Novel: An*

Historical and Critical Introduction, 2d ed., Contemporary Issues in the Middle East (Syracuse: Syracuse University Press, 1995), pp. 33–35.

73. Baron discusses the literature of home management in early women's journals in Egypt (*The Women's Awakening*, pp. 155–66). I analyze conduct manuals circulating in turn-of-the-century Egypt in *May Her Likes Be Multiplied*.

74. Marilyn Booth, "*Women in Islam*: Men and the 'Women's Press' in Turn-of-the-Century Cairo" (unpublished MS). This is a major trope, I argue, in the rewriting of masculinity in which these intellectual activists were engaged.

75. Fawwaz, *Al-Durr*, p. 122. The biographies in *Majallat al-sayyidat wa al-banat* (1903) and *Fatat al-sharq* (1911) do not mention him. From the 1920s, see Bahij, "Jan Dark," p. 120; Sadiq, "Jan Dark, fatat Urliyan; "Jan Dark," *Adab al-fatat*. If some from this decade subsume him in the "village family famous for piety and goodness," Yunus is more complex, for here Jeanne is "fleeing from her father the shepherd" ("Jan Dark 'la pusil,'" p. 104), which makes the father stand in for an implicitly critical attitude toward the peasant family and suggests a classist outlook on the part of the author.

76. "Jan Dark," *al-Sabah*, p. 14. There is disagreement over whether the relationship between Jeanne and her family was affectionate. Pernoud concludes from the trial documents that it was, and that her father felt an affectionate concern for her (*Joan of Arc by Herself and Her Witnesses*, p. 126). But, she notes, views to the contrary exist.

77. Musa, "Butulat Faransa," p. 66.

78. But the mothers of "Famous Women" are often invisible, which perhaps conveys the message that in previous generations mothers had not been in a position to further their daughters' educations. Exceptions are praised. See Booth, "May Her Likes Be Multiplied," pp. 870–71.

79. Musa, "Butulat Faransa," p. 66.

80. Nadia Margolis, *Joan of Arc in History, Literature, and Film: A Select, Annotated Bibliography* (New York and London: Garland Publishing, 1990), p. 243; Pernoud, *Joan of Arc by Herself and Her Witnesses*, p. 213; Warner, *Joan of Arc*, p. 105; Frances Gies, *Joan of Arc: The Legend and the Reality* (New York: Harper and Row, 1981), p. 21.

81. There are exceptions, as in the case of public political work mentioned above. Usually praised, it is, however, qualified by the assertion that the subject does not neglect her home. See Booth, "May Her Likes Be Multiplied."

82. It might be thought that as time passed, and as the biographical focus came to include more contemporary Arab and/or Muslim women with extradomestic professional careers (although this group was present in biography from the first decade of the twentieth century), the domestic imperative would become more muted. But it was in the late 1920s and the 1930s that the "woman-behind-the-man" became if anything more dominant as a biographical subject. This reflected (and helped to solidify) the crystallization of a dominant nationalist gender politics; but it also acted as a rearguard action, a move to defend women's movement into public life. For some, of course, highlighting women's domestic roles was a negative reaction to social change.

83. Warner notes that for a medieval woman who "contravened the destined subordination of her sex" by, for example, putting on male garb, this garb could act as "armour, both defensive and aggressive"; but simultaneously she could use domesticity as a defense (*Joan of Arc*, p. 153). Jeanne, though, "only insisted on it once" during her trial (*Joan of Arc*, p. 160), when she said, "[F]or spinning and sewing let me

alone against any woman in Rouen" (Pernoud, *Joan of Arc by Herself and Her Witnesses*, p. 16).

84. Sadiq, "Jan Dark, fatat Urliyan," p. 110. In the context of the narrative this is inaccurate; it was the commander of the fort at Vaucouleurs, nearest fortification to Domrémy, to whom Jeanne first went.

85. Ibid., p. 111.

86. "Jan Dark," *Majallat al-mar'a al-Misriyya*, p. 271. This text calls Jeanne's "firmness . . . proof of the true [or: sincere] nature of woman's will and her moral courage" (p. 273). These generalizations open out a second interpretive possibility for the text's construction of the struggle between weak and strong, by collapsing the colonizer/colonized binary into a male/female one. This is by now a well-recognized conjunction in postcolonial studies, and sources are too numerous to mention. I pursue this further in *May Her Likes Be Multiplied*.

87. Fawwaz, *Al-Durr*, p. 123.

88. Warner, *Joan of Arc*, p. 158.

89. Ibid., p. 147. Warner notes that in sixteenth-century (and later) European treatments of Jeanne, her "male dress is glossed over. She is armed and cuirassed as a practical measure. No inquiry is made into the disturbing and deep ambivalence of Joan's need to wear male dress far from the battlefield" (p. 213). In Egyptian biographies Jeanne's reversion to male garb after her imprisonment is explained as the ruse of her captors, not as her desire. Warner examines the cross-dressing issue in "Joan of Arc: A Gender Myth," in *Joan of Arc: Reality and Myth*, ed. Jan van Herwaarden (Hilversum: Verloren/University of Rotterdam, 1994), pp. 97–117.

90. Cf. one scholar's conclusion about the effect of certain early-twentieth-century English-language biographies of Jeanne: "the Maid of Orleans emerges a real girl as well as a genius, with the radiance of her young womanhood sublimated by her 'mission' to an ineffable whiteness." See Helen Harriet Salls, "Joan of Arc in English and American Literature," *South Atlantic Quarterly* 35 (1936): 175. See the pictorial images reproduced in Warner, *Joan of Arc*, between pp. 176 and 177; Regine Pernoud, *Joan of Arc*, trans. Jeanne Unger Duell (New York: Grove Press, and London: Evergreen Books, 1961), pp. 12–19, 52. Again, the emphasized motif of whiteness has a basis in the documents (Pernoud, *Joan of Arc by Herself and Her Witnesses*, pp. 83, 112).

91. A move, argues Warner, that shaped Jeanne's post-sixteenth-century image in France: "Joan's Amazonian likeness had to be softened to be countenanced at all: her transvestism, her armour, her inviolability had to seem something that in the final conclusion was offered on the altar of male supremacy. . . . Joan's life is a tribute to the traditional sphere of man, as opposed to woman. . . . she became a talisman for a host of causes conducted by men. . . . [Yet] because she was undeniably female, she was a figurehead for the women's side in one phase of the lasting struggle" (*Joan of Arc*, pp. 217–18).

92. "Jan Dark," *Majallat al-mar'a al-Misriyya*, p. 272. This digression gives immediacy to the abstraction quoted above, from the same biography, on women's strength of will.

93. Fawwaz, *Al-Durr*, p. 123. Also, in the 1920s, this recapitulates the theme of the happy nationalist peasant: "she wanted to return to her earlier life, among the sheep and fields of the folk of her dear village" (Hasan Muhammad Nur, "Jan Dark," *Majallat*

al-nahda al-nisa'iyya 4, no. 12 [1926]: 405–6; quotation p. 405). Again, writers in Egypt were making use of a motif popular in Joan's political "rehabilitation" in France (Warner, *Joan of Arc*, p. 217).

94. "The life history of this girl was pure; she did not dirty her hands with bloodshed" ("Jan Dark," *Fatat al-sharq*, p. 123; also, "Jan Dark," *Al-ʿArusa*, p. 3; "Jan Dark," *Adab al-fatat*, p. 98). *Al-Hilal* however claims she "killed seven hundred soldiers" ("Jan Dark, fatat Urliyan," p. 126). Musa also presents her as in the thick of the fighting ("Butulat Faransa," p. 70).

95. "Jan Dark, fatat Urliyan," p. 167.

96. Sadiq, "Jan Dark, fatat Urliyan," p. 110. A sketch of her childhood preoccupations substantiates Jeanne's role in battle: she "was concerned with the weak and cared for the sick" (Nur, "Jan Dark," p. 405). So does the increasingly explicit, descriptive emphasis on the domestic: as a girl returning home from tending the flocks, "she sat beside her mother sewing clothes and embroidering cloth and listening to stories of the war" ("Jan Dark," *al-ʿArusa*, p. 3). Cf. Boutet de Monvel's treatment (*Joan of Arc*, pp. 28, 36, 40).

97. Pernoud, *Joan of Arc by Herself and Her Witnesses*, pp. 17–20, 65; pp. 64, 86, 92.

98. Zuhayr, "Jan Dark munqidhat faransa," p. 99.

99. Ibid.

100. Ibid., p. 100.

101. Ibid. I have translated the verbal noun *ighra'* as "urging on," but the emphasis on Jeanne's femininity makes it hard to ignore a more common connotation, "tempting" or "alluring"; in no other biography does this term appear.

102. Pernoud, *Joan of Arc by Herself and Her Witnesses*, p. 63; see also pp. 62, 65, 84. "Yet, contrary to subsequent popular memory, Joan never actually took command; rather she assisted, advised, and, perhaps most important, chided those in charge when they delayed . . . " (Anderson and Zinnser, *A History of Their Own*, p. 155; see also Warner, *Joan of Arc*, p. 7).

103. On the reproduction and contestation of this gendered role in medieval and modern Arabic biography, see Booth, *May Her Likes Be Multiplied*.

104. Zuhayr, "Jan Dark munqidhat faransa," p. 100.

105. For a range of perspectives on this in the context of Egyptian feminisms, see Leila Ahmed, *Women and Gender in Islam: Historical Roots of a Modern Debate* (New Haven and London: Yale University Press, 1992); Badran, *Feminists, Islam, and Nation*; Baron, *The Women's Awakening*; Kumari Jayawardena, *Feminism and Nationalism in the Third World* (London: Zed Books, 1986); and Booth, *May Her Likes Be Multiplied*.

106. This had enormous political implications for the region, a fact that was not lost on local audiences. "[T]he defense of the [Ottoman] empire's integrity in Libya quickly became a popular political cause throughout the Muslim world." (Lisa Anderson, "Ramadan al-Suwaylihi: Hero of the Libyan Resistance," in *Struggle and Survival in the Modern Middle East*, ed. Edmund Burke, III [Berkeley and Los Angeles: University of California Press, 1993], pp. 114–28; quotation p. 120).

107. Badran, *Feminists, Islam, and Nation*, p. 50.

108. Anderson, "Ramadan al-Suwaylihi," p. 121.

109. "Fatat Qaraqish," *Fatat al-sharq* 6, no. 10 (1912): 361 (attrib. *Al-Ittihad al-ʿUthmani*).

110. "Jan Dar [*sic*] al-ʿarabiyya," *Fatat al-sharq* 14, no. 2 (1919): 42.

111. On ʿAliyya, see Fawwaz, *Al-Durr*, 368–72. Her father was Jawdat Pasha, governor of several Ottoman provinces, high official in Istanbul, and historian. Of ʿAliyya, Fawwaz says: "She blended Eastern knowledge with Western to the point where she became a source of pride for the secluded ladies of Islam. No woman, Eastern or Western, could match her. She now [1894] lives in Sublime Istanbul. May God increase her likes and through her spread knowledge to our female sex (p. 370). After this essay was in press, Carter Findley's work on ʿAliyya came to my attention. See especially Carter Vaughn Findley, "Fatma Aliye: First Ottoman Woman Novelist, Pioneer Feminist," *Histoire économique et sociale de l'Empire ottoman et de la Turquie (1326–1960): Actes du sixième congrès international tenu à Aix-en-Provence du 1er au 4 juillet 1992*, ed. Daniel Panzac (Paris: Peeters, 1995 [Collection Turcica vol. 8]), pp. 783–94; and "La Soumise, la subversive: Fatma Aliye, romancière et féministe," *Turcica* 17 (1995): 153–76.

112. "Fatat Qaraqish," pp. 362–363.

113. That the "Young Woman of Qaraqish" is anonymous, an everywoman, identifiable as only "Jeanne d'Arc" or "Khawla," enhances this collective emphasis.

114. "ʿArab" first signified the Bedouin, and that could have been meant here, but given the thrust of both versions, the wider and newer meaning seems to take precedence.

115. These biographies, for example, as they featured Western women's lives, both confirmed and complicated discourse attacking a superficial Westernization that some saw as ruining Egyptian womanhood—and threatening the identity and survival of the nation. This was and is a core theme in the cultural/political struggles of many Middle Eastern and/or Islamic nations.

116. "Al-Nabigha al-Misriyya al-Anisa Zakiyya ʿAbd al-Hamid Sulayman," *Majallat al-nahda al-nisa'iyya* 4, no. 12 [48] (1926): 412.

117. Powers, "The Joan of Arc Vogue in America," p. 178.

118. Warner, *Joan of Arc*, p. 259; *Crusade for Justice: The Autobiography of Ida B. Wells*, ed. Alfreda M. Duster (Chicago: University of Chicago Press, 1970), p. 3; David W. Dunlap, "Gray Skies and a Smaller Crowd, but High Spirits at Gay Pride March," *New York Times*, July 1, 1996, p. A13. For directing me to Wells, I am indebted to Alice Deck. Another recent example is the Joan of Arc episode of the PBS children's show *Wishbone*, which takes Mark Twain's Joan as the double for a contemporary American girl called on in an emergency to join a boys' soccer team.

119. Badran, *Feminists, Islam, and Nation*, p. 13.

120. Armstrong, *Desire and Domestic Fiction*, p. 23.

121. Eve Sedgewick, "Nationalisms and Sexualities in the Age of Wilde," in *Nationalisms and Sexualities*, ed. Andrew Parker, et al. (New York and London: Routledge, 1992), p. 241.

122. "ʿUzmat al-wataniyya," p. 81.

ISLAMISM, MODERNISM, AND FEMINISMS:
THE LATE TWENTIETH CENTURY

CHAPTER 6

Eluding the Feminist, Overthrowing the Modern?
Transformations in Twentieth-Century Iran

ZOHREH T. SULLIVAN

"Everything is pregnant with its contrary."
(Karl Marx)

THE Shaykh Fazl Allah Nuri Expressway cuts through modern Tehran. Five minutes away from the newly named Azadi (Freedom) Square, it intersects with the Jalal al-Ahmad Highway that goes past the Ali Shariati Hospital, the College of Commerce and Administrative Sciences, and the College of Educational Sciences. Shaykh Fazl Allah Nuri was the charismatic conservative cleric who positioned himself against Western modernity and was, in 1909, publicly executed for opposing the first Constitutional Revolution of 1906. "I speak of being afflicted with 'westisis' the way I would speak of being afflicted with cholera,"[1] writes Jalal al-Ahmad in *Westoxification* (*Gharbzadegi*), his famous critique of Pahlavi Iran's mindless mimicry of Western modernity. Any postrevolutionary Islamic government that chooses to name its expressways after Nuri and Al-Ahmad is probably, and self-evidently, being selective about which aspects of modernity to discard. Modernity, with its attendant goals of progress, autonomy, freedom, education, and justice, was quite simply reread as always already a part of the true Islam.

A model of secular modernity, however, had consolidated itself in nineteenth-century Iran through the Constitutional Movement that positioned itself against the practices of the decadent Qajar monarchy by looking to the West for models of nationhood and development. Modernity, however, came with unacknowledged ties to cultural colonization and petroleum politics. While on the macro-level the state bought the package deal, on the micro-level individuals resisted by channeling disturbance into various oppositional patterns of modernity, a countermodernity, as it were, one of whose impulses was shaped into revolutionary Islam.[2] The binary between traditionalism and modernity that sometimes shapes conventional discussions of Iran and the Iranian Revolution is therefore inadequate to a model I prefer, that of the coexistence and tension of each in a dialectical (but not mutually exclusive) relationship with its alterity.

I prefer to see modernity and the issue of women's freedom so integrally linked to it not as agendas but as new ways to package hidden internal agendas. Modernity, antimodernity, and feminism therefore need to be recast in terms of how groups respond to, react against, and use their ideologies. Modernity and feminism become vehicles producing a series of tensions between the ordering impulse of ideological systems and the clumsy challenges of real life. I will suggest not merely the relativity of the modern but the difficulty of reducing these modernities to their Western counterparts.[3] The liberation of women, though not necessary to the larger agendas of modernity, becomes a troubled sign of its possibilities, limits, blind spots, and discontents.

Both modernity and feminism, in Iran and elsewhere, exist in perpetual antithesis with excluded particularities that remain beyond their control, and that return to disrupt their management. The unexpected difficulty of absorbing large programs into experience can be seen in the disparity between how cultural work implements modernity and how it is integrated at the level of personal experience. This chapter therefore will oscillate between public and private narratives; it will rely, in part, on a series of oral narratives I collected, starting in 1990, with Iranian émigrés and exiles that form a book called *Exiled Memories: Identity, Revolution, Iran.* Although the interviews I conducted invited my informants' memories of childhood, revolution, and exile, modernity was a currency that circulated through all their transactions. I will use their voices as a way to reflect on alternative modernities and on the problem of gender in Iran, and as an introduction to groups who narrate competing conceptions of culture and identity that recall projects of modernity during the first Constitutional Revolution of 1905, during the Pahlavi era (1925–1979), and after the Islamic Revolution of 1979. Finally, by using stories of women as dialectical inversions of each other, I argue that although questions of gender and the articulation of gendered roles may come under the dominance of state apparatus, the state does not in the process secure the consent of all its women subjects. In other words, the Islamic State exercises hegemonic control over general politics, education, and culture, but, in the case of women, its hegemony is not tied (to use Ranajit Guha's elegant formulation) to dominance.[4]

GENDERING THE IRANIAN PAST: SHARIATI, NURI, AND KASRAVI

In October 1971, the shah of Iran and his queen staged the megalomaniacal 2,500-year celebration of Persian monarchy in Persepolis, a ceremony whose quail eggs stuffed with caviar and roast peacock and foie gras were catered by Maxim's of Paris, whose water and wine were flown in from France, whose entertainment was staged by Peter Brook, and whose benediction included a prayer in which the shah called upon Cyrus, the great Achaemenian king of kings, to "rest in peace, for we are awake." At the same time in a small religious center called Hosseineyeh Ershad, Ali Shariati was awakening Iranian dissidents and students to the principles of his countermonarchical manifestos, and calling upon the figure of Fatima, the daughter of the Prophet, as an emblem of revolutionary possibility.

Here we see two ways of recasting symbols from the past (Cyrus and Fatima), the shah overhauling pre-Islamic Iran to dramatize current "modernity," and Shariati recovering a woman, Fatima, whose conservative image he empowers with agency and revolutionary wrath against the patriarchal ruler. To the disenchanted masses angered at the petroleum imperialism hidden in the bright packagings of the shah's "Great Civilization," Shariati's fiery and erudite lectures and his reminder of daily life as a source of power and resistance offered alternative models of cultural identity. Imprisoned by the shah in 1974 and later exiled in France, Shariati is generally recognized (though he died in 1977) as the "ideologue" for the revolution. Overflowing crowds of dissidents and revolutionaries found new hope in his radical lectures at the Hosseinieh Ershad in the early 1970s. His audience had already been prepared for a new kind of Iranian-Muslim intellectual by the Islamo-Marxist narratives of the People's Mujahidin party and by Jalal-al-Ahmad.

In Paris, Shariati had edited *Iran-e-Azad* (Free Iran), had translated works of Che Guevara and Frantz Fanon, had debated with Fanon about using Islamic unity as a weapon against neocolonialism, and had studied with several famous scholars at the Sorbonne. In his series of influential lectures titled *Return to the Self*, Shariati called for resistance to Western cultural imperialism through a return "not to the self of a distant past, but a past that is present in the daily life of the people."[5] This is a self embedded in the social and material practice of everyday life whose power, as Foucault might put it, lies in "micro" operations and in the reconstitution of the self.

But that newly realized Islamic self was necessarily gender inflected. Woman, Shariati argued, was the easiest path to de-territorialization. "The West falls upon the soul of the Easterners like termites. . . . they empty out the contents . . . destroy all of the forces of resistance."[6] Shariati's much celebrated *Fatima Is Fatima* used the figure of the daughter of the prophet Muhammad not only as a model of revolutionary resistance to the monarchy in the 1970s but as a figure who could resolve the current problem of how women could enter modernity and remake themselves as neither Western nor traditional. Its vocabulary and arguments inform almost all subsequent manifestos by women after the revolution.[7] By authenticating a secular concept of womanhood as an alternative to the Pahlavi "westoxicated" images of woman, it offered a new and revolutionary model of Islamic womanhood; but it is also a text that once again uses the body of the woman as the site on which to compose national and ethical values. Woman, for Shariati, is at once the greatest hope for and the greatest threat to revolutionary possibility.

Yet it is not Western women he faults but their commodification. In spite of their power to effect social change, women, he claims, allow their desires to be so manipulated that they become vulnerable pawns in capitalist consumption and leisure. Blaming the poverty of modern Iranian culture for providing no alternative other than dead ritual and tradition to women and youth, Shariati addresses the collusion between the oppressor and the oppressed: "An oppressor cannot perform oppression in the air" (FF, 108). When, for instance, Chengiz Khan defeated Iran in the fourteenth century, Iran had opened itself to this defeat through internal decomposition, ignorance, and superstition.[8] The same historical decadence, he warns, recurs in current youthful vulnerability to Western ideological exploitation and cultural colonization at whose temple (to lust and sexuality) the first object to be sacrificed is woman (FF, 90). In language that recalls such social critics as Thorstein Veblen, George Bernard Shaw, and Karl Marx, Shariati reminds his audience of the link between the prostitute and the bourgeois lady, of the cost of unexamined sexuality and commodification. Referring to the marriage of Jackie Kennedy and Aristotle Onassis, he writes, "The First Lady of America can also be bought for a price. The difference between her and those who stand on the street is one of rate" (FF, 97).

Like Frantz Fanon, Shariati rejects the traditional model of woman built around past Islamic cultural traditions; but unlike Fanon, he argues that the traditional image of Islamic woman is an inadequate representation of the revolutionary activism offered within Islam and exemplified by Fatima and her daughter Zainab. More generally and more importantly he affirms Fanon's warning that

> In an underdeveloped country every effort [must be] made to mobilize men and women as quickly as possible; it must guard against the danger of perpetuating the feudal tradition which holds sacred the superiority of the masculine element over the feminine. Women will have exactly the same place as men, not in the clauses of the constitution but in the life of every day: in the factory, at school, and in the parliament.[9]

The "web" that imprisons and impoverishes modern woman, Shariati writes, is woven out of inherited traditions of conservatism, patriarchy, and ignorance (FF, 109–110). The confinement of women within the home, the gendered splitting of the private and public, and the exclusion of woman from the public sphere are all inadequately premised on the virtues of motherhood and chastity. How, he then asks, can a person "who is herself incomplete and useless, who is missing a part of her brain and who is excluded from literacy, books, education, discipline, thought, culture, civilization and social manners . . . be worthy of being the nourisher of tomorrow's generation?" (FF, 109)

In valorizing the figure of Fatima, not as daughter of Muhammad, wife of Ali, or mother of Hassan, Husain, and Zainab, but as "herself" (hence the title of the book), Shariati reminds his audience of the denigration to which Islamic culture (not Islam) has subjected the image of women. He contrasts the civility of Qur'anic respect for girls against an Arab poet's advice that fathers of daughters select the grave (over house and husband) as their most suitable son-in-law; and against Ferdowsi's *Shahnameh*: "It is better to bury women and dragons in the earth, / The world will be better off if cleansed of their existence" (*FF*, 124).

In opposition to the ubiquitous image of the traditional royal family whose patriarch claimed to respect only women who, as "natural" wives and mothers, were also "beautiful, feminine, and moderately clever,"[10] Shariati posited another way of seeing. He exposed the scandal of the traditional and unacknowledged traffic in women bartered in a form of unexamined homosocial exchange. The "fate of woman in our traditional, conservative society" is to grow up in her father's house "without breathing any free air," to go "to her husband's home (her second lord and master) in accordance with an agreement . . . between a buyer and a seller" (*FF*, 110). Once she is transferred to her husband's house, "the marriage licence or ownership papers show both her role and her price. She becomes a respectable servant. A married man means someone who has a servant who works in his house. . . . She is a household laborer and a nurse . . . without any wages; she has no rights" (*FF*, 111).

Though he is daring in his critique of the role of women in the traditional Iranian family, the contradictions in Shariati's stance toward women are also significant: on one hand, women are essentially vulnerable to the seductive powers of exploitation and consumerism; but on the other, they have power and agency to construct themselves as warriors, as is evidenced by a series of women scholars and scientists (*FF*, 82–86). So too, Fatima, as the ideal mother, wife, and daughter, can also become the emblem of "newly created revolutionary values" (*FF*, 129).[11]

Such values are needed, Shariati claimed in *One Followed by an Eternity of Zeros*, to defend the Muslim against neo-imperialism and cultural loss that come to Iran disguised as modernization. The history of Iran is narrated as a "fall" into colonialism. For Shariati, national authenticity was a necessary antidote to the designs of the multinational markets on individual desire; and cultural authenticity could be found in his philosophically eclectic and religiously armored construction of cultural identity. "Islam," Shariati said, "is the first school of social thought that recognizes the masses as the basis, the fundamental and conscious factor in determining history and society—not the elect as Nietzsche thought, not the aristocracy and nobility as Plato claimed, not great personalities as Carlyle and Emerson believed, not those of pure blood as Alexis Carrel imagined, not the priests or intellectuals, but the masses."[12] Here we see in Shariati's appeal to the masses and attack on the West an ironic link to Marxism, which, as an extension of Hegelian dialectics, is also (ironically) the latest bloom in Western Enlightenment thought. Through the early years of the revolution, Marxist categories and Shariati's language, argument, examples, and tropes became the scaffolding for Islamic feminism and humanism and were appropriated (though unacknowledged) by such groups as the Women's Society of Islamic Revolution, the Iranian women's delegation to the UN Decade for Women's Conference.[13]

Shariati locates the only weapon against global capital in individual agency and the "self." This is not an example of strategic essentialism in the service of a naive but necessary fiction of the self; this is a more popular, culturally constructed notion of self as a productive force in the service of nationalism deployed against the de-territorializing imperatives of Western global capital. Eloquent in his defiance of the monarchy *and* the traditional clergy, trained in a contemporary European vocabulary and in Islamic philosophy, Shariati played, according to historian Mohamad Tavakoli, "a crucial role in constructing an oppositional cultural and political identity based on a system of historical narration organized around Islam."[14]

That oppositional construction was prefigured by a clergyman of whom Shariati would have disapproved—the late-nineteenth-century figure recovered by the Islamic Revolution and celebrated in verse, drama, and modern expressways—Shaykh Fazl Allah Nuri. As leader of the clerical movement against the first Constitutional Movement, his politicization and organization of the clergy, some believe, prepared the way for the 1979 revolution. Why, he asked, did the Constitutionalists wish to base the Iranian Constitution on equality and freedom? "The foundation of Islam is obedience and not freedom; and the basis of its commandments is the differentiation of collectivities and the assemblage of the different elements, and not on equality."[15] Constitutionalism, Shaykh Fazl Allah claimed, was a European invention, "a fatal disease, a terminal injury," and he concluded that Western philosophy goes hand in hand with Western tyranny. Shaykh Fazl Allah was not the last to think so.[16] In aiming to halt the movement of Iran into Westernized "modernity" and plurality, Shaykh Fazl Allah asked for a return to *shariʿa* (divine law) as a defense against Western constitutional laws (*qanun*) that would turn authority over to the people and Parliament.[17] His stance against modernity and its corollary in women's freedom, articulated in a document titled "For the Awareness of Muslim Brothers," warned against the forces that "spread consumption of alcoholic drinks, promote prostitution, open schools for women, redirect the money that should be spend on religious projects into building of factories, roads, railways and other foreign projects in Iran."[18] (See Najmabadi's essay, chapter 3, this volume, for more on his reading of women's education.)

The historical moment that produced Shaykh Fazl Allah Nuri, modernity, women's education, and the woman's movement also produced its irreducible complexity on an individual level in the life of Nuri's granddaughter, Zia Ashraf Nasr, whom I interviewed in 1990. Her immediate family mirrored the schism in the country between the clergy who supported and those who opposed the constitution: whereas her grandfather on her father's side was Nuri, her grandfather on her mother's side was Sayyed Tabatabai, one of the leading theologians who backed the Constitutional Movement. In spite of family injunctions against the education of girls, Zia Ashraf persuaded her family to allow her to attend one of the first Muslim girls' schools, Madrassah-ʿi Namus, that had opened in 1907. A deeply religious woman who sees no contradiction between Islamic philosophy and the freedom of women in the public sphere, she renarrativized the progeny of the Prophet (it is standard knowledge that Muhammad had no male heirs; and Zeinul Abedin, the Prophet's great-grandson, is best known as a perpetually ailing imam) in order to foreground the power of his daughter and granddaughter, Fatima and Zainab. Mrs. Nasr faulted the 1979 revolution as "un-Islamic":

> This "Islamic" idea of women you quote to me from Khomeini. . . . the disparity between men and women. This should be labeled not "Islam" but "Khomeini." I believe, based on the life of the Prophet and the first leaders of Islam, that Muhammad himself did not discriminate against women. He considered his daughter Fatima superior to men. He made her the beginning. . . . Why? The Prophet had sons from other wives. He had daughters and sons. But he didn't give any of them as much power as he gave this girl. . . . After Fatima, her daughter was privileged—Hazrat Zainab who supervised the caravans, who took care of the family in the desert of Karbala, who brought the family in its imprisonment from Karbala to Medina. There were other men after Imam Hosein's martyrdom—Imam Zeinul Abedin, for instance. But it was a woman, Hazrat Zainab, who supervised the family, who took charge. Even in Yezid's court, it was she who lectured at him, and what a sermon she delivered. She was a woman, yet she was at the head of Islam. Then why should a woman, later on, stay home and the man go out? . . . Now the veil enslaves woman. Now women have been packaged and bundled so that one has to guess from the shape. . . . Is it a human being or a black bundle?

Like other girls in the early years of the century, Zia Ashraf Nasr had a gendered education: she was taught to read but not to write, in the tradition of limiting women's access to communication though not to learning. She learned to write only after her return to Tehran, after her family's exile in Iraq following the execution of her grandfather, and after the death of the grandmother with whom she lived. By then (1918) she was about fourteen years old and keenly aware of her sharp memory that enabled her to remember a page after glancing at it swiftly. Recalling her early education, she smiled as she told of making it through six grades in six months, and of the many women in her family who broke the family edict against girls' attending school: "Look at the number of strong women in our family who have doctorates in medicine, literature, and other fields. My aunt . . . was the first Iranian woman to go to the American school and learn English . . . to the American Missionary School." Zia Ashraf's temperament and life were formed in the crossfire of tradition, change, and modernity, at a time when women began their activities through the formation of organizations, the opening of girls' schools and the publication of women's periodicals.

The movement for women's rights in Iran has a long and well-documented history. Zia Ashraf Nasr experienced its beginnings in her friendship with Iran's leading feminist, Siddiqeh Dowlatabadi, in her involvement with women's societies, and in her struggle for women's enfranchisement. The same Constitutional Revolution that executed her grandfather also generated the start of women's secret societies and a surge in women's resistance to political and social subordination. When, in 1911, it was rumored that some of the members of Parliament were giving in, again, to Russian demands, women's groups took action. Three hundred women with concealed guns behind their *chadors* (veils) entered the buildings, confronted the leaders of Parliament, tore aside their veils, and threated to kill their husbands, their sons, and themselves if the independence of the Persian people were further eroded.[19]

At the turn of the century, political modernization became identified with nation building; but the discourse of nationhood, as Afsaneh Najmabadi demonstrates, was consistently gendered. Because the significance of symbolic gendering was never confronted and problematized, it was susceptible to slipping backward into Qur'anic rhetoric of male dominance or forward into the kind of consolidation expressed in the Islamic Republic.[20] Such casual acceptance of gender inequity forged unexpected bonds between secular and religious intellectuals. Ahmad Kasravi, the historian, reformer and jurist, active in the 1930s and 1940s, argued for modernity and women's education, and against the veil. But he also argued against women's right to enter the public sphere in politics, the judiciary, or the civil service.[21]

But women could, Kasravi conceded, participate through their political support of national and necessarily male agendas. Kasravi's importance as a secular modernist lay in his articulation of the need to centralize and integrate the many decentralized groups in the country: the elites, the masses, the clergy, the tribes, the clans, religious sects, and ethnic languages that constituted the "unintegrated" layers of Iranian society.[22] Gradually as secularism gained power, "the old tolerant attitude towards cultural heterogeneity was gradually supplanted by an intolerant crusade for national homogeneity: tribal nomadism became associated with rural gangsterism, regional autonomy with administrative anarchy, communal variety with political incompatibility, and linguistic diversity with oriental inefficiency."[23]

Iranian scholars read Ahmad Kasravi, variously, as the most controversial of modern intellectuals, as a theorist of modernity, and as a "dangerous iconoclast" appropriately murdered for trying to destroy traditional authority.[24] Because of his uncompromising opposition to "irrationality," he might be called a modernist who rethought Iranian modernism, one who, though a clergyman, celebrated Western science and supported the Constitutional Revolution in 1906, while he opposed women's liberation and suffrage, Western cultural imperialism, *and* the Shi'a clergy. Arguing for what Fischer calls "puritan rationalism," Kasravi attacked the clergy for superstition. He published over fifty books, a weekly journal, and a daily newspaper all elaborating on his theories of class, society, and "civilization," laying out his strategies for national integration. A celebrator of urban living, he coined the new Persian word *shahrigari* (urbanization) to contrast it with *biyabangari* (nomadizaton).[25] He also attacked, as reactionary, the most precious art in Persian culture—poetry—because he believed that the habit of recitation and recourse to poetic quotation was a way of avoiding thought. To clarify his position on the fetishizing of poetry and mysticism, he started a book-burning festival at the winter solstice.[26]

Kasravi's dream of unifying Iran was predicated on a paradox: he wished to take its distinctly divided factions and to integrate them into a modern democratic society with one language, one culture, and one central authority. In 1946 a man from an organization called the Fadayan-i-Islam (or the Devotees of Islam) shot Kasravi dead. Kasravi had been brought to court under indictment on charges of slander against Islam. The fable of his failure perhaps illustrates the course of civilization and its discontents— the "illusion" returning from the repressed to destroy its controller. Or alternatively, if we prefer another metaphor (from Kristeva), the banished or the abject returning violently from exclusion to enact its revenge against the center.[27]

MODERNIZING FROM ABOVE

Such denial of marginal and diverse forces has recurred through the reigns of the Pahlavis and the ayatollahs. As part of his modernizing programs, the shah set up, in the early 1970s, educational programs for women in villages. Pahlavi father and son, Reza Shah and Mohamad Reza Shah, combined the state policy of crushing opposition with enforced emancipation and modernization. Reza Shah's 1936 decree banning the veil is but a tiny example of how "modernization from above" was presented as the only way for Iran to enter the modern world.[28] Reza Shah learned from a visit in 1934 to Atatürk's Turkey that the road to modernity necessitated emancipation of civil law from the *shari'a* and thereby the disengaging of secular politics from religion. Political emancipation and equal rights, however, had their dark underside: state repression, a regularized police society, and a consumer-mad "westoxicated" culture.[29]

The *chador*, forbidden by Reza Shah as part of his enforced program for emancipating women, and associated with the backward and downtrodden during the Pahlavi era, was later used as an emblem of revolutionary protest by women of all castes and classes who marched against the Pahlavi regime.

Within the year following the revolution, they were to be surprised by governmental laws that required the *chador* for women who wished to venture outside their homes or enter offices and restaurants. Thus the *chador* is used by opposing camps for opposite reasons: the veil as a symbol of liberation from the dictatorial state and as an instrument for hegemonizing a revolution by those whose only aim was political power. The following story will suggest yet another take on the *chador*.

One of my interviewees, Pari (a pseudonym), spoke of her efforts, as assistant minister of agriculture, to head the literacy campaign for rural women: "Neither the government nor I knew what we were doing," she said. "The literacy campaign had staffed centers for educating village girls to become 'agents of development' who would then return to the villages to effect change." Six centers were therefore built outside villages in buildings that looked like English boarding schools, so different from their own environments that Pari found it "culturally shocking." The girls were required to learn how to use such Western facilities as tables and chairs, knives and forks, showers and Western toilets, none of which they had seen before. Also, the girls, who had never slept in beds, were now expected to sleep in bunk beds. Pari tells of how, when they persisted in falling off their bunk beds in the middle of the night, the administrators found a bizarre solution. They tied the woman on the top to her bed with her *chador*.

The image of the woman bound to her bed with the veil in the larger cause of progressive rights and freedoms, a paradox of modernity, captures the simultaneity of modernity and its underside, of the forces of reason and their bondage, of the necessary reconstruction of identity and the loss of community; it bears witness to modernity as its own gravedigger.[30] "Everything is pregnant with its contrary." In its social context, the image recalls the monumental hegemonic vision of Pahlavi Iran, and of the Enlightenment project of modernity that enforced selected citizen rights through repression and violence.

Another event revealed an even darker side of Pari's effort to educate village women. The story of the *chador* tells of the enforcement of knowledge whose dialectic is specific to modernity. This next story suggests a different dialectic endemic to resistance.

Here is her account of her visit as an "agent of development" going to the village in her official capacity:

> I went to the village and asked for S——. She didn't come out. The next day I returned and asked for her again, and she didn't come out. Then I found out that the girl had been beaten black and blue by her father, that she couldn't walk for weeks, and that she was ashamed to be seen because I had caused her such humiliation. . . . It was our organization that had made this man so angry. It was us as agents of development who couldn't understand village psychology. . . . The men

could not tolerate the fact that someone from outside the village would come and ask to speak to a woman and not to a man. . . . I later found out that when I wasn't present, the women I worked with would, for the smallest thing, ask permission from their fathers, brothers, and husbands. But then I would reappear and anger the men.

Pari was sent to the village to teach women's rights, which at its most basic level taught women their right *not* to be beaten or abused. But her very presence led to a reactionary violence—the abuse of the women. Pari assumed, as did the state, that social progress would neutralize the need for revolution. Her predicament was that of the modernizing agent taking on the burden of universal modernity, whose enlightened agenda necessarily produced darker consequences than she suspected. Or, as Geoffrey Harpham phrases it, "Enlightenment is always otherwise."[31]

Pari not only witnessed but inadvertently promoted the collision between the state and its citizens, between modernity and its other, between what Partha Chatterjee might call capital and community, and, on quite another but a connected register, between the premodern, subjugated woman and modernity. Pari's story tells us something too about the problem of modernization that Chatterjee writes of in *The Nation and Its Fragments*—the problem of the suppression of an independent narrative of community, the erasure of respect for the individual that can occur when the importance of individual freedom and individual rights is proclaimed.[32]

Pari tells the story of village women as part of a series of narratives that include herself and the women in her family. But the embedded stories are significant for their differences. Unlike her village counterpart, Pari's own search for autonomy from patriarchal oppression, her own subjection to coercive codes of female behavior and child abuse occurred in an urban setting that privileged her class, and that allowed her to find surrogate communities outside her city and country. But the village women relied on structures of kinship and community within the village. Outside the village a woman faced the multiple unknown threats of the city, whose effect was to alienate the villager from her former community, leaving nothing to fill the void.

Such alienation had also been the unexpected consequence of the White Revolution of 1962–63; the shah's programs of multiple modernization, coinciding with rapid industrialization and Westernization, resulted in poverty and chaos that followed mass migration from country to city. An Azari woman, Mrs. K., whose family owned a village near Tabriz, tells of the effects of the shah's White Revolution and land reforms on villagers.[33] She recalls that they sold their land and went to the city, where they lived in slums and, if they found jobs, worked as janitors. She described their depression and culture shock: "Now they [the villagers] come to my brother and complain that they don't know how to live in a city. On arriving in the city, one young man simply walked through a street expecting the cars to stop for him. Instead he was hit by a car and died."[34] The Iranian displaced by the shah's reforms could not survive the crash into modernity (any more than could his European counterparts) without the protection of a surrogate organization—perhaps even of the industrial "Fordist" organizations that had collapsed in the 1970s both in Europe and in Iran.

The land reforms, the White Revolution, and associated government projects, however, were premised on Western models of development that opposed a "backward" agriculture to a modern structure of unified (state) organizations. On the basis of the logic of downward flow from the economy's "centre of gravity," from the oil industry to rural sectors, literacy and programmatic learning were to be the first of many steps toward freedom and rights;[35] and the position of villagers, farmers, and women would (it was reasonably assumed) automatically right itself along with the spread of reading, writing, and reason. In fact, the program so angered the men in the village that it exacerbated the injustice it was intended to dispel. Though the "agents of development" came from above, descending from the skies in state helicopters equipped with institutional power, they failed to take into account the strength of revolutionary power brewing below.

Pari was vaguely aware that the young women in her village would disappear at certain points in the day, but she didn't give this much thought because their usual excuse was prayers. One day in 1978 she went to hold a workshop for women in a village near Shiraz. This time the students who were her village aides disappeared. Frustrated, Pari returned to Tehran and saw soldiers and cannons all over the streets. She asked the taxi driver what was happening. He answered, "Lady, haven't you been living in Iran?" Didn't she know there was trouble between the government and opposition rebels? She later realized that the women and student aides had disappeared at the same time of day, about 8 P.M. to gather around the radio and hear the BBC news. She should have known that 8 P.M. was not an appropriate time for Muslim prayers, but as a modernized, de-Islamicized Iranian, she didn't. The villagers, who were later to become part of the revolutionary movement, tuned in to radios that suggested an alternative entry into modernity—a new imagining of a society that does what modernity, as they received it, failed to do, one that follows the "exhaustion" of Pahlavi modernity but sees the possibility of an alternative narrative and activates new patterns of modernity. In the same vein, the message of that new society streamed in on tape cassettes recorded by Khomeini and surreptitiously distributed nationwide, and through underground radio stations and a system of new communication technologies that for the first time linked village life with global centers like London and Paris.

The historian Mohamad Tavakoli told me a slightly different story about "agents of development" that provides an important example of the appropriation and transformation of state powers, of how individuals used the instruments of Pahlavi modernization in ways other than those the state envisioned, how they took the packet and subverted its agenda. Mohamad's brother, who was part of the Education Corps set up as an arm of state modernization in the early 1970s, found that the opportunity to work in rural Iran yielded unexpected results. Inadvertently, the regime had promoted a hitherto impossible dialogue between the educated urban Iranian and the rural villager. His understanding of the problems of village life politicized his consciousness and spurred the formation of a new revolutionary identity in him and many others. His subsequent involvement with leftist groups was the direct and unintended consequence of the state's programs of development.

Iran's program of literacy and modernization served not only the interests of Big Oil and American foreign policy[36] but also the making of a revolutionary counterculture. The violent protection of U.S. oil investments turned into a narrative that energized the shah's Iran and mobilized the forces of modernity into a story of progress, development, modernization, and freedom.[37] But what the grand narrative ignored was the presence of another story that challenged its conceptual framework. Partha Chatterjee's narrative of community can perhaps be further complicated through a reading of resistance theory that refuses to allow the colonized (oppressed/subaltern) to be totalized as a stable category, and that investigates histories of insubordination and struggle against institutional and ideological domination.[38]

The state's many ideas of development,[39] all imposed from above, though theoretically plausible, were contradicted by the actual events fueled by the rage of those marginalized by modernization that built up to the Islamic Revolution of 1979. The revolutionaries were multiply determined subjects. The rage of displaced villagers and students drove them into a variety of leftist groups alongside the marginalized *ulema*, or clergy, and the intellectuals who opposed the shah's U.S.-supported, consumer-driven modernization. The opposition split into political spectra that resist easy classification, though for the sake of simplification we can list the conservative Right (the Bazaar) and the conservative Left (Jalal Al-Ahmad in one of his phases), the Islamic Right (Hezb Jumhuri Islami, the Ayatollahs Shariat Madari and Khomeini) and the Islamic Left (Mojaheddin, Ayatollah Taleqani and Ali Shariati), and, finally, a three-way split producing the nationalist Right (the shah), the nationalist Left (Fadayaan, the National Front), and the nationalist Islamic (Mehdi Bazargan and Ayatollah Taleqani).[40]

But none of these factions was antimodern. The revolution has been given many labels: against the standard reading of it as a reactionary, traditional, and antimodern revolution, Michel Foucault and Paul Vieille both describe it as a postmodern revolution, and for Anthony Giddens it was a sign of the crisis of modernity.[41] It was not antimodern because Khomeini and his cohorts built on a coalition with secular modernists and leftists, and their early pronouncements invoked, in addition to change and social justice, "the rights of minorities, the rights of women, and the holding of democratic elections."[42] Its leading theorists had recognized that the 1950s and 1960s had produced a cultural schizophrenia, and that an "other" modernity through Islam might be a way to confront "cultural imperialism" and to address what Shariati called the "modern calamities" of social and intellectual systems.

REVOLUTION AND WOMEN'S BODIES

In Iran's conflicted efforts to construct national, revolutionary, and Islamic modernities the figure of the "woman" has repeatedly been constituted as the overdetermined sign of an essentialized totality, as a metaphor for a beseiged nation, an embattled self, a delicate interiority, the uncontrollable other, the "unpierced pearl" to be bought and protected, or the sacred interior. As Farzaneh Milani observes, women dominate the cultural imaginary by becoming emblems of national identity: "Forcefully unveiled, they personify the modernization of the nation. Compulsorily veiled, they embody the reinstitution of the Islamic order."[43]

No matter how different the regime, it managed to produce a violent ambivalence in the processes by which the self, religion, and nation are ordered. For Nuri, Kasravi, Shariati, and even a modern feminist like Siddiqeh Dowlatabadi, their consolidation of identity and culture was won at the expense of otherness—which took the form of the feminine, the lower classes, or other ethnicities. Secular intellectuals such as Kasravi made gestures toward liberating women from the veil, but they continued to read women's place as essentially domestic and women's bodies as signs for potential exploitation, social disorder, commodification, and exchange.

A dramatic example of the violent repressions unpinning the gendered organization of Iranian cultural practice may be seen in the disruptive power of two women who transgressed the boundaries set by a patriarchal society. In their insistence on equality, independence, and women's emancipation, both women transgressed in ways that are specific to both feminism and modernity. When in the mid–nineteenth century Qurrat al-ʿAyn, a woman writer, orator, poet, teacher, and religious rebel, discarded her veil and her submission to Islam and became a celebrated preacher for Babism, she so angered the male elite that she was arrested and executed on orders of the shah. Before her death in 1852, the sight of her speaking unveiled before large crowds of men left more than a few men deranged. In the most notorious incident, one ʿAbdol Khaleq Esfahani is said to have protected his honor by cutting his throat with his own hands.[44]

Sixty years later in the city of Isfahan, another feminist, Siddiqeh Dowlatabadi, daughter of a well-known Muslim religious leader, had her life-threatened and was driven into exile. She was the contemporary woman most admired by Zia Ashraf Nasr, who recalled Dowlatabadi's return from Europe as one of the most important events in her life. The year was probably 1927, and Zia Ashraf was attending the *Dar-ol-Moallemat*, a teacher-training institution:

> I was very excited one day to hear that Khanum Dowlatabadi, the progressive leader of women's liberation in Iran, had returned from abroad and was giving a lecture in town. Some of our teachers got ready to go, and I asked to go with them. We went early and waited for her to arrive in this huge hall with balconies. She entered looking very dignified, very authoritative. She greeted a few people, went behind the desk, and began her lecture. There was silence as she began. But suddenly from the balcony a large pomegranate was thrown at her that landed on the lecture desk, exploded, and all the pomegranate juice splashed on her face and clothes. But Khanum Dowlatabadi was so collected and well composed that she did not pause in her talk; she continued as if nothing had happened. From that day on, I was won over and became devoted to this woman.

This powerful woman who so impressed Mrs. Nasr was the aunt to my main informant, Pari. Haji Mirza Hadi, Dowlatabadi's father, had been a Mojtahid (religious jurist) in Isfahan. He married first Khatemeh Begum, who bore him six sons and a daughter, Siddiqeh Dowlatabadi, before the mother fell sick and died. Dowlatabadi arranged for her father to marry his secretary's nine-year-old daughter, after which she took over the care of her father's child wife's two children—one of whom was Pari's mother.

Dowlatabadi raised the two girls and married a doctor, Dr. Etezad in 1898. But, so the story goes, she discovered that she was infertile and got divorced. In 1917, she started the first school in Isfahan for women, *Umm Al-Madaris* (Mother of Schools). One of the first graduates of the American College for Women, *Iran Bethel*, her friend, Mehrtaj Rakhshan, became the headmistress of this school. In 1919 Dowlatabadi started a society, *Sherkat Khavateen Isfahan* (Isfahan Women's Cooperative), whose purpose was to change practices she believed harmful to Iran, such as the marriage of girls before the age of fifteen and the import of foreign fabrics. At the same time she started the first major woman's magazine, *Zuban-i Zanan* (Women's tongue), in Isfahan in 1919. Through this magazine, she argued against the imposition of the veil, for the economic and emotional independence of women, for the education of women in ethics, literature, and science, and against the political dependence of Iran on other countries. The aim of this journal, then, was both feminist and nationalist. The biweekly magazine shocked religious groups in Isfahan.

Siddiqeh Dowlatabadi won further national notoriety by criticizing the prime minister (the *vusuq-al-dawlah*), who had signed a treaty giving certain rights to the British. The British retaliated by promising to distribute food to poor Iranians who agreed to gather at the post office in support of the *vusuq-al-dawlah*. When an emissary from Dowlatabadi arrived at the post office to read

out Siddiqeh Dowlatabadi's powerful petition for freedom from British interference and control, the crowd listened intently. After he finished reading, they
left without accepting any of the food offered by the British.

The government countered by banning Dowlatabadi's magazine because,
by discussing politics, she had transgressed its original purpose and limits.
After her life was threatened and her house stoned, she went into hiding. Finally she moved from Isfahan to Tehran, where she started new societies (*an-
juman*) for women and published a dictionary of contemporary women. In
1923, she left for Europe and traveled in France, Germany, and Switzerland.
She studied at the Sorbonne for a few years and returned to Iran in 1927. She
is known as one of the first women in twentieth-century Iran to address crowds
publicly without a veil. She gave speeches everywhere, even in the heart of
conservative Qum.

While in Europe, she attended the Tenth Congress of the International Alliance for Women's Suffrage in Paris (May 1926). There she met and started a
friendship with Margaret Ashby, the president of the International Alliance of
Women's Suffrage. Ashby, a New Yorker and mother of two, a housewife and
a politician, was also the founder of *Taking Care of Home and Children*. The
structure of this magazine influenced the journal Dowlatabadi subsequently
edited in Iran, *Name-i-Banovan* (Women's paper), which was produced under
the supervision of the government.

Not only was Dowlatabadi's magazine repeatedly threatened and its
publication banned for several months, but she received death threats for her
outspoken feminist and political editorials. When in 1936 Reza Shah issued
the decree banning the veil, Siddiqeh Dowlatabadi was safe. In 1946 she returned to Europe to attend the Tenth Congress of the Women's International
League for Peace and Freedom in Geneva. When she died in 1961 at the age
of eighty, Dowlatabadi asked that no veiled woman be allowed to attend her
death ceremonies or visit her grave. In 1993, her niece Pari went to visit her
grave, whose stone, though defaced by Hezbullahi thugs, still stands. She
asked the keeper of the graveyard whose grave this was. He replied, "I'm not
sure. But I think it is the grave of a lewd woman who danced naked in front of
cinema theaters."

A second reading of the Siddiqeh Dowlatabadi story reveals some
troubling fault lines. A courageous feminist and activist all her life, she consolidated her feminism along class lines. Her problem could be read as not
uncommon to the early history of feminism. Joan Scott, for instance, draws
attention to the history of feminism as "the history of the project of reducing
diversities (of class, race, sexuality, ethnicity, politics, religion, and socioeconomic status) among females to a common identity of women (usually in
opposition to patriarchy, a system of male domination)."[45] Yet Scott also
discusses the problem of feminism's repressing differences that could not
be eliminated. Such "repression" of sexuality and class can be seen in a pain-

ful and telling incident recorded during my conversations with Pari about her famous aunt.

Not only was the marriage between her seventy-year-old father and the nine-year-old daughter of his secretary arranged by Siddiqeh Dowlatabadi, the story continues with the following detail: when the girl was in labor before her first menstruation howling with pain and hanging from the beams in her bedroom, Siddiqeh Dowlatabadi ordered the family to leave her alone. Another relative, unable to bear her cries, went to her aid. When the young wife was fifteen—after giving birth to two daughters, one of whom was Pari's mother—she was widowed. Once again, Siddiqeh Dowlatabadi arranged for her to marry an old man. As Gayle Rubin might say, woman here was the gift, but the exchange partners upon whom this exchange would confer its "quasi-mystical power of social linkage," though not necessarily men, operated through a psychic economy where daughter identified with father, and whose power and privilege were male.[46] The locus of the girl's oppression was between power systems (father and daughter) within a sexual system that trafficked in women, more specifically, women of a lower class. Descended from the "lower-class interloper who had come into the family," Pari was always aware of her difference from and inferiority to the other Dowlatabadis. And "difference" perhaps became the category through which Dowlatabadi found more common ground with Margaret Ashby in Paris than with her father's child bride.

Feminist political activism waned during the Pahlavi era, partly because both the Left and the Right were gender blind, partly because various "societies" were subsumed into the state-sponsored Women's Organization of Iran headed by the shah's twin sister, Ashraf Pahlavi. Najmabadi describes the shift in attitudes toward women's rights as a movement from activism to tokenism: "In the first period [the 1930s], women's status was seen as a symbol of modernity of the new nation and the new state. In the second period [the 1970s], it became the symbol of the modernity of the monarch and his progressive benevolence towards women."[47]

Whereas women had been activists before and during the Islamic Revolution, they found themselves increasingly disenfranchised by the hardened positions taken by the revolution after its initial "spring of freedom." Newly hardened positions were articulated most publicly by Monireh Gurji, the woman representative responsible for drafting the new Constitution of the Islamic Republic: "I feel ashamed to talk about 'women's rights'. Have any of our brothers in this assembly mentioned 'men's rights'?"[48] The question elided was well articulated most recently by Mahnaz Afkhami: "[H]ow will Muslim women, particularly those among them who can communicate with others, influence events, and make a difference, be empowered to advance the cause of women's human rights? How can the process be enhanced, facilitated, encouraged? What possibilities exist or can be generated for women activists?"[49]

The struggle against the shah brought out the greatest political participation by women in the history of Iran. Hailed as the "pillars of Iranian society" by Ayatollah Khomeini, women were soon pilloried into submission, their symbol for revolutionary liberation (the *chador*) turned into a shroud of protective exclusion and bondage. Yet on International Woman's Day—March 8, 1979—thirty thousand women marched on the streets to protest compulsory veiling and other forms of punishing and disciplining women. The women who marched for women's rights were a heterogenous group who represented social and political organizations as different as the conservative Women's Society of Islamic Revolution and the radical Revolutionary Union of Militant Women, whose parent organization was the Maoist Communist Party of Workers and Peasants.[50]

For the women I interviewed who had participated in this and the next march, the event included moments of unwelcome epiphany.[51] Not only was the march followed by several days of hysterical responses from young Islamic fanatics who roamed the city in search of women they could assault, but it also revealed to them the indifference of leftist organizations to women's issues.

The Women's March of March 12, 1979, for instance, ruptured certainties for Afsaneh Najmabadi by starting the process of breaking up unexamined ideas of unified feminism, recognizing difference, and admitting the multiplicity of class and gender identities. The march had been organized to protest Khomeini's March 7th decree on *hijab* (regulation Islamic dress, not necessarily the *chador*) as a requirement. Najmabadi was about to take her turn (on behalf of a Trotskyist segment of the Socialist Worker's Party) as speaker on a platform. Suddenly something she heard made her so dizzy that she almost fell off the platform: she had heard a woman from another committee say, "Look at those painted faces in the crowd. I will never go on a march with those women." Afsaneh's first reaction was that "of course she was right. A great many women who had come to that rally were exactly the women whom for years we had come to call 'the painted dolls of the Pahlavi regime.'" But years later as she reflected on her dizzy spell, she wrote:

> Despite nine years of vehement argumentations against crossing class lines, something in my mind had broken down. All I cared about, there and at that moment, was for women of any class, of any ideological affiliation . . . to make a very loud presence felt. . . . For years I thought my dizziness had been caused by the deep anger I had felt. . . . On the body of what we called the Westoxicated painted dolls, we had *fixed* layer upon layer of meaning. . . . This dichotomous mapping of female bodies as representations of revolution and counter-revolution, of moral and immoral, was the common political and cultural language of Islamic and secular forces at the time, with no room for any "choreographical" destabilization.[52]

Four months later, on July 12, 1979, when three prostitutes were executed, none of the leftist presses with which Afsaneh Najmabadi was associated thought the event important enough to report. She and other activists like Nayereh Tohidi report their horror at the extent to which the Left had internalized patriachal priorities,[53] at their own inability to counter leftist arguments that head coverings and women's rights were minor issues in the context of the larger political arena of anti-imperial struggles.

Gradually, as evidenced by the writings of Khomeini and Motahari, all differences withered into a single truth: the only acceptable woman in the Islamic state was the Muslim woman who was the "pillar of the family," and who abided by all the laws laid down in the *shari'a*, who would accept the misogynist gender coding prescribed for her by the new government's version of Islam. By 1981 (two years after the revolution), the idea of debating compulsory veiling or women's marches or women's rights seemed a part of the quixotic fantasy that had briefly accompanied a lost revolution.

The role of motherhood, however, was chosen as a charged symbolic site for the Islamic Republic. Motherhood was politicized and valorized, as well as santified through association with the clergy's vision of Fatima as ideal mother, wife, and daughter, even as the "family" and "family values" were revived as the birthplace for a new and proper Islamic society. Haleh Afshar compares Khomeini's veneration of mothers as "pillars of the nation," "forts of virtue and chastity" who must raise "brave and enlightened men and weak and united women," with Hitler's similar claim that women were "entrusted in the life of the nation with a great task, the care of man, soul, body and mind."[54] Equality with men is deemed "degrading" to women because it alienates them from their essential nature. While educated and middle-class women likely to pursue higher education and careers were indignant at definitions of their true "nature," the poorest women in the lowest classes were attracted and empowered by Khomeini's decree that husbands were responsible for the care and feeding of their wives. And it was the promise of this protection that kept them ardent supporters of the clergy.

The thrust of the conventional public narrative I have offered above is contradicted and inverted by yet another private account. A story told to me by Mohamad Tavakoli about his sister's rise and resistance to patriarchy, it is also a story about the incommensurability between ideology as it does its cultural work and ideology as it gets absorbed into personal life. Mohamad Tavakoli was born in Chaleh Meidun (below the bazaars in south Tehran) into a family of eight sons and one daughter. All eight brothers and their father saw the little sister as the repository of their honor and therefore, from the age of seven on, the object of their concern, protection, and wrath if, for instance, her *chador* slipped. As was true of other girls in her conservative neighborhood, her movements in public were limited to trips to buy bread or go to school.

When the revolution started in 1978, she disappeared from her home for three days with no explanation. She was then sixteen years old. When she returned, her angry father and brothers discovered that she had been engaged in making Molotov cocktails near Jaleh Square during one of the decisive battles between the army and the people. During the family fight that ensued, she wrestled with her father, knocked him to the ground, and kicked him. The father, who ironically had been the most religious member of the family, found that the revolution had become his daughter's excuse for revolting against him. He left his home and went to his village of origin, promising never to return until his daughter left the house.

Her rejection of paternal power, however, did not preclude subsequent attachments to other centers of male power. In the early 1980s, Mohamad's sister flirted with the possibility of joining various leftist Islamic groups and temporarily even abandoned the *chador*. During the elections for the Assembly of Experts she came into contact with the Party of the Islamic Republic, liked their simplicity and clothing (the men, for instance, wore no ties), and became active in their cause. When she completed this trajectory by marrying a member of the Revolutionary Guard, she continued her education, became principal of a high school, and established an educational collective. Mohamad says that all the brothers are now afraid of her and warn him to be careful of what he writes in letters home. She has recently considered running for Parliament.

The strictures against women therefore contained and nourished their contrary. And in this inversion we see also an inversion of the narrative of bound women in Pari's story about her village work. The collapse of old certainties led to the invention of new spaces for the rethinking of women's issues and the male-engendered narratives of Islamic laws. Ten years after the revolution, women found other ways to avoid confrontation with the regime by critiquing *ijtihad* (legal decisions about the *shari'a*), by reinterpreting gendered readings of the Qur'an, and by demonstrating an active presence in "every field of artistic creation, professional achievement, educational and industrial institutions, and even in sports."[55]

Najmabadi draws attention to the new power women have gained through their manipulation of the gendered construction of Islamic political discourse, as a result of which they are configuring new readings of Islam and feminism. Studies of female suicide, of population control, of laws of custody and divorce, of opposition to changes in laws on marriage and polygamy, for instance, appeared in the pages of *Zan-i-Ruz* (Today's woman).[56]

Seventeen years after the revolution, evidence suggests that women are beginning not only to have an active presence in politics[57] but also to carve out new possibilities for themselves in social, legal, and political life through public debate in women's magazines, through social and civic activism, and through public office.[58] Small though the number appears, it is significant that

9 out of 280 members of the Majlis (parliament) are women. This number is 4 percent higher than the comparable figure in Turkey, which is assumed to be more "modern" than Iran. The cabinet includes one woman who serves as adviser on women's issues. After the Beijing conference, the Ministry of Health opened a new position for a female deputy minister. Rafsanjani's daughter, Fayezeh, won the second-highest number of votes in the Majlis during the most recent election.

The counternarrative to these happy statistics is that Rafsanjani's daughter, after being elected to the Majlis, was beaten after a press conference by a group of conservative thought-police who objected to her liberal positions on such issues as appropriate clothing for women who ride bicycles, and her opposition to certain aspects of the status quo: that women are excluded from the judiciary, that they are policed and arrested for improper *hijab*, and that the violation of Islamic gender relations is punishable by flogging. The Persian skill at versified sloganeering (demonstrated all through the marches preceding the Islamic Revolution) took a newly gendered turn during the conservative opposition to the election of Fayezeh Rafsanjani. The slogans began by collapsing two women, Fayezeh and Ayesheh ('A'isha)—the youngest wife of the Prophet, a model of reprehensible womanhood in Shiite Islam. One slogan therefore went as follows: "*Ayesheh ba shotor amad, / Fayezeh ba motor amad*" (Ayesheh came on a camel, Fayezeh came on a motorcycle.) Another slogan played on the likeness between her first name and the similar-sounding word meaning "prostitute"—*fahesheh*:

Ayeshe-i-shotor sawar (Ayesheh who rides a camel)
Faheshe-i-motor sawar (Prostitute who rides a motorcycle)

Fayezeh Rafsanjani and the debate about the propriety of women's riding bicycles (see *New York Times*, September 20, 1996) is but a small manifestation of a much larger debate about women and power. So too the link between the camel and the bicycle in the second slogan needs to be contextualized in terms of a larger conflict over female activity and transgression that goes back to the seventh-century Battle of the Camel, also known as the first civil war in Islamic society.[59]

The limited space women have carved for themselves has not been freely given. As Haideh Moghissi puts it, "The Islamic regime has not opened the gates. Women are jumping over the fences."[60] In particular, four journals are responsible for rearticulating the position of women: *Payam-i-Hajar* (Message of Hagar), *Zan-i-Ruz* (Today's woman), *Farzaneh* (Wise woman), and *Zanan* (Women).

While distancing themselves from Western feminism as a limited and Eurocentric category, articles and editorials in three of the four magazines call for a reexamination of male readings of the *shari'a* and the Islamic canon. Their central concerns vary: *Payam-i-Hajar*, for instance, focuses on "awakening the conscience of the Islamic Republic" to the plight of working women, rural women, state workers, and "other suffering sisters." *Zanan*, however, has taken on the radical task of "decentering the clergy from the domain of interpretation," questioning legality, justice, and canonical readings of the Qur'an, and advocating "reading the Qur'an as a woman."[61] Social critics (Mina Yadigar Azadi and others) challenge readings of specific verses in the Qur'an by refusing to allow claims about ethics to be normative and insisting on the need for historic specificity. By arguing against hegemonic authorities and by admitting into their pages forbidden female voices from the decadent period of monarchy, and from the writings of such Western feminists as Virginia Woolf, Simone de Beauvoir, and Susan Faludi, the new Islamic feminists are, as Najmabadi tells us, collapsing the oppositions between modernity and Islam, secular and Islamic feminism, and feminism and cultural authenticity. In these new alliances we might see a specifically non-Western alternative modernity that rereads and rethinks the failures of the past and present.

Finally, I return to my earlier point about the unexpected consequences of modernity—a package deal whose hidden agendas are surprisingly resisted by those who find ways to put new experiences in the old package. Those new experiences are the contraries with which modernity is always pregnant. Life makes for strange bedfellows. Just as Big Oil, the United States, and the shah had no intention of producing an Islamic Revolution, so too the Islamic Revolution had no intention of producing its unintended effect: a potential that, though compromised, is realizing itself in a kind of woman's movement specific to and produced by its historical moment—and in a newly politicized public reflected in the approximately 90 percent of people who went to the polls in May 1997, an election that, against conventional predictions, brought in the liberal Ayatollah Khatami. Women are neither "returning" to a past narrative, nor are they mimicking a Western model of feminism. Instead they struggle to articulate a women's movement in dialectical conflict with each.

NOTES

A shorter and earlier version of this paper was presented at a symposium on Alternative Modernities at Northwestern University in April 1996. For their generous conversations, comments, and criticisms on either the early or the late version of this essay, I want to thank: Lila Abu-Lughod, Susan Bazargan, Jim Hurt, Afsaneh Najmabadi, Robert Parker, Richard Powers, Mohamad Tavakoli, Joe Valente, and Paul Vieille.

1. Jalal Al-Ahmad, *Plagued by the West*, trans. Paul Sprachman, (Delmar, N.Y.: Coward, McCann, and Geoghegan, 1981), p. 3. Al-Ahmad was one of many intellectuals and social critics who theorized the importance of political Islam in terms made familiar by Marxist socialism. Other representative figures in this group were Mehdi

Bazargan and Abol Hassan Banisadr. His influential term *Gharbzadegi* has been translated alternatively as "westernitis" or "westoxification."

2. See Parvin Paidar's *Women and the Political Process in Twentieth-Century Iran* (Cambridge: Cambridge University Press, 1995) for a provocative linkage of two Iranian revolutions (1906 and 1979) with modernity, a movement that in Iran was "broadly defined . . . as a socio-political process which promised the establishment of economic prosperity, social and technological progress, social justice, political freedom and national independence" (p. 24).

3. Keya Ganguly insists on the *agrammaticality* of different cultural modernities to discuss the "messiness and incommensurable aspects of distinguishing, perhaps in the dark, the ruptures and syntheses produced in the encounter between a putatively universal grammar of subjectivity and its multiple, historically specific variations." "Carnal Knowledge: Visuality and the Modern in *Charulata*," *Camera Obscura* 37 (1996): 157–86.

4. See Ranajit Guha, "Dominance without Hegemony and Its Historiography," *Subaltern Studies* VI, ed. Guha (Delhi: Oxford University Press, 1980), pp. 210–309. Guha focuses on nineteenth-century colonial society in India, where he sees the state exerting domination without hegemony—the necessary consent of all classes.

5. Shariati, *Bazgasht bih Khvish*, p. 316, quoted in Mohamad Tavakoli, "The Constitutional Revolution of 1905–1906 and the Islamic Revolution of 1978–1979" (Ph.D. diss., University of Chicago, 1988), p. 124. This is not essentialist authenticity, and not a fixed definition of the self based on a fantasmatic past. That was the model of self used by the clergy and accounts for Shariati's excommunication by the religious Right.

6. Ali Shariati, *Fatima Is Fatima*, trans. Laleh Bakhtiar (Tehran: The Shariati Foundation, n.d.), p. 105. Hereafter cited parenthetically as *FF*.

7. Some of the documents by women compiled in Azar Tabari and Nahid Yeganeh's *In the Shadow of Islam: The Women's Movement in Iran* (London: Zed Press, 1982) include lengthy examples lifted from Shariati's book almost as if the authors had internalized his argument and metaphors.

8. Shariati's argument is reminiscent of Fanon's chapter "On National Culture," in *The Wretched of the Earth*, trans. Constance Farrington (New York: Grove, 1963), in which he examines the problems of constructing a new identity forged out of a dead past and a bourgeois travesty of an imagined European present.

9. Fanon, *The Wretched of the Earth*, p. 202.

10. Oriana Fallaci, *Interviews with History* (Boston: Houghton Mifflin, 1976), p. 272.

11. See William R. Darrow, "Woman's Place and the Place of Women in the Iranian Revolution," in *Women, Religion and Social Change*, ed. Yvonne Yazbeck Haddad and Ellison Banks Findly (Albany: State University of New York Press, 1985), pp. 307–20, for a valuable reading of the ambivalent discourse of women's rights in the Islamic Constitution and its sources in earlier writings by Shariati and Motahari.

12. Ali Shariati, *On the Sociology of Islam*, trans. Hamid Algar (Berkeley: Misan Press, 1979), p.49.

13. See, for example, Tabari and Yeganeh, *In the Shadow of Islam*, pp. 173, 176, 189, 190.

14. See Mohamad Tavakoli, "Modernist Refashioning of Iran" (unpublished MS).

15. Quoted in Said Amir Arjomand, *Authority and Political Culture in Shi'ism* (Albany: State University of New York Press, 1988), p. 357.

16. Derek Walcott refers to "Progress as history's dirty joke" and its excuse for extermination, genocide, war, and slavery; Levinas—using Hegel, Husserl, Heidegger, and Sartre as evidence—has also attacked Western ontology as a philosophy based, he claims, on "a horror of the other." Emmanuel Levinas, "The Trace of the Other," in *Deconstruction in Context*, ed. Mark C. Taylor (University of Chicago Press, 1986), pp. 346–47. Levinas proposes ethics in place of ontology, substituting respect for the other (justice) in place of desire (freedom).

17. The irony here is that while Nuri claimed that he did not wish to build Iran out of the *ash* (stew) of the British, he was glad to sell out land and monopolies to the Russians. For a reading of this entangled relationship, see Michael M. J. Fischer, *Iran: From Religious Dispute to Revolution* (Cambridge: Harvard University Press, 1980), pp. 5–51. See also Vanessa Martin's *Islam and Modernism: The Iranian Revolution of 1906* (Syracuse, N.Y.: Syracuse University Press, 1989). Although Nuri's stance later became the basis for what is now referred to as traditionalist ideology, he does not fit into the category of the "premodern" traditional because he takes modernity as a counter and articulates a position against it.

18. Quoted in Paidar, *Women and the Political Process*, p. 65.

19. See Eliz Sanasarian, *The Women's Rights Movement in Iran* (New York: Praeger, 1982), pp. 20–21. See also Haideh Moghissi, *Populism and Feminism in Iran: Women's Struggle in a Male-Defined Revolutionary Movement* (New York: St. Martin's Press, 1994); and Paidar, *Women and the Political Process*.

20. See Afsaneh Najmabadi's forthcoming *Daughters of Quchan: Re-membering the Forgotten Gender of the Iranian Constitutional Revolution* (Syracuse, N.Y.: Syracuse University Press) and her unpublished MS "Female Suns and Male Lions: The Gendered Tropes of Iranian Modernity."

21. See Moghissi, *Populism and Feminism in Iran*, pp. 82 ff. She quotes from Ahmad Kasravi, *Khaharan va Dokhtaran-e Ma* (Our sisters and daughters), 2d ed. (Bethesda, Md.: Iranbooks, 1992), pp. 13–31.

22. Ervand Abrahamian, "Kasravi: The Integrative Nationalist of Iran," *Middle East Studies*, October 1973, 271–95. This illuminating essay narrates the history of Iran as a story of linguistic, religious, and tribal factions and communal struggles. Abrahamian suggests what is at stake in political modernization by recalling differences in the use of the term "national integration," which for Clifford Geertz means the "aggregation of communal groups into nations" and for Leonard Binder suggests the closing of gaps "between elites and masses through the building of new national values and state institutions" (p. 272).

23. Ibid., p. 273.

24. Ibid.

25. Ibid., p. 280. See also Fischer, *Iran*, for its discussions of theological disputes.

26. For all these details, I am indebted mostly to Abrahamian, "Kasravi," and Roy Mottahedeh, *The Mantle of the Prophet* (New York: Pantheon, 1985), pp. 98–105. Abrahamian sees the book burning and Kasravi's desire to cleanse Persian of mystical poetry and foreign words as a typically extreme strategy whose effect was to alienate communists and intellectuals who would otherwise have supported Kasravi. He there-

fore sees the failure to compromise as the cause of Kasravi's downfall. For an account of a typical debate between Khomeini and Kasravi in the 1940s, see Fischer, *Iran*, pp. 130–33.

27. Julia Kristeva, *Powers of Horror: An Essay on Abjection*, trans. Leon Rodiez (New York: Columbia University Press, 1982).

28. See Nikki Keddie, *Roots of Revolution* (New Haven: Yale University Press, 1981), pp. 93 ff.; and Kumari Jayawardena, *Feminism and Nationalism in the Third World* (London: Zed Books, 1986), pp. 57–72.

29. See Geoffrey Galt Harpham, "So . . . What *Is* Enlightenment? An Inquisition into Modernity," *Critical Inquiry*, Spring 1994, 551–56, for a sharp reading of the Inquisition as embodiment of the paradox, self-division, darkness, and "dialectic" of the Enlightenment.

30. This familiar image from Marx has been used to advantage most recently in David Lyon, *Postmodernity* (Minneapolis: University of Minnesota Press, 1994), p. 21. Terry Eagleton uses the image to describe capitalism, which "gives birth to its own gravedigger, nurturing the acolyte who will one day stab the high priest in the back," in *Criticism and Ideology* (London: New Left Books, 1976), p. 133.

31. Harpham, "So . . . What *Is* Englightenment?" p. 333.

32. Partha Chatterjee, *The Nation and Its Fragments* (Princeton: Princeton University Press, 1993), p. 234.

33. In 1963, explaining his program in the language of popular revolution, the shah embarked on "the Revolution of the Shah and the People" that included reforms such as voting rights for women, the formation of a literacy corps, and land reforms. See also Afsaneh Najmabadi, *Land Reform and Social Change in Iran* (Salt Lake City: University of Utah Press, 1987), for a valuable study of the effects of the land reforms of 1962–72 on the economy of rural societies, and of the problems in translating into other cultures the European model for agrarian development.

34. We must recognize that this is the narrative of a landowner and not of a peasant. The White Revolution was also seen as liberation by many peasants, some of whom organized street demonstrations during the '60s in support of its aims.

35. See Haleh Afshar, "An Assessment of Agricultural Development Policies in Iran," in *Iran: A Revolution in Turmoil* (Albany: State University of New York Press, 1985), pp. 58–79. She points to misconceived national planning and to statistics that demonstrate, over a forty-five-year span, a lack of linkage beween central and rural economies: "The oil industry was a highly developed, capital-intensive producer of unprocessed oil, mainly for consumption of the West. Oil formed an enclave of development with no backward and little forward linkage to the indigenous sector" (p. 59).

36. After the CIA coup of 1953 Iran's political and economic enmeshment turned from Britain and the Soviet Union to the United States, whose paranoia about the Soviet threat from the 50s to the 70s translated into massive military and economic assistance. Before the 1953 coup, the country had been indirectly controlled by Britain and the Soviet Union. The shah is reported to have complained that ambassadors from the two countries handed him a list of candidates each time there was an election to the Majlis; see Mehran Kamrava, *Revolution in Iran: The Roots of Turmoil* (New York: Routledge, 1990), p. 30.

37. See Chatterjee, *The Nation and Its Fragments*, p. 235.

38. See Benita Parry, "Resistance Theory/Theorizing Resistance or Two Cheers for Nativism," in *Colonial Discourse/Postcolonial Theory*, ed. Francis Barker, Peter Hulme, and Margaret Iversen (Manchester: Manchester University Press, 1994), pp. 172–96; Lila Abu-Lughod, "The Romance of Resistance: Tracing Transformations of Power through Bedouin Women," *American Ethnologist* 17 (1990): 41–55.

39. See Anthony Giddens, *Central Problems in Social Theory: Action, Structure and Contradiction in Social Analysis* (Berkeley and Los Angeles: University of California Press, 1979), pp. 226 ff. Discussing the uneven development of different sectors of social systems, Giddens writes of two models of unfolding development in Marx: one a progressive model moving toward empowering workers, neighborhoods, unions, and the proletariat; and the other, a "second theory of revolution," that "anticipates a conception of uneven development," that "involves the idea that the conditions initiating revolutionary transformation are to be found in the conjunction of the retarded and the advanced: the sort of explosive situation Marx saw to exist in Germany in the late 1840s, and in Russia some thirty years later" (pp. 226–27).

See also Marshall Berman's persuasive and relevant argument about the "tragedy of development" in *All That Is Solid Melts into Air* (New York: Penguin, 1982): "In so-called underdeveloped countries, systematic plans for rapid development have generally meant systematic repression of the masses," a repression that he says takes two forms. "The first form has involved squeezing every last drop of labor power out of the masses—Faust's 'human sacrifices bled, / tortured screams would pierce the night'—in order to build up the forces of production, and at the same time drastically restricting mass consumption so as to create a surplus for reinvestment in the economy. The second form entails seemingly gratuitous acts of destruction—Faust's destruction of Philemon and Baucis and their bells and trees—not to create any material utility but to make the symbolic point that the new society must burn all its bridges so there can be no turning back" (pp. 75–76).

40. Although I am indebted to conversations with Mohamad Tavakoli for my understanding of differences, he warns me to resist such facile simplifications because each of the figures I name belongs just as easily in other categories.

41. See Ali Mirsepassi-Ashtiani, "The Crisis of Secular Politics and the Rise of Political Islam in Iran," *Social Text*, Spring 1994, 51–84, for an important reading of the revolution as a "historical turning point in the crisis of modern secular politics." Foucault's comment appeared, according to Ashtiani, in an interview in a Persian paper, *Akhtar*, no. 4 (Spring 1987): 43. Paul Vieille's comments were made in Champaign-Urbana, both in conversations and in public talks.

42. See Cheryl Benard and Zalmay Khalilzad, *"The Government of God"* (New York: Columbia University Press, 1984), p. 39. When Karim Sanjabi, the leader of the National Front, visited Khomeini in France, he emerged from their meeting with a shared understanding of Islam and democracy as foundations. This convinced secularists that the theologians would step aside once the revolution had been won. Later, however, Khomeini refused to include the word "democracy." It was, he said, a "a Western import and Islam sufficed." See Keddie, *Roots of Revolution*, p. 252.

43. Farzaneh Milani, *Veils and Words: The Emerging Voices of Iranian Women Writers* (Syracuse: Syracuse University Press, 1992), p. 4.

44. Ibid., p. 86.

45. Introduction to *Feminism and History*, ed. Joan Wallach Scott (Oxford: Oxford University Press, 1996), p. 4.

46. See Gayle Rubin, "The Traffic in Women: Notes on the 'Political Economy' of Sex," in Scott, *Feminism and History*, pp. 105–51.

47. Afsaneh Najmabadi, "Hazards of Modernity and Morality: Women, State and Ideology in Contemporary Iran," in *Women, Islam and the State*, ed. Deniz Kandiyoti (Philadelphia: Temple University Press, 1991), p. 63.

48. Nahid Yeganeh, "Women's Struggles in the Islamic Republic of Iran,"in Tabari and Yeganeh, *In the Shadow of Islam*, p. 55. Gurji was the chosen woman representative in the Assembly of Experts. She continued in this speech to say that Islam does not separate women's from men's rights. "We have only the rights of human beings."

49. Introduction to *Faith and Freedom: Women's Human Rights in the Muslim World*, ed. Mahnaz Afkhami (Syracuse: Syracuse University Press, 1995), p. 5.

50. My source is the section entitled "Women's Organizations in Iran," in Tabari and Yeganeh, *In the Shadow of Islam*. This useful book includes documents on the question of women spanning the period from Khomeini to the Tudeh Party. It also lists positions taken by thirteen major and ten smaller women's organizations on the Revolution.

51. See Afsaneh Najmabadi, "Without a Place to Rest the Sole of My Foot," *Emergences*, Fall 1992, 84–102, for an account of her participation in the march, her questioning of the mapping of female bodies as representations of revolution and counterrevolution, and her disillusionment with leftist organizations for their refusal to take public positions on the terror against women when three prostitutes were executed on July 12, 1979.

52. Ibid., pp. 91–92.

53. Ibid., p. 92.

54. See Haleh Afshar, "Khomeini's Teachings and Their Implications for Iranian Women," in Tabari and Yeganeh, *In the Shadow of Islam*, pp. 75–90. She quotes from C. Kirkpatrick's *Women in Nazi Germany* (London: Jarrolds, 1939), p. 100.

55. Afsaneh Najmabadi, "Feminisms in an Islamic Republic," in *Gender, Islam, and Social Change*, ed. Yvonne Haddad and John Esposito (New York: Oxford University Press, 1998), pp. 59–84.

56. See Paidar, *Women and the Political Process*, pp. 265–363, on the "Discourse of Islamization," for a valuable survey of the Islamic Republic's policies on women.

57. For this information, I am grateful to Nayereh Tohidi, who has recently visited Iran and written on the changing social positions of women (see n. 58).

58. See Moghissi, *Populism and Feminism in Iran*. See also Valentine Moghadam, ed., *Identity Politics and Women: Cultural Reassertions and Feminisms in an International Perspective* (Boulder, Colo. Westview Press, 1994); and Nayereh Tohidi, "Modernity, Islamization, and Women in Iran," in *Gender and National Identity: Women and Politics in Muslim Societies*, ed. Valentine Moghadam (London: Zed Books, 1994).

59. See D. A. Spellberg, *Politics, Gender, and the Islamic Past: The Legacy of ʿA'isha bint Abi Bakr* (New York: Columbia University Press, 1994), pp. 132 ff., for an insightful reading of conflicting interpretations of ʿA'isha's role in the Battle of the

Camel in Sunni and Shi'a sources. This event is read as the cause of the split in the Prophet's household after his death. Most of his wives opposed 'A'isha's involvement in politics on the grounds (according to Shi'a sources) that women belonged in their tents rather than on battlefields. "Retrospectively cast in the historical record as the defeated political activist, 'A'isha is scripted to defend an untenable legacy as a woman already defined by the errors of female transgression" (p. 137).

60. Moghissi, *Populism and Feminism in Iran*, p. 183.

61. For the details on magazines, I am entirely indebted to Najmabadi's "Feminism in an Islamic Republic."

CHAPTER 7

The Marriage of Feminism and Islamism in Egypt: Selective Repudiation as a Dynamic of Postcolonial Cultural Politics

LILA ABU-LUGHOD

IN THE CONTEXT of her analysis of the East/West dialectic that has secured the veil as a loaded symbolic marker of cultural identity and women's status in the contemporary Muslim world, Leila Ahmed has argued that "[c]olonialism's use of feminism to promote the culture of the colonizers and undermine native culture has ever since imparted to feminism in non-Western societies the taint of having served as an instrument of colonial domination, rendering it suspect in Arab eyes and vulnerable to the charge of being an ally of colonial interests."[1]

I want to explore here one facet of this vexed relationship between feminism and cultural nationalism, reexamining that familiar dynamic of postcolonial politics in which "the woman question" animates political and ideological contests couched in the language of cultural authenticity versus foreign influence.[2] In Egypt ever since the late nineteenth century when reformers and nationalist modernizers took up the question of women's status and role in society, there has been a struggle between those who seek to locate women's emancipation, variously defined, at the heart of the development of nation and of society and those who try to dislocate such a project as an alien Western import. However, the contemporary form this debate takes reveals something that is often overlooked: those who claim to reject feminist ideals as Western imports actually practice a form of selective repudiation that depends on significant occlusions.

Islamists today are the best examples of those who condemn feminism as Western, although Arab feminists complain that their progressive male colleagues can be just as dismissive.[3] I will argue, however, that what is characteristic of the Islamists is that they stigmatize sexual independence and public freedoms as Western but much more gingerly challenge women's rights to work, barely question women's education, and unthinkingly embrace the ideals of bourgeois marriage. Yet the latter three are elements of the turn-of-the-century modernist projects that might well carry the label "feminist" and whose origins are just as entangled with the West as are the sexual mores singled out in horror. This leads one to ask how the component parts of the modern feminism that developed in Egypt have become disaggregated such that only certain aspects can today be made to stand for a Western-tainted female emancipation—something groups like the Islamists gain such symbolic capital by denouncing.

One clue can be uncovered through a questioning of the Islamists' rhetorical claims to cultural authenticity and traditionalism. I will first describe some contemporary positions in Egypt on the question of women. Then I will present a critical reading of the work of Qasim Amin, the turn-of-the-century reformer known for his advocacy of women's emancipation. Through this I hope to show how dependent the Islamists, like their secular progressive counterparts, are on the ideas of such early modernizing reformers as these ideas have become transmuted, widely disseminated, and grounded in people's lives through the socioeconomic transformations of the last century.

MODERNIST VISIONS

Many Egyptian secularist liberals and progressives fear that women's rights are now under threat. They see signs of this in the growing popularity in the last two decades of the new forms of dress called Islamic or modest dress and the adoption in particular of the form of head covering called the *hijab*, institutionalized in the reversion to more conservative personal status laws, and publicized in calls made in Parliament, mosques, and the media for women's return to the home and their "traditional" roles.

Among the most influential sites for the articulation of their views are print media and television. Secularists have enjoyed access to these media since the 1950s and 1960s, although they have had to contend with government censors and periodic political repression. Thus one can look to state-controlled forms such as the enormously popular evening dramatic television serials for representations of their views on women—views that do not take the form of polemics and may not be completely conscious, and thus are especially revealing.[4]

As I have analyzed them elsewhere, television serials may not be as powerful and effective in influencing people as urban critics and those involved in producing them believe.[5] Yet they are both representative of the values of an influential segment of the middle class and enough subject to censorship to be in line with basic assumptions about social morality. Television writers are a diverse group, in their views and their politics, but the work of some recognized screenwriters who have been involved in television since the 1960s and regularly take up women's issues in their dramas is especially interesting to consider.

The two writers whose productions and views I will examine here are considered progressive and secular, sharing a disdain for the commercial values and productions of recent years, a deep concern about the increasingly conservative social climate in Egypt, and a fundamental belief in television drama as a tool of social education, a reflection of the fact that they came of age during the era of Nasser, Egypt's first president. They take up the key issues for women, issues that have been the subject of debate and transformation since the turn of the century: education, work, and marriage.

The mark of their progressive positions is that they treat the issue of women's work positively. Usama Anwar 'Ukasha, for example, widely regarded as the most brilliant writer of television serials, provides a glimpse of this in his most spectacular and complex serial, Hilmiyya Nights (Layali al-Hilmiyya), aired in the late 1980s and early 1990s. In over a hundred episodes its rich group of characters, people originally from a traditional Cairo neighborhood called Hilmiyya, were taken through the events of modern Egyptian history.

His unqualified support for education is reflected in his positive depiction of the achievements of the daughters of two working-class protagonists, women who went to university and began careers, one teaching in the university and the other working as a medical doctor whose goal was to open a clinic in her own community.

An important theme of Hilmiyya Nights, like many of his serials, is how women are to balance work and love, careers and marriage. The intractability of this social problem is dramatized most fully in the story line of the semi-tragic relationship between the young protagonists 'Ali and Zohra. 'Ali and Zohra are in love; they share their dreams and aspirations. Zohra finds in 'Ali the love and support she has never experienced. Others try to thwart the relationship, but it is finally Zohra's apparent dedication to her career that spells its end. In their conversations, Zohra has confided in 'Ali about the importance of an independent career for someone whose life circumstances have forced her to rely on herself. When 'Ali is offered a fellowship to do graduate study abroad, he asks Zohra to marry him and accompany him. Her father resists, and after a while, somewhat mysteriously, she stops pressuring her father. 'Ali gives up his opportunity to go abroad but then gets arrested while attending a political meeting.

It then becomes clear that behind Zohra's growing coldness to 'Ali is the fact that her boss, through flattery about her talents as a journalist and promises to promote her career, is seducing her. She agrees to a secret marriage with him, but when she gets pregnant, her family forces a shotgun public wedding, and then she goes abroad. An innocent 'Ali gets out of prison, discovers that Zohra has betrayed him, and, disillusioned in love and politics, becomes an unscrupulous businessman. He is made to represent in Hilmiyya Nights the corrupt and materialistic entrepreneurs who made fortunes under the free-market policies initiated by President Sadat after the death of Nasser.

Despite the negative message about women's career ambitions that this plot line might suggest, consideration of a later stage in ʿAli's and Zohra's lives and other relationships in *Hilmiyya Nights* shows ʿUkasha to be more balanced. The most telling defense of women's rights to careers comes in the marital troubles that develop between ʿAli and Shireen. She is the beautiful, talented, and principled young journalist of modest background ʿAli finally marries. Increasingly he tries to control her activities and to restrict her career. He demands, while he has fled the country to escape prosecution for his business crimes, that she give up her work. As ʿUkasha portrays these events, ʿAli looks like an unreasonable patriarchal bully. He spoils his second chance for happiness in love by treating his wife like a possession in an age, the 1980s, when women's rights to professions have been firmly established.

ʿUkasha knows how to touch emotions through the deployment of familiar popular images, like that of the *ibn al-balad*, the noble salt of the earth of urban Egypt, and the mobilization of shared assumptions; meanwhile he pushes ordinary people a little beyond their usual aspirations by holding up as models values that are more "enlightened" and modernist (and middle-class) than those of many of his viewers—and of the political conservatives who capitalize on these.[6] In *Hilmiyya Nights* one familiar chord he sounds is the shared aspiration for conjugal love and devotion to the nuclear family. We only finally begin to sympathize with an aristocratic protagonist's third wife when she shows her motherly concern by running away with her son because her husband is neglecting him. This is the cause, she accuses, of their son's brush with recreational drugs. ʿUkasha also knows how to inculcate values by shaping and giving emotional depth to viewers' fantasies. Our unfulfilled longing for a happy ending for ʿAli and Zohra works to intensify the sense of the desirability of a marriage based on true love and understanding.

Yet ʿUkasha pushes his viewers by showing that love and marital happiness should not be incompatible with women's work. He does not pretend that the resolution of the tension between the two is easy. He wants to make a distinction, however, the same defensive distinction that most Egyptian modernist reformers from the nineteenth century on have tried to make: between women's rights to work and to develop themselves and the dangerous forms of illicit sexuality that the mixing between the sexes might ignite. Unlike the Islamists to be discussed below, however, ʿUkasha paints his fallen characters like Zohra with sympathy. He shows the social genesis of the human weaknesses that led to their mistakes, rather than blaming the West, or the Devil, as might Islamists.

One of the few women writers of television serials of her generation, Fathiyya al-ʿAssal also uses her serials to present progressive views on social issues. A vivacious woman of sixty, mother of grown children, and committed political activist in Hizb al-Tagammu' (the leftist party), she is adamant that feminist issues cannot be divorced from general social and political issues. She criticizes fellow Egyptian feminist Nawal El-Saadawi, lionized in the West, for her exclusive focus on women's issues like marital abuse. This focus, she notes, corresponds (too) nicely to the depoliticized agenda of the American-based Ford Foundation, which sponsored El-Saadawi's short-lived feminist organization, the Arab Women's Solidarity Union. As Al-'Assal explains, "I'm against men beating their wives and women submitting to being beaten, of course. But that is not the only issue. For me the issue is how women can be liberated economically, politically, and intellectually; then they will be automatically liberated from men."[7]

Literacy and education for women are long-standing interests of Al-'Assal's. In fact, she traces her beginnings as a drama writer to her days as a literacy instructor who was frustrated that her students escaped the classroom to sit with the janitor whenever the radio serials were broadcast. She decided to try her hand at radio drama in 1957 and went on to television in 1967. She deplores the fact that people watch television more than they read, and tries to encourage reading in her television serials.

Al-'Assal is more uncompromising than 'Ukasha both on the importance of women's work—as a means of fulfillment *and* domestic bliss—and of companionate marriage. She looks to her controversial 1982 serial, *She and the Impossible* (*Hiya wa al-mustahil*) as the best example of her views. In it she combined her perennial push for education and economic independence for women with a strong vision of love as the only proper basis of marriage. The serial, as she described it, was about a man who divorced his illiterate wife once he got educated. After he left her, she persevered and got a job and then went to university while raising her son on her own.

After twelve years, the husband came back and wanted to remarry her because she was no longer uneducated ("ignorant"). As Al-'Assal explained,

> She refused and told him that the Zaynab whom he had chosen in the past now rejected him. . . . The husband then suggested they should return to each other in order to raise their son. She argued that they should get back together only if they loved each other, in which case they could live under one roof and raise the boy together. . . . My point was to emphasize the value of a home as a home. That is to say, a man and a woman should enter only on the condition that they love one another; otherwise it would be sheer betrayal. These are new values, of course.

While most serials on Egyptian television take for granted that the ideal form of marriage is one based on shared values and mutual love and respect, and all depict the core social units as couples, it is the more politically progressive Al-'Assal who seems most explicit in her promotion of the companionate marriage. Asked about the lessons on love and marriage she tries to teach in her serials, she said:

Regarding love, marriage, or anything for that matter, I try to force people to be honest with themselves. . . . Marriage is not a question of a diploma or a house. It is a form of understanding between you and the person you are marrying, that you actually love each other. Any other form of marriage I consider sinful and a betrayal. . . . That is my opinion on love. Economic necessity often leads a woman to marry a man who can support her well, because she cannot do so herself. What I want is for her to be able to set up a household herself. Then she won't have to sell her body to a man, under the guise of marriage.[8]

ISLAMISTS: THE OTHER END OF THE SPECTRUM?

Those supporting some sort of self-consciously Muslim identity and associated with a range of positions regarding the importance of structuring society and the polity in more Islamic terms now also produce popular forms of public culture. While progressive television writers and other intellectuals have worked through the official state-run instruments of mass media, the Islamists (except a few associated with the state) are forced to disseminate their messages through magazines, books, and booklets sold in bookstores and street stalls, pamphlets distributed in mosques, and sermons and lessons, often recorded on cassettes carrying notices like "Copyright in the name of all Muslims."

These two sets of politically motivated culture producers can be thought of as in dialogue with each other, although both conceive of themselves as oppositional voices in Egypt. What a comparison between their output on women suggests, however, is that there are surprising areas of overlap, even as they define their projects quite differently vis-à-vis modernity and the West.

The television writers just discussed define their projects as modernist. They respect aspects of the West and are quite familiar with its literature and culture, but see themselves as nationalists with Egypt's social good at heart. Enlightenment, advancement, and progress are central to their vocabularies, and they share a sense that their most dangerous adversaries on social issues are the Islamists who do not use the lexicon of "modernity" and yet target the same "masses" they try to uplift. For example, Wafiyya Kheiry, a liberal screenwriter, expresses her worries about the direction Egypt is taking by bemoaning the way that the social climate has changed television programming since the progressive 1960s and 1970s. Referring to a serial she had written in 1975 about the difficulties of establishing collegiality between men and women in the workplace, she said, "If I were to write a serial along these lines today, men would simply respond by asserting that women should go back to the home; then all these problems would be avoided. Now the fundamentalists would claim that all these problems are due to the fact that women are going out to work in the first place."[9] To these imagined conservatives Kheiry retorted,

"Just because someone gets run over by a car, should I forbid people to walk on the streets? Of course there are problems created [by female employment], but we must confront them."

She also expressed her anger about a recent confrontation with the television censors. She was working on a serial based on short stories by Egyptian women writers. The script of one story called "An Emancipated Woman" ("Imra'a mutaharrira") was turned down. As she described it, the story was about a liberal man who returns from abroad and falls in love with a conservative woman, always challenging her conservative views. She defends herself, saying that her conservativism is just the way she is. He then gets to know a more liberated woman and leaves the first. Once the first woman realizes that she has lost him, she changes herself radically and becomes quite cosmopolitan. When his relationship with the second woman fails to work out, he returns to the first, only to find her completely changed. He then leaves her too. The story was meant to show how men do not know what they want. But the censors rejected the episode, with the explanation that, as Kheiry put it, "it would create problems with the fundamentalists. . . . It would be problematic to depict a woman as moving from conservatism to liberalism. In fact, it was impossible for a woman to do so."

Al-ʿAssal, on the other hand, though she has had many run-ins with the censors, reserves her contempt for another group of veiled women involved in media: the so-called repentant artists who have captured the press and the imaginations of many in the past few years. These are a small group of famous actresses, singers, and belly dancers, stars of film and stage, who have given up their careers and taken on the new head covering called the *hijab*. In small booklets the decisions of these born-again stars are explored and marketed, one book sensationalizing the phenomenon by portraying these women as embattled. The blurb on the back cover reads, "After more than twenty actresses and radio personalities had adopted the veil (*hijab*) . . . war was declared on them. . . . Those carrying the banner of this war are 'sex stars' and 'merchants of lust.' "[10]

These actresses have done what an increasing number of urban Egyptian women have done: adopted the new modest Islamic dress as part of what they conceive of as their religious awakening.[11] Because they are such well-known figures, their actions have been publicized and capitalized on by the Islamists to further legitimize the trend toward women's veiling and to support their call for women's return to the home. Secularists and progressives, those opposed to veiling as a sign of "backwardness," suspiciously accuse these actresses of taking fat salaries from the Islamic groups for hosting study groups at which conservative religious authorities or unqualified women proselytize. Fathiyya al-ʿAssal sees them as gullible victims of the Islamic groups, who have preyed on their guilt about their genuinely dissolute lives with fiery talk about "Hell, God, and Judgment Day."

But such study groups have cropped up everywhere, and the decision to adopt the *hijab*, while initially, in the late 1970s, mostly a form of political action by intelligent university women, usually the first in their families to be educated, has now spread down to working women of the lower-middle classes and up to a few rebellious upper-class adolescents and movie stars. In rural areas, educated girls declare their difference from their uneducated relatives without jeopardizing their respectability by means of this form of dress.[12] In short, adopting the *hijab* now has an extraordinary number of meanings and coimplications that need to be distinguished.

Analysis of the discourse of these repentant stars suggests the complexity of the meanings and brings into relief a crucial dimension of the debates on women and cultural authenticity in contemporary Egypt. The women's narratives dramatically denounce performing as the work of the Devil and remorsefully regret their years in the milieu of the (night) world of "art," fame, and the limelight. The women express their joy at having become closer to God through renunciation of their professions.

I examine elsewhere ordinary Egyptians' responses to these stars, showing how media stars' wealth, independence from family, and links with Western lifestyles are conflated with sexual immorality to make them objects of ambivalence.[13] Recently the Islamist attacks on stars as symbols of sexual immorality have gained strength, Egypt's most famous and Westernized actress, Yusra, now having to fight a lawsuit that charges her with offending public morals. Her crime was appearing on the cover of a film magazine in skimpy clothes.[14]

Here I want to point out only one interesting aspect of the reformed actresses' self-presentations. A recurring theme in their narratives, bolstered by the interviews with their husbands that accompany their stories, is how their careers had caused them to neglect their husbands and children. In the book called *Repentant Artists and the Sex Stars!*, Shams al-Barudi, a former film star introduced as someone "associated with seduction roles," is reported as saying, "I now live a happy life in the midst of my family, with my noble husband who stood by me and encouraged me and congratulated me on each step . . . and my three children."[15] Her husband, a former actor and movie director explains, "I had long wished that Shams would retire from acting and live for her household." In talking about how she had changed, he said, "Shams has now become a wife who cares for her husband . . . and a mother who tends her children and lives her life like any other wife . . . she is a mother with a calling [to raise her children in a Muslim way]."[16] In a recent interview where he modifies his position on art and justifies his return to acting, he nevertheless ends with a similar statement: "My wife is the wealth God has bestowed on me. My beloved wife shares my life, for better or worse, and we adore our children, care for them, and show them every concern."[17]

This husband is echoing the conservative sentiments that have been widely expressed especially in the last two decades in the press and other media, sentiments perhaps widely felt, that women's proper place is in the home with their families. Actresses and other show business personalities epitomize the challenge to that model, and they are targeted because they represent the moral nightmare of the sexual looseness of professional women.

The problem is often presented as one affecting the next generation. As Soha Abdel Kader notes, when in 1985 a draft law was presented to Parliament calling for women to quit their jobs, keeping half their salaries, "the rationale behind the draft law was that working women were neglecting the care and upbringing of their children, thereby contributing to an increase in the incidence of juvenile delinquency and drug addiction among the young."[18] A short article by Anis Mansour, an establishment journalist, in the official government newspaper *Al-Ahram* in 1989 lays out the links between careerist mothers and unhappy children who turn to drugs, brothels, and "deviation." He stresses film stars' special culpability as people who send their children away to boarding school to feel unwanted.[19]

This call for women's "return" to the roles of wife and mother, also harped on by popular religious authorities such as Shaykh Al-Sha'rawi and the younger Dr. 'Umar 'Abd al-Kafi, who preaches his message on cassettes, is a cornerstone of a program constructed as "Islamic" or authentic. Such figures claim to be radically different from the progressive television writers who see women's work as essential to national development and social progress. Although there are important differences among Islamists that should not be ignored, I would still argue that the Islamists and other conservatives, and especially their women followers, are not as different from the liberals as they might think.[20] In particular, although they may claim to represent a "return" to the culturally authentic, rejecting the emancipation of women as a Western corruption, their positions are no more "traditional" than those of the progressives. They are certainly less positive about women's work than are the progressive television writers whose productions I described above, but on the value of education and conjugal love they hardly disagree.

As is often the case, men, and especially the male religious authorities, seem to be more conservative than the women to whom they preach. Someone like Shaykh al-Sha'rawi is obsessive in his condemnation of Western corruption and his insistence on the importance of women's veiling. He tries to persuade women that their place is in the home, using odd arguments—asserting, for example that Marilyn Monroe herself had wished she had been able to be a housewife.[21] Women's work is problematic for these figures because it involves them in a public world now distinctly separate, as it is in all modern capitalist societies, from the private world of home and family.

There has indeed been a backlash against working women, which many analysts relate to high levels of unemployment for men (exacerbated in Egypt by the dismantling of the public sector after Sadat's open-door policy and by fewer opportunities for migration to the Gulf). Many Islamists argue that women should not work outside the home, God having given them the noblest of occupations—raising His creatures. The reality is, however, that most of the women who have taken on the veil are in fact working or expect to work. Most families aspiring to achieve or maintain middle-class status cannot do without a second income.[22] And Egyptians have become used to women professionals in all areas. As Zuhur puts it, work for the Islamists is one of the "negotiable" issues.[23] Given these realities, at most what figures like Sheikh al-Sha'rawi can do is tell women that if they must work, they should comport themselves properly and have no physical contact with men in work situations.[24] This, of course, is not so different from what 'Ukasha suggests in *Hilmiyya Nights* in showing the sexual perils of working or what Wafiyya Kheiry suggests in showing the difficulties of establishing cross-sex collegiality (although both, it must be stressed, are more positive about professional women's work as an avenue for personal development).

The findings of one of the few serious surveys of veiled university women, reported on by both Leila Ahmed and Mervat Hatem and conducted in the early 1980s by Zaynab Radwan, show that the survey's subjects actually accept many components of what we might consider the modernist feminist project.[25] As Ahmed has noted, Radwan's study, while confirming that unveiled women were more feminist than their veiled counterparts on matters of women's education, work, political participation, and rights in marriage, showed that on most issues the majority of women shared what could be called feminist goals.[26] The margin of difference between the veiled and unveiled groups was often only slight. For example, 99 percent of unveiled women thought work outside the home was acceptable, but so did 88 percent of the veiled students. Badran has argued that in the late 1980s, there has even been a liberalization on gender issues within Islamist ranks. She points to Islamist women like Safinaz Kazim and Hiba Ra'uf who insist on women's rights to the public sphere.[27]

The support for women's education is more consistent. Radwan's 1982 study showed that 98 percent of unveiled women believed that women had the right to pursue the highest level of education possible; the figure for veiled women was 92 percent. And even the most conservative new charismatic religious figures, such as Dr. 'Umar 'Abd al-Kafi, whose daily appearance on a television show during Ramadan 1993 (hosted by Kariman Hamza, the only veiled public broadcaster) made him a media star, barely attack education for women.[28] He insisted only that women should not go far from home unaccompanied to attend university, and that wives should not work hundreds of miles away from their families.[29]

It is on matters of marriage, however, that one sees the most overlap between the liberal secular and Islamist positions. Although the television writers place more stress on women's equality and dignity in marriage and say little about motherhood, those advocating a "return" to Islam and tradition see conjugal love and the nuclear family as ideal.[30] Although much more research needs to be done before we can speak with confidence about expectations concerning love, marriage, and motherhood among those in the Islamic groups and the broad base of young people who find appealing an explicitly Islamic identity, the "born-again" stars and their supportive husbands quoted above suggest some of the ideals of domesticity that seem to be part of being pious in Egypt today. Hatem has also written about how central the husband-wife relationship was deemed by Zaynab al-Ghazali, influential leader of the Muslim Women's Association, to the "happy [Muslim] home," her advice going so far as to suggest that "the affairs of the couple and their marital agreements should not go beyond the couple."[31] And one could read Shayk Al-Sha'rawi's interpretation of the Islamic requirement of social equivalence (takafu') of marriage partners as referring not to wealth but to "an equality in essential nature, such as the mind, health, character, and values," and thus framing an ideal of companionate marriage in Islamic terms.[32] Elsewhere, Hatem has accused him of a "startling embrace of heterosexual (emotional) intimacy" because he regards women's care of men as "more primary than their reproductive task."[33]

Evidence of Islamists' concern with marital love can be found in the articles and advice columns that appear on the women's page of the newspaper published by Al-Azhar, Al-Luwa' al-Islami. These articles, on themes like how to achieve marital happiness or a stable and calm marital life, urge husbands and wives to be patient, forgiving, and tolerant of each other.[34] Although those interviewed, like the Islamist thinker Yusuf Qaradawi, outline women's duties as including serving their husbands, raising children, and keeping house—with statements like "virtuous women care only about satisfying, pleasing, and serving their husbands, taking good care of their home and family"[35]—they also urge husbands to be good-natured and to remember their wives' rights to kind words and tender gestures; [36] describe the proper management of household affairs as involving mutual consultation and cooperation rather than the domination of one partner;[37] condemn forced marriage; and, like the progressive writer Al-'Assal, assert that financial considerations should not be paramount in spouse selection.[38]

There is certainly no single Islamist voice on these matters. For example, although Qaradawi and 'Aliyya al-'Asqalani, the woman writer and interviewer responsible for many of the articles on the women's page, characterize marriage as properly based on the emotions of amity (mawadda) (described as a higher emotional state than love) and mercy (rahma) and meant to produce peace of mind (sakina) and serenity (tamanina), others, like Muhammad Ibrahim Mabruk, are happy to use the word love (hubb). In his recent book, Islam's Position on Love: A Revolt against the Materialism of Our Age, the Love of Man toward Woman and Woman toward Man, he denounces forced marriages and declares that Muslims, unlike Westerners, have always agreed about the value of love because they know it is not an illusion but a spiritual matter.[39] With images as trite as a Hallmark greeting card, he describes true love in the following terms: "A lover accepts the beloved's personality as a whole; he wishes the subject to stay just as it is, without trying to reform, guide, or advise";[40] "love is a constant attachment to and affection for the other . . . an ever renewing activity. It does not seek to possess the other. . . . "[41]

What all these Islamists share is the fact that the framework is religious, marriage being characterized as a spiritual blending (*imtizaj ruhi*) or as a resemblance between lovers' souls (*mushakala bayn nufus al-ʿushaq*), and all their positions are justified and supported by reference to Islamic texts, whether the Qur'an or traditions of the Prophet, or to the example of the Prophet. This is not insignificant, even when they readily use the authority of sexologists, psychologists, and medical scientists to confirm their points of view (as in Mabruk's arguments about the greater sexual fulfillment of those who have sex in the context of love).[42] Yet I would still maintain that their image of the ideal marriage shares its basic contours with the less explicitly religious norm.

From a somewhat bizarre television experience comes another kind of confirmation of the importance for Islamists of these "modern" values for marriage. One evening in 1990 there was a fleeting episode of a television serial that was not continued the following day. It began innocently enough, resembling any evening serial, with parents discussing with their grown children possible marriage partners, an outdoor scene at a club where a meeting had been arranged between a fashionably dressed young couple, and a slight twist on a predictable theme with the parents urging their handsome son to consider the daughter of their wealthy neighbors.

But suddenly all the usual terms of the evening serials were unsettled. The young man went to complain to his grandparents about his parents' materialistic motives. In language rich with pious phrases he revealed his dilemma. Quoting the well-known tradition of the Prophet Muhammad about what qualities to value in a woman, he asserted that he too valued piety above wealth and beauty. He confessed that he already knew who he wanted to marry. She was a pious woman, a veiled woman who was a classmate of his in medical school. This episode pitted arranged marriage against the love match, but it was the secular modern parents who wanted to arrange the match for their son and the Islamist son who wanted the love marriage with his colleague.

Although I was never able to discover the story behind this unusual drama, it was easy to see why it was yanked from the air, apparently after two episodes. Made by a private Islamic production company, it violated the segregation of religious from secular programming in its heavy incorporation of quotations from the Qur'an and the traditions of the Prophet. And it made positive mention of the modern urban religious men and women who, until 1992, were strictly ignored in television drama.[43] Yet what is so revealing about it is its suggestion that for the pious, educated, middle-class youths, the ideals of companionate marriage are just as vital as they are for the progressive secular nationalist feminists like Fathiyya al-ʿAssal.[44] In fact, sharing the values of a new generation and being, as the Islamist Zaynab al-Ghazali put it, comrades within a movement, should strengthen the bonds of marriage.[45]

HISTORICAL ROOTS

Many characterize the current call by conservatives for women to return to the home as a call for the "retraditionalization" of women's status and roles.[46] And indeed the assertion of the proper role of a woman as wife and mother, with the assumption of a happy nuclear family, husband and wife devoted to each other and to their children, is now—as the comment of the husband of the born-again film star Shams al-Barudi suggests, and the writings of Islamist thinkers indicate—couched in an Islamic religious idiom that gives it a pedigree. The duty of the mother is to raise good Muslim children, and the love between husband and wife is described in terms of emotions with Qur'anic resonances like mercy and amity.

But I would argue that this vision of family and women's proper relation to husband and children is profoundly modern and its sources are entwined with the West as surely as are the negatively perceived public freedoms of women the Islamists denounce. Yet this bourgeois vision of women's domesticity, rooted in a much earlier phase of Western and Egyptian feminist reform, has become so ensconced in upper-, middle-, and even lower-middle-class Egyptian society that none of those arguing for a rejection of Western ways seek to dislocate it. Instead, they assimilate it to "tradition" and try to find Islamic bases for it while vilifying as foreign the other side of what being a Western emancipated woman might mean. This is not to say that the Islamist inflection or translation of the ideals does not change the model in important ways; it is merely to note that the claims to a pure indigenous tradition are spurious.

To understand why I say this, one needs to understand the historical context of contemporary debates and the situation of women. A good place to begin is with a critical examination of the ideas of the most prominent instigator of Egyptian debates on women, the elite reformer Qasim Amin (also discussed in this volume by Afsaneh Najmabadi and Omnia Shakry, chapters 3 and 4), whose controversial *The Liberation of Women*, published in 1899 while Egypt was under British occupation, has led many to consider him the father of Egyptian feminism. More recently, a reassessment of his contributions has begun, with Timothy Mitchell questioning the colonial roots of his feminism and showing its link to a large-scale modernizing project intended to open up the women's world to the same surveillance and individualized subjection to the state as was imposed on the rest of the population, and to organize the family into a house of discipline for producing a new Egyptian mentality.[47] Leila Ahmed has followed, although without criticizing the overall projects of modern power in which Amin and his class were engaged, by accusing him of being "the son of Cromer [the British consul general] and colonialism," who used a particular kind of feminism to undermine his own culture along lines desired by the colonial powers.[48]

I will take up another aspect of his project, arguing that although he spoke of women's rights, education, and work, what he ultimately was most interested in promoting was the modern bourgeois family with its ideal of conjugal love and scientific child rearing. This is a form of family that some Western feminists, Marxists, and social theorists of the second half of the twentieth century have now come to criticize as a source of women's subjection because of the way it divides women from one another, gives them new tasks, places them under the control of husbands, and opens up the family to capitalist exploitation, state control, and new forms of discipline.

Like many reformers produced in the colonial encounter, Amin linked women's status to the progress of the nation, arguing that it was not an "exaggeration to claim that women are the foundation of the towering constructs of modern civilization."[49] He held up for admiration Europe and America where "women have contributed shoulder to shoulder with men to every branch of trade and industry, to every branch of knowledge and the arts, to every philanthropic activity, and to every political event."[50] Advocating especially an end to the veiling and seclusion of women, he detailed the potential gains for household heads and for the nation in the contributions women could make. "Our country," he wrote, "would benefit from the active participation of all its citizens, men and women alike."[51]

Despite the references to European women's public achievements, however, in the end he argued only for primary education for girls (albeit to be consolidated through later participation in public life) and never actually suggested that anyone except poor women and those without male support should have full educations and professions, the latter needing this opportunity so as not to turn to "improper occupations."[52] So how were women to help the nation develop?

For Amin, the principal benefits of Egyptian women's becoming educated and exposed to the world seemed to be two: they would become better mothers, capable of bringing up the kinds of good citizens required by the modern nation; and they would become better marriage companions for the educated modern man, capable of truly loving and understanding him. Both notions, informed child rearing and companionate marriage, can be considered novel imports, cultural forms transplanted from the West.

Shakry explores, in this volume (chapter 4), the way that he linked motherhood and nationalism and the fascination his contemporaries had with new ideas about the importance of child rearing.[53] As Mitchell has pointed out, and Shakry has elaborated, his criticism of Egyptian women's methods of child rearing is shot through with the obsessions with hygiene, rationality, and discipline that characterized the "enlightened" West and were adopted by colonial modernizers, indigenous or foreign.

Here I will be more concerned with his views on marriage. Although defensive throughout his book about his intent to stay within an Islamic framework, giving women only the rights they had according to the true principles of Islam, the Paris-educated Amin is blatant in his admiration for European society. Scathing in his condemnation of contemporary Egyptian women who were, in his words, incapable of truly loving their husbands, and of Islamic scholars who had reduced marriage to a contract by which a man has the right to sleep with a woman, he devotes many pages to painting a romantic picture of the kind of spiritual, mutual love he envisions between husbands and wives. He uses a passage from the Qur'an again to justify this: "He created for you helpmeets from yourselves that ye might find rest in them, and He ordained between you love and mercy." But the sources of this saccharine vision are clearly Western, and he uses the model of intense friendship to characterize it.[54] He dedicated his second book on the subject of women to his fellow nationalist Sa'd Zaghlul, whose friendship, he says, had led him "to consider the value of such a love when shared between a man and his wife" and which he then offers as "the secret of happiness that I declare to the citizens of my country, men or women."[55]

His call to end veiling and seclusion as well as to ban polygamy can be read as means to nurture the marital bond. Anticipating the anxieties about fidelity and chastity these reforms would incite, he again turns to the superiority of Europeans, arguing that they had realized, as their knowledge increased and "they began to evaluate and measure their way of life against rational criteria and accurate, unbiased information" that the chastity belt and other forms of control over women they had used in the past did not work or "guarantee their happiness. They concluded that their only route to happiness lay in having their wives share with them in their endeavors, assisting them in straightening out their muddled affairs, and complementing their inadequacies. To achieve this they began to prepare their women through education for their new role."[56]

Echoing the European Christian marriage vows, and quoting John Stuart Mill, he asks in *The New Woman*, "What better situation is there for a man than living with a companion who accompanies him day and night, at home and abroad, in sickness and in health, through good and bad, a companion who is intelligent, educated, and knowledgeable of life's challenges? . . . Can a man be happy if he does not have a woman next to him to donate his life to and who personifies perfection through her friendship? This type of life—which our men do not comprehend—is one of the greatest inspirations to great works."[57]

Amin in vivid terms portrayed the dismal state of marriage in his era. He argued that marital unhappiness was the rule, although he believed it was the upper- and middle-class urban men who suffered the most because the gap between themselves and their ignorant (uneducated) women was the greatest. They wanted order and systematically arranged homes; they wanted to share the ideas they cherished, their concerns about the society they served and the country they esteemed, their joys and pain. When they found their wives ignorant, wanting only money or attention from them, they came to despise them and turned away. This made their wives hate them. He concluded, "From then on life is like hell for both of them."[58]

One must wonder at the sources of his strange and negative depiction of marital life and the condition of women in Egypt. The resemblances between his descriptions and those of the missionaries and colonial officials, for example, are striking. Although the missionary women working in the Muslim world blamed the men as well as the system of seclusion, they too described the Muslim family as loveless and described upper-class women as idle. As evidence for the absence of love in marriage, besides numerous anecdotes about miserable marriages, they noted that "there is no word in the Arabic language for home." In a nice circulation of ideas, Annie Van Sommer's introduction to a 1907 collection of missionary women's accounts of their experiences in Muslim lands (*Our Moslem Sisters: A Cry of Need from Lands of Darkness*) cites the "Egyptian gentleman" Qasim Amin as an authority on the lovelessness of Muslim marriage.[59]

To highlight the novelty of Amin's vision of the proper role of wife and mother, a vision to which I suggest the current call to "retraditionalization" as well as the progressive visions of television writers are deeply indebted, I would like to pursue two strategies. One is to read against the grain Amin's complaints about women in his era, particularly the upper-class women with whom he is most concerned. This will suggest what one form of "traditional" (in the sense of pre-twentieth-century) gender relations might have been like. The second, and trickier, strategy is to sketch in what women's roles in one contemporary, nonurban community in Egypt are like. My intent is not to suggest that this community represents the past, whether pre-nineteenth-century or the Prophet's time, but rather to cautiously indicate the kinds of models of marriage and motherhood that developed in communities less affected by the modernizing reforms of the state. It should become clear that the current calls for "retraditionalization" do not have this kind of "tradition" in mind.

Amin's first complaint is that wives are too clingy, not respecting the work their husbands do, not granting them the freedom to read quietly. This may suggest that they expected more attention from husbands than the modern educated husband, with his ideological and social (read extrafamilial) concerns, now wished to provide.

He also thinks that women do not run their households efficiently and complains that they "have become accustomed to idleness . . . the source of all evil."[60] He proposes that the proper administration of large households is a serious occupation. Can one suggest that he would like to impose on women a new form of industriousness and new standards of household work that are more demanding of their time, keeping them bound to the home rather than permitting them time for visiting?

He accuses seclusion of being a source of moral corruption because it encourages upper-class women to mix with lower-class and less respectable women, to talk freely to peddlers ("women who are ignorant of their roots, their background, or their condition, and who have not adopted any points of good character"), and to be exposed to prostitutes (dancers) at wedding celebrations. He finds it problematic that "[t]he woman of the house sees no harm in visiting her servant's wife; in fact, she may be entertained by conversing with her and listening to her tales. She gives minimal consideration to the appropriateness or inappropriateness of the topics of conversation."[61] This anxiety over women's talk surfaces elsewhere in his complaint that idle women spend their time talking to their friends: "While with friends and neighbors, her deep sighs ascend with the cigarette smoke and coffee steam as she talks loudly about her private concerns: her relationship with her husband, her husband's relatives and friends, her sadness, her happiness, her anxiety, her joy. She pours out every secret to her friends, even those details associated with private behavior in the bedroom."[62]

Here I would like to suggest that Amin is signaling his desire to undermine the solidarities of a relatively separate women's world, distinguishing an emergent middle class, and dividing women by placing them into separate bourgeois nuclear families. He also seems to want to put an end to the sexually explicit language of that world that is often hostile to men. In her eloquent analysis of the parallel movement to modernize Iranian women, Najmabadi has argued that as women became educated and unveiled, they lost the rich and expressive language of their former homosocial world and imposed on themselves new forms of silence.[63]

Although he specifically distinguished the women of his class who were the main objects of his proposed reforms from rural women and desert Bedouin, women he saw as more the equals and partners of their men, I think that such women even today can offer further clues about what was novel about his notions of the proper charges of wives and mothers. This is not to deny that such groups themselves have undergone significant transformations in the last century. But since these communities have been positioned differently within colonial and postcolonial Egypt, they have followed paths separate from those of the urban middle and lower classes. Their assumptions about gender relations can offer hints about what might be included in the repertoire of "the traditional" or "indigenous."

I have shown in great detail elsewhere how one such community, the Awlad ʿAli Bedouin of Egypt's Western Desert, work with very different ideas about marriage and child rearing from those of contemporary urban middle-class Egyptians.[64] Marriages are arranged, in many cases between relatives, and love and respect can develop between marital partners if each fulfills his/her tasks well and respects the honor and dignity of the other. The basic loyalties, however, of men and women, are to kin. And the basic day-to-day socializing is oriented around same-sex groups, with women experiencing great freedom from the surveillance of men and expressing vibrant irreverence and resistance to the control of men in their separate sphere.

Women do most of the caring for children, but they do not see themselves as molding the characters of their children, making them industrious, or exposing them to proper stimulation and experience. They see their children's characters as in part due to heredity, in part influenced by the example set around them, but mostly God-given. Women take seriously their Qurʾanic duty to suckle their children for two years, but after that their main charge is to make sure that their children's behavior by their adolescent years is socially appropriate with regard to showing respect to others. Child rearing is not considered an occupation but only one of the many things, such as cooking, weaving, getting water, and paying social calls, that women do. They get help with the children from other women in the household but mostly from older children. If anyone is responsible for children's religious training, it is their fathers. And these women are certainly not trying to raise the future citizens of a proud Egypt or even good members of the Muslim *umma*, although they might sympathize with the latter concept.

In short, women are wives and mothers, but these roles do not require them to be devoted to their husbands or dedicated to the proper training of their children; and these roles are balanced by women's significant involvement in the affairs of their kin and of the women's community. Other studies of Arab women have suggested that in kin-based societies "public" and "private" do not have the same meanings they bear in other sorts of societies, and that in the former women's involvement in family affairs is a form of significant public action.[65]

Only now, with a younger generation of women who are becoming educated in state schools and gaining the literacy that allows them to be influenced by national ideologies, as well as being exposed to mass media, can one detect the entrance of the modernist ideals of marriage. Young, educated Awlad ʿAli women talk about mutual understanding (*tafahum*) as what they want most in a marriage. The only young woman in the community I lived in to achieve secondary education was also the only one to aspire to living with her new husband in a nice clean apartment alone, having only two children. She cherished her postcard collection, which like the collections of similarly educated girls in rural Upper Egypt, included romantic scenes of brides and grooms looking deep into each others' eyes.[66]

Amin's program, one can now see clearly, was for a liberation of women that would make of them good bourgeois wives and mothers in a world where state and class ties would override those of kin, capitalist organization would divide the world into the distinct spheres of private and public, and women would be subjected to husbands and children, cut off from their kin and from other women. His was a project of domesticating women that relied heavily, as Shakry and Najmabadi (this volume) show, on Western models of the time. Clearly it is this modernist and "feminist" tradition within which the Islamists work, even as they transform some of its elements. They do not gesture toward the sex-segregated world Amin denounced or toward the alternative model with different cultural and political roots that I have described for the contemporary Awlad ʿAli Bedouin in Egypt. As Homi Bhabha has argued for other postcolonial societies, access to any sort of real "tradition" has been made impossible by the historical cultural encounter with the West.[67]

CONCLUSION: BEYOND THE RHETORIC

It has been nearly a hundred years since Qasim Amin published his two controversial books. As feminist scholars have recently documented, he wrote in a context where women writers were already raising many of the concerns he raised. The struggles for women's rights and the transformation of women's lives were carried forward by a range of women writers and activists and an impressive series of feminist organizations in the early to mid–twentieth century, led by women like Huda Shaʿrawi, Saiza Nabarawi, and later Doria Shafik, who were far more radical than Amin in their demands for education and women's rights to the public sphere.[68]

Mostly tied by class to Europe and Europeans, even as many were anti-imperialist, they adopted not just the "feminist" projects of education and public roles for women but also the ideals of uplifting the lower classes and the key components of a new domesticity—companionate marriage and scientific child rearing. They thus retained and elaborated many of the ideals Amin promoted. Their journals carried dire stories about the tragedies of forced marriage and polygyny, carried information on how to run a proper household, and provided advice about child rearing. In short, as part of their call for awakening women and transforming their lives and possibilities, they encouraged modern bourgeois "rational" modes of housewifery and child rearing, similar to the modes of domesticity being developed and marketed through magazines in Europe and the United States at the time.[69] Most telling, they promoted the ideal of the conjugal couple, arguing against arranged marriage, polygyny, men's rights to easy divorce, and women's lack of access to the same. Their motives were different from Amin's, since they did not put themselves in the place of the modern man looking for a companion or blame women for marital unhappiness. They were more concerned with abuses of women. But they idealized companionate marriage as much as he did.[70]

It was Nasser who in the 1950s and 1960s could be said to have nationalized many of these feminist projects, removing at least from the goals of women's education and employment the taint of foreign influence with his own impeccable nationalist credentials. It was during his presidency that what Hatem calls "state feminism" was introduced, and independent women's organizations were suppressed.[71] His policies of mass education and guaranteed employment for graduates, regardless of sex, were based on a conception of woman as worker and citizen whose participation was essential for national development.

As many of Nasser's policies are being dismantled in the wake of Sadat's rapprochement with the United States and *infitah* (the opening up of Egypt to Western investment) and the restructuring that international agencies are requiring of Egypt under current president Mubarak, women are finding themselves at the center of debate again. But because of the history of reforms for women in Egypt and the socioeconomic transformations of the last century, the terms have changed.

Urban women today, of a variety of classes, veiled and unveiled, are generally more radical than Qasim Amin was on issues of education, work, and participation in some aspects of the public sphere, such as politics. If they were informed enough about Egyptian history to know about the early-twentieth-century Egyptian feminists whose activities and views have been so crucial, they would probably denounce them.[72] Yet they are the inheritors of the political gains made for women by these women who took up where Amin left off, as they are the beneficiaries of Nasser's policies of mass education and employment.[73]

Their views on motherhood and their romance with companionate marriage can be traced further back. These are arguments that Marilyn Booth and Omnia Shakry (chapters 5 and 4) show very clearly to have been part of the nationalist rhetoric of an earlier part of the century. The positive expectations about the marital couple carry the telltale signs of the bourgeois dreams of reformers like Amin and the women writers who advocated companionate marriage. For the conservatives of the middle classes these views are just the shared widespread assumptions about marriage of their class, assumptions that, as Baron has indicated, developed in the early twentieth century.[74] Although she asserts that these developed indigenously and were not influenced by the West, she provides no evidence of this alternative genealogy. I would suggest instead that it is very hard to deny their sources in the West, where they had developed historically as part of deep social and economic shifts. One would also have to explore the local socioeconomic conditions that favored this shift in ideology. Furthermore, as Dipesh Chakrabarty does for the Bengali adaptation of European ideals of companionate marriage, one should examine the important ways that the European ideals were reshaped when translated into the emerging Egyptian context, not to mention how they are inflected by being framed within an Islamic discourse.[75]

For the upwardly mobile lower middle classes, from whom the Islamists draw much of their support, I suspect it is changes in the nature of the economy and social organization that combine with the middle-class images offered as models by television and magazines that underpin this vision. After all, even the progressives' serials, which clearly reinforce the Nasserist legacy of support for women's work and education, take for granted, if they do not glorify, the ideals of the "modern" couple and the companionate marriage. It could well be argued that the religious leaders' stress on the couple arises from a need to accommodate to and appropriate widely shared popular attitudes and demographic realities, not just of the upper and middle classes but increasingly of the lower classes as well.[76]

Just as the *hijab* and the modest dress being adopted around the Middle East are modern forms of dress, representing, despite the rhetoric, not any sort of "return" to cultural traditions but rather a complex reaction to a wide set of modern conditions (including, to be sure, a confrontation with Western consumerism), so the Islamist call for women to return to their roles as wives and mothers does not represent anything resembling what could be considered "traditional." These roles were fundamentally altered in the twentieth century. To "return" to the home after the world has become fundamentally divided between a domestic and public sphere, after wage labor for all has transformed social and economic relations, after kin-based forms of social and economic organization have been attenuated, and after being a wife and mother has come to be thought of by some as a career, is to go to a new place and take on a radically new role.

The enmeshment with the West of an earlier period of such notions about the organization of family and the roles of women, like the colonial roots of many of the socioeconomic transformations that went along with these, are conveniently forgotten by the Islamists. This occlusion enables them to gain the moral high ground by seeming to reject the West, in their fixation on the chimera of sexual or public freedom, while not fundamentally challenging widely held ideals—like conjugal love, the nuclear family, the companionate marriage, and women's education—and economic necessities, like women's work, of late-twentieth-century middle- and lower-middle-class life in Egypt.

Cultures cannot simply displace or undermine each other, as the quotations with which this chapter opened might suggest. The complex processes of borrowing, translating, and creating new mixtures—what some theorists prefer to call cultural hybrids—cannot be subsumed under this sort of dichotomous image.[77] Nor can the ways in which new ideas are given firm bases by social and economic transformations as well as ideological familiarization, especially now through powerful forms of mass media. What the case of feminism in Egypt shows, however, is that the elements of borrowed, imported, or imposed "culture" are susceptible to disaggregation for political purposes. Elements that apply to only a tiny minority can be singled out for self-serving vilification as foreign, while those widely accepted, especially by the large middle and lower middle classes, are less likely to find themselves carrying the tainted label, "Made in the West."

It seems to be a common dynamic of postcolonial cultural politics that cultural transplants are selectively and self-consciously made the object of political contest. As analysts, we need to stand outside these struggles, writing the history of feminism in Egypt with an awareness of its multifaceted nature, historical stages, and complex intertwinement with the West while regarding the claims of the Islamists to cultural authenticity or countermodernity with healthy suspicion.

NOTES

For support in 1989–90 and 1993 for the research in Egypt on which this paper is based, I am grateful to the American Research Center in Egypt, the Near and Middle East Committee of the Social Science Research Council, and New York University (Presidential Fellowship). I have accumulated many debts for help with research and conceptualizing the issues since I wrote it in 1994. In particular I want to thank Iman Farid Abdel Karim, Hala Abu-Khatwa, Janet Abu-Lughod, Soraya Altorki, Fathiyya Al-ʿAssal, Beth Baron, Elwi Captan, Mervat Hatem, Deniz Kandiyoti, Wafiyya Kheiry, Saba Mahmood, Hasna Mekdashi, Tim Mitchell, Afsaneh Najmabadi, and Omnia Shakry. It goes without saying that none of these people or institutions is responsible for the views presented here.

1. Leila Ahmed, *Women and Gender in Islam* (New Haven: Yale University Press, 1992), p. 167.

2. For an early discussion, see Kumari Jayawardena, *Feminism and Nationalism in the Third World* (London: Zed Books, 1986). Partha Chatterjee in *The Nation and Its Fragments* (Princeton: Princeton University Press, 1993), Amrita Chhaachhi in "Forced Identities: The State, Communalism, Fundamentalism and Women in India," in *Women, Islam and the State*, ed. Deniz Kandiyoti (Philadelphia: Temple University Press, 1991), pp. 144–75, Lata Mani in "Contentious Traditions: The Debate on Sati in Colonial India," in *Recasting Women: Essays in Indian Colonial History*, ed. Kumkum Sangari and Sudesh Vaid (New Brunswick, N.J.: Rutgers University Press, 1990), pp. 88–126, and others have explored with acuity the way "the woman question" has figured centrally in anticolonial and now communal politics in India; Aihwa Ong in "State versus Islam: Malay Families, Women's Bodies, and the Body Politic in Malaysia," *American Ethnologist* 17, no. 2 (1990): 558–82, has shown how in Malaysia today a public obsession with the sexual freedom of (Westernized) young women factory

workers is used to reinforce the trend toward Islamic veiling; and Deniz Kandiyoti in *Women, Islam and the State* has argued most forcefully about how crucial women, as symbols and pawns, have been to nationalist politics across the Muslim world. For a recent collection on the Muslim world, see Valentine Moghadam, ed., *Gender and National Identity: Women and Politics in Muslim Societies* (London: Zed Books, 1994).

3. Margot Badran has written that even Egyptian professional women often resist the label "feminist" because of this taint. Margot Badran, "Gender Activism: Feminists and Islamists in Egypt," in *Identity Politics and Women: Cultural Reassertions and Feminisms in International Perspective*, ed. Valentine M. Moghadam (Boulder, Colo.: Westview Press, 1993), pp. 202–27.

4. Literacy rates still make newspaper (and book) reading the habit of a minority, while radios are in every home, popularized by Nasser (the first president of postindependence Egypt) in the 1950s and 1960s as a political instrument. Most people have access to television. Among the most widely watched television programs are the evening dramatic serials, which provide the occasion for a good deal of national discussion and debate of major social issues.

5. Lila Abu-Lughod, "The Objects of Soap Opera: Egyptian Television and the Cultural Politics of Modernity," in *Worlds Apart: Modernity through the Prism of the Local*, ed. Daniel Miller (London and New York: Routledge, 1995), pp. 190–210.

6. For more on *ibn al-balad*, see Sawsan El-Messiri, *Ibn al-Balad: A Concept of Egyptian Identity* (Leiden: Brill, 1978). For a discussion of this figure in another of ʿUkasha's television serials, see Walter Armbrust, *Mass Culture and Modernism in Egypt* (Cambridge: Cambridge University Press, 1996), chap. 2.

7. This and all other quotations are from two interviews with the author on June 27 and 28, 1993.

8. ʿUkasha has also expressed his concern over the materialistic motives of those contracting marriages, in an interview with Sawsan Al-Duwayk, "Al-hubb fi al-musalsalat." *Al-Idhaʿa wa al-tilifizyun*, January 23, 1993, p. 15. This is a theme that echoes early-twentieth-century arguments against arranged marriage.

9. All quotations are from an interview with the author on June 22, 1993.

10. The book was coauthored by ʿImad Nasif and Amal Khodayr and entitled *Fannanat taʾibat wa nijmat al-ithara!* It listed no publisher, but its publication date was 1991 and it was in its eighth printing in January 1993.

11. The phenomenon of "the new veiling" is extremely complex. Among those who have written insightfully on it, showing clearly how the religious motivation for it, stated by many as the reason, needs to be balanced by an understanding of how veiling contributes to greater freedom of movement in public, easier work relations in mixed-sex settings, respectability in the eyes of neighbors and husbands, greater economy, and social conformity, are Ahmed, *Women and Gender in Islam*; Fadwa El Guindi, "Veiling Infitah with Muslim Ethic" *Social Problems* 28 (1981): 465–85; Mervat Hatem, "Economic and Political Liberalization in Egypt and the Demise of State Feminism," *International Journal of Middle East Studies* 24 (1992): 231–51; Valerie Hoffman-Ladd, "Polemics on the Modesty and Segregation of Women in Contemporary Egypt" *International Journal of Middle East Studies* 19 (1987): 23–50; Arlene MacLeod, *Accommodating Protest: Working Women, the New Veiling, and Change in Cairo* (New York: Columbia University Press, 1991); and Sherifa Zuhur, *Revealing Reveiling: Islamist Gender Ideology in Contemporary Egypt* (Albany: State University of New York Press,

1992). Elizabeth Fernea's documentary film *A Veiled Revolution* is especially good at revealing many meanings of the new modest dress.

12. See Lila Abu-Lughod, "The Romance of Resistance: Tracing Transformations of Power through Bedouin Women," *American Ethnologist* 17 (1990): 41–55 and "Movie Stars and Islamic Moralism in Egypt," *Social Text* 42 (1995): 53–67.

13. Abu-Lughod, "Movie Stars and Islamic Moralism in Egypt."

14. John Lancaster, "Cloudy Days for Cairo Star: Film Celebrity Sued by Islamic Right, Stalked by Alleged Ex-Lover," *Washington Post*, January 31, 1996, p. 12.

15. Nasif and Khodayr, *Fannanat ta'ibat*, pp. 49, 61.

16. Ibid., pp. 60–61.

17. Interview of Hasan Yusuf with Amal Surur and ʿUmar Tahir, *Nusf al-dunya*, May 4, 1997, p. 21.

18. Soha Abdel Kader, *Egyptian Women in a Changing Society, 1899–1987* (Boulder, Colo.: Lynne Reinner Publishing, 1987), pp. 137–38.

19. This article was warranted important enough to be translated and published in the English-language newspaper. Anis Mansour, "Victims," *Egyptian Gazette*, November 6, 1989, p. 3.

20. See Mervat Hatem, "Egyptian Discourses on Gender and Political Liberalization: Do Secularist and Islamist Views Really Differ?" *Middle East Journal* 48, no. 4 (1994): 661–76, for an important assessment of this convergence.

21. Barbara Stowasser, "Religious Ideology, Women and the Family: The Islamic Paradigm," in her *The Islamic Impulse* (Washington, D.C.: Center for Contemporary Arab Studies, Georgetown University, 1987), pp. 262–96.

22. See MacLeod, *Accommodating Protest*.

23. Zuhur, *Revealing Reveiling*.

24. Stowasser, "Religious Ideology, Women and the Family," p. 269.

25. Ahmed, *Women and Gender in Islam*, and Hatem, "Economic and Political Liberalization."

26. Ahmed, *Women and Gender in Islam*, pp. 226–27.

27. Badran, "Gender Activism," pp. 205, 211–14.

28. For more on this announcer, see Fedwa Malti-Douglas, "A Woman and Her Sûfîs" (Washington, D.C.: Center for Contemporary Arab Studies Occasional Papers, Georgetown University, 1995).

29. This conservative's views are critically described in two articles by Ibrahim ʿIssa, "Mashayikh Kariman Hamza," *Roz al-Yusuf*, March 15, 1993, p. 23, and "D. ʿUmar ʿAbd al-Kafi shaykh al-nisa' . . . wa al-fitna al-ta'ifiyya," *Roz al-Yusuf*, March 29, 1993, pp. 23–25.

30. One should, perhaps, distinguish more carefully among ideals of marriage, noting the differences between a bourgeois notion of the couple and what could more accurately be called companionate marriage, carrying implications of equality between marital partners. But for the purposes of this argument, I am simply trying to locate the ideal of the couple.

31. Mervat Hatem, "Secularist and Islamist Discourses on Modernity in Egypt and the Evolution of the Post Colonial Nation-State," in *Islam, Gender and Social Change*, ed. Yvonne Haddad and John Esposito (New York and Oxford: Oxford University Press, 1998), pp. 85–99. Zuhur in *Revealing Reveiling*, p. 93, also argues that "the image of the veiled woman idealizes love within marriage."

32. Stowasser, "Religious Ideology, Women and Family," p. 277.

33. Hatem, "The Secularist and the Islamist Discourses on Modernity," p. 93.

34. Maha ʿUmar, "Min ajl hayat zawjiyya mustaqirra wa hadi'a," *Al-Luwa' al-Islami*, August 8, 1996, p. 17. I am grateful to Mervat Hatem and Saba Mahmood for guiding me to this material.

35. "ʿIndama tarfud al-mar'a khidmat zawjiha wa al-qiyam bi'shu'un al-manzil," *Al-Luwa' al-Islami*, August 8, 1996, p. 16.

36. Yusuf al-Qaradawi, *Fatawa muʿasira li-lmar'a wa al-usra al-muslima* (Cairo: Dar al-Israʿ, n.d.), p. 65; ʿAliyya al-ʿAsqalani, "Li kul mushkila hal," *Al-Luwa' al-Islami*, December 21, 1995, p. 17.

37. ʿAliyya al-ʿAsqalani, "Al-Tasallut yudammir al-ʿalaqa al-zawjiyya: sultat al-rajul fi al-bayt la tuʿadd istibdadan," *Al-Luwa' al-Islami*, July 6, 1995, p. 16.

38. Al-Qaradawi, *Fatawa muʿasira*, pp. 33–34.

39. Muhammad Ibrahim Mabruk, *Mawqif al-Islam min al-hubb* (Cairo: Al-Nur al-Islami, 1996), p. 19.

40. Ibid., p. 21.

41. Ibid., p. 26.

42. Ibid., p. 25.

43. For more on this exclusion, see my "Finding a Place for Islam: Egyptian Television Serials and the National Interest," *Public Culture* 5, no. 3 (1993): 493–513. See my "Dramatic Reversals," in *Political Islam*, ed. Joel Beinin and Joe Stork (Berkeley and Los Angeles: University of California Press, 1996), for a discussion of how this policy of exclusion shifted such that there is now a media campaign against "extremists."

44. Note also the similarities to the feminist discourse in the Egyptian press in 1930, which Badran summarizes as scorning "marriages made with an eye toward material advance or elevation in status." Margot Badran, *Feminists, Islam, and Nation: Gender and the Making of Modern Egypt* (Princeton: Princeton University Press, 1995), pp. 139–40.

45. See Zuhur, *Revealing Reveiling*, pp. 93–95. Deniz Kandiyoti (personal communication) also notes that marital choice within the circle of activists versus an older generation's attempts to control and arrange marriages on other bases is a classic theme in the political subculture of the Turkish Islamist youth.

46. See for example, Abdel Kader, *Egyptian Women in a Changing Society*, p. 137.

47. Timothy Mitchell, *Colonising Egypt* (Cambridge: Cambridge University Press, 1988), pp. 111–13.

48. Ahmed, *Women and Gender in Islam*, p. 153. Mervat Hatem's "Toward a Critique of Modernization: Narrative in Middle East Women Studies," *Arab Studies Quarterly* 15, no. 2 (1993): 117–22, also reassesses the meaning of education for women, criticizing the narrative of modernization shared by most feminist scholars of the Middle East that assumes that the introduction of education and other "modern" institutions has been absolutely positive for women.

49. All quotations are from Samiha Sidhom Peterson's translation of Qasim Amin, *The Liberation of Women* (Cairo: American University in Cairo Press, 1992). This one is from p. 58.

50. Ibid., p. 73.

51. Ibid., p. 10.

52. Ibid., pp. 47–48 and p. 13.

53. See also Beth Baron, "Mothers, Morality, and Nationalism in Pre-1919 Egypt," in *The Origins of Arab Nationalism*, ed. Rashid Khalidi, Lisa Anderson, Muhammad Muslih, and Reeva Simon (New York: Columbia University Press, 1991), pp. 271–88.

54. Amin, *The Liberation of Women*, p. 20.

55. Qasim Amin, *The New Woman*, trans. Samiha Sidhom Peterson (Cairo: American University in Cairo Press, 1995), p. xi.

56. Amin, *The Liberation of Women*, p. 58.

57. Amin, *The New Woman*, p. 55.

58. Amin, *The Liberation of Women*, p. 17.

59. Annie Van Sommer and Samuel M. Zwemmer, *Our Moslem Sisters: A Cry of Need from Lands of Darkness* (New York: Fleming H. Revell Company, 1907), esp. pp. 7 and 28.

60. Amin, *The Liberation of Women*, p. 32.

61. Ibid., p. 55.

62. Ibid., p. 33.

63. Afsaneh Najmabadi, "Veiled Discourse—Unveiled Bodies," *Feminist Studies* 19, no. 3 (1993): 487–518.

64. Lila Abu-Lughod, "A Community of Secrets," *Signs* 10, no. 4 (1985): 637–57; *Veiled Sentiments* (Berkeley and Los Angeles: University of California Press, 1986); and *Writing Women's Worlds: Bedouin Stories* (Berkeley and Los Angeles: University of California Press, 1993).

65. For example, see Soraya Altorki, *Women in Saudi Arabia* (New York: Columbia University Press, 1986), and Cynthia Nelson, "Public and Private Politics," *American Ethnologist* 1, no. 3 (1974): 551–63.

66. For more on this young Bedouin woman's views, see Abu-Lughod, *Writing Women's Worlds*, chap. 5; for similar examples from Upper Egypt, see Lila Abu-Lughod, "The Interpretation of Culture(s) after Television," *Representations* 59 (1997): 109–34.

67. Homi Bhabha, *The Location of Culture* (London and New York: Routledge, 1994), p. 2.

68. Badran, *Feminists, Islam, and Nation*; Beth Baron, *The Women's Awakening in Egypt* (New Haven: Yale University Press, 1994); Cynthia Nelson, "Biography and Women's History: On Interpreting Doria Shafik," in *Women in Middle Eastern History*, ed. Nikki Keddie and Beth Baron (New Haven: Yale University Press), pp. 310–333, and *Doria Shafik, Egyptian Feminist: A Woman Apart* (Gainseville: University Press of Florida, 1996).

69. Marilyn Booth in "'May Her Likes Be Multiplied': 'Famous Women' Biography and Gendered Prescription in Egypt, 1892–1935," *Signs* 22, no. 4 (1997): 827–90, presents rich detail on the contents of these journals, and particularly the use of biographies of famous women to suggest models for young women of the future.

70. For more on women's campaigns and writing on marriage, see Badran, *Feminists, Islam and Nation*, esp. pp. 135–40, and Beth Baron, "The Making and Breaking of Marital Bonds in Modern Egypt" in Keddie and Baron, *Women in Middle Eastern History*, pp. 275–91, esp. pp. 277–78. Badran notes that the 1930s saw a shift in emphasis from concern with the maternal role to that of the wife.

71. Hatem, "Economic and Political Liberalization."

72. Mervat Hatem's "Egypt's Middle Class in Crisis: The Sexual Division of Labor," *Middle East Journal* 42, no. 3 (1988): 407–22, p. 419, reports that most of the veiled college women surveyed denounced Qasim Amin but so did many of the unveiled women.

73. As a result, like just about everyone else in Egypt, they unthinkingly presume that education is good, despite the facts that the benefits of such a poor quality of education as is available in the overtaxed state system, leading to poorly paid employment at best, are dubious, and that the continuing debt to the West for the development of secular education is easy to see for those who want to. For example, none of those asserting the new Islamic identities complain that in the competitive university faculties where the veiled women are concentrated the influence of the West is most direct; it is there, in the scientific fields of medicine, engineering, and pharmacy that English is even the language of instruction.

74. Baron, "The Making and Breaking of Marital Bonds in Modern Egypt," pp. 275–91.

75. See Deniz Kandiyoti, "Gendering the Modern," in *Rethinking Modernity and National Identity in Turkey*, ed. Sibel Bozdoğan and Reşat Kasaba (Seattle: University of Washington Press, 1997), pp. 113–32, for an argument that the shift to new forms of marriage in Turkey may have preceded Westernization and calls for reform. Dipesh Chakrabarty, "The Difference-Deferral of a Colonial Modernity: Public Debates on Domesticity in British Bengal," *Subaltern Studies* VIII, ed. David Arnold and David Hardiman (Delhi: Oxford University Press, 1994), pp. 50–88.

76. See Marcia Inhorn, *Infertility and Patriarchy* (Philadelphia: University of Pennsylvania Press, 1996), esp. pp. 148–50. It would be worth exploring demographically the class breakdown of historical shifts from extended to nuclear households. For instance, Judith Tucker, in *Women in Nineteenth Century Egypt* (Cambridge: Cambridge University Press, 1985), p. 100, has argued in her study of the Egyptian peasantry and urban lower classes that even in the nineteenth century "[i]t was the small nuclear family, the husband and wife unit, that formed the basis of much business and property holding, not the large extended family of received wisdom and inheritance law logic."

77. Bhabha, *The Location of Culture*, has pursued this idea furthest.

Some Awkward Questions on Women
and Modernity in Turkey

DENIZ KANDIYOTI

IN THE CLOSING sections of his epic novel, *War and Peace*, Tolstoy waxes lyrical about the transformation undergone by the romantic heroine, Natasha, following matrimony and motherhood. Shunning society and all her previous accomplishments, she devotes herself entirely to her husband and children. It is sufficient for her husband to mention his agreement with Rousseau's views on the unnatural and deleterious effects of wet nurses for Natasha to insist on breast-feeding her babies, despite her delicate constitution and against everyone's advice. Count Leo Tolstoy, an aristocrat himself, extols at length the virtues of child-centered bourgeois domesticity. This is not about Rousseau's ideas, nor is it the dernier cri on children's education in Europe. It is first and foremost a critique of the artificial ways of the women of the aristocracy who, in the French manner (in the author's own evaluation), cling to the arts of seduction instead of relaxing into matronly, contented maternity. Put in the context of Tolstoy's populism and his general unhappiness about the imperial ancien régime, this depiction of healthy, "natural" domesticity, in contrast to the artifice and cosmopolitanism of the elite, fits in well with his romantic vision for a reformed Russia. Was Tolstoy's a "modern" vision? He may well have thought so, although it hardly featured women's emancipation. He writes, "Natasha in her own home placed herself on the footing of a slave to her husband, and the whole household went on tiptoe when he was occupied."[1] He goes on to inform us that not even aware of the debates on the so-called woman question Natasha would, in any case, have had no interest in them; she was completely engrossed in her little world and found total fulfillment within it.

This may seem like an oddly inappropriate prologue to what are meant to be reflections on a compendium of sophisticated articles on the complex relationships interconnecting feminism, modernity, and postcoloniality in the Middle East. Yet it is one that could be profitably reflected upon from the point of view of the many contradictions it contains. Europe is invoked in this passage as a potential source of both corruption (through the Frenchified aristocracy) and enlightenment (in the reference to Rousseau). Natasha's passionate espousal of domesticity is a source of great power, binding her husband and children to her through multiple moral obligations, but one that can be sustained only through a position of unquestioned and unquestionable subordination. The male author's fantasy of the ideal marriage is based on a vision of natural complementarity rather than equality, where Natasha represents the quintessentially feminine. Finally, the family is glorified as the ultimate foundation of all human relationships (and, by implication, of a healthier society).

There are traces here of a sensibility we encounter again and again in the writings of turn-of-the-century modernist reformers in the Middle East, especially those concerned with domestic mores and the condition of women. Indeed, Lila Abu-Lughod's reading of Qasim Amin in this volume (chapter 7) suggests that he might well have endorsed some of Tolstoy's domestic ideals. There are similar resonances in Malak Hifni Nassif's condemnation of upper-class Egyptians' reliance on nursemaids for the care of their children, as in Muhammad Tahir's emphasis on the centrality of mothering in his treatise on the education of children in Iran.[2] The vast Ottoman prescriptive literature on domestic mores, household management, and child rearing covers very similar ground.[3]

What, if anything, singles out Middle Eastern reformers is the relentless search for local roots for their reformist ideals and the references they make to a "tradition" that better approximates their modernist vision than do the current arrangements in their societies. Salvaging modernity by asserting its indigenous pedigree takes multifarious forms. It finds one of its most elaborate expressions in Turkey in the writings of Ziya Gökalp, the leading theoretician of Turkish nationalism, who invoked aspects of assumed ancient Turkish lore, namely, democracy and feminism, as inherent qualities of some transhistorical national essence.[4] Any corruption of these mores could be attributed to foreign accretions, specifically, Arab and Persian influences. Omnia Shakry, in this volume (chapter 4), points to a similar emphasis in Egypt where feminist projects were often conceptualized as an illustration that "true Islam," uncorrupted by Turkish backwardness and European colonization, was entirely compatible with modernity. These tendencies point to an attempt by nationalists both to deny colonial charges of backwardness and to remedy them through modernist reforms, a discursive move insightfully noted by Partha Chatterjee.[5]

These recurring tropes are undoubtedly significant and revealing. They may, however, also act to conceal more submerged concerns that are never fully articulated in prescriptive, pedagogical, or polemical writings. Here, I would like to probe further into the debates on modernity, postcoloniality, and feminism represented in this volume, by focusing on some omissions and silences in the literature. These crystallize around three main questions: To what extent are discourses on modernity in the Middle East conditioned not only by colonial encounters with the West but by societies' changing and troubled relations to their varied ancien régimes? To what extent were contested images and attributions of tradition and modernity also mediated through the internally heterogenous nature of Middle Eastern societies (in terms of class, religion, and ethnicity), creating more proximate images of difference than those propagated by the more distant imperial centers of Europe? To what extent were discourses that were ostensibly about "reforming" women (of which many illuminating examples are offered in this volume) also about reshaping gender by establishing new models of masculinity and femininity to better institutionalize the monogamous, heterosexual, nuclear family?

Doing full justice to these questions would require further research and the use of more varied sources than the works of the various reformers, pedagogues, and nationalist thinkers that are most commonly drawn upon as textual resources. I would, however, like to ouline a tentative agenda using illustrations drawn primarily from Ottoman and Turkish sources.

POSTIMPERIAL MALAISE AND THE WOMAN QUESTION

There is a sense in which my earlier evocation of Tolstoy may not be quite so far-fetched as might appear at first sight. Two very different dynastic formations—the Ottoman and the Romanov—were evolving distinctive discourses about the causes of imperial decline and articulating different positions on the "backwardness" of their respective societies. This suggests that the specificities of the societies in question may have played as determining a role as the history of their encounters with the West. Indeed, it could be argued that, far from being random, the selection of Western sources by local reformers reflected processes of internal negotiation and struggle between factions of political elites with different visions of the "good society." More detailed reflection on these processes of selection often reveals complex sources of influence, contradiction, and tension that may not be passed over, as they sometimes are, as battles between so-called traditionalists and modernists.

In the case of the Ottoman Empire, it is prominent Young Ottomans who are routinely invoked as the earliest advocates of women's emancipation, preparing the ground for later reforms. Şinasi's satirical play *Şair Evlenmesi* (The poet's wedding) written in 1859 is considered one of the pioneering critiques of the Ottoman arranged marriage system. Namik Kemal is also considered an ardent proponent of women's rights. He used the newspaper he edited, *İbret*, to call for reforms in women's education and denounce the state of ignorance of Ottoman women. His novels *İntibah* (The awakening) and *Zavallı Çocuk* (Poor child) offer critical commentaries on the unjust and oppressive aspects of marriage and family life. Yet it is important to remember that these writers were also the most outspoken critics of the Western-led reforms of the *Tanzimat* period.

The *Tanzimat* reforms initiated in 1839 deepened incipient trends of centralization and secularization of the Ottoman state apparatus. The independent position of the *ulema* (the clergy) was undermined by both the introduction of state control of the *vakif*, the religious endowments that constituted their major source of income, and the inception of secular education in parallel to the *medrese* system. Power was increasingly concentrated in the hands of a new class of Ottoman imperial bureaucrats, relatively secure within a secularized bureaucratic hierarchy. In the process of its modernization, the apparatus of the Ottoman state appeared to be more monolithic and authoritarian, as well as more enmeshed in ties of economic dependence to the West, than ever before. The Imperial Rescript of Gülhane, the official document that ushered in the *Tanzimat*, by guaranteeing the life, honor, and property of all Ottoman subjects regardless of their creed and religion was, in effect, extending legal assurances to non-Muslim and non-Turkish mercantile groups affiliated to European commercial interests. The *Tanzimat* bureaucracy was meeting the expectations of Western powers in a manner that alienated the groups and classes that were marginalized by the new "modernized" structures (such as the urban lower-middle classes, petty civil servants, artisans and craftsmen, and the lower ranks of the *ulema*), creating deep cleavages in Ottoman society.

The Young Ottomans who reacted against the authoritarianism and humiliating abdications of *Tanzimat* policies were, as Şerif Mardin demonstrates in his classic study, inspired by mutually contradictory sources of influence that did not coalesce into an internally coherent ideology. They were influenced by European ideas of nationalism and liberalism, which they attempted to incorporate into an Islamic theory of state and legitimacy. They also adopted a contradictory stand vis-à-vis the idea of progress, "on one hand praising abstract 'progress' and the material advances of Europe and on the other hand looking back wistfully on the harmoniousness of an imaginary, ideal Islamic state."[6] Indeed, Mardin characterizes their political philosophy as pre-Enlightenment, since they perceived no discrepancy between the theory that the king's power comes from God and the theory that it arises by a contract with the people, and describes their position as conservative. Yet it is the Young Ottomans who are cited as the earliest feminists. For them, the amelioration of women's status was a tenet of Ottoman patriotism that required the mobilization of society in attempt to salvage the state.

It is more difficult to level against the Young Ottomans the charge made by Leila Ahmed against the Egyptian reformer, Qasim Amin, of being "the son of Cromer and colonialism."[7] The former risked imprisonment and exile in their protests against an Ottoman autocracy that they also perceived as a tool of Western imperial domination. They invoked European notions of liberty only to shore up the flagging Ottoman polity, which was hardly an instantiation of Western liberal principles. They were also part of a new urban class of literati who used the print media to create a climate of public opinion in favor of constitutionalism. This would culminate in the overthrow of Abdülhamit's absolutist rule by the Young Turks in 1908. It should suffice to note their selective—and inconsistent—appropriation of European and Islamic concepts in the service of a political project that would eventually lead to a republicanism that they could neither have anticipated nor, indeed, have approved. The same process of selectivity in borrowing ideas from the West, suggested by these references to the Young Ottomans, continued during the era of the Young Turks.

It is worth noting here that the West was not some monolithic entity but one from which different and contradictory discourses emanated: from the modernist, individualistic pronouncements of Anglo-Saxon liberalisms to the antimodernist, organicist approaches of German romanticism to the corporatism of French sociologists. It should not surprise us, therefore, that elective affinities were formed not only on the basis of the exposure of certain elites to different intellectual milieus in Paris, London, or Berlin but also in response to local dilemmas that became the subject of political contestations.

In his seminal work on the Second Constitutional Period (1908–18), Zafer Toprak draws our attention to the fact that Turkish nationalism, which arose from the liberal currents of 1908, also represented a reaction against liberalism, especially the economic liberalism that cost the Muslim artisan so dear.[8] The dominant ideology of the Committee for Union and Progress (CUP) contained a blend of solidarism inspired by French corporatist thought and Ottoman guild traditions.[9] The current of *Milli Iktisat* (national economics) also made references to the German model and derived its inspiration from the work of Friedrich List. Ziya Gökalp suggested that a modern nation could not be founded on communally based ethnic divisions of labor that allocated Ottoman Turks mainly to positions in the state bureaucracy and the army, thereby marginalizing them from the economy; this could only lead, he thought, to forms of mutual parasitism. The major thrust of the CUP effort was therefore the creation of an indigenous middle class of Turkish-Muslim entrepreneurs. The expansion of women's employment and of their opportunities for higher education was clearly part of this process of national consolidation and was a product of the need for new cadres rather than the result of some modern vision of women's equal participation. One must also emphasize the effects of the dislocations and human losses occasioned by the Balkan Wars and World War I, which pushed Ottoman women into occupations and services that were formerly considered the exclusive domain of men. This set the scene for CUP policies exhorting women to contribute to the war effort both as workers and as prolific mothers.[10]

This does not, however, mean that Ottoman feminists did not have their own agenda. As is clearly demonstrated by Serpil Çakır's detailed reading of the women's journal *Kadınlar Dünyası* (Women's world), published between 1913 and 1921, not only did women demand access to employment but some of the bolder writers asserted that they should settle for no less than equal pay for equal work.[11] In the pages of the journal, women used allusions to the West both as a rhetorical ploy to highlight the restrictions in their own lives and to suggest that "catching up with the West" could be achieved only through their own empowerment: "Oh. . . . Who will save our poor nation from the yoke of European economic domination? Our men? No, we do not expect any further effort from them. Maybe if womanhood were to be elevated and a new future generation formed, that might be different. . . . But at the moment our only hope is in womanhood. Let us not just scream and shout but engage in a productive, active movement to habituate ourselves to work and workmanship."[12] Although many themes—such as patriotism and the formative influence of mothers—that Beth Baron and Marilyn Booth find in the turn-of-the-century women's press in Egypt[13] were echoed in the pages of *Kadınlar Dünyası*, there were also writers who took a more confrontational stance vis-à-vis men (by engaging in direct polemics with them) and espoused openly feminist points of view. Ottoman women's opinions could be just as varied as those expressed by their contemporaries in Europe, ranging from maternalist, separate-spheres feminisms to more individualistic and libertarian positions.

Ottoman feminists' selective appropriation of Western sources has, as yet, not been the subject of systematic investigation. Marilyn Booth, in this volume (chapter 5), provides us with an insightful illustration of the complexities of such appropriation in her discussion of the ways in which Jeanne d'Arc could be transformed into an Egytian heroine. The "Famous Women" biographies that Booth draws upon also have the potential for invoking a "supra-ethnic, supra-geographical, supra-class community of women based on shared experience."[14] Nonetheless, we may also concur with Mervat Hatem that, more often than not, the images which Middle Eastern and European women formed of themselves and each other were forged in an encounter that encouraged the projection onto each other of what they found most threatening for themselves.[15] These perceptions of both commonality and difference were undoubtedly complicated by the presence of local religious and ethnic minorities with differing relationships to European powers, some enjoying the protection and patronage of colonial administrations. The influence of the West was, therefore, mediated through multiple and varying levels of "othering" that must have had an impact on women's positionality, daily lives, and apprehensions of the "modern." These mediations and the complex social landscapes they reveal rarely find their way into textual sources with pedagogical or didactic leanings but are no less important for it.

COLONIAL MEDIATIONS AND SOCIAL HETEROGENEITY

In contrast to the literature on South Asia which acknowledges that the colonial encounter took place against a background of Hindu/Muslim differences,
shaping and redefining those,[16] there is little critical reflection on how the
everyday landscape of modernity in the Middle East (including tastes, styles,
mores, and consumption patterns) was shaped through relations among different classes and communal groups (Muslims, Levantines, Armenians, Jews,
and Copts, to name but a few). Although scholars working on local women's
presses are quite aware of the heterogenous composition of early feminist
movements,[17] this does not necessarily lead to a process of sustained reflection
on the effects such heterogeneity might have had.

In a useful acknowledgment of this complexity, Hatem surveys the writings
of turn-of-the-century Egyptian women, European women who had married
Egyptian men, and Levantine women of Syrian and Palestinian origin. She
draws our attention to the fact that the British singled out the Levantines in
Egypt, some of whom had received Christian missionary schooling, as potential allies by virtue of their being Christian (when in fact this group also included Muslims). She goes on to demonstrate that Levantine women writers in
Egypt were no less pro-Arab and nationalist but felt freer to adopt modernist
positions and advocate syntheses of East and West than did their Egyptian
sisters who had longer direct experiences of British colonialism.[18] They articulated a positionality that was not only different but subject to manipulation and
reinterpretation by the colonial power.

Colonial mediation and the refashioning of local differences had material
consequences that actively informed nationalist and feminist struggles. In the
Ottoman Empire, which by the nineteenth century had an economy that was
thoroughly penetrated and controlled by European powers, this led to a different positioning of various sections of Ottoman society vis-à-vis foreign mercantile interests. Let us take the example of a minor episode that is considered
to be a typical instance of women's militancy in late Ottoman Turkey. This
episode was triggered by the refusal of the telephone company (which was run
by a French firm) to recruit Turkish Muslim women on the grounds of their
lack of knowledge of foreign languages. There was an outcry that pressured
the company to hire seven Muslim women. This modest gesture was followed
by a campaign of protest in the pages of *Kadınlar Dünyası* accusing the company of being biased against Muslim women:

> Although by now over two hundred Muslim women have applied and asked for
> jobs, despite government guidelines, they were not accepted on the grounds that
> they lacked knowledge of Greek and French. In short, Muslim womanhood found
> no favor with the telephone company. . . . It is well known that the girls from

Muslim families who do receive French education are from upper-class family backgrounds. They would be reticent to apply for such jobs and to be employed. Those who are from social strata that depend on work and on being employees have had no education except in Turkish, which is the official local language.[19]

I find this episode, and the above quotation, significant from the point of view of the multiple identities that are being articulated within it. The writers of this open letter position themselves as Muslim women yet distinguish themselves from women of the upper class with whom they may not share interests. They are the women of an emerging urban petite bourgeoisie and middle class who benefited from access to formal education different from both the private tuition of the elite and the foreign missionary–based education of the better-off sections of minority communities. There is also a suggestion here that women of the minority groups even of a similar class background (specifically Greeks, but also possibly others) may have been the object of favoritism on account of their foreign-language skills. They may conceivably have emerged in an adversarial position on the urban job market.[20]

Going beyond the quotation itself, one may well wonder where the locus of encroaching Westernization might have been in late Ottoman society. Among the upper-class women following the latest Paris fashions and reading the novels their French governesses made available to them? Among the religious minorities with freer access to missionary schooling and presumed affinities with the West in terms of cultural tastes? Or among the writers of the above letter who invoke their Turkish/Muslimness to demand their rightful place in the public world of work and openly proclaim their feminism? There is, of course, little doubt that they all represent facets of an Ottoman modernization that was powerfully shaped by colonial mediations and nationalist aspirations.

In order to find more nuanced descriptions of the malaise of late Ottoman modernization with its subtexts of class and community, one must often turn to the novel. I have argued elsewhere that images of women in the Turkish novel provided a running commentary on changing perceptions of Westernization.[21] Depictions of the *alafranga* (Westernized) woman, which start out as portrayals of upper-class idleness and frivolity in the post-*Tanzimat* novel, culminate in accusations of treachery and collaborationism by the time of the occupation of Anatolia by foreign powers and the War of National Liberation. It is important to note, however, that this running commentary also took as its object the changing material culture of the Ottoman Empire, expressed through consumption patterns, fads and fashions, styles of dress, and public comportment. These became complex markers of class and community where the "modern" got translated into new and more diverse lines of cleavage within Ottoman society. These cleavages were also intergenerational, as is sensitively illustrated in Alan Duben and Cem Behar's analysis of the Europeanization of domestic mores in Istanbul households.[22] The changes they describe range from interpersonal relations to more mundane activities such as eating habits: the Muslim Ottoman middle classes gradually abandoned the *sini* (floor table) and the use of their fingers in favor of knives, forks, and eating at a Western-style table. They utilize the term "civilizational shift" to capture the cultural mood of late Ottoman society.

These complex transformations in the social landscape rarely find full expression in the pedagogical and polemical writings of reformers. This is precisely because so much nationalist thought is based on the elision of the present in favor of a glorified mythical past or a utopian future. Yet it is the complexities of the modern that continue to haunt contemporary political movements and are persistently recycled in a variety of populist discourses, including those that now favor an Islamist idiom. It is, therefore, within the cultural field of modernity that we must attempt to locate the search for new family forms and contested notions of masculinity and femininity in Turkey.

REMAKING WOMEN OR REFASHIONING GENDER?

In her critique of Qasim Amin in this volume, Lila Abu-Lughod argues that it was not so much women's emancipation but the promotion of the modern bourgeois family with its ideal of conjugal love and scientific child rearing that lay at the heart of his reforming project. She goes on to suggest that this redefined domesticity had as one of its implicit objects the undermining of women's homosocial networks that may have encouraged cross-class mixing and the subversion of men's authority. Although this may well have constituted one of the strands of Qasim's polemic, the extensive literature on the so-called family crisis in Ottoman Turkey suggests that a great deal more may have been at stake here. There are, indeed, so many facets to the debates on the Ottoman family that one must be prepared, as in peeling an onion, to discover many hidden layers beneath the thin outer skin.

At one level, the Ottoman family was used in debates as a sometimes thinly disguised and, at other times, explicit metaphor for the Ottoman state. The early reformers who bemoaned the plight of women felt disenfranchised themselves by Ottoman autocracy and invited parallels between the democratization of the state (the demise of the Absolute Patriarch, realized by the Young Turk Revolution) and the democratization of the family. The Ottoman patriarch became the object of both nostalgia and rebellion; he was both the guarantor of a secure moral order and the perpetrator of stifling conventions. The cultural turmoil and confusion created by the post-*Tanzimat* period manifested itself in contradictory longings and expressions of moral panic. Jale Parla's insightful analysis of the *Tanzimat* novel captures this ambivalence well by drawing our attention to the fact that the fatherless home featured in numerous

plots where the novelist assumed the paternal role of guidance to his dis-
oriented society.[23] Thus behind many reformers' condemnation of arranged,
loveless matches also lay their unresolved ambivalence about the paternal
authority that curtailed their freedom of choice in both their familial and their
public lives.[24]

At a more overt level, the promotion of the monogamous, nuclear, companionate family became an article of official policy that was provided with elaborate ideological underpinnings and bolstered by early attempts at family reform in 1917. As Zafer Toprak points out, the Young Turks wanted to follow
up their political revolution with a social revolution (*içtimai inkilab*) or what
they termed the "New Life" (*Yeni Hayat*).[25] The tenets of the 1908 revolution
mandated that the "New Family" (*Yeni Aile*) or the "National Family" (*Milli
Aile*) replace the older patriarchal form. Ziya Gökalp, who drew his inspiration
from Durkheimian sociology, envisioned a form of social solidarity that was
based on the "collective conscience" and required a common set of norms and
moralities. The family as the smallest "cell" of a consensual society should
henceforth be based on the precepts of "Moral Turkism" (*Ahklaki Türkçülük*).
Moral Turkism when applied to the family would represent a return to ancient
Turkish culture where monogamy, equality in the marriage union, and democracy in the family were assumed to be the rule. Although Gökalp considered
that the advent of Islam constituted a progressive development for the lives of
the women of Arabia, it is to pre-Islamic Turkic sources, to Central Asian
legends and sagas, that he turned for inspiration. He was clearly at pains to
demonstrate that the companionate nuclear family was not only the most suitable form for a modern nation but one that had its origins in the depths of
ancient Turkish culture.[26]

But what was the actual substance behind the critiques leveled against the
Ottoman family? Duben and Behar, basing their analysis on demographic data,
including household compositions, interject, "Gökalp could not have known
that his '*konak* type' multiple family household was itself a rather illusory
thing in Ottoman Istanbul."[27] They point to a similar discrepancy between the
assumed customary arrangements that were the target of modernists' reforming zeal and the actual patterns of family formation in late Ottoman Istanbul.
According to the writers of the time, polygyny and arranged marriages between teenage girls and much older men were commonplace. In fact, they turn
out to have been extremely rare occurrences. Duben and Behar express their
own puzzlement in the following terms:

> The advice and recommendations which appeared in the popular press and in
> books and magazines during the late nineteenth and early twentieth centuries
> corresponded almost exactly to the demographic realities of the time. Most of
> those who wrote on this topic, however, were somehow convinced that the prac-
> tice—and the unspoken rule—in Istanbul was teenage marriage. Many of the

articles and books we have quoted were written in criticism of teenage marriages and there is little doubt that, though most of them are anonymous, they were penned by the "modernists" of the time.[28]

I argued elsewhere that the source of this discrepancy must be sought not in the realm of misconception but in the urge to articulate a new morality and a new discourse on the regulation of sexuality.[29] Indeed, although Duben and Behar provide numerous illustrations, they do not stress the extent to which polemics on the family were systematically couched in a quasi-scientific language on "appropriate" reproductive heterosexuality. For instance, they quote a leading daily, *Vakit*, which in 1920 featured the following: "The purpose of marriage is the perennity of the human race. People should marry therefore at the age most suitable for raising healthy children. The proper age for marrying is twenty-five for men and twenty for women. . . . Late marriages are just as harmful as ones too early. Besides, the ages of the spouses must be well-balanced. The husband should be from three to ten years older than the wife."[30] In this and many other texts sexuality is firmly linked to procreativity, and expert medical opinion is repeatedly invoked to determine the scientific basis of best practice.[31] In this context, the imagined world of "custom" emerges as a dangerous place seething with reprehensible and "unhealthy" practices. Focusing on the emulation of Western patterns of domesticity as an inspiration for family reform tends to hide from view more subterranean preoccupations with the varieties that local custom could take. We have to entertain the possibility that defining responsible social adulthood in terms of monogamous heterosexuality may not only have been a matter of proscribing co-wives, concubines, and child brides but may also have been about taming other, unruly forms of male sexuality.

Indeed, although a great deal has been said about the homosocial worlds of women in the Middle East, we know surprisingly little about the worlds of men. Nevertheless, despite our relative ignorance, we get occasional glimpses of a more fluid world where rank, ethnicity, and sexualities could map out a complex social landscape, one in which palace boys who had liaisons with powerful patrons could themselves become respected patriarchs surrounded by their wives and children. Redefining domesticity in the fashion advocated by modernist reformers could target these more complex gender regimes in favor of the monogamous, heterosexual couple as the normative ideal. That this ideal appears to have been largely realized among the urban middle classes in turn-of-the-century Ottoman society did not deprive the polemic on the family of its momentum; the reformers could formulate their vision of modernity only with reference to an assumed prior state, even if it was one that existed mainly in their own constructions of custom.

We have yet to chronicle, as Foucault did for the Christian West, the point at which "[s]ex was driven out of hiding and forced to lead a discursive existence"[32] in Middle Eastern societies, if indeed it was ever in hiding in the same sense as that understood by Foucault. There is little doubt, however, that in Ottoman society overt preoccupations with marital sexuality did coincide with the emergence of new governmental technologies that redefined subjects as a "population" with its own phenomena of health, morbidity, life expectancy, and fertility. Not only the survival but the viability of the nation depended upon the judicious regulation of population, a task given added urgency by the loss of both life and territory in the closing decades of the Ottoman Empire. However, at the center of the problem of population lay sex: it was necessary to monitor ages at marriage, levels of fertility, and maternal and child health. Moreover, it was not merely the material aspects of procreation that came under scrutiny but the psychological and emotional tone of family life itself, which mandated new orientations and disciplines for both women and men. I would, therefore, suggest that what was at stake was not just the remaking of women but the wholesale refashioning of gender and gender relations.

The refashioning of gender necessarily involved the articulation of new im ages of masculinity and femininity. These images were, in fact, dual since they contained both ideals to aspire to and identities to be condemned and cast aside. To achieve definition and focus, the image of modernity was dependent upon its repudiated double. Moreover, the process of articulation of new images and norms was complex and diffuse since it manifested itself in a multiplicity of institutional arenas, from the classroom to the fashion magazine, from legislation such as the republican dress code to daily encounters on city streets.

In Turkey, while the question of changing femininities and the effects of republican Kemalist reforms on images of womanhood has become a subject of inquiry,[33] the masculine ideals of Turkish nationalism have rarely received explicit attention. In the prescriptive literature I referred to earlier, it was invariably men's paternal roles that came under scrutiny. The Ottoman father figure was depicted by reformers and novelists alike as a remote, authoritarian, and foreboding figure who displayed little overt emotional closeness to his spouse or children and expected total respect and obedience. Naguib Mahfouz's portrayal of the turn-of-the-century Cairene patriarch in his famous novel *Palace Walk* is noteworthy in this respect for its illustration of the split between the home, a place of parental authority and obligation, and the homosocial world of men where the needs for intellectual companionship, recreation, and expression of sexual desire (through liaisons with women entertainers) are fulfilled.

The "new man" of the republican period was, in contrast, expected to be an attentive spouse and engaged parent who was emotionally close to and directly involved with his children. The letters that Ziya Gökalp, a precursor in this respect as in many others, wrote to his family from his exile in Malta exemplify this new affective tone through a myriad of intimate details: exhortations to his wife not to neglect visiting the dentist, concern about children's schoolwork, simple poems and tender missives addressed to his daughters.[34] While this did not mean that remote and authoritarian fathers had ceased to exist, they were, according to Duben and Behar, "looked upon with disfavour."[35] A new domestic intimacy involving both companionship between spouses and a child-centeredness based on a new conception of children's physical and emotional needs mandated changes in the comportment of both men and women.

I suggested elsewhere[36] that a subtle shift was taking place in the locus of "tradition." The unreconstructed masculinities of Ottoman patriarchy were attributed no longer to urban elites, who defined themselves as "modern," but increasingly to village life through portrayals of the downtrodden rural woman. Just like the wearing of neckties, the manner in which men interacted with women could mark them out as belonging to specific social categories. Codes of class and gender cut across and fed into each other, adding new dimensions of meaning to both.

Images of the "modern" woman carried their own ambiguities and tensions. In literary and polemic writings, predominantly penned by men, the world of tradition was a place where women were portrayed both as victims and as culpable of social inertia through their idleness and ignorance. Theirs was taken to be a self-enclosed world of petty intrigue and superstition. Male longing for the "modern" woman expressed itself insistently through clamorous demands for "love," demands thwarted by tight social controls over access to the opposite sex and over the choice of marriage partners. The writer Ömer Seyfettin expresses his rage and despair, which he directs at women, in the following terms: "Do you know who, in our surroundings, above and beyond religion, traditions, customs, the *ulema*, the elderly, the reactionary, and the gendarmes of the government, want this ban on love? Women. Turkish women. They are the most fearsome enemies of love and beauty."[37] We may well ponder the injustice of these charges in a society where women's sexual purity was, and still is, related to family honor and where familial control over matches may afford women a degree of protection from arbitrary treatment by husbands. Besides, the men who desired freer access to companions of their choice never intended that women should be anything other than monogamous and chaste. If, as I speculated earlier, there was a muted preoccupation with male sexualities, concerns over women's sexual freedom were expressed overtly and, at times, vehemently. A persistent anxiety over sexual morality lodged itself at the heart of images of the "modern" woman. With segregation and the veil removed, women incurred the constant risk of overstepping dangerous boundaries, which now required diffuse but persistent monitoring. Modern femininities in Turkey continue to be haunted by this unresolved tension.

Modern women were thrust upon a public world of men whose habits of heterosocial interaction were restricted and shallow. This created unprecedented problems of identity management for women who had to devise new sets of signals and codes in order to function in the public realm without compromising their respectability. I argued elsewhere that the fact that women were no longer secluded or veiled might have mandated new forms of puritanism that could be activated as a symbolic shield in a society where femininity was, by and large, incompatible with a public presence.[38] Najmabadi has gone much further by suggesting that unveiled women in Iran may have imposed new forms of silence on themselves and lost the expressive language of their homosocial world. She writes: "In other words, when the female voice found a public audience, it became a veiled voice, a disciplined voice. Erasing or replacing its sexual markers, it sanitized itself."[39]

This replacement of the physical veil by its metaphoric counterpart, chastity, was, at best, an unstable solution and one that failed to effectively dissociate modernity from potential sexual transgression. The modern woman's presumably disciplined and de-eroticized body could constantly reinvent and refashion itself by selecting from the many images offered by global consumerism and invite renewed charges of both immorality and "inauthenticity." Expressions of femininity, just like masculinities, became multivalent signifiers of class, cultural tastes, and styles but did so under an ambivalent male gaze that continued to sexualize the female body and presence. Given the nature of this dilemma, it is hardly surprising that the search for new and more enabling expressions of femininity should take contradictory and sometimes conflictual forms. There is a sense in which the new veiling of the 1980s and 1990s may be bringing this inherent contradiction to its logical conclusion, although the political uses to which such veiling might be put cannot necessarily be read off from the cultural dilemmas that may partly give rise to it.

CONCLUSION

The field of women's studies in the Middle East has, for a long time, remained locked into either relatively uncritical endorsements of modernization or defensive apologias of what was presumed to represent "tradition."[40] The binary categories of traditional/modern and East/West cast a long shadow, not least because they continue to inform the language of political rhetoric and common sense. The studies in this volume achieve, each in its own way, a radical break from and definitive unsettling of this framework. They do so by illustrating the complexities, contradictions, and ambiguities of modernity and, ultimately, the futility (and political unwisdom) of attempting to cast postcolonial phenomena in terms of (Western) foreignness or (indigenous) authenticity, categories that themselves emerge as dubious artifacts of the colonial gaze. They chart a terrain that expands our horizons, stretches our imagination, and, therefore, invites further intellectual adventurousness.

This invitation emboldened me to push the boundaries yet further by drawing attention to three relatively neglected sets of issues. The first revolve around the dangers of reification of the West, of insufficient attention to the specificities of colonial encounters and to local processes of selectivity that become the object of internal negotiation and struggle. Although many studies in this volume make specific references to the ambiguities and contradictions of the usages of the West, their insights could be usefully extended to include contextualized analyses of how these usages are deployed in contemporary political contests.

A corollary of the reification of the West is the homogenization of societies in the Middle East. I suggested that it is precisely because the encounter with the West built upon and refashioned internal lines of cleavage (such as class, religion, and ethnicity) that modernity emerged as a highly conflictual category, laden with emotional as well as political meaning, despite nationalist secularisms' attempts at containing and occluding such divisions. Colonial mediations of this social heterogeneity have left bitter legacies that are still being worked through in modern political movements. Capturing the complexity of the social landscapes of modernity will, therefore, require a great deal more probing into social history, and awareness of this complexity invites us to be mindful of the limitations of prescriptive textual sources as guides to lived reality.

Finally, I argued that "remaking women" tells us one part of a more complicated story about the refashioning of gender in the Middle East. Underlying reformers' and polemicists' writings on the modern family, monogamy, and educated mothers and housewives—painstakingly captured and deconstructed in this volume—is a new regulatory discourse on sexuality that attempts to institutionalize monogamous heterosexuality as the normative ideal. That some aspects of this ideal, such as the preference for consensual rather than arranged marriages, have been widely and thoroughly internalized is illustrated in Abu-Lughod's treatment of modern Egypt, attesting to the inroads made by modernist reformers. However, refashioning gender also implies the creation of new images of masculinity and femininity that involve the repudiation of the old as well as the espousal of the new. These images and styles are selectively appropriated by different sections of society, making gender a contested and polyvalent marker of class, social extraction, and cultural preference. The unresolved tensions around establishing workable codes of heterosocial modernity are fueling a search for alternatives that may take contradictory and conflictual forms. The politicization of gender in the Middle East speaks to, attempts to heal, and, at the same time, exacerbates the confusions and uncertainties of modernity. This makes the study of gender more crucial than ever to our understanding of society and opens up vast and exhilarating vistas on questions yet to be answered and issues yet to be explored.

NOTES

1. Leo N. Tolstoy, *War and Peace* (London: Penguin Books, 1982), p. 1373.

2. See Shakry and Najmabadi, chaps. 4 and 3 in this volume.

3. For an excellent and comprehensive account, see Alan Duben and Cem Behar, *Istanbul Households: Marriage, Family and Fertility, 1880–1940* (Cambridge: Cambridge University Press, 1991); and an original contribution on the early republican period, Yael Navaro, "'Using the Mind' at Home: Dialogues on Taylorism and Housework in Early Republican Turkey" (unpublished MS, 1992).

4. Ziya Gökalp, *Türkcülüğün Esasları* (İstanbul: İnkilap ve Aka Kitabevleri, 1978). For commentaries on Gökalp, see Taha Parla, *The Social and Political Thought of Ziya Gökalp 1876–1924* (Leiden: E. J. Brill, 1985), and on women, Deniz Kandiyoti, "End of Empire: Islam, Nationalism and Women in Turkey," in *Women, Islam and the State*, ed. Deniz Kandiyoti (London: Macmillan, 1991), pp. 22–47.

5. Partha Chatterjee, *Nationalist Thought and the Colonial World: A Derivative Discourse?* (London: Zed Books, 1986).

6. Şerif Mardin, *The Genesis of Young Ottoman Thought* (Princeton: Princeton University Press, 1962), p. 402.

7. Leila Ahmed, *Women and Gender in Islam* (New Haven: Yale University Press, 1992), p. 153.

8. Zafer Toprak, *Türkiyede Milli İktisat (1908–1918)* (Ankara: Yurt Yayınları, 1982).

9. Zafer Toprak,"Türkiyede Korporatizmin Doğuşu," *Toplum ve Bilim* 12 (1980): 41–49.

10. The Unionists adopted pro-natalist policies to palliate severe population losses. The Ottoman Islamic Association for the Employment of Women provided inducements for earlier marriage (by 21 for women and 25 for men) by providing trousseaux for brides, financial assistance, and salary increments both at marriage and for each new birth. The association also facilitated introductions to prospective partners and introduced penalties for noncompliance with these guidelines. See Zafer Toprak, "Osmanlı Kadınları Çalıştırma Cemiyeti, Kadın Askerler ve Milli Aile," *Tarih ve Toplum* 51 (1988): 162–66.

11. Serpil Çakır, *Osmanlı Kadın Hareketi* (Istanbul: Metis Yayinlari, 1994).

12. Ibid., p. 266, my translation.

13. Beth Baron, *The Women's Awakening in Egypt* (New Haven: Yale University Press, 1994); Marilyn Booth, "'May Her Likes Be Multiplied': 'Famous Women' Biography and Gendered Prescription in Egypt, 1892–1935," *Signs* 22, no. 4 (1997): 827–90.

14. Booth, "'May Her Likes Be Multiplied,'" p. 7.

15. Mervat Hatem, "Through Each Other's Eyes: Egyptian, Levantine-Egyptian, and European Women's Images of Themselves and Each Other (1862–1920)," *Women's Studies International Forum* 12 (1989): 183–98.

16. See, for instance, Ayesha Jalal, "The Convenience of Subservience: Women and the State of Pakistan," in Kandiyoti, *Women, Islam and the State*, pp. 77–114.

17. Thomas Phillip, "Feminism and Nationalism in Egypt," in *Women in the Muslim World*, ed. Lois Beck and Nikki Keddie (Cambridge: Harvard University Press, 1987),

pp. 285–308. Baron, *The Women's Awakening in Egypt.* Also see Booth, "'May Her Likes Be Multiplied.'"

18. Hatem, "Through Each Other's Eyes," pp. 188–92.

19. Serpil Çakir, *Osmanlı Kadıin Hareketi*, p. 292, my translation. As a postcript, let us note that a law was finally passed in 1916 making Turkish the official language of correspondence, which meant that foreign firms had to either fold up or recruit local Turkish-speaking employees.

20. This certainly represents a significant departure from the homosocial world of Ottoman women with divisions of labor cutting across communities. Fanny Davis mentions, for instance, the role of Jewish women peddlers visiting the more homebound Ottoman ladies and functioning as conduits for exchanges, gossip, and loans as well as fortune-telling and other recreational services. Fanny Davis, *The Ottoman Lady: A Social History (1718–1918)* (London: Greenwood Press, 1986).

21. Deniz Kandiyoti, "Slave Girls, Temptresses and Comrades: Images of Women in the Turkish Novel," *Feminist Issues* 8 (1988): 35–50.

22. Duben and Behar, *Istanbul Households*, chap. 7.

23. Jale Parla, *Babalar ve Oğullar* (Istanbul: Iletişim Yayinlari, 1990).

24. For a fuller treatment of this question, see Deniz Kandiyoti, "The Paradoxes of Masculinity: Some Thoughts on Segregated Societies," in *Dislocating Masculinity: Comparative Ethnographies*, ed. Andrea Cornwall and Nancy Lindisfarne (London: Routledge, 1994), pp. 197–213.

25. Zafer Toprak, "The Family, Feminism and the State during the Young Turk Period, 1908–1918," in *Prémière rencontre internationale sur l'Empire Ottoman et la Turquie moderne*, ed. Edhem Eldem (Istanbul: Institut National de Langues et Civilisations Orientales; Maison des Sciences de l'Homme, 1990).

26. This attempt was by no means unique to Turkey but finds parallels in Iran, in references to pre-Islamic Persian mythologies, and in Egypt with the invocation by nationalists of the pharaonic past. For a discussion of the tensions between modernist and organicist tendencies in nationalism, see Deniz Kandiyoti, "Identity and Its Discontents: Women and the Nation," in *Colonial Discourse and Post-Colonial Theory: A Reader*, ed. Patrick Williams and Laura Chrisman (New York: Columbia University Press, 1994), pp. 376–91.

27. Duben and Behar, *Istanbul Households*, p. 212.

28. Ibid., p. 139–40.

29. Deniz Kandiyoti, "Gendering the Modern: On Missing Dimensions in the Study of Turkish Modernity," in *Rethinking Modernity and National Identity in Turkey*, ed. Sibel Bozdoğan and Reşat Kasaba (Seattle: University of Washington Press, 1997), pp. 113–32.

30. Duben and Behar, *Istanbul Households*, p. 139.

31. Shakry's article in this volume (chap. 4) provides numerous illustrations of how in both Europe and its colonies the production of a healthy nation became linked to a discourse on eugenics and maternalism. The Ottoman literature on marriage and child rearing expresses strikingly similar concerns.

32. Michel Foucault, *The History of Sexuality*, vol. 1 (London: Allen Lane, 1979), p. 33.

33. Yeşim Arat, *The Patriarchal Paradox: Women Politicians in Turkey* (Rutherford, N.J.: Fairleigh Dickinson University Press, 1989); Ayşe Durakbaşa, "Cumhuriyet

Döneminde Kemalist Kadın Kimliğinin Oluşumu," *Tarih ve Toplum* 9 (1988): 167–71; Şirin Tekeli, "The Meaning and Limits of Feminist Ideology in Turkey," in *Women, Family and Social Change in Turkey*, ed. Ferhunde Ozbay (Bangkok: UNESCO, 1990), pp. 139–59.

34. *Ziya Gökalp'in Neşredilments Yedi Eseri ve Aile Mektuplari*, ed. Ali Nüzhet Göksel (Istanbul: Işıl Matbaasi, 1956), pp. 15–42.

35. Duben and Behar, *Istanbul Households*, p. 236.

36. Kandiyoti, "Gendering the Modern."

37. Ömer Seyfettin, *Aşk Dalgası* (Istanbul, 1964), p. 56, my translation. First published in the literary magazine *Genç Kalemler* in 1912.

38. Deniz Kandiyoti, "Patterns of Patriarchy: Notes for an Analysis of Male Dominance in Turkish Society," in *Women in Modern Turkish Society*, ed. Şirin Tekeli (London: Zed Books, 1995), pp. 306–18.

39. Afsaneh Najmabadi, "Veiled Discourse—Unveiled Bodies," *Feminist Studies* 19, no. 3 (1993): 487–518; quotation on p. 489.

40. For a fuller treatment of the historical reasons behind this state of affairs, see Deniz Kandiyoti, "Contemporary Feminist Scholarship and Middle East Studies," in *Gendering the Middle East*, ed. Deniz Kandiyoti (London: I. B. Tauris, 1996), pp. 1–28.

Contributors

LILA ABU-LUGHOD is professor of anthropology and Middle East Studies at New York University. Her books include *Veiled Sentiments: Honor and Poetry in a Bedouin Society* and *Writing Women's Worlds: Bedouin Stories* (Berkeley and Los Angeles: University of California Press, 1986 and 1993, respectively). She is currently working on a study of the cultural politics of Egyptian television, exploring the relationship of popular television serials to local debates about gender, class, national identity, and modernity.

MARILYN BOOTH is an independent scholar and translator affiliated with the University of Illinois, Urbana-Champaign, where she teaches in the Program in Comparative Literature. She has authored *Bayram al-Tunisi's Egypt: Social Criticism and Narrative Strategies* (Reading, Eng.: Ithaca Books, 1990) and *May Her Likes Be Multiplied: Biography, Prescription, and Gender Politics in Egypt, 1870–1990* (Berkeley and Los Angeles: University of California Press, forthcoming). She has published four volumes of translated fiction and memoirs by contemporary Egyptian women and has received two translation awards. She is writing a book on Zaynab Fawwaz and translating writings by Mayy Ziyadah, both Lebanese feminists who lived in Egypt early in this century.

KHALED FAHMY is assistant professor of modern history in the Near Eastern Studies Department at Princeton Univerity. He is the author of *All the Pasha's Men: Mehmed Ali, His Army and the Making of Modern Egypt* (Cambridge: Cambridge University Press, 1997). Besides military history, his research interests include the medical and legal history of modern Egypt.

MERVAT HATEM is associate professor of political science at Howard University. She has written widely on gender and politics in the Middle East and in Egypt. Her latest article is "The Professionalization of Health and the Control of Women's Bodies as Modern Governmentalities in Nineteenth Century Egypt," in *Women in the Ottoman Empire*, ed. M. Zilfi (Leiden: Brill, 1997).

DENIZ KANDIYOTI is senior lecturer in the Department of Anthropology and Sociology at the School of Oriental and African Studies, University of London. She is editor of *Women, Islam and the State* (London: Macmillan, 1991) and *Gendering the Middle East* (London: I. B. Tauris, 1996) and has written extensively on issues of gender in the Middle East. She is currently doing research on the Central Asian republics of the Former Soviet Union.

AFSANEH NAJMABADI is associate professor of Women's Studies at Barnard College, Columbia University. Her publications include an edited volume, *Women's Autobiographies in Contemporary Iran*, Center for Middle Eastern Studies Monograph Series (Cambridge: Harvard University Press, 1991). She is currently working on a book, *Male Lions and Female Suns: The Gendered Tropes of Iranian Modernity*.

OMNIA SHAKRY is a Ph.D. candidate in the Department of History, Princeton University. Her current research interests concern the formulation of a post-colonial national modern and include the history of bio-politics and govern-mentality in Egypt. Her dissertation explores the production and organization of rural and urban space in twentieth-century Egypt.

ZOHREH T. SULLIVAN is associate professor of English at the University of Illinois at Urbana-Champaign. Her publications include *Narratives of Empire: The Fictions of Rudyard Kipling* (Cambridge: Cambridge University Press, 1993) and numerous articles on pedagogy, race, and imperial life, and modern British and postcolonial writers. She has recently completed a new book, *Exiled Memories: Recovering Stories of Iranian Diaspora*, and her current project is on migration and postcolonial literature, focusing on such writers as Salman Rushdie, V. S. Naipaul, Tayeb Salih, Buchi Emecheta, and Bharati Mukherjee.

Index

PRINCETON STUDIES IN
CULTURE/POWER/HISTORY